Breaking Intersubjectivity

Radical Subjects in International Politics

Series Editor: Ruth Kinna

This series uses the idea of political subjection to promote the discussion and analysis of individual, communal and civic participation and activism. "Radical subjects" refers both to the character of the topics and issues tacked in the series and to the ethic guiding the research. The series has a radical focus in that it provides a springboard for the discussion of activism that sits outside or on the fringes of institutional politics, yet which, insofar as it reflects a commitment to social change, is far from marginal. It provides a platform for scholarship that interrogates modern political movements, probes the local, regional and global dimensions of activist networking and the principles that drive them, and develops innovative frames to analyze issues of exclusion and empowerment. The scope of the series is defined by engagement with the concept of the radical in contemporary politics but includes research that is multi- or interdisciplinary, working at the boundaries of art and politics, political utopianism, feminism, sociology and radical geography.

Titles in Series
Taking the Square: Mediated Dissent and Occupations of Public Space
    Edited by Maria Rovisco and Jonathan Corpus Ong
The Politics of Transnational Peasant Struggle: Resistance, Rights and Democracy
    Robin Dunford
Sustainable Urbanism and Direct Action: Case Studies in Dialectical Activism
    Benjamin Heim Shepard
Participation and Non-Participation in Student Activism: Paths and Barriers to Mobilizing Young People for Political Action
    Alexander Hensby
The Crisis of Liberal Democracy and the Path Ahead
    Bernd Reiter
Becoming a Movement: Identity and Narratives in the European Global Justice Movement
    Priska Daphi
Liminal Subjects: Weaving (Our) Liberation
    Sara C. Motta
Autonomy, Refusal and The Black Block: Positioning Class Analysis in Critical and Radical Theory
    Robert F. Carley
A Post-Western Account of Critical Cosmopolitan Social Theory: Being and Acting in a Democratic World
    Michael Murphy
Breaking Intersubjectivity: A Critical Theory of Counter-Revolutionary Trauma in Egypt
    Vivienne Matthies-Boon

Breaking Intersubjectivity

A Critical Theory of Counter-Revolutionary Trauma in Egypt

Vivienne Matthies-Boon

ROWMAN & LITTLEFIELD
Lanham • Boulder • New York • London

Published by Rowman & Littlefield
An imprint of The Rowman & Littlefield Publishing Group, Inc.
4501 Forbes Boulevard, Suite 200, Lanham, Maryland 20706
www.rowman.com

86-90 Paul Street, London EC2A 4NE

Copyright © 2023 by Vivienne Matthies-Boon

All rights reserved. No part of this book may be reproduced in any form or by any electronic or mechanical means, including information storage and retrieval systems, without written permission from the publisher, except by a reviewer who may quote passages in a review.

British Library Cataloguing in Publication Information Available

Library of Congress Cataloging-in-Publication Data

Names: Matthies-Boon, Vivienne, author.
Title: Breaking intersubjectivity : a critical theory of counter-revolutionary trauma in Egypt / Vivienne Matthies-Boon.
Description: Lanham, Maryland : Rowman & Littlefield, 2023. | Series: Radical subjects in international politics | Includes bibliographical references and index.
Identifiers: LCCN 2022023378 (print) | LCCN 2022023379 (ebook) | ISBN 9781786610324 (cloth) | ISBN 9781538173008 (paper) | ISBN 9781786610331 (ebook)
Subjects: LCSH: Political violence—Egypt—History—21st century. | Political violence—Egypt—Psychological aspects. | Counterrevolutionaries—Egypt. | Psychic trauma—Egypt. | Egypt—History—Protests, 2011-2013—Psychological aspects.
Classification: LCC DT107.87 .M385 2022 (print) | LCC DT107.87 (ebook) | DDC 962.05/6019—dc23/eng/20220714
LC record available at https://lccn.loc.gov/2022023378
LC ebook record available at https://lccn.loc.gov/2022023379a

This book is dedicated to all those known and unknown political prisoners that are languishing in the most horrid conditions in Sisi's jails and to all those family members and friends that suffer with them. It is also dedicated to all those Egyptian activists who in the face of a politics of death have sought to embrace a politics of life.

Contents

Acknowledgements xi

Introduction 1
   Structure of the Book 5
   Further Remarks 16

PART 1: TOWARDS A CRITICAL THEORY OF TRAUMA AS BROKEN SUBJECTIVITY **23**

1 Trauma Studies and the Philosophy of the Subject 31
   Towards Intersubjectivity: Habermas's Critique of the
      Philosophy of the Subject 31
   The Positivist Revolution and the Emergence of PTSD 36
   Cognitive Trauma Theory: Intersubjectivity Within 54
   Lazarus Never Dies: Anti-Mimeticism in Post-Structural and
      Political Trauma 58

2 Towards a Critical Trauma Studies: Trauma as Intersubjective
   Alienation 65
   On Heideggerian Trauma Theory: Struggles of Intersubjectivity 66
   Traumatic Status Subordination: Nancy Fraser 71
   Traumatic Alienation: Rahel Jaeggi 76
   Traumatic Instrumentality: Jurgen Habermas 80
   Conclusion 89

PART 2: COUNTER-REVOLUTIONARY TRAUMA IN EGYPT 93

3 A Legacy of Traumatic Status Subordination in Egypt: From Nasser to Mubarak 101
Maldistribution: Neoliberal Economics 103
Misrecognition: Security State Violence 105
Destroying Potentiality: Traumatic Alienation 108

4 Revolutionary Becoming: The Politics of Prefigurative Intersubjective Parity 111
Revolutionary Precursor: Kifaya 111
Egypt's 2011 Revolution: Politics of Intersubjective Parity 113

5 Supreme Council of Armed Forces: The Politics of Traumatic Status Subordination 125
Political Proceduralism: Colonising the Political Public Sphere 126
Direct Physical Force: Disorientation and Isolation 139
Neoliberal Economic Rationalism 151

6 Mohammed Morsi: The Politics of Traumatic Status Subordination 155
Political Proceduralism: Morsi's Struggle for Power 156
Direct Physical Force: Turning Violence Inwards 161
Neoliberal Economic Rationalism 165

7 The Military's Deadly Return 169
Tamarod and the 30 June Protests 169
The Rabaa Massacre 172

8 Abdel Fattah El Sisi: The Politics of Traumatic Status Subordination 179
Political Proceduralism: Sisi's Colonisation of the Political Public Sphere 180
Repressive Juridification of the Public Sphere 184
Direct Physical Force 190
Neoliberal Economic Rationalism 201
Conclusion 207

PART 3: BREAKING THE REVOLUTIONARY LIFEWORLD AND POTENTIAL OF CREATIVE BECOMING 209

9 Breaking the Lifeworld: On the Existential Burden of Violence and Death 219
Living death: Experience Torture 220

*Being against Death: Clashes and the Politics of Violence,
    Death and Disorientation* 224
Martyrs, Revolutionary Betrayal and the Burden of Death 234

10 Deepening Intersubjective Imparity: Turning Violence Inwards 245
Social Revenge and the Inwards Direction of Violence 247
Rabaa: Mass Murder and the Destruction of Potentiality 260
Social Death and the Impossibility of Change 270
Coping with the Counter-Revolution: Depoliticisation 290

11 Conclusion 297

Bibliography 305

Index 329

About the Author 337

Acknowledgements

This book has been over eight years in the making. During this time, I have had too many conversations and discussions with friends, colleagues and activists about the contents of this book to account for all of them here. Yet, without a doubt, the greatest, most humbling impact have been the interviewees themselves, who entrusted me with their deeply personal and often difficult stories. I remember the conversations with each and everyone of you, where we sat, what we drank or ate, how we talked and often how you laughed, cried or got angry. There are no adequate words to describe these moments. And it is your particular faces, that in a Levinasian sense, bestowed a deeply felt love and responsibility not only to try and listen but also to try and make sense of all the madness that was (and still is) happening in Egypt. And I can only hope that the result is helpful to you, to others, to anyone trying to make sense of the politics of death and destruction that has been so violently inflicted on you, and those that you love, with such great force. I can only hope that I, in some way, do justice to your experiences, your stories and your feelings.
I would also like to express my deepest thanks to all my Egyptian friends, including those that were not interviewed for this study. Due to security concerns, I cannot mention your names here, but I hope that you will know who you are. Your suffering was the very reason this book came into existence, and I thank you for your trust, friendship, kindness, laughter and love. I treasure all of our times spent, from driving in the 'Rolls Royce' (quite the opposite!) across Egypt's motorways to singing Scottish folk songs while playing the oud, and spending time at your houses, in my rented room, at cafes, going for walks and also just doing nothing. I miss you all dearly.

I also want to send a special thanks to an Egyptian friend who provided logistical help and advice during the time of conducting the interviews. I am forever grateful to you, and just again wished the reality we lived in was different. You are a truly wonderful human being and I miss you greatly.

Admittedly, writing this book has been a very difficult process. Its content has resulted in bouts of physical and existential sickness. And in that respect, I would also like to thank Brother Emile of the Taizé Community, who implicitly and explicitly taught me perhaps the simplest but most difficult and arduous lessons of all: how to (try and) keep singing in the face of injustice.

Academically, this work has benefitted from many conversations over a great span of time. Too many to mention here. However, the most important conversations this work has benefitted from are those I had with: Naomi Head, Gennaro Gervasio, Jannis Julien Grimm, Jeroen Gunning, Patrick Hayden, Stephan Millich, Annelies Moors, Andrea Teti, Peter Verkinderen, Erin Wilson and a large array of Egyptian scholars and activists whose names I will not mention here due to security concerns. I do hope you will know who you are.

I also benefitted from the feedback of my colleagues at my previous employer, the University of Amsterdam, especially Nel VandeKerckhove, John Grin and Marlies Glasius but also the political theory working group where parts of this book were presented just before its publication. The BA and MA students that I taught at the University of Amsterdam also deserve a special thanks. I remain grateful for the discussions with all of those who took part in the courses 'Conflict and Violence in the Middle East' and 'Revolutions in the Middle East: Gender, Conflict and Mental Health' in particular. I will treasure many of our moments discussing, pondering and thinking together. The last couple of years, these courses were taught from a phenomenological trauma perspective on authoritarian repression and violence. Hence, these discussions had an indirect impact on the manuscript presented in front of you.

I also would like to thank the Socrates Association for my Professorial Appointment at the Radboud University. I am also especially indebted to my current colleagues at the Faculty of Philosophy, Theology and Religious Studies at the Radboud University in Nijmegen, and in particular Heleen Murre-Van den Berg, Mathijs van de Sande, Tamar Sharon, Jean-Pierre Wils and Evert van der Zweerde for their collegiality and support during the last stages of this book and the pandemic, which hit my household particularly hard in the debilitating form of Long Covid. With regards to my Long Covid, a special thanks also goes to Rowman & Littlefield and those who helped in the production process for their patience and understanding.

I furthermore would like to express my gratitude to four scholars who, each in their own way, taught me the value of philosophy as a way of life (rather than a career) during my earlier years and whose influence remains formative. Those scholars are Professor Robert Fine †, Professor Gillian Howie †, Professor Simon Hailwood and Dr Charles Turner.

Yet, my deepest love, of course, goes to my husband Tim and my daughter Jenna, for all those times lost, and all that you had to endure during the writing of this book (including in the context of a pandemic). I cannot even begin to describe the impact that writing this book has had on our family life. I love you deeply.

Introduction

My friend was pacing up and down the living room of the house he shared with two friends in the Cairene area of Dokki. The pain was visible on his face. He was often absent minded, lost in his own thoughts and his own world. Even when in company, he appeared isolated, alone and most of all hurt, and there was nothing we (his friends) could do about it. He was suffering from all that he had seen, all that had happened, all those hopes that had been destroyed and, above all, his utter inability to do anything about it. Helpless, alone, he not only felt depressed but also experienced a crippling existential guilt towards those who had died as well as those that survived and those that would yet have to be born. He appeared to be suffocating under the weight of all that had gone wrong in Egypt's post-revolutionary aftermath.

Another friend suffered from periods wherein he appeared frantic, confused, upset and angry. He was unable to make sense of what was happening around him. One time, he rang me in the middle of the night. He was panicking about his future. The revolution had cost him so much: he had lost friends who were like family, his education, his career. How can he continue? Yet how can he give up? Giving up meant betrayal – betrayal of all those that died, betrayal of being able to live properly. But the dream was in tatters and he was broken. Sobbing over the phone, he poured his heart out in desperate misery. Caught in an existential no-man's-land he started to blame himself, regarding himself as a failure. He said he was a foolish man, who had naively pursued some abstracted dreams. These not only resulted in many deaths but also meant he let his family down. His education was halted, he was unemployed, without a wife and lacking an apartment. No matter what one said, this belief subsequently dominated his way of being in the world as he was lost to debilitating depression.

These personal experiences with just two of my close Egyptian friends in the spring of 2013 led me to research the existential and emotional impact of the revolution and the counter-revolutionary crackdown on activists in Cairo. The origins of this research are thus founded in friendship.

The everyday conversations and interactions with those around me – the people I cared about – appeared to take on special significance in light of public commentaries and academic analyses that were published during Egypt's counter-revolutionary aftermath. Using models of democratisation, such commentaries and analyses frequently employed a normative yardstick along which the progression of Egypt's so-called democratisation was measured (Abuzaid, 2011; Mohamed, 2012; Sarihan, 2012; Sarquís, 2012). While these models might themselves not be inaccurate, the trouble was that they did not take into account what it was existentially like to live through Egypt's post-revolutionary sandstorm (sandstorms typifying the Egyptian 'spring' much more than the Westocentric imaginary of flowers, bees and butterflies). And since they failed to take into account such experiences, their macro-level exploration of what was going awry in Egypt's post-revolutionary transition risked implicitly adding to activists' sense of guilt and failure. Frequently, activists were implicitly partially blamed for the failure of the revolution: deemed too reactive (rather than proactive), they had an unclear democratic agenda and a horizontal (leaderless) organisational structure which resulted in inefficiency (Abdelrahman, 2013; Davies, 2014; Khan et al., 2020; Springborg, 2017; Totten, 2012; Völkel, 2020). While there is no doubt that these analyses were in some sense correct and sometimes incredibly insightful,[1] what remains hidden from view is how the military sought to purposefully shift the existential structures of being in the world. They failed to reflect on what it was like to encounter overwhelming bloodshed and death, what it was like to wake up the morning after the night before wherein two of your best friends had been killed. Or, how it felt finding your way home after you were left for dead in an alleyway by Egypt's security forces. Detached and abstracted accounts of democratisation (Abuzaid, 2011; Brownlee, 2012; Sarquís, 2012; el Medni, 2013; Moghadam, 2013) thus failed to take into consideration how the first three post-revolutionary years were constituted by a lot of 'booms and busts' (interview 2), and how, as one interviewee put it, it meant that you would: 'Wake up in the morning and you think "ok the situation is this", and then by the afternoon it turned 180 degrees, for it to have changed 360 degrees at night' (interview 27). In other words, they paid insufficient attention to the human, existential, *lived* impact of counter-revolutionary violence – and particularly how its disorientating and atomising effects deeply affected political participation and activism (particularly in the long run). Ignoring the deeply embodied and existential experience of the (counter)revolution, these analyses overlooked how such experiences impacted one's political Being-in-the-World. Instead, what emerged was an abstracted and limited understanding of Egypt's counter-revolutionary aftermath, which moreover highlighted a great lacuna in democratic theory and theories of democratisation: namely, its relative negligence of the existential, phenomenological impacts of lived political pain and injury and how these impact processes of political mobilisation and democratisation.

Since then, there have of course there have been some scholarly articles on the impacts of emotions and affect within the Egyptian and Arabic uprisings (Pearlman, 2013, 2016; Matthies-Boon, 2017; Matthies-Boon and Head, 2018; Solomon, 2018; Coşkun, 2019). Yet, these analyses largely provide a cognitivist perception on emotions wherein emotions affect cognitive decision-making, mobilisation and rational choice calculations. Since these analyses remain operative at the level of philosophical intentionality, they fail to sufficiently account for how the grave violence inflicted during the (counter-)revolution does not merely affect one's *thinking about* the world, but rather one's *being in* the world. As psychological cognitivism has become so commonplace today (Radstone, 2007; Garnham, 2019), it has become hard to think of ourselves differently than brain-wiring units (Bracken, 1988; Bracken and Thomas, 1999, 2002; Thomas and Bracken, 2011). Yet, I will argue in this book, if we want to understand how processes of democratisation were curtailed in Egypt we must take into account the ways in which counter-revolutionary demobilisation was achieved through the strategic, multilevelled infliction of trauma (encompassing the political, social and subjective spheres), which affected activists *existential being in* the world.

And so, motivated to try and make sense of my friends' experiences and frustrated with these blatant lacunae in political analyses, I started to conduct life-story interviews with forty young Cairene activists (eighteen to thirty-five years) between October 2013 and February 2014. This period was a significant turning point in Egypt's post-revolutionary trajectory: the Egyptian military had just ousted the Muslim Brotherhood president Mohamed Morsi and inflicted mass murder on the Brotherhoods' supporters during the clearances of the Rabaa and Ennahda sit-ins on 14 August 2013, while the current president Abdel Fattah El Sisi was in the process of consolidating his repressive authoritarian (deadly) political rule. Many interviewees experienced this as a consolidation of the end: the end of revolutionary potential. It was thus a significant period for taking stock of the emotional and existential impacts of counter-revolutionary violence.

Importantly, political activity – or activism – is here understood in the broadest possible sense and comprises both structurally organised formal politics and participation in informal politics. Hence, some were formally engaged in political movements such as the 6th of April, NGOs or political parties, while others were active informally through online platforms, participation in demonstrations or local committees. None of them were, however, personally affiliated with industry-related social movements. Interviewees covered the political spectrum in Egypt and included liberals, socialists, Islamists (both Muslim Brotherhood and Salafist) and military regime supporters. Religiously, they varied from practising to non-practising Sunni Muslims, Christians (Coptic and Evangelical), agnostics and atheists. Socio-economically, the majority were clearly situated in the middle class (living in areas such as Mohandiseen, Heliopolis, Maadi or 6th of October), some were from lower-class areas such as Bulaaq or Imbaba, while others were from higher middle-class families who lived in exclusive compounds outside of Cairo. Importantly, the focus was on young activists, not because the 25th of January revolution was exclusively a youth movement (Beissinger et al., 2013) but because in Egypt's hierarchically structured society the destruction of their hopes and aspirations had been particularly marginalised from internal political debates which often remained dominated by the voices of the 'older' activists (Matthies-Boon, 2017).

Importantly, interviewees were not selected (using a snowball approach) on 'having suffered trauma' but rather on being politically active in the broadest sense as possible. The traumatic, debilitating phenomenological impacts of the violence they endured only became transparent during the interviews themselves and were made sense of through the development of a critical theoretical understanding of trauma afterwards.

The violence experienced by these activists was grave, with twenty-six out of forty participants commenting on the pervasiveness of death in their lives. Between 2011 and 2014, twelve interviewees were teargassed, eleven were directly injured, seven were detained (and beaten), four were tortured, four were sexually abused and three experienced near-death. Furthermore, twelve had friends who died, twelve had friends who were injured, nine had friends who were detained and seven had friends who were tortured. Also, seven had family members who were injured, three had family members who were detained, two had family members who died, two had family members who were tortured and one had a family member who nearly died.

In order to understand the existential impact of this violence, interviews were conducted using a testimonial life-story method. In this approach, the personal narrative has analytical priority over any qualitative interview questions, thus allowing for multifaceted and contradictory reactions to be included as the interviewee elaborates on his or her experiences at length (Benezir, 2009). This also makes it possible to pay attention to what Benezir (2009) calls trauma markers: silences, self-report, a change in voice and intonation, a loss of emotional control and a change in body language. All such markers have been included in the verbatim quotations from the interviews, which were conducted in a mixture of English and Egyptian Arabic.

Sometimes, however, interviewees' quotations have had to be shortened due to a lack of available space and to keep focus. Interviews conducted in Arabic have been translated into English as literally as possible. It is important to include trauma markers as it indicates existential disorientation: when one is subject to trauma, the ability to accurately express oneself linguistically often collapses too, making it critical to identify that which may or may not find linguistic expression (Edkins, 2003: 8; Moore, 2005; Andrews, 2010). Through its close attention to personal narratives, the life-story method furthermore facilitates a culturally sensitive account of activists' phenomenological experiences, wherein the macro-level social and political analyses may be connected to individual experiences of traumatic violence which are embedded in social and political contexts.

STRUCTURE OF THE BOOK

When analysing the phenomenological impact of the counter-revolutionary violence activists suffered, it quickly became apparent that it had been traumatic: many interviewees experienced extreme disorientation, numbing, the loss of speech, the inability to act and the emptying out of meaning from their lives. Yet, nearly just as quickly, it became apparent that the cognitivist understanding of trauma as Post-Traumatic Stress Disorder (PTSD) was not only severely limited but in fact grossly inadequate in accounting for these activists' traumatic experiences. Nevertheless, the term of trauma itself appeared to remain appropriate (and should not be thrown overboard) given the deep existential disorientation and demoralised speechlessness activists experienced. And so, I spent several years developing an alternative, critical theoretical understanding of trauma and traumatic injustice, using the philosophical frameworks of both Jurgen Habermas and Nancy Fraser as a metatheoretical analytical lens.

Hence, Part 1 first outlines a theoretical critique of trauma studies, and particularly the concept of PTSD, before developing a critical theoretical account of trauma as broken intersubjectivity. One might wonder here why one would take recourse to Frankfurt School's critical theory when speaking about trauma. In a certain sense, the answer is quite simple. Habermas's critique of positivism (Habermas, 1976a, 1987a) and the philosophy of the subject (Habermas, 1995; Crossley, 1996, 2012; Finlayson, 2013; Fritsch, 2019) is directly applicable to trauma studies and its notion of PTSD. At the same time, a critical theoretical understanding of trauma as broken *inter*subjectivity not only avoids these pitfalls but also provides us with a thin political conception of trauma, which, while capturing the universal essence of trauma, remains sensitive to its particular (divergent) cultural, social and political embedding.[2]

But, before I outline this critical theoretical understanding of trauma, let me briefly state why the by-now commonplace understanding of trauma as PTSD is deeply flawed, not just in the case of Egyptian activists but generally. The essence of the problem is that the cognitivist understanding of trauma (understood as PTSD) remains wedded to a philosophy of the subject. The philosophy of the subject assumes that there is an essential, atomistic and sovereign self, who is not only detached from the social and political reality wherein he or she finds him- or herself but also that the solipsist gaze of the detached individual establishes objective facts about the self, others and the world (Habermas, 1995; Crossley, 1996; Fritsch, 2019). The trouble with this point of view is that it abides by a subject–object metaphysics, wherein both the object and subject are reified into detached, atomised entities, whose essence or properties may be understood using an objectifying lens (Finlayson, 2013: 29). In other words, both object and subject are artificially abstracted from their intersubjective embeddedness and constitution and undergo (universalistic) essentialisation. Hence, the associated aporias of a philosophy of the subject include an unwarranted universalist projection of a particular understanding, an abidance by abstracted decontextualised individualism and an objectifying reification. In trauma studies, I argue, all these problems are reproduced: not only does trauma studies project a particular Westocentric understanding of trauma as universally valid, it also decontextualises both the study and experience of trauma as it reifies trauma into an intrapsychic cognitive affair of the mind – which supposedly is to be analysed through detached models of (quantifiable) diagnostic criteria.

As Part 1 explains, this results in a threefold problematic. First, this solipsist cognitivist conception of trauma gives rise to the problem of a double injury:[3] the victims of an injustice are now also told that there is something wrong with their mind or brain and become (at least implicitly) responsible for its repair. Second, mired as the cognitivist conception is in detached universalism, trauma studies fails to properly account for both the political contextual constitution of its own theoretical concepts and its underlying political claims.[4] Hence, trauma studies projects forth a universalist historical teleological account of trauma, which on closer inspection remains solely focused on Western experiences such as the First and Second World War, the Holocaust and the Vietnam War, with a complete absence of accounts of imperialism, colonialism and slavery to just name a few (Radstone, 2007; Craps, 2014; Bracken et al., 2021). Third, it developed and popularised the notion of trauma as an external (even extraordinary) past event, which overwhelms the processing capacities of the mind or the brain. This is deeply problematic: eventism overlooks both the structural nature of the threat to life (such as poverty or authoritarian repression) and its 'normalcy': its continuous nature in much of the world, and particularly the Global South. It is precisely this normalcy that is, as Stef Craps reminds us, so poignantly highlighted in Aminatta Forna's novel *The Memory of Love* (Forna, 2011), set in Sierra Leone, wherein the character Atilla says to the Western flown in psychiatrist Dr Lockman, 'you call it a disorder my fried. We call it life' (Craps, 2014: 53). Moreover, as scholars in South Africa such as Gillian Straker (2013) noted, in such contexts, therapeutic safety is not only an illusion (with the frequent bugging of therapists' offices) but traumatic symptom reduction is also dangerous in that, for instance, anxiety and suspicion is a necessary survival mechanism.[5]

There is no doubt that some of the points of critique mentioned here have featured in other commentaries (Stolorow and Atwood, 1996; Summerfield, 2001; Bracken and Thomas, 2002; Thomas and Bracken, 2004; Stolorow, 2007, 2011; Straker, 2013; Craps, 2014; Bracken et al., 2021). Yet, these have often been offered as stand-alone, separate points of critique. They have not yet been systematically connected to its underlying causation: namely trauma studies' abidance to a philosophy of the subject. It is on this basis that I propose we understand trauma not as impaired subjectivity but as broken intersubjectivity, since only a radical intersubjective reconceptualisation of trauma will release us from the solipsist confines of the philosophy of the subject.

Trauma studies' adherence to the philosophy of the subject was particularly solidified when trauma scholars committed a simple category mistake, and trauma became regarded as an objective (medical) fact instead of a violation of intersubjective norms. Or, to put it in stronger Habermasian language, it became regarded as a validity claim belonging to the realm of objective truth rather than a claim belonging to the intersubjective socio-normative realm of righteousness and justice.[6] This category mistake is a direct upshot of the positivist revolution that swept through the American Psychological Association (APA) when the concept of PTSD emerged and was included in the DSM III in 1980 (Young, 1995; Kihlstrom, 2010; Alford, 2016). Supporters of the 'positivist revolution' formed the working group charged with the establishment of new diagnostic criteria (Alford, 2016: 11–12). These diagnostic criteria were supposed to determine a psychological disorder on the basis of nosological symptomology (the observation of symptoms) (Alford, 2016; Stein et al., 2016) and followed a purposive rationale in that calculative rational considerations of cost-efficiency, predictability and universal quantifiability trumped previous forms of open-ended, ambiguous and interpretative processes of reaching therapeutic understanding.

The trouble is that the concept of trauma as PTSD, popularised by this working group, includes its own aetiology in its definition: it entails both the effects (the symptoms) and the causal traumatic event (Radstone, 2007). This not only gives rise to tautological reason, but its diagnosis also clearly transcends the limits of nosological symptomology of the APA's new diagnostic manual was supposed to abide by. The diagnosis of PTSD does not rest so much on empirical observation of supposed observable medical symptoms but rather on the interpretative attribution of causality to a particular event (and this bypasses objective medical observation). As chapter 1 will explain, this the ascription of causality to a particular event or experience is extremely problematic given the presence of pre-existing character traits, different possible responses to the same event and the persuasive power of the therapist. Indeed, this problem became particularly pronounced when trauma studies fell down the rabbit hole of the 'repressed memory debate' (Loftus and Ketcham, 1996; Alford, 2016: 83). Herein, therapists the owners of ultimate truth, supposedly able to discern the truth of a traumatic event repressed (and thus forgotten) by the sufferer him- or herself. This debate was only finally closed after questionable evidence of supposed repressed traumatic memories had entered the American legal system as evidence, including alien abductions and UFOs encounters.

Yet, the same scholars that had been leading defenders of the repressed memory debate – such as Bessel van der Kolk – now turned to neuroscience as their saviour (Alford, 2016: 83). Surely, hard the 'empirical evidence' of neuroscience could close this interpretative ambiguity. Yet, the problem here is that the pixels of the fMRI scans used in trauma research are not only too imprecise to attribute the exact brain functions that trauma scholars would like to attribute to amygdala and hippocampus, it also provides us with nothing more than a correlation (Alford, 2016: 87). That is, even if parts of the brain light up like a colourful Christmas tree, there is still no *causal* established to a particular event. As John F Kihlstrom explains, all that has been done is translate psychological assumptions from one language into another language – like English into French (Kihlstrom, 2010: 773).

What it did achieve however was a further reification of trauma as an 'object' located in the mind of the individual, and which may be solved through psychical introspective intervention. Or rather, it solidified its rooting in a philosophy of the subject, with all the above-mentioned problems thereof. As this chapter will show, the trouble is that these cognitivist presumptions have become so dominant in academic studies and everyday life that they have even been replicated even in scholarly strands of thought normally hostile to the philosophy of the subject, such as postmodern or poststructuralist conceptions of trauma.[7]

Hence, in order to resolve these dilemmas, this book proposes a critical theoretical understanding of trauma wherein trauma is perceived not as impaired subjectivity but as broken *inter*subjectivity. In doing so, this monograph clearly takes inspiration from existing existential (or Heideggerian) trauma theory such as that of Patrick Bracken (Bracken and Thomas, 1999, 2002; Bracken, 2002b; Thomas and Bracken, 2004, 2011) and Robert

Stolorow (Stolorow, 2007, 2011a, 2011b, 2013), which stressed the intersubjective constitution of traumatic experience. However, these philosophies remained tied to the philosophy of the subject in the sense that, while they stressed the intersubjective nature of trauma, they still primarily focused on the internal subjective experience of trauma. Or rather, the emphasis remains on the individual experience of trauma in relative separation from its social and political constitution.

Hence, I seek to complement, or perhaps extend, their philosophical considerations by providing a distinctly critical theoretical, or Habermasian, take on trauma-broken intersubjectivity. Herein, trauma is regarded as the violent betrayal of the counterfactual presupposition of being treated as an equal peer in relation to others. Trauma thus entails a violation of what Nancy Fraser calls participation parity (Fraser and Honneth, 2003: 36–37), as the perpetrator (either a group or an individual) seeks to impose power over the victim (either a group or an individual). In this sense, trauma is hence always already political (either in a formal or informal sense). It comprises the violent imposition of a traumatic status subordination,[8] which is constituted by both grave forms of misrecognition (taken here to mean the failure to recognise our equality as human beings) and maldistribution (the unfair distribution of political and economic resources). Trauma thus entails the betrayal of the counterfactual presupposition of the equal value of each human being in relation to others[9] – and may both be inflicted through violent events (such as torture or killings) and structural violence (such as violent marginalisation and excruciating poverty). Indeed, incidental and structural violence often beget each other and constitute a toxic mix through which the lifeworld ruptures and breaks down, leaving one in an incapacitated state of atomised disorientation.

There are three important comments to make here. First, while always unpleasant and unjust, not all forms of status subordination are necessarily traumatic. Rather, injustice only becomes traumatic when it removes the capacity to speak back at its infliction – when it has such an incapacitating effect one loses one's bearing in the world and the ability to address the injury suffered. Second, a Habermasian/Fraserian perspective clearly locates trauma in the realm of social and political justice, without neglecting its deeply personal impact. And lastly, such a Habermasian perception also brings the purposive (or instrumental) rationality that underpins trauma to the fore. Traumatic status subordination entails a violent manifestation of power in the pursuit of instrumental goals. These goals may be more limited or broader in scope: they may comprise direct power over the victim but also the pursuit of broader social, political or economic power. And indeed, often it comprises both.

Trauma is thus a tool of (political) repression par excellence. For, in the violent, strategic destruction of intersubjective equality, trauma destroys the (communicative) foundations of the lifeworld as a background of interpretation and a horizon of possibility. This means that, in the face of traumatic violence, our meaning-making practices are shattered, resulting in a deep sense of traumatic alienation and a shift in the underlying structure of experience away from possibility towards an overwhelming sense of the *im*possibility of meaningful change. It thus results in traumatic alienation: such an overwhelming sense of alienation that one loses the capacity to speak back. With regards to the notion of traumatic alienation, this book is heavily indebted to Rahel Jaeggi's important critical theoretical work on alienation (Jaeggi, 2014). Herein, alienation is understood as the inability to manifest ourselves in the world: the world overtakes us, it comes to stand over and above us, and induces a sense of helplessness in us. It is through this traumatic alienation that the unitary existential structure of experience is shifted away from one of possibility towards impossibility. Here, I also particularly draw on Matthew Ratcliffe's excellent phenomenological work on depression and illness (Ratcliffe, 2008, 2014), where he explains how the horizon of possibility is destroyed: demoralisation is felt so acute that any sense of *the possibility* of meaningful change dissipates from underneath one's feet. And this, I argue is precisely what the counter-revolutionary actors (primarily the Egyptian military, but also its temporary subsidiary the Muslim Brotherhood) achieved when they violently inflicted multilevelled traumatic status subordination on Egyptian activists. This multilevelled traumatisation spanned across the political and social spheres, leaving them in an existential state of atomised, demoralised depoliticisation.

In order to fully grasp the multifaceted nature of traumatic status subordination, I propose we make an *analytical* distinction between political, social and individual traumatisation. Political traumatisation entails the violent infliction of intersubjective imparity in the political terrain, resulting in a total breakdown of political participation in the public sphere (and thus a removal of the capacity to speak back at the political injustices inflicted). Social traumatisation entails the fundamental betrayal of the counterfactual presupposition of intersubjective parity in one's relation to others in the social sphere. It deeply breaks the presumption that in the eyes of the other we hold the value as an equal peer, a valued human being in reciprocal relationships of recognition.[10] Hence, when social traumatisation occurs, it has a profoundly disorienting and alienating effect: one cannot manifest or establish oneself in social relation to others anymore. The social networks and relations of trust that were once taken for granted break down and are marked with radical unsafety: leaving one in a state of atomised alienation with depoliticising effects (see chapter 10). These existential effects that are captured by individual traumatisation, which refers to subjective experience of a ruptured lifeworld. An analysis of individual traumatisation thus describes the phenomenological experience of traumatic status subordination from a first person's point of view. In Egypt, it was the amalgamation of this multilevelled imposition of traumatic status subordination, which extended to all these spheres, that resulted in the destruction of the revolutionary horizon of potentiality and the retreat of activists into a state of demoralised, depoliticised, atomisation.

Importantly, experientially political, social and individual trauma are of course difficult to disentangle from a first person's perspective. Nevertheless, this analytical differentiation is useful in that it not only highlights the primary political (rather than subjective psychological) nature of trauma in Egypt, but also how it is related to, and indeed gave rise to, social and individual traumatisation. It thus helps us to break through the fetishism of cognitive individualism that has haunted trauma studies and wedded it firmly to the philosophy of the subject. Since trauma is now no longer regarded as a validity claim that falls within the remit of objective (medical) truth but rather an social-normative claims of (in)justice, the analysis of trauma foregrounds its intersubjective constitution. Importantly, in no way does this diminish the validity of the claim to trauma itself. Rather, it precisely does justice to, and fully accounts for, the destructive nature of trauma by breaking out of the myopic vision wherein trauma is reduced to an object located in the individual's mind. For it provides both a reconstruction of the phenomenological (inter)subjective experiences of trauma and the ways in which these experiences are socially and politically constituted, thus providing a more comprehensive understanding of the devastating nature of trauma. Such an account thus combines a third-person explication of the social and political constitution of trauma as well as its disastrous first-person phenomenological effects.

It is for this reason that Part 2 provides an account of the mechanisms of political trauma in Egypt (chapter 2), before social and individual traumatisation is addressed in Part 3. The second part thus examines the structural political constitution of trauma through a close analysis of traumatic status subordination in the political public sphere. It firstly argues that the violent, systematic, and multilevelled betrayal of intersubjective parity is not a new phenomenon in Egypt but rather has characterised Egyptian politics at least since the time of Abdel Fattah el Nasser (and also before that). While under Nasser's socialist rule, Egyptians experienced a relative improvement of economic distribution, it came at the cost of grave misrecognition inflicted by his ever-expanding authoritarian security state – including torture, killings and other forms of physical abuse. However, with Anwar Sadat's neoliberalisation of the economy (Joya, 2011, 2017a; Soliman, 2011; Kandil, 2013), Egyptians started to suffer both crippling maldistribution and violent misrecognition, which under Hosni Mubarak's Nazif government accelerated even further (Joya, 2011; Tansel, 2019). Crippled both by economic uncertainty and physical violence, Egyptians suffered what I call traumatic alienation – with many living an atomised life characterised by social and political estrangement and an inability to have their voices heard. This changed when, after having experimented with social movements such as Kifaya and 6 April in the early 2000s (El Mahdi, 2009; Sonay, 2018), Egyptians ventured out onto the streets en masse on 25 January 2011, Egypt's national day of celebrating the police. During the following eighteen revolutionary days, a prefigurative public sphere emerged[11] wherein the counterfactual presupposition of intersubjective parity was instantiated with all its transformative effects. Egyptians were pulled out of their atomised shells and engaged in collective creative self-becoming, as they raised their voices against the decades of traumatic injustice inflicted that Mubarak (and his predecessors) inflicted on them. As intersubjective parity was actualised in the revolutionary prefigurative public sphere, the existential structures of experience moved away from *im*possibility towards *possibility*, away from a deprivation of hope towards hope of meaningful change.

This transformation, however, also posed a great potential challenge to the political and economic interests of the Egyptian military that, after the ouster of Mubarak, had taken control over Egypt's political transition. Having been displeased with Hosni Mubarak's son's possible succession (and his likely intention to redistribute the military's economic interests to his civic business elite) the military had refused to intervene on behalf of Mubarak during the eighteen days (El-Menawy, 2012; Stacher, 2020). Yet, once Mubarak was out of the way, the military immediately sought to consolidate its own instrumental interests through the infliction of traumatic status subordination in the political sphere. Traumatic status subordination was imposed through a threefold violent tactic: the infliction of overwhelming physical force, of political procedural monopolisation and of neoliberal economic rationalism – all of which violently marginalised Egyptians from the political terrain and rendered them speechless. While the events of overwhelming physical force left activists in a state of existential disorientation, political and economic colonisation ensured that activists were violently marginalised from the formal political terrain, thereby compounding their speechlessness. The realm of formal politics was now strategically controlled by the military who – through concealed strategic actions – had co-opted the Brotherhood as its temporary subsidiary,[12] and pushed for quick elections all the while safeguarding its own political and economic interests through a series of constitutional amendments (Khalifa, 2015; Abul-Magd, 2018; Stacher, 2020). Moreover, neoliberal economic rationalism deprived activists of the material resources necessary to raise their voice in the public sphere, while increasing general economic anxiety amongst the general population enabled the military to lay the blame for Egypt's 'chaos' and 'instability' at the feet of activists, thereby further fracturing and destroying revolutionary unity and solidarity.

Throughout Egypt's post-revolutionary aftermath, this tripartite structure of traumatic status subordination remained remarkably alike under Morsi and Sisi alike. As soon as Brotherhood president Mohammed Morsi was elected and inaugurated in August 2013, he in fact repeated the infliction of traumatic status subordination on Egyptian activists through a procedural political colonisation of the political public sphere, the infliction of grave physical as well as the continuation of neoliberal economics. When Morsi rose to power, the military remained in control of Egypt's political and economic developments as it had firmly clipped the new president's wings. Morsi was inaugurated as a relatively powerless president, namely a president without a parliament and without a constitution. Parliament had been disbanded on a technicality while the constitution was still to be written, and indeed the constitutional process itself was deeply steered by the military. Realising his powerlessness, Morsi's marriage of convenience with the military quickly turned sour. Within this context, the Brotherhood adopted an increasingly defensive attitude of suspicion, wherein it not only regarded *all* of Egypt's opposition as part of the deep state (including those that had always immensely critical of this deep state) but also excluded non-Islamist voices from the constitutional drafting process. In November 2012, Morsi even went so far as to issue a presidential declaration, wherein he sought to immunise his decisions from any legal challenge. While arguably intended to strike back at the military's attempt at political control, this was a classical authoritarian move that alienated the revolutionary opposition (and indeed large sections of the population) ever more from the Brotherhood. Moreover, lacking sufficient access to and control over Egypt's security apparatus, the Brotherhood increasingly depended on civilian Brotherhood supporters for 'security', which meant that grave political violence, such as torture, killings and serious injuries were now inflicted by ordinary civilians rather than state institutions, thereby setting motion violent social polarisation that tore Egyptian society apart. All the while, Egyptians suffered increasing economic disparity under Morsi's regime due to its continuation of neoliberalisation, albeit this time with an Islamist culturalist veneer.

The resulting frustrations were then manipulated by the military using its associated media outlets and behind the scenes meddling (for instance the Tamarrod protest movement), so that the stage was set for the heroic return of the military, personified in Abdel Fattah El Sisi himself, now cast as the saviour of national stability and security. The military was depicted as Egypt's strong institution that would rescue Egypt Islamist abyss of chaos. Yet, unsurprisingly perhaps, as soon as Sisi rose to power, he sought to destroy the potential of revolutionary becoming once and for all, and thus particularly intensified the infliction of traumatic status subordination. Sisi inflicted the gravest forms of direct physical force: he inflicted mass murder, death and destruction. He actively pursued what I call a 'politics of death' and imprisoned over 100,000 citizens on the most dubious of charges as part of the active quest for, what I call, the 'prisonification' of Egyptian society. This direct physical violence was furthermore facilitated by his procedural colonisation of the political sphere, which included gravely (and violently) manipulated elections and the repressive juridification of the public sphere, wherein political assembly, protest and countering the government's message became punishable by law. At the same time, Sisi accelerated Egypt's economy's neoliberalisation, while placing it fully under the military's control.

Hence, all post-revolutionary regimes, from SCAF to Morsi and then Sisi, adopted a counter-revolutionary strategy of traumatic status subordination, wherein revolutionary activists were violently excluded from the political sphere and lost their political voice. Importantly, the instrumental aim of the counter-revolution was not to merely destroy the intentional object of revolutionary politics (through the violent marginalisation of activists from the political public sphere) but rather to destroy the *potentiality* of revolutionary becoming as such. That is, it sought not only to politically exclude revolutionary politics as such but rather to ensure that the revolutionary genie was put firmly back into the bottle of authoritarian repression. It thus sought to alter the underlying structures of being in the world through the destruction of their lifeworld's horizon. It broke the lifeworld's revolutionary horizon by tearing apart communicative and intersubjective relations: it imposed overwhelming deadly physical force (resulting in a breakdown of the shared symbolic order, and a deep sense of existential disorientation) and encouraged social polarisation through which intersubjective imparity became reproduced in the social sphere. And so, the third part (chapter 9) discusses the impacts of deadly violence from a first-person phenomenological perspective: how exposure to torture and (near)death (including the experience of being teargassed) clashes and the experience of near-death situations resulted in a deep existential disorientation – a breakdown of the symbolic order of the lifeworld through which we derive meaning in and from the world. After this, it explores how such a breakdown of the symbolic order not only occurs through the experience of violent events but also the gradual accumulation of violence – and how it was the accumulative death of others that evoked a profound sense of (Levinasian) ethical responsibility (Burggraeve, 1999, 2003; Levinas, 2005; Edelglass, 2006): namely a refusal to let the particularity of those who died sink in the generalised pit of anonymity. Yet, the ability to ascribe meaning to these deaths through a forward projection of revolutionary becoming was violently curtailed by the counter-revolution – thereby resulting in the accumulative breakdown of the lifeworld's functioning as a background for interpretation. The accumulative weight of death thus pulled interviewees ever deeper into an existential state of nihilistic meaninglessness that hampered their ability to engage in the world.

However, as chapter 10 of Part 3 indicates, the frustration and anger that accumulated due to the counter-revolutionary obstruction of political progress resulted was then carefully manipulated inwards – into society – by the military and its allies through violent social polarisation characterised by vicious cycles of revenge. The result of this was social traumatisation: social relations of trust were violently broken as citizens now battled each other to the point of great injury and even death. Egypt descended downwards into a vicious spiral of revenge. Revenge, as explained in this chapter, entails the attempt to regain intersubjective power vis-à-vis another through violent means after one suffered status subordination (which gives rise to (relative) feelings of powerlessness). Revenge may be directed at the perpetrator, as well as redirected elsewhere, onto subjects taken to represent the perpetrator as well as more vulnerable others. In this sense, revenge is thus both the outcome and the continuation of a distorted mode of communicative action typified by status subordination, particularly when it is purposefully redirected away from the (political perpetrator) into the social sphere. Hence, as a destructive cycle of violent revenge spread through the social sphere, interviewees were subjected to traumatic status subordination there too. This not only meant that the injustices suffered in the political sphere remained unrecognised but also that they were subjected to yet another layer of violent intersubjective imparity, which compounded the injustices suffered in the political realm.

It was through this strategic infliction of multilevelled traumatic status subordination, that the lifeworld's horizon of potentiality was destroyed. Since violence had become pervasive, unpredictable and affected the entirety of their existence, there was not a single space wherein they did not suffer the potential of the violent intersubjective parity. In light of such overwhelming pervasive violence, interviewees suffered increasing anxiety (also expressed in dreams and nightmares), a deep sense of existential unsafety, deep demoralisation, depression and utter exhaustion. And in the absence of (even the possibility of)effectively addressing this in the social and political sphere, some resorted to drugs and alcohol to numb their existential pain, while a handful of others tried to mend the symbolic framework of their lifeworld through artistic expression (chapter 10) The majority however resorted to depoliticisation and atomisation: a withdrawal from both participation in and exposure to formal and informal politics, as well as a retreat from social relations and an individualistic (atomised) refocusing of their individual lives: towards small achievable goals such as finishing their education, getting an apartment and seeking employment. The uncomfortable truth is not only that interviewees herein repeated the same process of individualised atomisation that they criticised their parents for but also that while some regarded this political retreat and individualist refocus as a temporary measure to gain some breath or to re-strategise, the Sisi's violent politics of death and prisonification ensured that the potential for revolutionary uprising in Egypt would be closed.

And so, one of the most pertinent questions here also is, how long Sisi can maintain his politics of death? In light of so much death and destruction, critical voices in Egypt have been rendered mute. Perhaps in this situation, a Levinasian responsibility to ensure no harm befalls others falls squarely on those who are not subject to the regime, those who have a freedom to manifest themselves in ways impossible in Egypt. And perhaps a notable responsibility might in particular be placed upon international governments, companies and organisations to hold Egypt's deadly government to account for the crimes against humanity it is committing. Yet, as it stands, these actors have been proven to be interested only in their own short-term goals of political and economic power. That is, these actors have by and large proven unwilling to take firm action against Sisi's regime of death, and instead have proven all too willing to engage in the dance of death, either under the banner of counter-terrorism, anti-migration, sustainable energy, gas deals or other lucrative business deals. And so, the question we must ask ourselves is who, in the face of so much death, is willing to stand up for life?

FURTHER REMARKS

Now, before we turn to the particular chapters, there are a few additional comments to make here. First, the reader has probably already sensed that this book is 'rather strange': it is difficult to situate it within particular disciplinary boundaries. It is neither a purely philosophical normative account of trauma nor solely an empirical description of Egypt's multi-layered process of traumatisation. Nor is it a straightforward case of applied philosophy, wherein a particular philosophical framework is imposed on particular empirical phenomena or a particular case is selected as evidence for a certain normative position. Rather, the philosophical lens presented in this book slowly developed over the course of the eight years that this book was in preparation. The empirical material itself was hence not only made sense of through the theoretical framework but was itself constitutive of the philosophical framework's development. In this sense, this work has developed in a true critical theoretical manner, wherein theory and practice inform each other so as to hopefully enable a deeper understanding of processes of domination and repression with ultimate aim of seeking to contribute to the overcoming of such repression.

In this sense, the book has followed Habermas's critical theoretical method of reconstruction (Habermas, 1979, 1990a; Pederson, 2008). Yet, while

Habermas used the reconstructive method to distil the rational normative (and universalising) kernel of the presuppositions of everyday speech (upon which he developed his theory of communication and discourse ethics) (Habermas, 1979, 1984, 1987b), reconstruction has here been employed as a way of discerning the underlying mechanisms and structures of traumatic status subordination, thereby exposing how traumatic status subordination violates our presupposition of equal existential parity. And so, it provides a thin, universal, reconstructive account of the dynamics of traumatic status subordination, in the full realisation that any such manifestation always necessarily occurs within a specific social and political context. Hence, while the underlying dynamics of human-induced traumatic status subordination follow a universal pattern, the ways in which it is exercised will differ from case to case and must always be examined and understood within its specific contexts.[13] In this sense, it avoids both the charges of unwarranted philosophical abstraction (with the risk of a universal projection of the particular) and the dangers of philosophical relativism wherein trauma would be a purely cultural or social relative phenomena as there would be no universalising lessons (of intersubjective parity) to be drawn from it.[14]

Importantly, the adoption of a Habermasian reconstructive method also means that this book nor indeed trauma research remains fallible, as its findings remain open to contestation in debate. Like, Habermas's theory of rational communication and discourse ethics, this monograph thus operates within a post-positivist social scientific framework wherein any findings and assertions are by definition fallible: any conclusions reached and insights offered remain subject to public deliberation (Habermas, 1998b: 38).

This brings us to the second point that since this monograph comprises an interdisciplinary account of counter-revolutionary traumatisation, it addresses a variety of different audiences as once. And addressing different audiences of course also means opening up different avenues of critique: while political scientists might find it too philosophically heavy, Middle East Studies scholars might object to Frankfurter Schule theoretical framework, philosophers might find it philosophically light, while activists might find it too academic.

To the political scientists, I would say that political philosophy helps us go beyond the mere descriptive, beyond the realm of intentional political objects, so as to hopefully better grasp the existential depth of authoritarian repression. While there is an abundance of political science literature that remains at the analytical level of philosophical intentionality (for instance, literature on authoritarian upgrading, authoritarian learning, authoritarian repression, etc.), there has been no literature on how such processes affect one's being in the world, how it shifts one's existential structures of the possibility of experience (Ratcliffe, 2008, 2014). Yet, if we want to understand the gravity and the depth of effects of such political violence, whose existential impacts also affect political mobilisation as such, it is essential that the existential impact of authoritarian rule is taken seriously in the political science literature. And this relates to the fact that insofar as emotions have been incorporated into social movement theory, they too have remained at the level of philosophical intentionality (see Eyerman, 1982, 2015; Rehin et al., 1993) – the realm of our mental *cognitive* directedness to the world – rather than how we might experience shifts in the underlying existential structures of possible experience. It is hence through the incorporation of critical theoretical philosophy that this monograph would like to break out of such a cognitivist impasse.

Middle East scholars might find it questionable to use Western philosophical frameworks – and particularly that of Jürgen Habermas, which is so steeped in a teleological theory of evolution and modernity – to make sense of their experiences and the counter-revolutionary events that took place in Egypt, and Cairo in more specifically. Now, of course the contextual origins need not necessarily impact a philosophy's usefulness as an analytical lens, but where it does – and in the case of Habermas's theory of modernity (Habermas, 1979, 1984, 1987b, 1990b) it certainly does – this is directly addressed in this monograph not only through a *meta*-theoretical adaptation of his works but also the explicit emptying out of his theoretical framework of the teleological Westocentric presumptions that pester his theory of modernity (Boon, 2009). Once we have emptied Habermas's critical theory of such teleological notions, we are left with a horizontal account of communicative reason, wherein the kernel of radical intersubjective equality is posited, that is, particularly useful for the analysis of trauma. It is useful since it enables us to break free from the straightjacket of the philosophy of the subject and empowers us to see trauma for what it is: namely, the infliction of a grave *injustice* wherein one is not regarded and treated as an equal human being, as a being of equal existential worth. We speak of traumatic status subordination when this injustice has been so grave that it removed the capacity to speak back.

In this sense, it highlights the fact that human-induced trauma[15] in all its forms is always already political in that it always already involves a power relation. Hence, whether it is the traumatic abuse of a minor or the infliction of Sisi's regime of death, trauma always entails a violent betrayal of the fundamental existential equality of a human being is distorted. And in this sense, trauma is always already political, either informally or formally. A Habermasian perspective is useful since it highlights this political nature of trauma, through its illumination of trauma's underlying instrumental rationality: it is an abusive power relation that comes in different shapes and sizes but is geared by the purposive pursuit of silencing and incapacitating the victim (the latter of whom could be both a group and an individual). How these power dynamics exactly operate varies from context to context and cannot be philosophically predetermined. Moreover, in some cases the scope of power relation extends 'only' to the victim, while in other cases, this domination over the victim also serves the pursuit of broader political and economic power – as it did in Egypt.

To be sure, as explained earlier (when discussing the reconstructive method), this book indeed does assume – in a *critical* humanist fashion – that there is a universal dynamic of trauma that might be valid in different circumstances. However, in outlining this dynamic, this book does not put forward a thick conception based on (thick) cognitivist presuppositions about the universal workings of the inner mind but rather on thin, fallible, social-normative considerations of intersubjective imparity.[16] Yet, as stated before, this research is necessarily fallible and post-positivist in orientation, it ought by no means be regarded as the final word on trauma. Rather, this monograph seeks to merely provide one stepping stone towards opening up debates on trauma within Middle East Studies that are no longer hampered by the restrictions and errors of philosophy of the subject.

And then to turn to the philosopher's objections. Indeed, this account of trauma perhaps goes somewhat outside of the usual bounds of philosophical discussions on Jurgen Habermas, Nancy Fraser or Rahel Jaeggi in that this book employs these works meta-theoretically. The professionalisation of Philosophy has led to a decline in Philosophy as a way of life, or as a lived praxis, and an increased focus on detailed textual analysis. While such detailed discussions of critical theory are extremely useful in highlighting internal contradictions, shortcoming, biases and other philosophical problems, the risk is that they become somewhat myopic – divorced from the concrete social and political reality it is supposed to pertain and talk to. And so, while often I greatly appreciate these philosophical debates and love to revel in them myself; this monograph nevertheless deliberately moves in the other direction: it seeks to (meta-theoretically) employ philosophical insights so as to shed new light on the dynamics of violence and repression. It thus employs critical theoretical concepts such as Jurgen Habermas's ideal speech situation, his concept of the colonisation of the lifeworld, Nancy Fraser's status subordination and Rahel Jaeggi's account of alienation in such a way as to elucidate the dynamics of authoritarian and counter-revolutionary traumatisation.

In doing so, this monograph not only seeks to bring abstract concepts such as the lifeworld down to earth (Edwards, 2007)[17] but also seeks to engage the Frankfurter Schule literature (and especially the second and third-generation theorists) directly with developments in a non-Western setting. For, though critical in its orientation, one of the limitations of the Frankfurter Schule has been its underlying occidental parochialism (Allen, 2016; Vazquez-Arroyo,

2018; Ingram, 2019), whose reasoning, argumentation and application have remained limited to social and political debates and current affairs situated in Europe and Northern America. This has narrowed its critical gaze, and hence I believe it is crucial for the development of German critical theory[18] to pull off these blinkers and opens its horizons. It should particularly do so through an active engagement with the practical lived realities and experiences of violence in the non-Western world. Only then can we develop a truly reflective critical theoretical framework that is transformative and emancipatory in nature. This monograph hence attempts to make a step in that direction, through a critical theoretical engagement with the embodied, carceral practices of authoritarian repression and violence in Egypt.

And here we come to the last audience of the book, activists or ordinary concerned Egyptian citizens. Admittedly, this book is academic in character, with Part 1 in particular being rather heavily steeped in philosophy. There is always a tension between the depth of an academic analysis and the desired scope of audience one engages with, with academic language and analysis often restricting public access. And admittedly, when this research started the aim was somewhat different, rather more practical, than what is presented here in its current academic form. Initially, the aim of the project was to gather life stories of ordinary Egyptians and to then distribute the analyses of these life stories through social media or YouTube so as to try and help mend societal bridges where these had been deliberately broken by Egypt's counter-revolution. These interviews were taken during the heat of societal ruptures in Egypt, and the hope was to contribute towards overcoming such hardened divisions by help people see the human being behind the suffering, the bloodshed and the violence. Yet, it soon became evident that with the acceleration of deadly counter-revolutionary politics under Sisi, it was no longer possible – or at least not without a risk to do serious harm to others – to undertake such an endeavour. Hence, this research changed from a publicly oriented undertaking to an overtly academic one. This shift undoubtedly benefitted its philosophical argument, since, in all likelihood, in its practical form my research would have also probably simply replicated the 'trauma is PTSD' myth. Yet, the price might very well be a restriction in its intended audience. And I can only hope that those who might not share my passion for philosophy will bear with me in the first Part, which is theoretically heavy, and will find a useful account of the existential dynamics of repression in Egypt in Part 2 and 3. And I can only hope that it will contribute a little to the recognition of grave traumatic injustice Egyptians suffered when in the violent crushing of their intersubjective equality, they were purposefully deprived of hope – the hope of living nothing less than a human, non-deadly, life. And so, it is my deepest hope that this book will not only speak truth to power, and help relay the grave injustice of the counter-revolution and Sisi's rule, but also make sense of Egyptian activists' experiences. I hope that it may in this way contribute a little to amplifying their particular voices, especially given that these were so violently destroyed and muted.

NOTES

1. Particularly, Abdelrahman's analysis provides a very insightful and nuanced detailed account of the obstacles posed by the movements horizontality (Abdelrahman, 2013).

2. Though, in a true Habermasian fashion, such an account always necessarily remains fallible – and will be subject to revision in light of objections and other insights that might occur (Habermas, 1992, 2017).

3. Here I reapply Fraser's critique of Honneth, and the double injury therein, in the realm of trauma studies (Fraser, 2003b).

4. This point draws inspiration from Hegel's critique of abstract universalism, wherein generalised philosophical frameworks become separated from concrete material and find no point of application, which has motivated Habermas's intersubjective formulation of universal reason as rooted in concrete, grounded communication – and though Habermas in his own philosophy ends up repeating this problem in his later philosophy as he moves towards social frameworks of abstraction, this point emphasises the importance of the contextual embeddedness of intersubjective formations (Habermas, 1988).

5. Also see Eagle Prof and (Kaminer, 2013; Stevens et al., 2013; Straker, 2013; Hecker et al., 2017; Kaminer et al., 2018; Pat-Horenczyk and Schiff, 2019).

6. On the difference between truth and socio-normative righteousness, see Habermas (2003: 237–276).

7. For an excellent philosophical analysis of the ways cognitivism has been incorporated into post-structuralist literary trauma theory, see Radstone (2007).

8. For Fraser's own understanding of status subordination, see Fraser and Honneth (2003: 18–19).

9. This assertion of the counterfactual presupposition of equality in debate is grounded in Jurgen Habermas's reconstructive account of the presuppositions necessary in debate (Habermas, 1993, 1995, 1998), which has inspired Fraser's conception of participation parity. For a detailed scholarly evaluation of the latter concept, see (Armstrong and Thompson, 2009).

10. As explained earlier, while in a sense all form of trauma is political in that it constitutes a power relation and social in that it entails a distortion of *intersubjective* parity – here social trauma is an analytical distinction imposed on an intertwined traumatic reality so as to talk about traumatisation as it is experienced in the social sphere. The social sphere is thus differentiated (though always interconnected) with the political sphere of political contestation and decision-making, and the individual realm of subjective emotional experience.

11. On the prefigurative nature of the Egyptian revolution, see van de Sande (2013).

12. Joshua Stacher's book *Watermelon Democracy* (2020) is particularly insightful on this process of co-optation.

13. Note that this book is primarily concerned with human-induced trauma. However, the boundary between human-induced trauma and natural trauma is often porous – in that human actions (and frequently those informed by instrumental rationality) often result in natural trauma's or the aggravation thereof. For instance, hurricane Katrina had such a disastrous effect on certain communities because they had been structurally marginalised for so long. Moreover, even where we can make the distinction more clearly, while in natural trauma there is arguably no intentional actor behind the suffering (unless one believes in an intentional transcendental god) the effects – of disorientation and feeling an powerlessness to manifest oneself in the world – still result from the experience of an unequal power relation wherein the capacity to act, to influence one's surroundings, is violently curtailed.

14. And thus in this sense, the reconstruction of traumatic status subordination follows Habermas's own logic of quasi-transcendentality wherein reason is always directed towards the universal, yet concretely manifested in real discursive formations – thereby finding a middle ground between universal abstraction and concrete particularity (see Habermas, 1998b).

15. See footnote 13 on the relation between human-induced and natural trauma.

16. Again, here I am adopting Habermas's post-positivist reconstructive method, wherein fallibility is emphasised (Habermas, 1979, 1992).

17. As Gemma Edwards pointed out: 'Colonization needs to be brought out of the realm of abstract theory and made sense of in terms of actual issues and policies affective actual struggles' (2007: 113).

18. I refer to it here as German critical theory so as to highlight I am referring to the Frankfurter Schule tradition specifically, rather than say the French tradition of critical thought.

Part 1

TOWARDS A CRITICAL THEORY OF TRAUMA AS BROKEN SUBJECTIVITY

INTRODUCTION

As explained in the introduction, the motivation behind this book was to explore the existential impact of counter-revolutionary violence on Egyptian activists. To that end, forty life-story interviews were conducted with young Cairene activists between October 2013 and February 2014. These activists covered the socio-economic and religious divides in Egypt as well as Egypt's political spectrum: it included liberals, socialists, social democrats, Islamists and Salafists. Importantly, interviewees were not chosen on the basis of having 'suffered trauma' as such, but rather on having been politically active. Political activism was understood here in the broadest sense possible and thus varied from direct involvement in formal party politics, to participation in informal street politics (such as protests and sit-ins) and producing political content (such as art, blogs or opinion pieces). When analysing the phenomenological impact of the counter-revolutionary violence that activists suffered, it quickly became apparent that it had been traumatic: many interviewees experienced extreme demoralised disorientation and an inability to make sense of the world around them, resulting in a profound speechlessness.

Yet, nearly just as quickly, it became apparent that the common cognitivist understanding of trauma as PTSD was not only severely limited but failed to effectively account for these activists' traumatic experiences. The trouble was, it transpired, that it remained wedded to a philosophy of the subject (Habermas, 1995; Fritsch, 2019). The philosophy of the subject assumes that there is an atomistic and sovereign self, whose abstracted essence may be known through a detached, introspective, objectifying gaze (Habermas, 1995; Finlayson, 2013: 29). The trouble with this point of view is that it abides by a universalist subject–object metaphysics, wherein both the object and subject are reified into detached, atomised entities, whose essence or properties may be understood using a detached objectifying (monologically constructed) lens. Simply put, the problem is that both the 'object' studied and the studying 'subject' become artificially abstracted from their intersubjective embeddedness and constitution, and undergo (universalistic) essentialisation (Habermas, 1995). This results in the well-known and commonly associated aporias, such as the unwarranted universalist projection of a particular, a reliance on an abstracted decontextualised individualism and objectifying reification of the object studied.

In trauma studies, abidance by a philosophy of the subject has resulted in a fourfold problematic. First, since it produced an individualist, cognitive understanding of trauma as an injury of the inner workings of the mind, it directly posed the danger of what Nancy Fraser calls a 'double injury' (Fraser, 2003a) wherein insult is added to injury. Those who already suffered a violent injustice are now also told that there is also something wrong with their mind (or brain), and they become responsible for its repair through therapeutic practice (which often, though not always, takes the form of cognitive behavioural therapy). And while therapeutic practice can be extremely useful repairing intersubjective imparity – through the recognition of the patient's suffering and worth by a therapist, it nevertheless (implicitly) shifts the burden of responsibility onto the victim.

Second, as the cognitivist conception is mired in detached individualist universalism, trauma studies fails to properly account for the political contextual constitution of its own theoretical concepts. That is to say, trauma studies fails to critically reflect on Westocentric origins of its own theoretical constructs (and the limitations thereof) and instead projects forth a universal cognitivist conception of trauma that is rooted in a (again Westocentric) teleological history. And so, the argument goes, trauma is a universal human condition of cognitive impairment that existed throughout history, but has gone through periods of scholarly amnesia (Leys, 2000). Yet, as trauma studies progressed, the truth of its universal condition has been supposedly revealed to or discovered by trauma theorists through the experiences such as the Railroad Injury, Shellshock of the First World War, the Second World War's Holocaust and the Vietnam War. The trouble here is not only that, as Allan Young pointed out (2014), trauma studies violently reduces a diversity of experiences (and variety of *sense-making* of those experiences) under one theoretical construct of PTSD, but also that in this historical teleology there is a complete absence of non-Western experiences (such as colonisation, imperialism and slavery to just name a few) (Summerfield, 2001; Bracken, 2002b; Craps, 2014; Tseris, 2015).

This leads us directly to the third problem, namely trauma studies' persistent portrayal of trauma as an (extraordinary) *external, past, event*

(Radstone, 2007; Alford, 2016), which has supposedly overwhelmed the processing capacities of the mind or the brain, thereby resulting in the error of its cognitive software (Bracken, 2002b). This 'event-ism' is deeply problematic: it overlooks the structural nature and continuous experiential reality of trauma – such as the threat to life due to poverty or authoritarian repression – in much of the world, and particularly (though not solely) the Global South. As Stef Craps noted in his seminal work on trauma, what some might call trauma, others might call life (Craps, 2014: 53). Moreover, as psychologists in South Africa (such as Gillian Straker (2013)) noted, this construction of trauma as a *past* event fails to recognise not only the continuous nature of trauma in many parts of the world, but also the extent to which therapeutic safety is often directly compromised (particularly through mechanisms and networks of authoritarian surveillance). Indeed, they argue that in these contexts, trauma studies insistence on symptom reduction may in fact be outright dangerous – since under such circumstances anxiety, suspicion and hyper-alertness are necessary survival mechanisms (Eagle and Kaminer, 2013; Stevens et al., 2013; Straker, 2013; Kaminer et al., 2018).

And then fourthly, the problem is that so long as trauma studies remains tied to the introspective, detached ontological confines of a medicalised philosophy of the subject philosophy of the subject, it cannot account for the political claims it itself wants to make. From its very inception, namely its emergence out of the Vietnam War veterans lobby, trauma studies has been motivated by a distinctly political claim: the pursuit of *justice* for victims of violence (Alford, 2016). The trouble is that it cannot logically pursue such claims from within the perspective of a solipsist, introspective medical objectivism. Rather, such claims towards justice make an appeal to the socio-normative order that extends beyond the remit of medical facts and enters into the realm of intersubjective meaning-making and socio-normativity. Or, claims of justice are of a socio-normative nature rather than an objective-factual one (Habermas, 1987b: 120), and thus cannot be accounted for within the remit of biomedical objectivism.

Indeed, this issue points directly to the fact that trauma studies actually committed a simple category mistake when it – due to the American Psychological Association's positivist 'revolution' in the 1980s – firmly positioned trauma in the realm of an objective truth claims rather than socio-normative validity claims. As Habermas has explained, the validity of socio-normative claims rests on intersubjective processes of deliberation (centred around issues of normative rightness and are thus directly related to intersubjective interpretative processes of meaning-making), whereas objective truth claims are constative claims about observable facts (Habermas, 1987b: 120). The trouble for trauma studies is that the concept of trauma as PTSD includes its own aetiology in its definition: trauma refers to both the event and its effects (or symptoms) simultaneously. This not only gives rise to tautological reasoning, but the diagnosis of trauma also clearly transcends the limits of nosological symptomology (or observable medical facts). Its diagnosis does not rest so much on empirical observation of supposed observable medical symptoms but rather on the interpretative attribution of causality to a particular event. As chapter 1 explains, this attribution is extremely problematic especially given the presence of pre-existing character traits that remain unaccounted for, different possible responses to the same event and the persuasive power of the therapist. Indeed, this debate on the causal event reached its pinnacle (or rather, its low point) when trauma studies got itself stuck in some notorious muddy waters: the repressed memory debate (Loftus and Ketcham, 1996; Pendergrast, 2017). This debate was only finally closed after questionable evidence of supposed repressed traumatic memories had entered the American legal system as evidence, including alien abduction and UFOs encounters (Loftus and Ketcham, 1996).

Yet, the same scholars that had been staunch advocates for the repressed memory debate – such as Bessel van der Kolk – now turned to neuroscience as their saviour (Alford, 2016: 16). Surely, hard 'empirical evidence' would close this interpretative ambiguity once and for all. However, the problem here is that the pixels of the fMRI scans used in trauma research are not only too imprecise to attribute the exact brain functions that trauma scholars would like to attribute to amygdala and hippocampus, it also provides us with nothing more than a correlation (Kihlstrom, 2006, 2010; Alford, 2016). That is, even if parts of the brain light up like a colourful Christmas tree, still no *causal* link may be established to a particular event. All that has occurred is a translation of psychological assumptions into a different language, like a translation from one language to another such as English into French (Kihlstrom, 2010: 773). It did however significantly contribute to a further reification of trauma as a pathological 'object' located in the individual's mind, which may be resolved through psychical introspective intervention. The neuroscientific turn thus solidified trauma studies' rooting in a philosophy of the subject, with all the above-mentioned problems thereof. As chapter 1 will show, the trouble is that these cognitivist presumptions have so dominated the field of trauma studies that they have been replicated even in areas normally hostile to the philosophy of the subject, such as postmodern or post-structuralist conceptions of trauma (Radstone, 2007).

Hence, this part is divided into two chapters, with the first outlining the persistence of the philosophy of the subject and its aporias in trauma studies, and the second section proposing a critical theoretical conception of trauma not as impaired subjectivity but as impaired *inter*subjectivity. More specifically, chapter 1 will offer a critical theoretical critique of both PTSD as well as the development of trauma studies as such. Such an endeavour is urgent because while trauma studies' essentialism, unwarranted universalism and Westocentrism have been critiqued from a variety of different angles (Bracken, 1988; Craps, 2014; Tseris, 2015; Bistoen, 2016; Lewis-Fernández and Kirmayer, 2019; Bracken et al., 2021), it has not yet been successfully linked to trauma studies' abidance by a philosophy of the subject as such. Chapter 1 will thus commence with an overview of Habermas's philosophy, including his critique of the philosophy of the subject, before outlining how the positivist revolution within the APA wedded trauma studies precisely to such a philosophy of the subject through its concept of PTSD. It will then explain how, haunted by a weak epistemological foundation, trauma studies sought to solidify its scientific basis through recourse to neuroscience. Yet, not only did this leave the problem of causality unresolved, it also plunged the concept of trauma ever deeper into the quagmire of the philosophy of the subject and its associated aporias. As the cognitivist perception of trauma as PTSD then became so dominant, or commonplace, in both academic and popular circles, it became increasingly difficult to even imagine alternatives. Though the definition of PTSD was modified in the APA's diagnostic statistical manual (DSM) several times, the cognitivist perception of trauma as PTSD was left unquestion and was, despite its unscientific basis, posited as a taken for granted truth. And so, those trauma approaches that emphasised the intersubjective breakdown of meaning-making in trauma did so in introspective cognitivist terms (Horowitz, 1983; Janoff-Bulman, 1992), while strands of thought normally hostile to the philosophy of the subject – such as post-structuralism – in fact replicated its main presuppositions when they actively embraced the cognitivist perception of trauma (see Radstone, 2007).

Hence, chapter 2 develops a critical theoretical understanding of trauma as broken *inter*subjectivity. In doing so, I take its inspiration from Heideggerian trauma scholarship, such as that of Robert D. Stolorow[1] and Patrick Bracken[2] which have excellently emphasised the intersubjective rupture of meaning in trauma. Yet, though an important stepping stone, the problem is that their work regards this rupture of meaning from the first person's subjective (phenomenological) perspective only. That is, it only discusses how trauma is experienced from within, by the person suffering, in and thus fails to provide a closer analysis of its social and political constitution. Heideggerian trauma studies thus arguably remains, at least implicitly, tied to a philosophy of the subject.

And thus, this monograph extends these Heideggerian insights in a more radical critical theoretical direction, namely through a meta-theoretical appropriation of the philosophical ideas of Jürgen Habermas (1979, 1984, 1987b, 1992, 1995), Nancy Fraser (Fraser and Honneth, 2003) and Rahel Jaeggi (2014). Using their philosophical insights as a departure, the chapter 2 develops a critical theoretical understanding of trauma as a violent betrayal of the counterfactual presupposition of being treated as an equal peer in intersubjective relation with (an) other(s). Trauma thus entails the imposition of a deeply violent power relation, wherein one experiences an alienating and disorientating loss of agency. As one loses the ability to shape or influence one's surroundings, one loses one's existential orientation in the world. The victim (which can be both an individual as well as a group) is incapacitated and rendered speechless, muted. Trauma, no matter its scope, is hence always already political. It entails a grave violation of what Nancy Fraser calls participation parity (Fraser and Honneth, 2003: 36–37), the equality of peers, through the mechanism of status subordination (Fraser and Honneth, 2003: 18–19). Rather, the perpetrator (either a group or an individual) seeks to violently subordinate the victim through both practices of misrecognition (taken here to mean the failure to recognise our equality as a human beings) and maldistribution (the unfair distribution of political and economic resources).

Importantly, while always unpleasant and unjust, not all forms of injustice or, status subordination are necessarily traumatic. Rather, we only speak of traumatic status subordination when the *capacity to speak back* at the infliction of injustice is removed – when it has such an incapacitating impact that one loses one's bearing in the world and the ability to address the injury suffered.

Crucially, while Fraser's philosophy (Fraser and Honneth, 2003; Fraser, 2010, 2014) and particularly her notion of status subordination, helps us elucidate the *mechanism* of traumatic status subordination, and Rahel Jaeggi's theory of alienation helps illuminate trauma's deeply alienating effects (Jaeggi, 2014), it is Habermas's philosophy (Habermas, 1979, 1987b) that shines a light on its underlying instrumental rationality. The infliction of trauma is part of a calculative rational, or purposeful, pursuit of power – with may range in scope (from power over the victim to the wider calculative aims of political and economic power). Habermas also helps us understand how such a strategic onslaught (wherein the fundamental presuppositions of meaning-making are destroyed) results in a breakdown of the lifeworld (Habermas, 1987b), which gives rise to the experience of alienation so well described by Rahel Jaeggi (2014). Understood in such a critical theoretical manner, it becomes apparent that trauma entails nothing less than the purposefully inflicted breakdown of the lifeworld. Its aim is to incapacitate the victim through the violent infliction of status subordination that destroys the fundamental presupposition of intersubjective equality, and ruptures the shared symbolic realm of the lifeworld, leaving the victim hanging in a state of existential isolation and disorientation. For, as I will explain in this chapter, when the lifeworld's background dissipates into thin air, it leaves us hanging in existential no-man's-land as the potential of meaning-making disappears from underneath our feet. And it is precisely this potentiality that Egypt's counter-revolution was intent on destroying through the systematic infliction of multilevelled traumatic status subordination (see Part 2), which spanned across the political and social spheres. For, with the disappearance of the lifeworld's horizon of potentiality, a deep relationlessness (re)occurred, wherein re-atomisation, demoralisation and depoliticisation held sway and creative collective becoming was destroyed (Part 3).

Such a critical theory of trauma not only sheds light on the underexposed existential dynamics of counter-revolutionary repression in Egypt, it also has a number of philosophical advantages. First, as it releases us from the confines of the philosophy of the subject, it enables us to clearly perceive and distinguish trauma's causality from its effects. While trauma is caused by a grave violation of intersubjective parity, its effects are existential disorientation and atomisation that result in speechlessness and incapacitation.

Second, it avoids the 'eventism' that has haunted trauma studies (Leys, 2000; Radstone, 2007): trauma understood as broken intersubjectivity may both be inflicted through violent events (such as torture or killings) and structural violence (such as violent marginalisation and excruciating poverty). Indeed, often incidental and structural violence beget each other and constitute a toxic mix through which the lifeworld is purposefully broken down, leaving one in an incapacitated state of atomised disorientation.

Third, such a Habermasian-/Fraserian-inspired conception of trauma firmly positions it within the realm of justice and socio-normative claims. This does not in any way deny or diminish the horrific effects trauma has on the victim, but rather it is able to do justice to this suffering through a more comprehensive understanding of trauma, as both the cause and effects are placed within an intersubjective social and political context. It thus enables us to perceive human-induced trauma in all its different forms (whether that is child abuse or counter-revolutionary repression) as a political tool of domination. In doing so, it not only avoids the above-mentioned problem of a double injury, it also enables us to theoretically ground the underlying political motivations of trauma studies: namely the pursuit of justice and rectification of injustice.

Fourth, it enables us to grasp the universal dynamics of trauma, without projecting forth a particular (thick) Westocentric conception of trauma. That is, while human induced trauma in all its different forms entails a gross violation of intersubjective equality through status subordination, its specific forms and shapes will be context dependent. Needless to say, any such claim that I am making to universality here can only be understood in a (Habermasian) post-positivist sense: they remain fallible and open to debate.

And so, after the critique of trauma in chapter 1 and a philosophical outline of a critical theory of trauma in chapter 2, Part 2 of this book will outline how Egypt's counter-revolution applied this tool of domination in a multi-levelled manner, namely through the political procedural colonisation of the political public sphere, the infliction of grave deadly violence and neoliberal economic marginalisation. Part 3 will then discuss how the weight of death and overwhelming violence, in the context of political colonisation and economic deterioration broke down the lifeworld's horizon of interpretation. And particularly as the military redirected frustration and anger inwards and encouraged violent social polarisation, it destroyed the last possible remnants of revolutionary unity, thereby crushing the potential of creative collective becoming. Indeed, a deeply incapacitating sense of demoralisation set in: one wherein the very potentiality of meaningful change had dissappeared into thin air.

NOTES

1. Stolorow, 2007, 2011, 2013, 2018, 2020b, 2020a; Atwood and Stolorow, 2014a, 2014b; Stolorow and Atwood, 2014, 2018; Orange et al., 2015.
2. See Bracken, 1988, 2002b, 2002a; Bracken et al., 1995; Thomas and Bracken, 2004; Thomas et al., 2004; Bracken et al., 2021.

Chapter 1

Trauma Studies and the Philosophy of the Subject

TOWARDS INTERSUBJECTIVITY: HABERMAS'S CRITIQUE OF THE PHILOSOPHY OF THE SUBJECT

As stated in the introduction of this book, I draw on the insights of Jurgen Habermas *meta-theoretically*. This means I position myself slightly outside the usual terrain (or confines) of Habermasian scholarship: I will neither develop a detailed study on deliberative democracy as such nor will I enter into the details of his discourse ethics or deliberative philosophical framework here. Rather, I draw inspiration from Habermas's works and use these as a meta-theoretical lens that enables us to rethink trauma in a critical theoretical and intersubjective manner. In this book, Habermas's insights on the constitutive intersubjectivity of social life (Habermas, 1992), his associated critique of the philosophy of the subject (Habermas, 1995) and his theory of the colonisation of the lifeworld (Habermas, 1979, 1984, 1987b) serve two important, and distinct, points. First, it offers a critique of trauma studies' adherence to an introspective foundational philosophy of the subject. Second, it is used to construct an alternative, critical theoretical account of trauma as purposefully inflicted intersubjective imparity. While chapter 2 is focused on the latter point, this chapter will explain how (through a genealogical tracing) trauma studies fell victim to Habermas's critique of positivism and has remained tied to a philosophy of the subject (with all its associated aporias) ever since.

The first section of chapter 1 will thus explore some of the key insights of Habermas's philosophy which will then be brought to bear on trauma studies and a critical theoretical account of trauma will be developed (chapter 2). At the essence of Habermas's philosophy lies the assertion that life, including personal, social and political life, is profoundly and fundamentally intersubjective

(Habermas, 1979, 1984, 1987b, 1995, 1998). The notion of a pure or essential self whose essence we may know through inwards inspection is a mythical abstraction that has dangerous alienating effects (Habermas, 1992). Drawing on the intersubjective theory of socialisation of George Herbert Mead and developmental psychology of Lawrence Kohlberg and Jean Piaget, Habermas asserts that even insofar as we are able to speak of a self, this self is always already formed in a process of socialisation (Habermas, 1979, 1993). For, we only become aware of our 'selves' through communicative relations with others. Drawing on Mead, he argues that it is through processes of communication with others in our life – initially through a conversation of gestures when we are smaller and later through a conversation of signals (or, words) – that individuation occurs and our idea of our individual self may be formed. The 'I', or subjectivity, is hence not an object waiting to be discovered through introspection but rather formed in concrete social interaction with others (Habermas, 1998b: 153). Put differently, the self – and one's sense of 'I' – is hence not constituted by an essential core of 'inner truth' but is rather inherently intersubjectively shaped in direct relation to one's social surroundings (Habermas, 1992: 171). It is also precisely this process of socialised individualisation that we are enabled to adopt a critical stance not only to the social patterns of the 'we' – or the traditions we are socialised in – but also to our self and our actions (Habermas, 1992). In other words, it enables critical (self) reflection. Thus, importantly, the capacity of critical reflection upon the self does not occur in isolation from others through cognitive introspection but intersubjectively through socialisation and communication with others in the world.

Hence, for Habermas, the notion of a pure self as epitomised in the philosophy of consciousness by, most notably, Rene Descartes or Emmanuel Kant is a false construction that hides our radical intersubjectivity and fundamental social embeddedness from view (Habermas, 1992, 1993). Both Descartes and Kant sought to establish how the object of perception is made apparent to the experiencing subject by laying bare the foundations of experience. In doing so, they adopted an inward-looking stance that buttressed the notion of an individual autonomous self, capable of reflecting on pure consciousness in isolation from its social surroundings and intersubjective constitution. After all, Descartes's rationalism argued that consciousness arises for us through thought (thus giving rise to mind/body dualism) (Descartes, 2008), while Kant – seeking to steer his way through both Descartes's rationalism and Hume's empiricism – insisted that perception and experience of objects are made possible through the transcendental, a priori, conditions of time, space and concepts[1] (Kant, 1724). In both these philosopher's works, Habermas argues,[2] experience is reduced to an object that may be delineated and grasped by the autonomous atomised self through introspective reflection – or rather, through the interior mental realm of ideas and perceptions (Finlayson, 2013: 29). This move leads to a form of metaphysical dualism wherein the mind becomes detached from its location in the corporeal, intersubjectively constituted world – and objects come to be regarded as standing over and against a plurality of thinking and acting subjects (resulting in a subject–object metaphysics) (Habermas, 1995; Finlayson, 2013: 29). The upshot of this is a threefold reduction:

> Ontologically, the world is reduced to the world of entities as a whole (as the totality of objects that can be represented and of existing states of affairs); epistemologically, our relationship is reduced to the capacity to know existing states of affairs or bring them about in a purposive-rational fashion; semantically, it is reduced to a fact stating discourse in which assertoric sentences are used – and no validity claim is admitted besides propositional truth, which is available *in foro interno*. (Habermas, 1995: 154–155)

Hence, a philosophy of consciousness reduces the world around us into objects that are to be grasped and manipulated by the perceiving, objectivating, atomised and sovereign subject.

Habermas argues that the philosophy of consciousness thereby adheres to a purposive rationalist orientation since it presumes that there is an object out there waiting to be grasped and worked upon by the neutral, detached and disembodied subject. It is also purposive rational since it takes the perspective that the object out there is to be worked upon by the subject to achieve a particular goal (including for instance the goal of self-clarification). The problem is that by adopting such an orientation, neither the subject nor the object is brought down to earth and regarded as susceptible to concrete historical, social and political intersubjective formations (see Habermas, 1992b: 30). And so, we end up with abstracted, universalised, generalised and objectified knowledge of the self and the object that remains stuck in a world of oppositions (namely, oppositions between the object and subject, the phenomenal and noumenal, and the universal and the particular) as the radical intersubjective nature of our ontological embedding and epistemological frameworks is obscured (Habermas, 1995). The result is an objectifying projection of universally valid truth, based on a monological and abstracted prescription that ignores the manner in which subjects, objects and perceptions are always already entangled in a contextual web of interpretation.

In his critique of positivism (Habermas, 1976a), Habermas explicitly points out that these problems were perpetuated by the positivist social sciences as they reproduced this metaphysical dualism of the philosophy of consciousness through the presupposition of a neutral subject and object relations. In doing so, positivist social sciences also adopted a purposive rational orientation, wherein in this supposedly neutral relation, the object exists out there to be worked upon by the subject in pursuit of a particular goal.

Now, in his critique of the philosophy of consciousness, Habermas thus also explicitly argues against such a purposive rational orientation (when it concerns matters of meaning-making and socio-normative claims) and instead insists that any interpretation always already occurs against the unescapable background of a mutually constituted lifeworld (Habermas, 1984, 1987b, 1995, 2017) – or, the world into which we are thrown. Hence, according to this reading, positivist social sciences (such as positivist psychology) contribute to the essentialist reification of social reality wherein both subject and object are essentialised and abstracted from their intersubjective grounding. And thus, psychology's notion of cognitive, introspective abstraction results in distortions of our understanding of ourselves, others as well as the surrounding world. And thus, Habermas insist that we ought to

> [replace] the paradigm of self-consciousness, of the relation-to-self of a subject knowing and acting in isolation [. . .] by a different one – by the paradigm of mutual understanding, that is, of the intersubjective relationship between individuals who are socialised through communication and reciprocally recognise one another. (Habermas, 1995: 154)

And so, it is upon this basis that Habermas builds his theory of communicative rationality and deliberative democracy. Herein, he puts forward the bold thesis that it is possible to salvage the potential of rationality, despite the destructive nature of modernity and the perhaps sometimes appealing threat of relativism (Habermas, 1984, 1987b, 1990a). Rather, he insists that in light of modernity's destructiveness and plurality, we do not have to throw reason overboard, but rather we can rescue it through a radically intersubjective conception of reason. He makes an important distinction here between instrumental and communicative rationality. While the former entails the adoption of an objectivating attitude towards the object in the strategic pursuit of a predetermined end (as we discussed above), the latter is based on mutual perspective-taking as participants engage in (real and actual) dialogue to come to an understanding (Habermas, 1979, 1988b).

Importantly, in contrast to the universalist, positivist (Descartian) point of view, communicative rationality is thus not located in the solipsist inner mind, but rather grounded in the actual processes of intersubjective reason giving (Habermas, 1993). And taking seriously the post-modern critiques of Enlightment grand narratives, it also means that in Habermas's account of communicative rationality, no single person is the owner of ultimate truth or justice, but rather it is formed intersubjectively within particular contexts. Yet, despite the fact that rationality is always constituted in particular processes of debate, it does not mean Habermas's theory falls down the slippery slope of relativism. Instead, while recognising that communicative rationality is always formed in particular contexts, he adheres to a (thin) universalist notion of reason, which also immediately forms the basis of critique: a critique of the (violent) distortions of reason.

Now, this thin universalist notion of communicative reason is founded upon his earlier theory of universal (or formal) pragmatics, wherein he reconstructed the necessary rational presuppositions of everyday speech (Habermas, 1979).[3] Here, he explained that as we engage in dialogue, the hearer automatically evaluates any utterance made by the speaker with reference to objective truth, intersubjective norms and subjective sincerity (Habermas, 1987b: 122–123). Or, more simply put, when someone says something to us, we ask ourselves: is what this person says it factually correct, normatively right and truthful? It is against the background of these three validity spheres that the speaker has to redeem his utterance. Importantly, this means that while instrumental rationality is based on a relation of domination (wherein the subject takes an instrumental attitude towards an object in the strategic pursuit of a particular goal) communicative rationality rests upon the presupposition of radical mutual reciprocity and intersubjective parity (Habermas, 1984, 1987b). It is only under the conditions of free and equal participation in public debate wherein all affected are able to engage as equal peers that we can come to rational understanding. And thus, a norm is only valid when all affected can agree on its foreseen consequences in unhindered, free and open debate. It is hence on this basis that Habermas argued for the rationality (and indeed necessity) of democratic deliberation and the necessity of an accessible, vibrant and open public sphere (Habermas, 1993, 1996, 2001b).[4]

Essential in his theory of communication is the understanding that any such deliberation, or indeed sense-making, always already occurs against the interpretative background of the lifeworld. Neatly mapping his theory of universal pragmatics onto his philosophy of communicative action, Habermas thus argues that we always come to an understanding of our own identity (the subjective world), of others and social norms (the intersubjective world) and the external world (the objective world) against the background of an intersubjectively formed lifeworld (Habermas, 1987: 120). Drawing on Martin Heidegger, Edmund Husserl and Hans-Georg Gadamer in particular, the lifeworld for Habermas comprises the inescapable taken-for-granted, unquestioned background assumptions into which we have been socialised and which provide us with our orientation in daily life (Habermas, 1987b, 2017). It is constituted by the objective stock of cultural knowledge (or tradition), the sphere of social integration comprising institutionalised social memberships and the sphere of socialisation forming one's personal identity in intersubjective relations with others. The lifeworld is not a solid entity set in stone, but rather is subject to change as segments become problematised in our engagements with others and the world around us (Habermas, 1987b:

122–123). Yet, the lifeworld is a reservoir of taken-for-granted norms and presuppositions that we draw on when we enter into public debate and orientate ourselves in our everyday life (Habermas, 1987b: 126). The functioning of the lifeworld as a communicative realm is thus dependent on the free flow of debate wherein all are considered equal. It is only then that we may reach understanding and engage in intersubjective meaning-making processes.

Again, Habermas sharply distinguishes communicative rationality from instrumental rationality. He argues that if instrumental reason encroaches on and shortcuts communicative reason it colonises segments of the lifeworld, which has deeply alienating effects (Habermas, 1976b, 1979, 1987b). Habermas here couples his argument about the nature of linguistic reason with a sociological critique of societal developments (Cooke, 1994). His primary argument here is that the purposive rational or instrumental logic of the system (the state, its bureaucratic political power and the economy with its money and market logic) has become uncoupled from communicative reason and started to encroach on the meaning-making structures of the lifeworld. This has had a number of undesirable and alienating effects: within the cultural sphere, it leads to a breakdown of meaning as the taken-for-granted stock of knowledge is destroyed. Within the social sphere, it results in anomie: a breakdown of social bonds, a tearing of social identity and a fragmentation of social values. In the personal sphere of socialisation, it destroys one's identity, giving rise to mental illnesses, feelings of helplessness and alienation as well as demoralisation (Finlayson, 2005: 57; Habermas, 1987: 130).

Now, chapter 2 will elaborate upon the usefulness of the lens that Habermas's theory of colonisation offers for understanding process of counter-revolutionary traumatisation in Egypt, which is then applied to Egypt in Part 2 and 3. There, I will argue such traumatisation is best conceived as the purposeful destruction of the lifeworld through a deeply violent and fundamental betrayal of intersubjective parity, which left activists are muted, disoriented and ultimately demoralised. That is, in the instrumental pursuit of economic and political power, the military purposefully and systematically destroyed the communicative realm so as to inhibit the *potential* of creative self-becoming, thereby instilling a deep existential sense of demoralised relationlessness (wherein the potential of meaningful change itself had dissipated) in activists.

THE POSITIVIST REVOLUTION AND THE EMERGENCE OF PTSD

However, we first have to consider the ways in which trauma studies falls victim to Habermas's critique of positivism (Habermas, 1976a, 1988b). Habermas's critique of positivism centres around the ways in which it continues the philosophy of the subject: employing a detached observer's lens, positivism reifies intersubjectively constituted meaning into a detached 'object' whose essence and properties are transparent to this (equally detached) observant subject. Hence, as positivism extends the logic of the natural sciences to the social sciences, it reifies meaning and meaning-making practices by regarding them as following naturally observable laws (Habermas, 1988b). As Andrew Edgard explains, 'such laws are expressed not in terms of concrete and meaningful relationships between human being, but only as interconnections between the abstractly quantified, and mathematically formulated properties of a system' (Edgar, 2005: 19). Importantly, as positivism expands technocratic reason into the realm of social sciences not only commits an 'error in the philosophy of science' (Edgar, 2005: 20) but is rather itself part and parcel of the lifeworld's colonisation. Positivism artificially restricts the range of acceptable validity claims to constative speech acts (pertaining to objective truth). It thereby directly encroaches on the interpretative, intersubjective realms of regulative speech (referring to social norms) and expressive speech (pertaining to subjective truth), and reduces the scope of human action and interaction to purposive rational thought. In doing so, it transforms matters of meaning and meaning-making into objects for technocratic, administrative control under the objectivating gaze of the scientist (Habermas, 1976a). Certainly, Habermas does not eschew positivism altogether, but rather expresses concern that the scope of its validity claims ought to be restricted to the observation of (natural) facts and that as soon as its logic encroaches onto matters of socio-normative righteousness or subjective truth, it will have deeply alienating and reifying effects.

The problem with trauma studies, I argue, lies directly in way in which it falls victim to Habermas's critique of positivism, thereby replicating the most common fallacies associated with the Philosophy of Subject. In trauma studies, these aporias primarily consisted of an unwarranted universalist projection of a particular (Westocentric) understanding, including an overemphasis on the traumatic event (as opposed to violent traumatic structures) and the inability to account for the intersubjective contextual constitution of both subject and object. This resulted in a problematic account of causation as well as the inability to account for its own underlying political aim of pursuing justice. These problems, I propose in this section, are only solved once we undo the category mistake trauma studies has committed: once we remove trauma from the realm of supposed objective medical facts and recognise its belonging in the sphere of socio-normative justice. I cannot emphasise enough that this by no means undervalues the experienced severity of trauma. Rather, we seek to avoid the pitfalls of the philosophy of the subject by conceiving it through a radical intersubjective lens, namely not as broken subjectivity but impaired intersubjectivity. It means taking trauma out of its cognitive straight jacket and no longer regarding its resolution to entail the cognitive restructuring of thought patterns or brain wiring but rather the eradication of abusive traumatic power relations. Or rather, by conceiving trauma in an intersubjective light, it becomes apparent that what trauma requires is in fact much more difficult and demanding task, namely the undoing of social, political and economic injustice.

But before, we get to these issues, we first ought to note that the fact trauma studies (in its current forms) falls victim to Habermas's critique of positivism is hardly surprising. After all, the very concept of PTSD arose in the midst of the positivist revolution that swept through the APA when it was composing the DSMII in 1980 (Bracken, 1988; Young, 1995; Alford, 2016). While the DSMI and DSMII were based on the open-ended, intersubjective practices of psychoanalysis and psychodynamic practices, the DSMII adopted a radically different approach: it was to be based on a rigorous natural scientific framework that yielded both statistically reliable, predictable and above all quick results (Bracken, 2002b). For, actively spurred on by the health insurance companies that were growing increasingly impatient and frustrated with both expensive and unpredictable mental health bills (as well as 'statistically unreliable results'), the APA charged the small working group headed by Robert L. Spitzer with the task of improving the DSM efficiency based on 'objective' natural scientific standards (Schulman and Hammer, 1988; Mayes and Horwitz, 2005; Alford, 2016). Hence, deeply influenced by neo-Kraepelian positivism, this small working group radically overhauled the existing frameworks of interpretation and replaced the open-ended intersubjective frameworks of psychoanalysis and psychodynamics with a cognitivist diagnostic framework whose reliability was no longer rooted in (open-ended) clinical practice but quantifiable, objective scientific research (Bracken, 2002b: 51–53) – also referred to 'evidence-based approaches'. Importantly, such 'evidence-based' research is somewhat misleading, since the diagnostic criteria are in fact now no longer based on the 'evidence' of longstanding therapeutic practice (Bracken, 2002b: 47) but rather based on quantifiable statistical results composed in a scientific laboratory (Young, 1995). Rather, mental disorders were now to be diagnosed through nosological observation (just as physical illnesses), using objective, observable and universally valid symptomatic criteria as laid out in the DSM guideline (Bracken, 2002b). And so, an abstracted model of observable symptomology arose that replaced the complex interpretative and contextual frameworks of psychoanalysis. The emphasis was thus placed on a (supposedly) neutral, objective, a-theoretical and universal framework of psychiatric diagnostic criteria, according to which one could diagnose mental illness just as one could diagnose physical disease. Psychology thus not only embraced positivism, but in doing so explicitly attempted to (re)model itself on the natural biological and medical sciences (Young, 1995; Bracken, 2002b; Alford, 2016).

In this sense, the DSMIII constituted nothing less than a radical turning point in the history of psychology and the psychiatric sciences. Through abstraction and rationalisation, it addressed 'questions of psychiatry's scientific status, such as concerns about the reliability of diagnoses' (Spitzer, 2007: viii). Reliability became established through medical analogy and statistical reasoning, which permitted 'researchers to liberate cases from contexts and to decompose distinctively messy lives into uniform and universal constitutive elements' (Young, 1995: 112). Not only were diagnostic criteria decontextualised and universalised, diagnostic practice also increasingly involved the usage of cost-effective impersonal (frequently computerised) questionnaires (Young, 1995: 129). These would be filled in by a patient before he or she even set foot in the therapist's office and would offer a guideline for the treatment plan that was to follow. Indeed, such statistical templates were believed to aid objective psychological diagnoses, that no longer depended on the interpretative interference of the psychologist or psychiatrist, while of course having the added benefit of cost-efficiency. For the (mathematical) outcome of questionnaires also often indicated the number of therapeutic sessions the patient was entitled to claim on insurance companies. All this, before the patient and therapist even met. As Spitzer himself put it, in this sense, the

> [DSM III is] considered to have revolutionized the psychiatric profession. It serve[d] to define how researchers collect their samples, what conditions insurance companies will reimburse, what conditions courts and social agencies treat as illnesses, and how individuals themselves interpret their emotional experiences. (Spitzer, 2007: viii)

Such an overhaul of the diagnostic manual is significant since 'contemporary manuals, like the DSM, also mark out, shape and configure a territory for psychiatry to occupy' (Rose, 2019: 71). And so, the consequences of the APA's avid pursuit of positivism was far-reaching: it led to an emergence of an entire mental health industry that moulded therapeutic practice along techno-bureaucratic lines. Researchers and funding boards increasingly adopted a standardised, universalist, positivistic diagnostic mental health discourse geared towards procedural efficiency, rather than intersubjective meaning-making and interpretation (Young, 1995; Bracken, 2002b; Stolorow, 2011b). And psychiatrists and psychologists were encouraged, and even trained, to adopt an observer's perspective towards the diagnosis of mental disorders, rather than one of mutual perspective-taking and interpretative, intersubjective meaning-making.[5] Guidelines of therapeutic standards and practices were increasingly directed by an instrumental rationality based on calculative goals of (cost-)efficiency, predictability and quantifiability.

This development was directly motivated by the psycho-positivists' desire to demystify psychological diagnosis, analysis and intervention and set clear professional standards (based on scientific reason). Spitzer's positivists bemoaned the fact that during the psychoanalytical and psychodynamic dominance of the APA (around the period of DSMI and DSMII), psychological analysis relied heavily on a costly, non-quantifiable, non-standardisable and 'dubious' process of interpretation between therapist and patient (Schulman and Hammer, 1988; Mayes and Horwitz, 2005). Not only was this therapist–patient supposedly couched in unprofessional intimacy, the concepts and processes of interpretation and meaning-making were non-quantifiable, necessarily contextual and thus ambiguous and open to dispute. The problem with psychoanalysis was, positivists argued, that it relied too heavily on an arbitrary interpretative framework that was neither falsifiable nor replicable.

Admittedly, there is a real risk that within psychoanalysis the therapist may be led to adopt an epistemologically privileged position,[6] wherein he or she becomes the (monological) bearer of ultimate truth, wherein alternative explanations or opinions are brushed aside. Or put differently, the danger was that the therapist, through this all-encompassing analytical framework, will cease to be reflective on the possibility of its own interpretative errors and leave no room for alternative views and experiences.

Yet, rather than facing this issue of 'ultimate truth' head on by working towards a more intersubjective understanding of therapeutic practice and psychological diagnosis (wherein *intersubjective parity* would be upheld therapeutic relations and an diagnosis would be subject to therapeutic deliberation), positivist psychologists merely replaced one ultimate truth with another. The interpretative truth of psychoanalysis and psychodynamics was merely replaced with the ultimate 'objective' truth of cognitve positivism. Cognitivist positivism thus moved psychological practice in the other direction, towards the 'scientism', wherein diagnoses are to be determined through detached introspective observation based on supposed universally valid and statistically tested criteria. Needless to say, this did not alter psychologist's privileged epistemological position as such, but that did seem not matter much since now his or her findings were (supposedly) based on replicable science and quantifiable statistical criteria rather than 'dubious' criteria of interpretation.

Yet the problem is that in its move towards 'hard-core' natural science, the intersubjective realm of therapeutic practice and therapeutic meaning-making was increasingly colonised by instrumental purposive reason. For, as psychological diagnosis moved out of the interpretative and relational sphere of meaning-making towards the realm of natural scientific observation, it artifically restricted the range of acceptable validity claims to those directly concerned with particularly cognitive (biomedical) facts. Constative validity claims around the biological (and later neuroscientific) workings of the mind were thus prioritised over (and encroached upon) regulative and expressive validity claims. As mental health became (increasingly exclusively) perceived through the objectivating prism of cognitive biomedical facts, notions of thought patterns and brain wiring (including its chemical imbalances) trumped philosophical and socio-normative considerations of the meaning of life, justice or even the soul (Bracken, 2002b). Indeed, socio-normative questions or even the expressive content of phenomenological experience were sidelined or even blatantly outcast as non-scientific: for, only 'value-free' and 'objective' medical facts were allowed, and deemed to have much greater validity and priority.

And so, a medicalised, positivist perception of mental illness arose which not only artificially restricted the range of acceptable validity claims but thereby also the scope of human action. Through its epistemologically restrictive framework, cognitive positivism directly contributed to both the detached individualisation and depoliticisation of psychological practice. A detached universalist understanding of psychological disorders (and therapeutic practice) arose wherein 'illness' was firmly located within the inner cognitive realms of the individual mind (and later brain). Psychological disorders thus became regarded as the result of (temporary) faulty cognitive patterning of the mind (or later, brain wiring) (Bracken, 2002b; Alford, 2016; Bistoen, 2016).

Yet, if the problem lay inside the mind, so did its resolution. For if psychological disorders arose from faulty cognitive structuring, then all that needed to be done was to restructure the mind in a more positive direction. Hence, cognitive behavioural therapy and positive psychology became increasingly popular. With the help of a therapist, one would adopt an objectivating perspective, acquire knowledge over the processes and structures of one's own thoughts and redirect these thoughts in such a more positive direction. And thus, positivist psychology abided by a philosophy of the subject that radically overhauled the earlier psychoanalytic and psychodynamic frameworks. Psychoanalysis and psychodynamics in its various forms – whether in the more orthodox versions which stressed the inner drives or the neo-Freudians which stressed social relations – have always stressed that the ego is never really a master is in its own house (Antze, 2003: 105) due to its inherent (unconscious or social) otherness within, cognitive positivism (like all philosophies of the subject) posits a sovereign and autonomous self-knowable to itself through objective introspection (Radstone, 2007). Indeed, it not only posits the possibility of knowing oneself but also holds that the self is self-contained, manageble, malleable and in control. The self became regarded as an atomistic unit, detached from its social surroundings. Yet, though deeply flawed, this individualist cognitive conception of mental disorder as faulty brain-wiring or defective cognitive structures has become so dominant that for many it has become difficult to even imagine alternatives.

The appeal of individualist, cognitive positivism lies in its simplicity, its cost-effectiveness, and the way in which it suits (and perhaps even serves) the capitalist ideology of the strong self, who can always make it if he (or she) tries (Illouz, 2007; Ehrenreich, 2010; Dalal, 2018). For the resolution is simple, and cognitive psychologists say effective. Indeed, longwinded, ambiguous and deeply contextual therapeutic processes wherein concepts such as unconscious drives and social processes of domination played an important role were now a thing of the past. All that was needed was a relatively short-term cognitive behavioural intervention, wherein the client changes his or her patterns of thought and reality itself is changed. Efficiency is a key term here (Dalal, 2018). Yet the extent to which these quick results are also successful in the longer term remains an issue that is heavily debated: while on the short-term, cognitive therapeutic interventions appear to yield good results, in the longer term, psychoanalysts argue, the results are less promising (Fonagy et al., 2015).[7] Because cognitive behavioural therapy operates at a relatively superficial level of (individualist) cognitive restructuring, psychoanalysts argue that patients often experience a recurrence of symptoms later on as deeper underlying issues remain unresolved.

While this debate on effectiveness has not been settled, it cannot be denied that cognitive positivism moved psychology in a truly Descartian direction: you are what you think. Of course, from a Marxian perspective this assertion is deeply problematic. Indeed, from this perspective, cognitive behavioural therapy may even be regarded as nothing less than false consciousness, wherein the neoliberal capitalist idea of a strong autonomous (and transparent) self, who carries individual responsibility for his or her own reality, becomes internalised into our very sense of subjectivity (Illouz, 2007). The fact is that no matter how hard we try, reality cannot be changed through our thought – or cognitive structures – alone. Rather, it requires material manifestation, namely collective action and a striving for equality and justice. Moreover, by focusing on the cognitive workings of the mind or brain, attention is redirected away from such collective struggles as the burden of responsibility becomes placed upon the individual's shoulders.[8] It thus contributes directly to the individualisation of stress. For, within a positivist observer's perspective focused on the individual mind such social struggles, as well as the intersubjective constitution of both subject and object, evade from view. Rather, what emerges from such an introspective objectivating perspective is a detached, essentialist understanding of both the self and psychological disorders, deemed to be unconstrained by any contextual limitations.

Hence, both the knowledge, formation and the cure of psychological disorders were now artificially detached and abstracted from their intersubjective embedding. The problem with this is that psychology ended up producing a universalist idea of mental illness on the basis of a particularly myopic Westocentric image of the Self and mental disorder (Bracken and Thomas, 1999, 2002; Bracken, 2002b; Thomas and Bracken, 2004; Bracken et al., 2021). Not only did it ignore the vast plurality of possible phenomenological experiences of existential suffering – and their varied interpretations – in the world, it also failed to sufficiently consider the relation between mental illness and social or political injustice.

Of course, the critic might object here that I am saying nothing new here. After all, these issues have been addressed already, often from within perspective of (Foucauldian) critical or cultural psychology (Thomas and Bracken, 2004; Sorrell, 2006; Craps, 2014; Bracken et al., 2021), which has highlighted the problematic nature of psychology's abstraction of the Self, its solipsism, its Westo- or Eurocentrism and its insensitivity to social and political contexts, cultural differences and phenomenological experiences (Craps, 2014, Bracken, 2002b; Stolorow, 2011a, 2011b). And indeed, such studies have been immensely productive and are an inspiration to this work here. However, in a sense these studies have been pointing at the symptoms but not its underlying cause. For what they have missed to establish is that underlying these issues is psychology's abidance by a philosophy of the subject as such. The upshot of this is that even as they critique Psychology's Westocentric or detached parameters, they often reproduce the main premises of the philosophy of the subject, as the locus of analysis the individual subjects internal experience(s) of psychological disorder or suffering (Bracken, 2002b; Stolorow, 2011a, 2011b). It is for this very reason that a Habermasian-inspired intersubjective perspective offers a more fruitful perspective: it enables us to see that it is Psychology's adherence to a philosophy of the subject that is particularly problematic here.

Hence, what is needed is to knock cognitive positivism of its pedestal somewhat. To be clear, this is *not* to say that all the insights gained by the positivist psychological sciences are entirely superfluous or erroneous, nor to deny that injustice and harm can have deep (distortive) subjective effects. But rather, that we ought to be aware of the underlying ontological and epistemological limitations, and particularly of the ways in which the positivist logic has encroached on the socio-normative and expressive realms of validation that have affected our self-understanding. As cognitive positivism's dominance restricted the range of acceptable validity claims, its instrumental objectivating perspective encroached into the regulative sphere of social norms and the expressive sphere of our subjectivity. It thereby gave rise to a mechanistic or technocratic conception of our self as atomistic units of cognitive patterning or brain wiring rather than intersubjectively constituted creatures engaged in concrete practices of interpretative meaning-making. In doing so, it upheld a detached, sovereign image of the self, which from a critical theoretical perspective is deeply problematic. For, the self is never self-same and always already other. Not only is the concept of a unified self is always already based on a negative relation to non-identity (Adorno, 1973), but the very emergence of the 'I' – of our sense of self – is always already grounded in concrete intersubjective relations of meaning-making and interpretation with others (Habermas, 1987b, 2003). The problem is that as cognitive positivism gained dominance, it restricted the range of acceptable validity claims to constative speech and impoverished the way in which we make sense of the world and ourselves. Or rather, it resulted in the problematic encroachment of constative speech over other validity claims, and thereby artificially reduced the scope of human action and subsumed meaning under instrumental processes of administrative control.

Now, these problems are particularly pronounced when it comes to trauma. Trauma is commonly conceived as PTSD, which as concept arose during the APA's positivist revolution – when a small working group, headed by Nancy Andreasen and deeply rooted in anti-Vietnam War activism lobbied for its inclusion in the APA's new diagnostic manual (DSMIII) (Schulman and Hammer, 1988; Young, 1995; Mayes and Horwitz, 2005; Alford, 2016). Though the definitions of PTSD have been modified somewhat over the years, the latest DSM (DSMV) regards PTSD as a cognitive disorder of the mind, wherein a confrontation with actual or threatened death, serious injury or sexual violation (either directly or indirectly through relatives and friends) results in the following symptoms: intrusion (flashbacks, nightmares and dreams), avoidance (of thoughts and places related to the trauma), negative moods and thoughts (including anger, depression, guilt, shame and negative thoughts about the self, others and the world – including feeling alienated from others and the inability to trust others) and arousal and hyperactivity (such as anger, carelessness, annoyance, concentration and sleeping problems) (American Psychiatric Association, 2014).

Previous definitions of PTSD have also characterised it as a disorder that may arise from a threat against bodily integrity, while the current definition of PTSD employs a much narrower definition stating it must entail an actual threat to life or serious *physical* injury. Moreover, previously (in the DSMIII), it was regarded as an experience that would fall 'outside the range of usual experience' and one that 'most people would find distressing' (American Psychiatric Association, 1980). This clause has since been removed. Yet, despite this deletion, the notion of trauma as an 'extraordinary' event, as an event outside the bounds of common experience, nevertheless remained persistent not only within trauma studies scholarship but also in everyday life.

One reason for this 'event-ism' is the direct relation between the traumatic (causal) event and its traumatic effects that was established in the definition of trauma. That is, trauma includes its aetiology in its own definition: it refers to both the effects (the symptoms) and the causal event (Radstone, 2007). This not only gives rise to tautological reasoning, but its diagnosis also clearly transcends the limits of nosological symptomology. And indeed, it was upon this basis that Robert L. Spitzer initially objected to the inclusion of PTSD as a diagnostic category. Not only could its symptoms of avoidance behaviour, intrusions and arousal easily be categorised under other classifications (notably, depression, stress and anxiety related disorders) (Alford, 2016: 19; Young, 1995), its ascription to a causal event also went beyond the boundaries of nosological reason. Spitzer was right in this. The ascription of a causal event could not be based on the observations of symptoms but rather was an interpretative act that went beyond the limitations of nosological reasoning. Yet, having previously declined it in 1975, when two of the working group members (Robert Jay Lifton and Chaim Shatan) had already approached Robert L. Spitzer, he eventually gave in to overwhelming public pressure and lobbying by the Vietnam War veteran group (Alford, 2016: 11). A subcommittee was formed and PTSD was eventually included in the DSMIII as a separate category. As Alford reminds us, it is important to remind ourselves here that

> PTSD did not come about as the result of psychological research, or at least that was not the main reason. The diagnoses of PTSD resulted from the pressure by Vietnam veterans, and a few psychiatrists who supported them, to explain the torment so many young men experienced after serving a tour of duty in Vietnam. (Alfred, 2016: 20)

But what then set trauma apart from other diagnostic categories? What was its distinguishing feature that supposedly now set it apart from other diagnoses, such as stress or anxiety? It was the direct causal reference to a particular causal event, which meant that rather than being based on nosological reasoning alone, it included an interpretative ascription of a causal event in its diagnosis (March, 1990; Alford, 2016; Stein et al., 2016). In this sense, PTSD is an somewhat odd fish in the DSM pond, as through its references to the event in its definition it clearly transgresses objective symptomatic observation. Indeed, Spitzer's initial hesitation should have functioned as the first warning about the category mistake trauma studies was about to commit. It tried to squeeze a concept with socio-normative foundations into constative speech of biomedical language (Kihlstrom, 2006, 2010; Kihlstrom and Park, 2016).

This causal reference to a traumatic event is rather problematic. First, it raises the issue of tautological reason: an event is traumatic because of its symptoms which are *traumatic* because of its associated event. Secondly, the difficulty in attributing causality to a particular event is clearly highlighted when we take into consideration that not all people that experience a particular event will have PTSD symptoms, while for others traumatic symptoms are delayed. Not only that, but it is also impossible to determine whether PTSD in fact *causally* emerged from this actual event or from pre-existing personality traits or from other pre-existing mental problems (Young, 1995; Radstone, 2007; Alford, 2016). The point here is not to refute that traumatic experiences might be constituted by a violent event, for they very well might, but rather that the diagnosis of trauma as such depends on an interpretative act wherein a particular *meaning* is ascribed to this event. Again, in doing so, the diagnosis of trauma goes beyond the bounds of strictly 'observable' nosology. It includes an interpretative act wherein therapist and client ascribe a particular meaning to a particular event as having resulted in particular symptoms. It thereby bypasses the logic of nosological observation and enters into the intersubjective sphere of social norms and meaning-making. As Habermas explains, however, processes of meaning-making are intersubjectively constituted (Habermas, 1984, 1987b, 1988b, 1993, 1995). Not only is meaning ascribed directly in intersubjective relation with others (in this case, for instance, the therapist) but is also always constituted against the intersubjectively constituted background of the lifeworld, which forms the grid of orientation through which we make sense of the world. The trouble is that when such interpretative communicative acts become couched in positivistic language, they are reified into facts and their interpretative nature is hidden from view. Hence, as soon as trauma is cast in terms of constative speech, its interpretative and intersubjective constitution masquerades as a (biomedical) objective fact.

Aware of the weak epistemological ground that the concept of trauma rests upon, trauma studies tried to establish firmer scientific ground underneath its feet. And so, given its aversion to the interpretative nature of psychoanalysis and psychodynamic therapy, it moved towards natural science as its saviour (Radstone, 2007; Kihlstrom, 2010; Alford, 2016; Kihlstrom and Park, 2016). Hence, rather than resorting to a greater intersubjective framework of analysis, that would solve the unstable epistemological ground underneath its feet, trauma studies turned to neuroscience in the attempt solidify the uncertain scientific ground it was standing on. In search of objective, observable empirical evidence that would supposedly leave little to speculation, neuroscience became a popular field within trauma studies. Neuroscience allegedly verified the impact of the traumatic event on cognitive processing through the observation of clear, observable, scientific and biological processes.

Importantly, within trauma studies, this turn towards neuroscience not only entailed a further objectification of trauma as a biological process, it also marked a shift away from the *psychological mind* towards the objective *scientific, neurological, brain* (Bracken, 1988, 2002b; Alford, 2016). In doing so, a particularly anti-mimetic conception of trauma was strengthened, wherein trauma was regarded as being constituted by an *external* event that overwhelmed the cognitive functioning of the *inner* mind (or neurological wiring of the brain) (Leys, 2000; Radstone, 2007). It replaced earlier mimetic psychoanalytic visions of trauma as repressed and unconscious subjectivity over which the individual was never fully in control. In a typical cognitive positivist fashion, such an anti-mimetic understanding of trauma upheld and fostered the idea of an autonomous, sovereign individual or self who was only temporarily beset by an external event. As Radstone explains, trauma theory thus '[abandoned] any emphasis on the radical ungovernability of the unconscious. In trauma theory, it is the event rather than the subject, which emerges as unpredictable or ungovernable' (Radstone, 2007: 5). As such, the individual is normally fully in control, and only suffers a temporal setback of its autonomy due to this external event. The point of cognitive behavioural therapy, now grounded in a neuroscientific understanding of trauma, is hence to get this person back into control – back into the driving seat of his life. The compatibility between both the neoliberal capitalist understanding of the strong self – who is always 'able to make it if he tries' – and the cognitive behavioural understanding of the self who is normally in control (as well as its supposed cost efficiency), might go some way in explaining the increasing popularity and widespread usage of cognitive behavioural therapy under accelerated capitalism. After all, both neoliberal subjectivity and cognitive behavioural therapy are deeply grounded in the instrumental rationality of a philosophy of the subject.

Now, in terms of this anti-mimetic conception of trauma, its main assumption is that upon experiencing a shocking event, the brain is incapable of processing it into normal memory and hence stores it in raw memory, resulting in intrusions such as flashbacks and nightmares as well as dissociation (Caruth, 1995, 1996). As Patrick Bracken explained, trauma studies uses a computer analogy to explain that such an event would basically damage the 'software' of the brain, whose 'hardwire' is perceived as universal (Bracken, 2002b: 34). Particularly important here is the damage caused by the traumatic event to the stress regulative capacities of the hippocampus (which aids orientation, locates memory in space and time, provides orientation and regulates stress reduction), the emotional regulative functions of the amygdala (which regulates emotional relations and aids in the detection of danger) and a decreasing function of the prefrontal cortex (which regulates our fear responses) (Vermetten, 2009).

As C. Fred Alford (2016) and J. F. Kihlstrom (2006, 2010) have pointed out, the trouble is that while there has been a flurry of neuroscientific trauma studies, it has in fact not been able to resolve the causal ambiguity underlying the notion of trauma since it is beset by a number of serious problems. First, as Alford explains, the fMRI scans used in trauma studies (which determine brain activity through contemporaneous streams of bloodflow measured by voxels[9]) are in fact grossly imprecise in terms of their measurements and modularity (Alford, 2016: 94). The amygdala and hippocampus cannot be sufficiently discriminated at the level of a 3-mm voxel, which is the measurement of the used fMRI scans (Alford, 2016: 95). Moreover, since the amygdala in particular has in fact been attributed with a wide range of different functions (and is considered as nothing less than a mini-brain within a larger brain), such precise discrimination and measurement is necessary for scientific accuracy and clarity. Alford is of course not the first to highlight the gross inaccuracy of the fMRI scans. Using these very same scans, Craig Bennet in his legendary (Nobel Prize winning) study detected a lot of neuroactivity as measured by voxels in nothing less than a *dead fish* (Alford, 2016: 94). There are scans that have a higher resolution and thus are more accurate in detecting neuro-activity, but as Alford explains, they have yet to be used within trauma studies (Alford, 2016: 94).

Moreover, the assumption in neuroscientific trauma studies is that blood flow to the brain is an indicator of activity[10] (Alford, 2016: 85). Yet, it may also be the case that 'important brain functions may not require large amount of blood flow to support them' (Alford, 2016: 94). And so, 'most neuroscientists assume a linear relation between oxygen use and degree of neuronal stimulation, but that is a working assumption, not an empirically established fact' (Alford, 2016: 94). Of course, every study rests on assumptions, yet the trouble is that 'most published studies applying fMRI to trauma do not discuss these assumptions and so the average reader is left without a context within which to evaluate them' (Alford, 2016: 94).

And most importantly, 'even when the criteria of best science are met, the significance of neuro-imagining, and CNS in general is unclear' (Alford, 2016: 88). The trouble here is simply that the lightening up or colouring of brain segments during scans offers us nothing but *correlations* between trauma theory and brain activity. It does not offer us *psychological causation*. Put simply, a causal relation between a specific event and traumatic 'symptoms' cannot be (and thus has not been) provided in neuroscientific terms. As Kihlstrom explains, the problem is that neuroscience as employed in trauma studies (merely translates the already existing psychological concepts and presuppositions into another language, neuroscientific terms) not unlike translating English into French (Kihlstrom, 2010: 774). And so, while neuroscientific findings become presented as objective empirical findings, upon closer inspection it transpires these are in fact steered by psychological assumptions that remain unaccounted for (Kihlstrom, 2010; Alford, 2016). Hence, while it is often presumed that 'objective' cognitive neuroscience poses limits on psychological interpretation, the reality has in fact been the other way around: psychological theory determines the interpretation of neuroscientific phenomena (Kihlstrom, 2006, 2010; Hatfield, 2007; Kihlstrom and Park, 2016).

Perceived from this angle, it is perhaps not so surprising that trauma studies got itself stuck in the murky waters of the repressed memory debate during the 1990s. Spearheaded by neuropsychologists such as Bessel van der Kolk, the argument was that in light of a traumatic event, the brain would fail to perform and close off, leading to dissociation (or, a forgetfulness of the event) in its wake. It was then the task of the therapist to discern this repressed memory and reintegrate it into 'normal' narrative memory through cognitive behavioural interventions (Radstone, 2007; Alford, 2016). While initially influential in the legal persecution of sex offenders, the enthusiasm for this argument rapidly waned when the claims of repressed memory grew more outlandish inside the court rooms, even including so-called repressed experiences of alien abductions and secret satanic cults (Interlandi, 2014). Critics rightfully pointed out that it was the psychologist's interpretation that directed the recalling of these events, which were difficult to corroborate scientifically. And so, in 2014, it was finally concluded that the dissociation model 'attributes to trauma a central etiological role in the absence of sufficient evidence' since it 'leaps *too quickly from correlational data to causal conclusions*' (Lynn et al., 2014: 896).

Now the point here is not to dismiss neuroscience as such. Indeed, there might very well be interesting neuroscientific *correlations* to between traumatic experiences and brain activity that are worth exploring. Rather the issue is that trauma's *causal* relation to a particular experience cannot be grasped through constative, neuroscientific reasoning. Indeed, employing Habermasian language here, I argue that trauma does not fall within the remit of objective truth but rather of intersubjective interpretation and social normativity. Hence, the causal ascription of trauma to an experience is also an interpretative act that falls within the remit of intersubjective meaning-making. Uncomfortable as this realisation might be to some, trauma does not squarely fall within the remit of biomedical facts but rather falls within the realm of social normativity. Again, as we will see later on in this chapter and the remainder of the book, this by no means diminishes the serious existential impacts of traumatic experiences and the validity of the traumatic truth claim. Rather, it suggests that we can only properly conceive and address these if we regard trauma intersubjectively as a matter of socio-normativity. Trauma is the violent violation of our counterfactual expectation to be treated as equal peers in our communicative relations, as a result of which the lifeworld's functioning is so deeply disrupted that we lose our capacity to act in the world. Trauma is hence above all an issue of meaning-making – or rather the destructive loss of meaning-making in the world. To reduce issues of meaning to biological claims of objective truth is to make a category mistake, with deeply reifying effects. This reification is vividly illustrated by Kihlstrom in a small hypothetical 'dialogue' between the neuro-philosophers Paul and Patricia Churchland in California, whereby Patricia comes home from work tired and says to her husband:

> Paul, don't speak to me, my serotonin levels have hit bottom, my brain is awash in glucosteroids, my blood vessels are full of adrenaline and if it weren't for my endogenous opiates, I'd have driven my car into a tree on the way home. My dopamine levels need lifting. Pour me a glass of Chardonnay, and I'll be down in a minute. (Kihlstrom, 2010: 773)

This fictional dialogue relays, in perhaps more vivid terms, Habermas's point that meaning cannot be grasped from an objectivating, positivistic perspective. Meaning cannot be turned into a 'thing' (at least not without distortive effects), but rather has to be understood intersubjectively from a first person's perspective. That is, sense- and meaning making has to be comprehended from the point of view of intersubjective experience.

Yet, with the neuroscientific move, supposedly value-free objectivating statements were prioritised, regarded as superior, and thus encroached upon normative regulative and subjective expressive claims. We thus see an 'inter-theoretic reductionism, which asserts that the language of psychology and other social sciences is at best an obsolete folk science, and worst misleading, illegitimate and outright false' (Kihlstrom, 2010: 774) (despite of course itself being steered by such 'folk science'). This resulted in both a reification of meaning-making practices (which are now reduced to neurological activity and mental processing) and subjectivity (wherein we increasingly regard ourselves in biomedical terms of neurological wiring rather than agents engaged in intersubjective meaning-making). In other words, an objectivating image of ourselves as detached, atomistic, singular, biological entities emerged in which our constitutional intersubjectivity and perception of ourselves as meaning-making agents are cast aside. Hence, the move towards neuroscience resulted in trauma studies getting ever more deeply entangled in a philosophy of the subject, and the promotion of an anti-mimetic conception of trauma, wherein the sovereign, autonomous individual is (temporarily) impaired by an overwhelming external event.

Hence, the turn to neuroscience also reinforced the tendency of 'event-ism' already present within trauma studies. (Leys, 2000; Radstone, 2007). Within event-ism centrality is ascribed to the overwhelming catastrophic *event* (or a short series of events) rather than structural and ongoing forms of traumatic stress – such as life-threatening poverty, political repression and community violence. Yet, in the majority of the world, trauma is not an extraordinary event but rather a structural and continuous part of everyday life. Indeed, one might even go so far as to state that in some of these contexts, it is not the occurrence of trauma that is an extraordinary experience, but rather its relative absence (Craps, 2014). As Stef Craps notably stated:

> For most Sierra Leonians, the 'normal' experience is one of oppression, deprivation, and upheaval; freedom, affluence, and stability – the Western standard of normality – are actually the exception rather than the rule. 'You call it a disorder . . . . We call it Life': instantiation of the critique of the event-based model of trauma and associated methods of treatment, which risk obscuring the chronic suffering and structural violence experienced by the Sierra Leonean population, and, indeed, by much of the world. (Craps, 2014, p. 5)

The anti-mimetic conception of trauma thus not only upholds a reductive understanding of trauma as a cognitive disorder but also prioritises a (supposed causal) event over structural experiences of social and political violence and injustice – such as life-threatening poverty, political repression and community violence that are so rampant in the world. This emphasis on the shocking event, originally also conceived as laying outside the realm of ordinary experience, reveals the position of (Westocentric) privilege that trauma studies was speaking from.

It is also precisely this that activist psychologists in South Africa (writing in the context of South African Apartheid), such as Gillian Straker (2013), criticised when they coined the term 'Continuous Traumatic Stress' (CTS) (Eagle and Kaminer, 2013; Stevens et al., 2013; Hecker et al., 2017; Kaminer et al., 2018; Pat-Horenczyk and Schiff, 2019). They critiqued the cognitive reduction of trauma to an overwhelming event, its temporal location in the past, its presupposition of therapeutic safety and its focus on symptom reduction. They argued that trauma studies' cognitive reduction of trauma to an overwhelming event that is temporally located in the past overlooks experiences of trauma are continuous, ongoing and pervasive, particularly (though not solely) without temporal respite (Stevens et al., 2013). Rather, structures of trauma may be relentless, particularly in contexts of political violence. Moreover, what is broken in such contexts is not the cognitive mind or brain, but the social contract between the state and the individual or community (Stevens et al., 2013). Yet, since the anti-mimetic understanding of trauma moves trauma inwards into the solitary mind, it remains blind to such social, political and economic contexts of continuous traumatic stress.

Moreover, within such situations, it is often precisely the authorities charged with the protection of people that are main perpetrators (or at least facilitators of trauma through their informal collusion). The impact of traumatic violence is hence often aggravated by the fact that violations are accompanied by 'resignation, collusion, non-retribution and licence for further violation at a systemic level' (Eagle and Kaminer, 2013: 94). And thus, 'systems designed to create a sense of accountability and to minimise harm to citizens are ineffectual and overstretched, at best, or corrupt and collusive with informal systems of power, at worst' (Eagle and Kaminer, 2013: 93). Hence, in such situations, there is a structural lack of accountability, which means that any attempt to address traumatic grievances potentially comes at a high risk for oneself or others. Often, even talking about trauma risks attracting further retribution and traumatic violence by these actors or their formal or informal accomplices (Eagle and Kaminer, 2013). The trouble is that the anti-mimetic understanding of trauma thus often overlooks the fact that trauma is frequently inflicted by social and political actors who may 'strike again', also compromising the other presumption of trauma theory: therapeutic safety. Therapeutic safety might be inhibited through repressive practices such as the co-option of therapists into networks of informers, as well as the raiding, closing down or bugging of therapists' offices (Eagle and Kaminer, 2013). Traumatic violence may thus be pervasive, structural and omnipresent.

Given its omnipresence, CTS scholars warn that the anti-mimetic perception of symptoms as pathological and its subsequent emphasis on symptom reduction is a potentially dangerous one. For, in contexts of pervasive structural traumatic violence, expressions (such as paranoia) that would be classified as pathological are not only a normal, nonpathological expression of continuous fear, but also constitute a crucial survival mechanism. In contexts of pervasive, continuous violence, one must be continuously on guard for the sake of one's own survival. Not doing so might very well compromise one's own safety or that of others. Hence, they argue that a different therapeutic approach is needed, wherein the aim of therapeutic intervention is not symptom reduction as such, but rather risk management (Eagle and Kaminer, 2013). In situations of pervasive and unpredictable political violence, it becomes difficult to distinguish real traumatic threats from imagined or perceived future ones (Straker, 216). Within such contexts, therapists should take seriously the patient's own risk assessment and work towards a realistic threat discrimination rather than reduction of symptoms. In such contexts, 'the denial or minimalisation of danger might be more problematic than exaggeration, even if such defences allow for reduction of anxiety' (Eagle and Kaminer, 2013: 93).

And so, they urge us to move away from the notion of trauma as a diagnostic cognitive concept, towards a phenomenological one wherein the subjective experiences of trauma are placed within an intersubjective context of violence. Unfortunately, CTS scholarship remains very much at the fringes of trauma studies. Yet its insights are immensely valuable, especially (though not solely) when studying counter-revolutionary trauma in Egypt, since it directs our attention to both the political contextual formation of traumatic experiences and the limitations of the cognitivist conceptual tools itself. For the problem is that locked within the solipsist epistemology of a philosophy of the subject, trauma studies is unable to account for both the intersubjective, contextual, social and political constitution of trauma and trauma theory.

This inability to reflect on its particular constitution is also reflected in trauma studies' Westocentric (and teleological) historiography. Herein PTSD is again not treated as a constructed idea (strung together by a variety of specific discourses and practices) (Young, 1995) but rather as an objective stable, universal, timeless and objective phenomenon waiting to be discovered like other natural scientific phenomena. The dominant teleological narrative within trauma studies holds that the historical discovery of the universally valid concept PTSD has been progressive, and has merely suffered periods of amnesia or disinterest in the scholarly community as attention periodically waned (Leys, 2000). The culmination of this linear discovery of trauma was the inclusion of the concept of PTSD in the DMSIII, where it finally secured its 'rightful' place as a diagnostic category. What is striking in this victorious, teleological account of trauma studies' development is its Westocentric selection of both traumatic events and scholarship. It commonly starts with the emergence of trauma in John Eric Erichsen's book on the distress of railway spine injuries (Keller, T et al., 1996), which was then taken up as a distinctly psychological problem in the works on hysteria by J. M. Charcot, Pierre Janet and Sigmund Freud (Leys, 2000). After this the study of trauma lapsed into a period of forgetfulness, only to arise as the psychological study of the soldiers' 'shell shock' syndrome in the wake of the First World War.[11] Hereafter, the interest in trauma studies declined again, only to be picked up in the wake of the pinnacle of trauma, the Holocaust. Yet it was not until the Vietnam War and particularly the veterans' lobby that trauma was placed properly on the scholarly agenda and was included in the DMSIII (Leys, 2000: 5). The difficulty with this account of course is that it is incredibly myopic. There is a notable absence of non-Western traumatic experiences such as the slave trade, colonialism, the genocide of America's native population or indeed even the Nakba (Sayigh, 2013) to name a few. Equally absent is a serious consideration of the different contextual manifestations and understandings of suffering – or how meaning is ascribed to it. This is of course not surprising, since (again) the detached objectivating gaze of positivism imposes analytical restrictions that impede precisely such much-needed interpretivist endeavours. Rather, trauma (and trauma studies) become divorced from their intersubjective constitutive context as trauma studies adopts a philosophy of the subject, wherein trauma is reified as an object suitable for objective detached introspective observation, namely the impairment of the mind.

COGNITIVE TRAUMA THEORY: INTERSUBJECTIVITY WITHIN

Now, the astute reader might of course object here that intersubjectivity has not been *entirely* ignored within the cognitivist tradition of trauma studies. After all, important scholars such as Mardi Horowitz (1983) and Ronnie Janoff-Bulman (1992) have each insisted that trauma entails a breakdown of our internal cognitive schemata or assumptive world *in relation to* our surrounding world. Yet, the problem is that they adopt a cognitivist reductive understanding of intersubjectivity, wherein intersubjectivity is only taken into account insofar as it impacts the internal cognitive patterning of the mind. Hence, in doing so, they approach intersubjectivity from within the confines of a philosophy of the subject, rather than breaking free from it. They regard intersubjectivity from the inside out, so to speak – from a reductive mentalist conception of cognitive structures.

Importantly, both Horowitz and Janoff-Bulman adopt an anti-mimetic understanding of trauma wherein trauma is regarded as an event entailing shocking information that does not fit our cognitive schemata (Horowitz, 1983) or assumptive world (Janoff-Bulman, 1992). This schemata or assumptive world subsequently breaks down, resulting in intrusive and dissociative symptoms. To be sure, for Janoff-Bulman this assumptive world is socially constituted in that it comprises the generalised assumptions into which we have been socialised from an early age onwards. Through our (intersubjective) engagements with 'good enough' carers, we have come to believe (with only a few exceptions) that the world is benevolent, our relations with others are meaningful and the self is worthy. These form our generalised expectations in life: they are the 'basis of our subsequent interactions in and interpretations of the world' (Janoff-Bulman, 1992: 21, 39). She explains that of course we *rationally* know these assumptions to be delusional, yet *emotionally* we rely on them to build and maintain a stable and predictable world around us that enables us to function on a daily basis.

Usually, she argues, we cognitively modify our assumptive world in a gradual manner as we journey through life. However, such a change is rapid, sudden and fundamental when a traumatic event shatters our assumptions and ruptures our basic trust in our relations to others, the world and the self. In light of such a traumatic disruption, she argues, we cognitively re-stabilise our assumptive world through the automatic intra-cognitive coping mechanisms of dissociation (emotional numbing) and intrusions (such as nightmares and flashbacks), which help the brain process the event in gradual piecemeal manner (Janoff-Bulman, 1992).

In addition to automatic coping mechanisms, we need the non-automatic coping mechanisms of reinterpretation and reintegration. Reinterpretation entails the belief that a traumatic experience has resulted in a positive outcome, which can take the form of personal lessons learnt as well as a reorientation of one's life towards another good. Reintegration entails the incorporation of the traumatic event into one's cognitive schemata through a socially supportive environment.[12] She notes that the absence of such a supportive social environment constitutes a 'second injury to victims': namely the 'reinjuring of victims through the failure to receive expected support from social agencies, communities, society in general and even from family and friends' (Janoff-Bulman, 1992: 147).

On first sight, Janoff-Bulman's assumptive world appears to resemble Jurgen Habermas's notion of the lifeworld. After all, like the assumptive world, the lifeworld comprises the inescapable taken-for-granted, unquestioned background assumptions into which we have been socialised. And like the assumptive world, it provides us with our orientation in daily life. Moreover, like the assumptive world, lifeworld is not a solid entity set in stone, but rather is subject to change as segments become problematised in our engagements with others and the world around us. And indeed, just as Janoff-Bulman argues that the assumptive world breaks down in light of trauma, so I suggest that the effect of trauma (conceived not anti-mimetically but rather as broken intersubjectivity) is the lifeworld's collapse, its seizing to function.

Yet, the crucial difference here is that the assumptive world is a reductive cognitivist conception, wherein trauma is placed inside our heads and analysed from an introspective objectivating perspective. Not only does Janoff-Bulman's analysis adopt an instrumental approach insofar as it commences from the point of view of the necessity of medical intervention rather than coming to a broader understanding of a breakdown of meaning (Bracken, 2002b: 9). In contrast, a Habermasian notion of the lifeworld encompasses not merely our subjective (cognitive) structures but also our concrete socio-normative relations to others. That is, a Habermasian lifeworld is not merely the internal mental realm of cognitive patterning, but is much broader (and in a sense more 'earthly') than that: it includes the social and contextual embedding wherein we are situated. The lifeworld thus also entails the background of our daily communicative practices that are located within the actual social, intersubjective context wherein we are embedded. And thus, when the lifeworld breaks down, it is not our cognitive capacity to process information that breaks down but rather our intersubjective sense-making in communicative relations with others. The lifeworld is thus the intersubjectively formed existential grid of orientation in the world, which is as much social and it is subjective: it is truly intersubjective.

The limitations of Janoff-Bulman's introspective cognitive approach come clearly to the fore in her discussion of victim blaming, which she argues is frequently employed in the aftermath of trauma. According to her account, victim blaming is a tool used to minimise the impact of harmful information that does not correspond to one's image of a just world (Janoff-Bulman, 1992: 150). Underlying victim blaming is a belief in self-outcome contingency, namely the belief that there is a direct correlation between a person's character or actions and the outcome of events (i.e. bad things happen to bad people, and a bad thing 'y' happens because a person did or did not do 'x') (Janoff-Bulman, 1992: 8). Such self-outcome contingency is most often employed retrospectively: once people near the outcome of events, they tend to overestimate the prior likelihood of that outcome (Janoff-Bulman, 1992: 150). Victim blaming (including a victim's self-blame) is thus a way to cognitively reduce the randomness and meaninglessness of life and (re)instill the idea that we have some control over what we do.

Her account of victim blaming might make intuitive sense in an age where psychological cognitivism has become the dominant frame of reference. However, due to its reductive cognitivist perception, her account only addresses victim blaming from an individualist introspective perspective, namely as an activity inside the cognitive mind. It thereby fails to acknowledge the distinctly intersubjective (and indeed political) nature of victim blaming. As I explain in more detail in chapter 10 of Part 3, victim blaming also serves a political purpose: it is a tool employed to ensure that the victim of trauma is not able to speak back at the injustice inflicted. Victim blaming is a politically convenient redirection of responsibility from the perpetrator to the victim, the subordinate. In this redirection, it not only justifies and normalises the violence inflicted but also further disempowers the victim through a social segregation from others. For, the injustices suffered by the victim not only remain unrecognised, the victim now also suffers a lack of social support that would otherwise strengthen his or her (or their) capacity to speak out. Rather, in the ascription of blame, a social relationlessness is imposed onto the victim, and it is this segregation or rupture of communicative relations that is essential to the mechanisations of repressive political violence. Victim blaming is thus not merely an cognitive tool used in situations of cognitive dissonance, it is a political tool that is part of traumatic status subordination.

Unsurprisingly, therefore, victim blaming is particularly rife in authoritarian contexts, such as that of both pre- and post-revolutionary Egypt, where it often takes a particularly conspirational form. Conspirational victim blaming goes even further than 'ordinary' victim blaming: it centres around an authoritarian or politically repressive discourse wherein the (supposed) deep 'existential' threat posed by the victim is emphasised. The victim is portrayed as threatening either the group's security (for instance, national security) or identity (such as national identity). The political purpose of conspirational victim blaming is redirecting responsibility away from the state (or perpetrator) to the victim, and in doing so boosting allegiances to authoritarian structures and creating social tension or social discord wherein the potential of creative collective becoming is hampered. Hence, conspirational victim blaming is not so much about stabilising cognitive patterns, but more about legitimising and normalising violence as well as deepening the victim's speechlessness. Of course, Janoff-Bulman might retort here that one of the reasons why politically motivated victim blaming might be so successful is an intrinsic cognitive desire for a just world or coherent assumptive world. However, this would not only have to be empirically proven but we also cannot be sure that other factors are not at play here such as the fear of retaliation by the powerful perpetrator (such as the security state apparatus), the unfair distribution of (alternative) information about perpetrated violence and the ways in which this violence was framed. The problem is that so long as cognitive psychology only adopts the detached introspective gaze of the philosophy of the subject, it cannot take into account intersubjectivity proper, it cannot account for such political constellations as it provides a one-sided, limited account of the phenomena it is trying to explain. And the problem with this account is also that it is largely a depoliticised one. So long as the positivist image of trauma as object located in the mind triumphs, its intersubjective constitution and embedding cannot be properly accounted, and hence its political constitution escapes from view.[13]

In this sense, I thus fundamentally disagree with C. Alfred Alford's assertion that while it is not much of a scientific diagnosis, PTSD is a good political diagnosis since it draws attention to the suffering of the poor and the marginalised (Alford, 2016). Not only does this overlook the extent to which trauma studies itself is (and has been) militarised and forms arguably at least as much (if not more) part of the (repressive) status quo as of critique, it also reduces political injustice to an impairment of the individual's mind or brain. It thereby often individualises and medicalises structural problems of social and political injustice, resulting in the aforementioned issue of double injury. For, so long as trauma studies operates from within the prism of the philosophy of the subject and consciousness, it lacks the necessary analytical tools for social and political critique. It can neither direct us to trauma's causality (the injustice of having been treated existentially inferior and unequal human being) nor account for trauma's intersubjective social and political embedding. It thus fails to fulfil the implicit normative aim that underpinned trauma studies since its inception, namely its attempt to try and achieve justice for those who have suffered wrongs. For, justice cannot be achieved within the realms of consciousness alone. Rather, it requires us to break out of the mind, or bounds of the philosophy of the subject, and get our hands dirty in the intersubjective world, the world of social and political affairs. It requires us to recognise the fundamental intersubjective constitution of our inner, social and political worlds because it is from this vantage point that a (thin) normative standard for social and political justice (namely intersubjective parity) can be upheld

LAZARUS NEVER DIES: ANTI-MIMETICISM IN POST-STRUCTURAL AND POLITICAL TRAUMA

What is striking, however, is that rather than moving in a more radically intersubjective direction, the presuppositions of cognitivist and neuropsychological trauma studies have become so dominant that even approaches ordinarily critical of the philosophy of the subject have adopted them. So, while post-structuralism normally critiques anything even remotely related to a philosophy of the subject, in the case of trauma studies it has adopted the cognitivist presumptions. Indeed, rather than problematising these assumptions, it only sought to complement them with post-structuralist literary insights (Radstone, 2007).

Perhaps this is not so surprising when we note that post-structuralist trauma theory[14] arose on American campuses during its culture wars in the 1990s. It was thus part of the humanities' movement to try and prove its worth vis-à-vis the natural sciences. In the case of post-structuralist trauma theory, this meant it emphasised its *complementary* (rather than critical) status vis-à-vis neuroscientific trauma studies (Radstone, 2007). And so, while neuroscience supposedly supplied an objective account of the traumatic impact on brain wiring and biological markers, post-structuralist literary trauma theory would (through its literary concepts and expressions) provide the tools for understanding the subjective expressions and experiences of trauma. Hence, a supposedly constructive role division was constructed wherein neuroscience provided the objective scientific analysis of trauma, and literary trauma theory was able to put the subjective experiences of trauma into words. Post-structuralist literary tools, trauma theory argued, were particularly useful in making the unspeakable heard, bear witness to the unwitnessable and in doing so help to 'work through the trauma' (Caruth, 1995, 1996).

As Susannah Radstone explains, central to this understanding of trauma was a peculiar American post-modernisation of Freud (particularly using Paul de Mann and Jacques Derrida) that was mixed with the anti-mimetic neuroscientific perception of trauma as an external overwhelming event that breaks the linearity of memory (Radstone, 2007). And so, trauma became regarded as 'the story of a wound that cries out, that addresses us in the attempt to tell us of a reality that is not otherwise available' (Caruth, 1996: 4). It is an event that is not yet assimilated into normal memory, which 'defies and demands our witness. . . . [this] cannot be spoken directly, but must indeed also be spoken in a language that is somehow literary: a language that defies, even as it claims, our understanding' (Caruth, 1996: 5). It is also an event that nevertheless leaves 'absent traces' and may only be experienced through an involuntary remembering of that which cannot be remembered – a remembering of traceless events. Post-structuralist trauma theory hereby not only aestheticised the traumatic event (thereby reinforcing its fetishisation within trauma studies), it also ascribed a dubious role to the literary theorist,[15] who now becomes the primary authoritative figure to decipher the 'real' meaning of trauma.

It also gave rise to theoretical contradictions that, as Susannah Radstone (2007) explained, remained underexamined. Radstone wonders whether these contradictions were not scrutinised due to the grave subject matter of trauma studies, namely the suffering of others. I wonder whether this is simply due to the dominance of cognitivist psychology in both trauma studies and everyday life, wherein its assumptions are taken as for granted truths rather than projected truths whose fundamental presuppositions are in need of critical investigation. Yet, Radstone rightly insists that literary trauma theory must nevertheless be subjected to the same kind of rigorous academic critique that other subjects are subjected to, especially since post-structuralist trauma theory seeks to reconcile the irreconcilable, namely a mimetic and anti-mimetic understanding of trauma. While the anti-mimetic (neuroscientific) account upholds the subject as sovereign, autonomous and self-same, which is (temporarily) impaired through an external event, its complimentary addition – its Freudian component – instead insists on the radical otherness or unknowability within. As we noted earlier, within Freudian analysis, the subject's unknowability is not a result of impaired memory, but rather the ego is never really master in its own house to begin with (Antze, 2003: 105). Hence, in post-structural trauma theory, a curious development happens: Freud's 'unconscious conflict, repression and fantasy is replaced by an understanding of memory as related to brain functioning' (Radstone, 2007: 3). And so, the subject is supposed to be sovereign and autonomous while not being sovereign and autonomous at the same time. Moreover, Paul Antze explains, this is also problematic because, in contrast to neuroscience and cognitive psychology, psychoanalysis offers not simply a model of representative reality but rather of interpretative understanding (Antze, 2003). Psychoanalysis is thus much more than a technique or a mental science, it is a set of intersubjective and interpretative practices that are impossible to reconcile with anti-mimetic positivism (Antze, 2003).

What is furthermore striking is that while post-structuralist thought is generally opposed to essentialising grand narratives, post-structural trauma theory enthusiastically reinforces and reproduces the grand narrative of a (Westocentric) teleological historiography of trauma, and places a particular emphasis on the Holocaust as *the* ultimate traumatic experience. The absence of any serious consideration as to non-Western traumatic experiences is striking to say the least.

Also remarkable is post-structural trauma theory's simplistic Manichean dichotomy between good and bad and between the victim and the perpetrator. The victim is 'in no way complicitous with the violence directed against her' (Leys, 2000: 299) nor does he or she potentially reproduce the traumatic cycle of violence. Rather, a binary world of good versus evil is created which stands in direct contrast to psychoanalytic models of the mirroring self (whereby aggression is also internalised). As I explain in chapter 10 of Part 3, even where the distinction between the perpetrator and victim is clear insofar as in Egypt it is clearly the military that inflicts traumatic status subordination, the inability to address the injustice results in a perpetuation of traumatic violence by the victims onto others in other areas of life. For, when one is unable to address the perpetrator of injustice, who gravely subordinated and subjected the victim to a traumatic inferior position, the victim often seeks to reestablish his, her or their intersubjective power onto others. This occurs either through the redirection of violence onto an (often weaker) person, or through cycles of revenge, and often it comprises both. More than merely an outlet of frustration, this is also a (distorted) attempt to regain intersubjective power in relation to others, to undo the inferiority experienced. Perceived intersubjectively, therefore, a Manichean dichotomy can often not be held up.

Moreover, the additional trouble with post-structuralism is that rather than locating its normative critique in the violation of intersubjective parity, it situates it in the realm of sentiments alone. Post-structural trauma theory explicitly imposes an ethical burden of responsibility on the witness to listen to the victims cries and to unconditionally stand by his or her (or their) side. Normative rightness thus becomes rooted in the emotional appeal of the victim's narration of his or her pain. This, however, is a dangerous normative ground. Clearly, such unconditional allegiance to the victim may not only be blind to other forms of traumatic suffering but may itself also (re)produce further injustices. That is, the experience of traumatic violations is not only reproduced by the victim through the redirection of violence onto others and through cycles of revenge but may also be politically employed to construct in- and out-groups, wherein under the rhetorical guise of 'existential defensiveness', the most horrendous crimes are committed. To take the obvious example here: trauma theory posits the Holocaust as the ultimate traumatic experience that demands a special kind of witness, one that bears ethical responsibility even before the narrator utters any words since its atrocities are unspeakable (Laub, 1995; Felman and Laub, 2013). Clearly I am not questioning the utter horror of the Holocaust as a systematic mass destruction of life here. Yet, we have to acknowledge how the memory of the Holocaust has also been used politically and was integrated into Israeli nationalist discourse, which legitimised violence and abuse (including the nakba, land appropriation and house demolitions) of the Palestinians (Bashir and Goldberg, 2018). The question is often asked why and how victims of such horrendous trauma can reproduce trauma themselves. Well, just as often as trauma may lead to a more cosmopolitan solidarity of suffering, it may also contribute to a hardening of (violent) divisions as trauma is internalised as a deep existential crisis that justifies 'defensive' violent responses. So long as trauma theory remains stuck within the confines of a philosophy of the subject, we cannot account for such phenomena as its analytical scope is artificially confined to the introspective perception of the subject. Hence, there will be no analytical tools nor a normative standard at our disposal with which to analyse the social and political constitution and implications of trauma.

And the trouble is that insofar as political and social theoretical accounts of trauma have been developed, these have also adopted precisely the anti-mimetic premises of literary trauma theory, including its fetishisation of the traumatic event. For instance, Jenny Edkin's Foucauldian account of trauma is a pioneering work that if not inaugurated at least firmly cleared the path for the *political* study of trauma (2002, 2003, 2004). Adopting a Foucauldian approach, she argues that through its shock, trauma as an external event suspends normal time and thereby also authority, as it leaves a gap in narration – an emptiness or an absence – that the authorities desperately seek to fill through the construction of particular discourses. Using the examples such as the attacks on the twin towers, she insists that the authorities seek to end this suspension through the construction of specific discursive practices, including monuments of commemoration and rituals of national remembrance. Her work is important in that it directs our attention to trauma as a site of political contestation that is embued with power and power relations. And so, Jenny Edkins is critical of the ways in which these political discourses are formed. Yet, her account of trauma nevertheless reproduces some of the dominant anti-mimetic assumptions of cognitivist trauma theory. That is, in her work, trauma is above all regarded as an external overwhelming event (Edkins, 2002, 2003, 2004). A closer reading reveals that underlying this account is a projection of the cognitivist perception of trauma on societal or political scale: just as the traumatic event is supposed to have split off narration through the impairment of a person's cognitive memory, so the traumatic event results in a splitting of narration in the community. The trouble is that her account thereby overlooks the fact that trauma might not be comprised of an event but rather be structural, pervasive and continuous. It fails to see that trauma might in fact be a manifestation, rather than a suspension, of authority. That is, though her work is extremely important, it is arguably less suitable for the study of trauma in authoritarian contexts: as it insufficiently recognises the ways in which authorities *themselves* might be involved in the purposeful structural and continuous infliction of trauma – particularly, though not solely, in repressive authoritarian contexts, such as that of Egypt. Here too, we see that as the cognitivist notion of PTSD, has become so commonplace, its presuppositions are left unchallenged since it has become difficult to even imagine alternatives.

We see the same dilemma in Emma Hutchinson's recent work on political trauma, which also reproduces the anti-mimetic understanding of trauma as an external shocking event (one which again can either split communities apart or bring them together) (Hutchison, 2013). She argues that while a traumatic event can isolate people and result in a withdrawal from the public sphere, 'it can also construct or consolidate forms of political community. [. . .] traumatic events can generate shared meanings and bonds between individuals' (Hutchison, 2013: 36). While she is right in the possible political effects of trauma, I would argue that because of an uncritical adoption of anti-mimetic premises her account fails to grasp how atomisation and fragmentation does result not from a rupture of memory as such but rather from the rupture of intersubjective parity, and how mobilisation resulting from trauma is precisely centred around the (re)gaining of this intersubjective parity.

Of course, a very different political account of trauma is provided by both Jeffrey Alexander (2004) and Piotr Sztompka (2000a, 2000b, 2004), as they emphasise the importance of mobilisation in trauma. They insist that *social trauma* emerges when 'collective actors "decide" to represent social pain as fundamental threat to their sense of who they are, where they come from and where they want to go' (Alexander, 2004: 10). Hence, they acknowledge that trauma involves 'a meaning struggle', but state that this occurs through the collective mobilisation around a painful experience, in which the nature of the pain and the nature of the victim and the attribution of responsibility is identified (Alexander, 2004: 13–15). And so, for Sztompka and Alexander, trauma is above all a performative act of mobilisation and a speech act through which victims seek 'persuasively project the trauma claim to the audience-public' (Alexander, 2004: 12). This account also again regards trauma anti-mimetically as trauma, for them, is clearly 'rooted in an event or series of events' (Sztompka, 2000: 449) that shock the cultural tissue of society. Importantly, in their accounts, such events do not become traumatic because of the experience of pain as such, but rather because 'this acute discomfort enter[s] into the core of the collectivity's sense of its own identity' (Alexander, 2004: 10). Through its articulation in the public sphere it becomes a focal point of collective mobilisation. But this clearly presumes at least a modicum of freedom and agency where one is able to collectively construct a narrative around the trauma experienced. It thus presumes precisely the ability to articulate grievances and injuries in the public domain without risk for one's own life or that of others often. Their account thus relies on at least a minimally liberal context, wherein individuals or groups would be able to mobilise around their injuries. In the way it is currently formulated, it is doubtful that in their account a trauma not expressed is a trauma experienced all. This is clearly problematic since traumatic status subordination above all induces a profound speechlessness and robs one of the capacity to act in the world. Hence, like the political accounts of trauma discussed previously, their account is not so suitable for a deadly authoritarian context such as that of Egypt.

And so, what is needed is a recognition that trauma consists of a violent violation of intersubjective parity, wherein the ability to manifest oneself (collectively) in the world is destroyed. As the following chapters will illustrate, human induced trauma is a tool of domination, wherein the potential of creative becoming is crushed through the severe violation of intersubjective parity, leaving one hanging in a state of atomised disorientation and demoralisation. However, in order to analyse its infliction in counter-revolutionary Egypt (Part 2) and its existential manifestation amongst Egyptian activists (Part 3), the following chapter will provide us with the necessary analytical tools through a critical theory of trauma.

NOTES

1. For more information on Habermas's interpretation of Kant and how he detranscendentalises Kant in his theory of communicative reason, see Habermas (2003).
2. See, particularly, part I in Habermas (1992).
3. For an excellent overview of Habermas's formal pragmatics, see (Cooke, 1994).
4. Footnote needed refeudalisation.
5. Of course in the process of therapy, the therapist might still engage in a process of meaning-making with the patient, but this is most often (at least in the case of cognitive behavioural therapy) nevertheless shaped around the understanding of trauma as an cognitivist 'objective medical problem' of the mind or the brain.
6. This was also the basis upon which Habermas eventually rescinded the modelling of his philosophical framework on the example of psychoanalysis (Habermas, 1974).
7. For a popular, accessible, account of this debate see Burkeman (2016).
8. For an interesting account of how the trend of mindfulness fits within this same paradigm, see Purser (2019).

9. A voxel is a combination of a cube and a pixel and contains millions of neurons (see Alfred, 2016: 94).

10. In this sense, fMRI scans differ markedly from MRI scans most of us are familiar with (Alford, 2016: 85).

11. This aim behind this study was incidentally the speedily returning soldiers to the front, thereby saving military expenditure – which highlights the instrumental purposive rationality underlying the study and treatment of trauma.

12. In my own previous work on trauma in Egypt, I still erroneously adopted such a cognitivist framework of interpretation (Matthies-Boon, 2017).

13. Notably, such political constitution may refer both to its infliction by distinctly political actors (such as the authoritarian state) and its dynamic of violent incapacitation.

14. (See Caruth, 1995, 1996, 2001; Laub, 1995; Felman, 1996; Felman and Laub, 2013).

15. As Radstone put it: 'There is one sense in which trauma analysis's investment of power in the analyst or reader is explicit. Trauma theory emphasises the dialogic nature of testimony. Yet notwithstanding its analogous relation to testimonial witnessing, trauma analysis appears to dispense with the insights of contemporary media and literary studies concerning the complex processes of meaning negotiation that take place between texts and their various spectators/readers, and invests the analyst with immensely and conclusively authoritative interpretative capacities. It seems that it is the analyst, and the analyst alone, who is able to discern trauma's absent traces. In this regard, trauma theory seems to return us to an almost Althusserian moment, in which the authoritative analyst alone is invested with the capacity to perceive the truth of representation' (Radstone, 2007: 24).

Chapter 2

Towards a Critical Trauma Studies
Trauma as Intersubjective Alienation

In this monograph, I thus propose a different conception of trauma, wherein it is conceived as broken *inter*subjectivity. Herein, the violent infliction of traumatic status subordination collapses the interpretative framework of the lifeworld that we use in everyday life to make sense of the world and to manifest ourselves in the world in relations with others. As the lifeworld collapses, we lose the underlying grid of meaningful orientation, and thus experience a deep sense of existential disorientation. Unsurprisingly, as the lifeworld's shared symbolic order through which we used to make sense of the world evaporates from underneath our feet, we can no longer properly orientate ourselves in the world and experience a profound sense of speechlessness. With the lifeworld's collapse, the horizon of potentiality – the possibility of creative collective becoming and meaningful change – is thus also destroyed. In this sense, trauma through its betrayal of the counterfactual presupposition of intersubjective parity thus shatters the lifeworlds functioning, thereby throwing us into a depoliticised atomisation (wherein one retreats into a 'protective' shell of individualism) and disrupting (the potential of) creative (collective) becoming. This then sets in motion a vicious downwards spiral of relationless demoralisation and alienation.

In the below, I will first explain that this distinctly critical theoretical conception of trauma finds its initial inspiration in Heideggerian trauma theory, which not only criticises psychological cognitivism but also directs our attention to the phenomenological rupture of meaning in trauma. After this, I will outline the mechanisms of traumatic status subordination (with recourse to Nancy Fraser's philosophy (2003a, 2003b, 2010, 2014)), as well as its existential (subjective) effects (with reference to the work of Rahel Jaeggi) and, lastly, trauma's underlying purposive rationality (using Jürgen Habermas's philosophy). As noted earlier in this monograph's introduction, the advantage of such a critical theoretical conception is not only that it avoids trauma theory's category mistake, but it also enables us to situate trauma within its intersubjectively constitutive context, regard trauma as a distinctly political tool (as it is comprised of a destructive power relation) and clearly distinguish the cause (the injustice, the violent violation of intersubjective parity through status subordination) from its effects (disorientation, speechlessness and demoralised atomisation). In Part 2, this novel philosophical conception of trauma will then be employed to make sense of the ways in which trauma has been inflicted by the Egyptian counter-revolution (namely through a procedural colonisation of the public sphere, the infliction of grave violence and neoliberal economic rationalism). Part 3 will then examine the deep existential impact this multilevelled traumatic status subordination had on interviewees, and how particularly the weight of death in a context of political hopelessness resulted in demoralised atomisation – a retreat of activists into their own individualist shells. In Egypt, multilevelled traumatic status subordination was thus a counter-revolutionary tool par excellence, as it crushed the very potential of collective creative self becoming.

ON HEIDEGGERIAN TRAUMA THEORY: STRUGGLES OF INTERSUBJECTIVITY

A primary source of inspiration for my critical theoretical conception of trauma is Heideggerian trauma theory as developed by scholars such as Robert D. Stolorow and Patrick Bracken (Bracken and Thomas, 1999, 2004; Bracken, 2002b; Stolorow, 2007; 2011; Bracken et al., 2021). Heideggerian trauma theory starts from the point of view that we are always already involved in the world: we can only make sense of ourselves, others and the world insofar we draw on and are embedded in a background structure of meaning that is intersubjectively constituted.[1] We are thus always already 'bound up with the meanings, values and practices of the world' (Aho, 2014: 49). Heideggerian trauma theory thus counters the Descartian subject–object dichotomy, since it 'rejects configuration of the human being as a self-contained subject that is separate and distinct from objects' (Aho, 2014: 49). Rather,

> [i]n striking contrast to Descartes' detached, world-less subject, for Heidegger the being of human life was primordially embedded and engaged 'in-the-world'. In Heidegger's vision, human 'being' is saturated with the world in which it

dwells, just as the inhabited world is drenched in human meanings and purposes. (Stolorow, 2007: 2)

This also means that 'I am limited and constrained by the world that I find myself in, and this influences how I interpret myself and make sense of who I am' (Aho, 2014: 50). There is no abstracted vantage point of objective truth, rather as reflective and conscious beings (for whom the question of Being arises) we always already find ourselves in the world. Hence, for Heideggerian trauma theorists, the question is

> not about the nature of things in the world as objects and thoughts, it is the question of how the world makes sense for us, of how it is meaningful. [. . .] The meaningfulness of the world is primary. In other words, we experience the world first and foremost as a whole and only then do we encounter particular things within that world. Entities show up as meaningful for us only against a background context. (Bracken and Thomas, 2005: 124)

And so, Heideggerian trauma theory starts from the point of view of how meaning is ruptured in trauma, how the world no longer makes sense to us. Trauma is hence not regarded as an object suitable for biological, neurological or cognitive examination but rather as an embedded, phenomenological experience wherein meaning evaporates from underneath our feet. In trauma, we lose our bearing in the world: the way in which we used to make sense of the world and derive meaning from and in the world is no longer available to us (Bracken, 2002b; Stolorow, 2007). Rather, in trauma our symbolic realm collapses which means that we can no longer find our home in the world. Trauma is thus above all characterised by an uncanny, overwhelming sensation of surreality and estrangement from our surroundings, others and even ourselves. The world we once inhabited, the relations we had with others and the understanding we once had of ourselves all appear to have evaporated into thin air, leaving us hanging in a deep sense of existential homelessness – of alienation. For, as Stolorow remarks, in trauma, we experience the 'massive deconstruction of the absolutisms of everyday life [, which] exposes the inescapable contingency of existence in a universe that is random and unpredictable and in which no safety or continuity of being can be assured' (Stolorow, 2007: 16).

Heideggerian trauma theorists explain that in trauma we come face to face with the distinct and concrete possibility of our own impending mortality – the possibility of our own impossibility. As we come face to face with death, our symbolic realm (our background of taken-for-granted assumptions) crumbles from underneath our feet. For Heidegger, this was largely a positive development, in that it would open up the possibility of *authentic* Being through the cultivation of a 'Being-towards-Death' (Heidegger, 2010: 249).

In the orientation towards death, we would be freed from the daily diversions of the 'They' (or, Das Man) – or 'what happens daily', what one commonly does – as the singularity of our particular existential being would be disclosed to us (Heidegger, 2010: 370).[2]

Importantly, trauma theorists move away from Heidegger's embrace of the possibility of authentic Being, not least because especially in its plural form as an authentic Volk or (German) nation it became closely connected to his Nazi politics in the Second World War (Stolorow et al., 2010). Another example of this association between his concept of authenticity and Nazi violence was also his insistence on the sacrificial soldier being a prime, heroic, example of 'Being towards death' (Crépon, 2013) one that I will also refute in Part 3 when I argue that in Egypt's revolution we did not so much see a 'Being towards death' as a collective 'Being against death', namely a collective fight to not let death and a deadly life pass without a good fight. And it was in this 'Being against death' that the frontliners, as well as the martyrs, acquired a heroic status. But, having emptied Heidegger's philosophy of the problematic notion of authenticity, trauma theorists employ Heidegger's insights to relay the deep existential burden that trauma imposes upon its victims. For, in the face of trauma, and our impending death, the way we used to make sense of the world and derive meaning from it evaporates into thin air. Rather, 'the totality of involvements, the entities within the world, the way [we used to engage] with the world, falls away' (Sherman, 2009: 2). We experience a deep existential confrontation wherein nothingness closes in on us: we cannot get a hold on things anymore, we lose our bearing in the world and are thrown in into a deep atomising state wherein our relations to our surroundings are severed.

Hence, trauma is often closely connected to a profound feeling of anxiety. Importantly, anxiety differs from fear in that while fear refers to a concrete object in the world (for instance, the fear of a policeman), anxiety has become a generalised order of being which lacks any such specific object. Anxiety includes a general 'feeling of uncanniness, in the sense of "not-being-at-home" [. . .] In anxiety, the experience of "Being-at-home" [. . .] in one's tranquilized "everyday familiarity" [. . .] with the publicly interpreted world collapses, and "Being-in enters into the existential 'mode' of the 'not-at-home' . . . [i.e., of] 'uncanniness'"' (Stolorow, 2007: 35). As Heidegger writes 'Anxiety [. . .] fetches Dasein out of its entangled absorption in the "world". Everyday familiarity collapses' and one 'enters the existential "mode" of not-being-at-home' (Heidegger, 2010: 183). In such a state, every single thing or person we encounter as well as our very notion of self loses its significance and meaning. All things and we ourselves sink into indifference. Anxiety is thus 'completely indefinite' 'is nothing and nowhere' and turns out to be 'being-in-the-world as such' (Stolorow, 2007: 34).

Significantly, anxiety, for Heidegger, is thus not a mental disorder but rather an affective condition wherein one finds oneself (Heidegger, 2010: 134). Important in Heidegger's understanding of affective conditions is the concept of a mood. It is through our moods that the world is disclosed to us. Importantly, moods are thus 'not somehow added to our experience of the world but rather constitutive of this experience' as such (Svendsen, 2012: 422): they open up the realm of possible experience. Hence, in different moods, different possibilities of experience are opened up to us: in the mood of love, we experience the world radically different than in a mood of anxiety or depression. Heidegger argues that some moods – notably anxiety and depression – reveal the existential nature of our existence, namely our singular particularity. Perceived from a Habermasian perspective, this latter point is problematic: Heidegger explicitly *embraces* such a disclosure of existential singularity as opening up the avenues for authentic Being, which brings us right back to the atomistic individualism characteristic of a philosophy of the subject.

Yet, Heideggerian trauma theory is useful in that it explicitly offers us the insight that trauma ruptures the usual sense-making of the world and throws the victim into a deep state of atomisation wherein one experiences an overwhelming sense of relationlessness[3] to the world, to others and to ourselves. Moreover, Heideggerian trauma theory also indicates how this relationlessness alters the underlying structures of possibility:[4] in trauma, we experience a profound closure or rupture of potentiality. This is due to the way in which our meaning-making is inherently connected to the 'ecstases of temporality: the manner in which our sense of past, present and future always refer to each other – and form a horizontal schema of interpretation' (Heidegger, 2010: 347). That is, they always already 'stand out-side' or transcend themselves. Each dimension only makes sense in relation to the other, thereby constituting a meaningful whole in which all three are indissolubly united (Stolorow, 2007: 19). And so, any sense we make of our existence at all, we do so on the basis of this temporal cross-referencing: it is through reference to a past, that we can shape a present and project ourselves into the future. Hence, when in trauma the symbolic order we inhabit collapses, the horizon of future potentiality crumbles also: we can no longer make sense of the present through the past, nor can we project ourselves into the future. Instead, as meaning evaporates underneath our feet, so the possibility of meaningful potential dissipates also. Rather, with trauma, we frequently experience ourselves as being stuck in an eternal, non-changeable present. Our very being becomes 'freeze framed into a constant reliving of present' (Stolorow, 2007: 20), which 'contributes to the sense of alienation and estrangement from other human beings [. . .] that typically haunts the traumatized person' (Stolorow, 2007: 20). The temporal frame of reference through which we project ourselves towards future possibilities in the world with others is ruptured and thus losing this temporal reference, we lose the ability to inhabit the common symbolic order with others. We are existentially stuck in a temporal no man's land.

Heideggerian trauma theory clearly liberates us from the confines of cognitivist positivism, wherein analysis remained stuck at the philosophical level of intentionality: the analysis of cognitive objects. Indeed, through its phenomenological account, it relays not only how trauma is always embedded and intersubjectively constituted, but also that it gives rise to a deep sense of existential anxiety and atomising estrangement as our symbolic social order breaks down. Heideggerian trauma theory thus points our attention to the fact that what is altered in trauma is the underlying structure of possible experience.

This insight is crucial for our purposes here. As we will see in Part 3, it helps us understand how counter-revolutionary trauma in Egypt accumulated in a depoliticised demoralisation among activists (and is thus so effective as a political tool of repression). As activists were subjected to multilevelled traumatisation that affected the political, social and private realms simultaneously, their intersubjective relations were severed, the symbolic order was violently ruptured and they could no longer even perceive the possibility of meaningful change – and thus retreated into their protective shell of depoliticised atomisation. Unable to project themselves forward into the future, they withdrew from the political and social sphere as a deep existential sense of meaninglessness encroached upon them.

Yet, the trouble with Heideggerian trauma theory is that while it emphasises our intersubjective embedding and highlights the shift in the existential structure of experience that trauma effectuates, it describes the experience of trauma solely from a first-person perspective. That is, it relays the existential breakdown of the symbolic order, and how it gives rise to alienation, atomisation and relationlessness solely from the point of view of the person experiences it internally. In doing so, Heideggerian trauma theory inadvertently remains restricted to a subjective, individualist, description of trauma. In a sense, this is not so surprising. After all, Heidegger's philosophy itself was solipsist: not only did he embrace the singularity of authentic Being, but his analysis also commenced from the point of view of the singular person for whom Being became a concern. The difficulty is hence that since Heideggerian trauma theory remains restricted to an introspective point of view, it forfeits an analysis of trauma's social and political constitution. In other words, while it moves towards a theory of trauma based on intersubjectivity, it in fact remains tied to a philosophy of the subject. This monograph seeks to move beyond this purely individualist introspective conception by complementing the important Heideggerian insights on the existential effects of trauma with a critical theoretical consideration of trauma's radically intersubjective constitution.

TRAUMATIC STATUS SUBORDINATION: NANCY FRASER

And so, I put forward a different understanding of trauma based on a metatheoretical appropriation of Habermasian/Fraserian critical theory, wherein trauma becomes conceived as broken *inter*subjectivity. Trauma, I propose, entails a fundamental betrayal of the counterfactual presupposition of being treated as an equal human being in relation to others. Or, rather, putting it in stronger Habermasian language, trauma violates the intersubjective counterfactual expectation of equal reciprocity that is inherent in speech, wherein we seek to reach understanding as such (Habermas, 1979, 2004: 7).[5] Such a counterfactual presupposition of intersubjective parity is foundational for our communicative relations and necessary for a well-functioning lifeworld. And so, whereas the lifeworld normally adjusts and changes gradually in intersubjective relation to others and the outside world, in trauma – in the violation of this essential presupposition – we experience its collapse. The presupposition of intersubjective parity is so violently and deeply betrayed that the lifeworld crumbles from underneath our feet: our symbolic order of interpretation dissipates into thin air and we lose our orientation and bearing in the world. In trauma, we thus suffer all the existential impacts as outlined by Heideggerian trauma theory. We are incapacitated, unable to manifest ourselves in intersubjective relation with others and the world. We experience an overwhelming atomising alienation, as a deep relationlessness to others and the world around us is violently manifested. The potential of meaning and establishing meaningful relations is foreclosed.

In trauma, the presupposition of intersubjective parity is violently broken through the (strategic) infliction of traumatic status subordination. This is a term that I derive from Nancy Fraser's philosophical framework of recognition and particularly her concept of status subordination which entails the violation of participation parity (Fraser, 2003a: 29–31). Fraser's philosophy of recognition is crucial for our understanding of trauma since she explains how participation parity (the ability of all to engage in deliberations with an *equal status as peers* (Fraser, 2003a: 29) may be broken through the imposition of status subordination, which comprises both processes of misrecognition and maldistribution. For Fraser, misrecognition comprises those cultural injustices 'rooted in social patterns of representation, interpretation and communications' (Fraser and Honneth, 2003: 13) while maldistribution is primarily 'rooted in the economic structure of society' (Fraser, 2003a: 13). Examples of misrecognition hence include 'cultural domination, nonrecognition (being rendered invisible via authoritative representational, communicative and interpretative practices of one's own culture); and disrespect (being routinely maligned or disparaged in stereotypical cultural representations and/or in everyday life interactions', whereas maldistribution entails practices of 'exploitation, economic marginalisation, deprivation' (Fraser, 2003a: 13). She insists that while maldistribution and misrecognition have often been studied separately from each other – with some focusing on identity politics and others on the socio-economic structures of inequality – she argues that they most frequently occur simultaneously and ought to be studied in tandem. Participation parity is hampered through both processes of misrecognition and maldistribution, since vulnerable individuals and groups may suffer harm to their identity and their economic status concurrently. Here, she mentions the example of women, who may suffer

> sexual assault and domestic violence, trivialising, objectifying, and demeaning stereotypical depictions in the media; harassment and disparage in and on everyday life; exclusion or marginalisation in public spheres and deliberative bodies; denial of the full rights and equal protections of citizenship

as well as economic inequality, a glass ceiling and unequal access to jobs in the labour market and so on (Fraser, 2003a: 21). Hence, injustice frequently occurs

> in forms *where neither of these injustices is an indirect effect of the other, but where both are primary and co-original.* Neither a politics of redistribution alone nor a politics of recognition alone will suffice. Two-dimensional subordinated groups need both. (Fraser, 2003a: 19)

What misrecognition and maldistribution amount to is *status subordination*: wherein the affected (subordinated) party is not able to relate to others as *equal peers* in debate (anymore) (Fraser, 2003a: 32). Or rather, status subordination creates 'a class of devalued persons who are impeded from participating on a par with others in social life' (Fraser, 2003a: 30). This, she notes, is an urgent issue of injustice. For, clearly positioning herself within a Habermasian deliberative tradition, she explains that justice may only be achieved when all participants are able to relate as equal peers in debate and reach understanding of a particular norm.

In this monograph, I employ Nancy Fraser's philosophical insights meta-theoretically to elucidate the underlying mechanisms of traumatisation. In doing so, I deliberately extend the analytical scope of her philosophical focus on the political public sphere to all forms of social interaction. For, what I call traumatic status subordination may occur not only in the political and social public spheres but also in the realm of private life. Indeed, it may occur in any realm of significance, such as one's home, neighbourhood, educational places, places of work and the streets and other places. Traumatic status subordination is above all characterised by the violent destruction of our counterfactual presupposition of being a human of equal worth in relation to another. It thus violently destroys what I call – drawing on Fraser's notion of participation parity – intersubjective parity, wherein one is treated as a human being of equal value in relation to another or others. This counterfactual presupposition of intersubjective parity is fundamental to the well-functioning of our communicatively constructed lifeworld, wherein we derive meaning and significance in and from the world in intersubjective relation with others. In traumatic status subordination, this counterfactual presupposition is however violently destroyed through the infliction of grave misrecognition and maldistribution.

Importantly, these concepts are employed somewhat differently here than in Fraser's original philosophy. So, while misrecognition in Fraser's philosophy refers to cultural injustices rooted in discursive social structures (Fraser, 2003a: 16), the concept here entails the fundamental *failure to symbolically recognise the other as an equal human being as such* (which may or may not be focused around a specific social or cultural identity). In traumatic status subordination, such misrecognition coincides with the infliction of violent maldistribution. Maldistribution is here understood as *the unequal distribution of the material resources of power*, which physically and materially enables the perpetrator to submit the victim to his (or their) violent will. Traumatic status subordination comprises a toxic mix of both symbolic misrecognition and maldistribution, wherein intersubjective inferiority is violently imprinted upon the victim(s). For example, in torture, the victim's material incapacitation is combined with the purposeful infliction of symbolic violence, such as calling the victim names or using demeaning words that further reinforce the victim's inferiority. It is through this toxic mix of misrecognition and maldistribution that traumatic status subordination is imprinted upon the victim, and intersubjective parity is violently broken.

Needless to say, this does not mean that all forms of intersubjective inequality are necessarily traumatic. Not only would such an expansive understanding render the concept vacuous, it also would clearly not reflect lived reality. Furthermore, not all instances of intersubjective inequality, particularly when ascribed to certain social roles, are necessarily damaging. After all, there are plenty of cases wherein an unequal status relation may even be considered beneficial. A good example here is the function of a teacher vis-à-vis the pupil, or a parent vis-à-vis their child. In such instances, the unequal status is ascribed through a particular social role, while – if all goes well – the underlying presupposition of having equal value as a human being remains intact (and is even cherished). Indeed, in cases wherein these roles are carried out well, the potential of intersubjective reciprocity is fundamentally built into these roles: with the parent or teacher not treating the child or student as an object suitable for domination but rather as a person in the process of becoming an equal peer. Moreover, should the roles in such contexts be reversed, the relation of inequality would shift also.

But even though harmful cases of status subordination might be unjust, but not necessarily traumatic. Rather, I argue, impaired intersubjectivity is *traumatic* only when it destroys our capacity to speak back at the injustice inflicted: when it destroys the functioning of the lifeworld to such an extent, we lose our bearing in the world, and suffer disorientation, atomisation and incapacitation in its wake. Hence, intersubjective imparity is only traumatic when we can speak of a traumatic rupture of the lifeworld – when alienation is no longer limited to just a fragment of our (personal, social or political) existence, of our lifeworld, but when it takes over, when it destroys the lifeworld's functioning to such an extent that we are thrown into a state of muted atomisation, unable to manifest ourselves in our surroundings and address the injustices inflicted. The world overwhelms, as the lifeworld's horizon of potentiality dissipates in front of our eyes and we experience an excruciating sense of silenced alienation. In its violent betrayal of the counterfactual presupposition of intersubjective parity, trauma destroys the foundation of the lifeworld's interpretative grid necessary for the establishment of effective intersubjective relations with others and the surrounding world. In doing so, traumatic status subordination thus destroys our (collective) manifestation in the world, our creative (collective) self-becoming and self-realisation.

There is of course a philosophical question here as to how this emphasis on trauma's rupture of self-becoming may be squared with Nancy Fraser's objections to accounts of self-realisation – or the grounding of recognition in patterns of 'deprecation by others' (Fraser, 2003a: 29, 30–33). Fraser, after all, emphasises the need for a thin deontological account of justice that avoids the prescription of more substantive visions of the good life – or, theories of self-realisation. This critique of hers is mostly directed towards Axel Honneth's theory of recognition, whose work is grounded in a substantive theory of a supposedly universal human need for self-confidence (rooted in parental love), self-respect (rooted in legal relations and rights) and self-esteem (rooted in patterns of social relations and solidarity). Honneth believes that all these elements of recognition are necessary for the healthy development of our personality and that a violation of any of these is highly damaging to our ethical self-realisation. Fraser rightfully worries that such a substantive vision of self-realisation is particularistic and not necessarily universally valid. Rather, it normatively prescribes a particular thick vision of the good onto others, thereby overlooking and potentially damaging the diversity of worldviews.

Fraser is also concerned that Honneth's account of recognition ends up contributing to the psychologisation of injustice (Fraser and Honneth, 2003: 31), as it fails ground the perceived ills in untoward social and political conditions – or, a practical theory of justice. That is, the origins of social and political injustices become transposed onto the individual's subjectivity, now deemed impaired. This, she argues, results in a double injury wherein insult is added to injury: the person who suffers an injustice is now also told their subjectivity is impaired (Fraser and Honneth, 2003: 31). As we have seen, it is precisely this problem of adding insult to injury that also persists in trauma studies when it reduces trauma to a problem of the mind. And so, Fraser explicitly grounds her conception of justice not on a substantive, particularistic vision of the good life, but instead on the Habermasian insight that a social and political order is only just when all affected are free to deliberate on a norm and its anticipated side effects as equal peers. This deontological model does not prescribe us with a thicker more substantive notion of the ethical life,[6] as it is merely based on an egalitarian notion of the intersubjective *equality* of all people, which itself is rooted in the counterfactual presuppositions of speech itself. Hence, she asserts that misrecognition is constituted by 'institutionalised patterns of cultural values in ways that *prevent one from participating as a peer in social life*' (Fraser, 2003: 29). And its overcoming depends on the fulfilment of two conditions, namely (1) that institutionalised patterns of cultural values express equal respect for all and (2) that the distribution of material resources ensures the independence and voice of participants.

Now, while I share Fraser's criticisms of Honneth's model of recognition, I believe we can nevertheless salvage a thin conception of self-realisation by basing it on purely on intersubjective parity. While Honneth indeed prescribes a thick and essentialising account of self-realisation that may not be acceptable to all, it is also possible to regard self-realisation in a non-substantive way: as the ability to manifest oneself intersubjectively in the world with others, *without* attaching substantive notions to this (such as the need for confidence, respect and love). Rather, these more substantive notions are to be determined by those affected in their particular contextual settings and need not be philosophically be predetermined. Indeed, one does not need to philosophically establish the exact substantive content of self-realisation (and rather leave this for people themselves to decide), but simply stipulate a thin formal condition: namely, that effective self-realisation depends on the absence of existential status subordination, including its traumatic forms. Importantly, this does not imply the absence of differentiating social roles or contextual differentiation of social hierarchies but rather that these are not so grave that they manifest themselves through violent power relations wherein the existential intersubjective parity of being together in the world, of equal human beings, is damaged. And so, while the scope of concrete application would extend beyond Fraser's more limited emphasis on the political public sphere (and enters into the social and private sphere), the analytical foundation of the concept self-realisation does not stray from Fraser's own thin conceptualisation of justice. That is, philosophically, such a minimalist formulation of self-realisation would not go beyond the quasi-deontological boundaries of Nancy Fraser's own account, and instead be perfectly situated within it. Self-realisation would merely depend on the freedom to engage in communicative relations with others as equal intersubjective peers, so that one may manifest oneself in the world and engage in (collective) self-becoming. Adding such a thin conception of self-realisation to Fraser's account also helps us shine a clearer light on the particularly destructive effects of injustice, including its traumatic variants that are under examination here.

TRAUMATIC ALIENATION: RAHEL JAEGGI

Particularly useful in this reformulation is Rahel Jaeggi's important work on alienation (Jaeggi, 2014), wherein she sketches out a thin account of alienation as the inhibition of self-manifestation in the world. Jaeggi explains that within philosophy, alienation has been conceived as

> indifference and internal division, but also powerless-ness and relationlessness with respect to oneself and to a world experienced as indifferent and alien. Alienation is the inability to establish a relation to other human beings, to things, to social institutions and thereby also – so the fundamental intuition of the theory of alienation – to oneself. An alienated world presents itself to individuals as insignificant and meaningless, as rigidified or impoverished, as a world that is not one's own, which is to say, a world in which one is not 'at home' and over which one can have no influence. The alienated subject becomes a stranger to itself; it no longer experiences itself as an 'actively effective subject' but a 'passive object' at the mercy of unknown forces. One can speak of alienation 'wherever individuals do not find themselves in their own actions' or wherever we cannot be master over the being that we ourselves are (as Heidegger might have put it). The alienated person, according to the early Alasdair MacIntyre, is 'a stranger in the world that he himself has made'. (Jaeggi, 2014: 3)

What Jaeggi distils from these various philosophical visions is that alienation comprises the inability to appropriate the self and the surrounding world. Significantly, appropriation is here not understood to mean ownership or instrumentalisation of resources, but rather intersubjectively as an effective transformation of both self and other in a mutually constitutive encounter. Hence, alienation as a breakdown of appropriation entails a failure to identify with one's actions or desires, the inability to be present in one's actions, to steer or direct one's life and actions (Jaeggi, 2014: 51). Alienation is a failure to realise oneself:

> One is not an agent in what one does, is not present in one's life but is instead driven by it, does not identify with what one wants, and is not involved in what one does, this does not imply that one is somehow 'really' someone else. And yet, there is an identifiable discrepancy, an analysable deficit or contradiction, in what one does. (Jaeggi, 2014: 159)

Hence her argument is that 'living one's own life means identifying in a certain way with oneself and the world – being able to appropriate the world' (Jaeggi, 2014: xxi) to realise oneself in it and to shape it.

Importantly, her theory of alienation avoids the substantive essentialism that has haunted alienation theory since its inception. Alienation theories – in both their Marxist and existentialist forms – often upheld an (implicit) belief in an unalienated, authentic or true self or society that one is alienated from. This 'unalienated' essence of man is hence one that we have become estranged from and must strive towards or return to (depending on the progressive or conservative nature of the critique) (Jaeggi, 2014: 2). Jaeggi instead sheds this idea and provides the powerful argument that alienation does not mean we have become alienated from a real inner core or independent ontological entity that is our unalienated self. Rather, our selves are formed through the *act* of our identifications, which are embedded in and constituted by intersubjective relation. Hence, the 'true' self is not an essential core but 'a set of characteristics with which the person genuinely identifies' (Jaeggi, 2014: 165). And so, when we are alienated, we fail to identify with our practice(s) in the world and we fail to manifest ourselves in it. So, for instance, social roles are alienating because we cannot appropriate these roles, we cannot shape them, give them a meaning of our own and we cannot fully identify with them. They appear to stand over us, in a pre-given fashion that pulls our sense of agency from underneath our feet. Hence,

> the problem is not that he does something that he is not but that he is not present in what he does [. . .] One is not alienated *from something* (one's authentic self) but rather in one's performance of actions and hence in what one does or *how* one does it. (Jaeggi, 2014: 158)

And so, rather than referring to an idealised essential or authentic self, alienation consists of a *relation of relationlessness* wherein appropriation has been inhibited or halted.

Now, while Fraser's philosophy was useful for understanding the mechanisms of traumatic status subordination, Jaeggi's insights are particularly important for elucidating its effects. For what occurs in trauma is precisely this relation of relationlessness. Through the violent betrayal of intersubjective parity, and the lifeworld's collapse in its wake, we can no longer establish effective relations with the world, others and ourselves. Rather, as the underlying grid of interpretation collapses, we lose our bearing in the world. We can no longer identify ourselves in the world, in our relations with others and in our own actions. Instead, the world appears to have been transformed into an unchangeable void, a big gaping hole wherein the potential of meaningful change has disappeared into thin air. In face of traumatic status subordination, and the violent rupture of intersubjective relations, one loses the capacity to manifest oneself in the world. Rather, the appropriation of the world and ourselves in it is inhibited, and the world comes and stands over and above us as an alien force of malevolent, unchangeable meaninglessness.

Importantly, while all forms of alienation may be distressing, they are not always traumatic. We only speak of traumatic alienation when appropriation is inhibited to such an extent it can no longer be contained to one element or fragment in one's life, but rather pertains to one's entire existence as such. In traumatic alienation, we lack the appropriate interpretative symbolic resources to identify with anything at all. For, the lifeworld which provides us with the background of social knowledge and cultural traditions that help us orientate ourselves and navigate through (everyday) life collapses. The lifeworld is not just compromises one aspect of one's life or is forced to shift according to different circumstances. Rather, in face of traumatic status subordination it ceases to function. As this interpretative framework falls away, we lose our effective relations to others and we find ourselves existentially tumbling down a void, a nihilistic hole of stifling atomisation, relationlessness and meaninglessness. And so, traumatic alienation happens when the interpretative horizon (or the shared communicative realm) of the lifeworld breaks down to such an extent that we can no longer effectively draw from it as a resource for our actions. Lacking this resource, we can no longer identify with anything: we become so gravely atomised and estranged that it incapacitates us. We can neither find our bearing in the world, nor derive meaning from our relations with others. Instead, we experience an overwhelming sense of estrangement that is typified by social withdrawal and excruciating atomisation. Our intersubjectivity is broken, and we experience a deep existential relationlessness so well described by Heideggerian trauma theory (Bracken, 1988, 2002b; Bracken and Thomas, 2005; Stolorow, 2007, 2011; Thomas and Bracken, 2011). As we experience such overwhelming relationlessness and inability to intersubjectively manifest ourselves in the world, we lose our voice. We lose the capacity to speak back at the injustice(s) inflicted. We become numbed, thrown back into existential meaningless atomisation, as the horizon's potentiality of creative self-becoming evades from view.

Yet, unfortunately, in her analysis Jaeggi focuses on the *subjective experience* of alienation over and above an account of its intersubjective, social and political constitution. Indeed, throughout her work she explores alienation from the point of view of the person experiencing it, from the first-person experience. And so, despite the acknowledgement that we can only realise ourselves through intersubjective relations to others, she arguably pays insufficient heed to the socio-normative dimensions of her theory of alienation. Yet, since successful appropriation and identification depend on *uninhibited intersubjective* relations, one of the normative implications would be that just social and political orders ought to be devoid of status subordination (obviously including its traumatic variant). For, we are only able to effectively influence, shape and appropriate the world, our surroundings and ourselves through undistorted intersubjective relationality wherein all are regarded and treated as equal peers. it is only through equal intersubjective relations that we are able to assert our agency and identify with our engagement in the world – including our social order and political institutions. Hence, overcoming alienation – including traumatic alienation – means ensuring that intersubjectivity is no longer impaired: that we are enabled to engage in (collective) creative self-becoming.

It was exactly this, I argue, that we saw in the eighteen days of the Egyptian revolution in 2011 – when following the events in Tunisia and the murder of Khaled Said, people slowly overcame their fear, ventured onto the streets and squares of Egypt on the day of the national celebration of the police, demanding an end to the grave injustices inflicted on them by Mubarak's security apparatus and neoliberal business elite. Gradually overcoming their fear, Egyptians arose out of their muted state of atomised isolation, overcome social divisions and instead established a prefigurative public sphere wherein the counterfactual ideal of intersubjective parity was manifested. Having been deprived of the potential of meaningful change for so long under Mubarak's authoritarian rule, suddenly a new horizon of potentiality burst out into the open as people engaged in the process of creative (collective) self-becoming. Radical potentiality – the potential of change – was suddenly a lived, embodied, existential reality on Egypt's streets. Yet, as Part 2 indicates, it was also precisely this creative self-becoming, and the potential for radical change (namely a politics based on intersubjective parity) that frightened the military. Hence, as soon as the Mubarak had been disposal, the military set about inflicting multilevelled traumatic status subordination on Egyptian activists in the effort of quelling this potential. That is, it purposefully broke intersubjective parity through the colonisation of the public sphere, the infliction of the gravest kinds of violence and the active continuation of neoliberal politics. All in the effort of putting the revolutionary genie back into the authoritarian bottle and destroying the potential challenge to its own political and economic interests.

This then brings us to our last point here. Namely, since Jaeggi (2014) only considers alienation from the subject's perspective, the underlying purposive rationality of trauma would escape from view. As she prioritises an elucidation of the subjective experience of alienation, a reliance on her analysis alone would foreshorten reflection on the fact that alienation – and in our case, traumatic alienation – is frequently purposefully inflicted in the pursuit of instrumental goals of political and economic power. That is, alienation most frequently results from policies or actions geared towards a calculative goal, wherein others become objectified as a means to an end – wherein the perception of others as an equal peer is violated. And certainly, the infliction of traumatic alienation does not occur out of the blue but is rather motivated by the desire to mute the victim in pursuit of greater influence or power.

TRAUMATIC INSTRUMENTALITY: JURGEN HABERMAS

Hence, while Nancy Fraser's philosophy explicates the mechanisms of traumatisation and Rahel Jaeggi's account illuminates the effects of traumatisation, it is Jurgen Habermas's philosophy – and particularly his theory of the colonisation of the lifeworld – that sheds a useful light on trauma's underlying (instrumental) rationale. As noted earlier in this chapter, his theory of the lifeworld's colonisation distinguishes instrumental or strategic rationality from communicative rationality geared towards reaching understanding (Habermas, 1979, 1984, 1987b). While the former is oriented towards achieving a particular strategic end and operate according to a calculative-purposeful reasoning, the latter entails the process of intersubjective meaning-making, interpretation and reaching understanding. While the former is particularly tied to the system of calculative rationality (i.e., administrative and economic power), the latter comprises the communicative realm of the lifeworld. As the instrumental logic of the system (or purposive rational reasoning) starts to encroach on and cut short the communicative realm of the lifeworld, distortions in meaning-making start to occur. It is then that Habermas speaks of the colonisation of the lifeworld, which is characterised by a range of pathologies: a breakdown of the taken-for-granted stock of knowledge, a rupture of social relations and social identity and the rise of mental distress (Habermas, 1987b: 130; Finlayson, 2013: 57).

Perceiving trauma through a Habermasian lens thus illuminates the fact that the perpetrator is not acting communicatively, but rather instrumentally. That is, it brings to light that human-induced trauma is not an accident but is rather purposefully inflicted in the instrumental pursuit of power.[7] Underlying the imposition of trauma is thus a distinct, violent, instrumental rationality. In trauma, the perpetrator engages in violent instrumental action as he, she or they seek to establish a ferocious power relation over the victim. In this power relation, the victim undergoes the gravest forms of symbolic and material violence (constituting misrecognition and maldistribution) at the hands of the perpetrator, who purposefully seeks to inhibit the victim's capacity for self-manifestation and creative (collective) becoming so as to maintain a superior power position. Trauma is hence an instrumental tool or means in the strategic, violent, pursuit of power. Put briefly, the point of the infliction of trauma is to incapacitate the victim, to destroy the victim's agency and ability to manifest him-, her- or themselves in the world. It mutes and silences the victim by inflicting such a deep betrayal of the counterfactual presupposition of intersubjective parity that the victim loses the capacity for orientation in the world – all as a means to protect or gain a superior power position.

Habermas's philosophy is especially useful here, not only because his theory of colonisation illuminates the instrumental rationality underlying the infliction of trauma but also because it enables us to relate trauma's efficacy as a political tool directly to the ways in which its imposition destroys the coordinating functions of the lifeworld. The reason why trauma is so efficient – and hence widely employed – as a tool of repression is because the deep and violent betrayal of intersubjective parity results in the collapse and malfunctioning of the victim's lifeworld, which we draw on for our everyday practices of meaning- and sense-making in the world. The thin presupposition of existential intersubjective parity – hence, the fundamental presupposition of our parity as a human being as such, unaffected by contextual differences social hierarchies and concrete social roles – is essential for the well-functioning of the lifeworld. It is crucial for our ability to engage in intersubjective relations with the world, others and manifest our self. Once this is deeply violated, the communicatively constituted symbolic realm of the lifeworld malfunctions: the horizon of interpretation falls away from underneath our feet. As the lifeworld's grid orientation and the shared symbolic order collapses, we lose our bearing in the world and experience a deep severing of (the possibility of) intersubjective relations. Hence, in trauma, we find ourselves thrown into a crippling state of nihilistic isolation, wherein all meaning has evaporated from underneath our feet and we are left dangling in a state of speechless anxiety so well described by Heideggerian trauma theory. Trauma is thus an efficient tool of repression precisely because its instrumental infliction destroys the functioning of the lifeworld, and in the absence of a shared affective symbolic order, we experience an evaporation of meaning and annihilation of our intersubjective relationality to others, the world and ourselves. It is in this manner that the infliction of traumatic status subordination destroys the potential of creative (collective) becoming and manifestation in the world. And so, as Stolorow explained, in trauma we experience a deep rupture in our intersubjective relations as we can no longer find a shared relational home (Stolorow, 2013). Rather, since the lifeworld ceases to function, we are no longer able to inhabit a shared symbolic order with those around us. Hence, one of the main characteristics of trauma is a crippling sensation of nihilistic atomisation, wherein we are rendered speechless. In trauma, one thus experiences a fundamental sense of existential alienation, as one doubles up inside one's atomised self. Traumatic status subordination thus shifts the horizon of possible experience away from one of potentiality towards one of impossibility: the impossibility of creative (collective) becoming and the potential of meaningful change. Rather, traumatic status subordination violently betrays the counterfactual presupposition of intersubjective parity, and in doing so destroys the lifeworld's grid of meaning-making and interpretation, which means we lose our bearing in the world and our capacity for intersubjective becoming. And as this potential for meaningful engagement in the world, and the possibility of change is destroyed, we experience a deep sense of speechlessness – a disorientating silence. And so, human-induced trauma – in all its forms – is instrumentally inflicted in pursuit of a power relation, wherein the victim's voice, the victim's ability to influence the surrounding world is violently destroyed and the perpetrator's interests are maintained.

Shining a particularly Habermasian light on the manifestation of trauma helps us understand not only that the infliction of trauma follows an instrumental rationality but also that its infliction is so effective precisely become it inhibits the potential of creative becoming through the strategic destruction of the lifeworld. Hence, employing a Habermasian lens, it becomes clear that trauma is not so much the destruction of the cognitive capacities of the mind, as it is a purposeful obliteration of the lifeworld's functioning – the annihilation of the victim's manifestation in the world. The infliction of trauma thus serves a strategic purpose, namely the destruction of the victim's agency and voice as part of an instrumental pursuit of power.

Yet, the application of such a Habermasian lens of course raises the question as to whether the deployment of his theory of colonisation will not risk, at least implicitly, projecting a particular Westocentric normative framework onto the counter-revolutionary context of Egypt. After all, his theory of colonisation is deeply rooted in his rather more controversial account of modernity, wherein he depicts a particularly Westocentric, teleological account of societal development (Boon, 2009; Allen, 2016).[8] Indeed, the uncritical adoption of this theoretical construction would be deeply problematic, and rightfully subject to decolonial critique. However, as I have argued in more detail elsewhere (Boon, 2009), even if Habermas's theory of modernity is extremely problematic due to its inherent Occidentalism, this does not mean we have to throw his *entire* theoretical oeuvre and philosophical insights overboard. Rather, I suggested, we can salvage his insights on communication and the presuppositions of speech, wherein the kernel of his normative critique is situated, by analytically separating these from his theory of social evolution and modernity. I thus propose we insert an analytical divide between his horizontal theory of communication wherein Habermas develops a thin reconstructive account of the presuppositions of rational speech as such and his more substantive, diachronic, particular account of substantive societal development. In the former, I argue (admittedly somewhat controversially), Habermas takes on the role of a philosopher, while in the latter, he acts as an ordinary participant in social and political debate – subject to preconditions of rational deliberation he himself has outlined in his rational reconstruction. And so, we ought to theoretically distinguish two different analytical levels in Habermas's account that he himself unfortunately connected – and which hence resulted in a persistent contradiction between the universalism of Habermas's thin reconstructive account of his discourse ethics and the substantive particularity of his social and political analyses and commentaries (Boon, 2009). Admittedly, some might deem such a hard cut in Habermas's oeuvre rather difficult, and indeed it does require some diligent work to tease out the different analytical strands Habermas himself has so intimately connected.[9] Yet, doing so is fruitful since it not only enables us to overcome the contradiction between his claim towards universality and reliance on thick substantive (West) European particularity but we are also able to uphold the potential of rational critique on the basis of the presuppositions of rational speech alone (without particular substantiation). And importantly for our considerations here, it is exactly herein that the notion of intersubjective parity is located in Habermas's works. Here, he stipulates that a valid norm may only be established through concrete deliberations in free and open public debate wherein all affected are included and wherein participants *relate to each other as equal peers*. Important in coming to an understanding is the notion of mutual perspective-taking, wherein – as Simon Susen explains – the other is understood 'not only as a conversational interlocutor (Gesprächspartner) but also as an existential interlocutor (Lebenspartner)' (Susen, 2009: 102). It is grounded in the counterfactual ideal of '"unlimited communication community" (Kommunikationsgemeinschaft) that we necessarily implicitly refer to in everyday speech, which is nothing less than the idea of "unlimited life community" of mutual coexistence (Lebensgemeinschaft)' (Susen, 2009: 102). Thus, inherent in Habermas's philosophical framework is the notion of intersubjective parity, which is premised on the radical ontological equality of each human being. And so, I argue, the counterfactual presupposition of existential intersubjective parity not only pertains to rational public debate in the political public sphere but rather is a necessary background assumption for all our meaningful intersubjective engagements with others. It is essential for our ability to engage in intersubjective self-manifestation and creative (collective) becoming in the world as such. And so, when this thin underlying counterfactual presupposition is violently damaged in traumatic status subordination, the lifeworld's interpretative grid of orientation collapses – throwing one into a state of nihilistic atomisation characterised by grave existential disorientation and speechlessness (as described above). And so, when I employ Habermas's theory of colonisation to make sense of counter-revolutionary traumatisation, I thus redeploy it in purely horizontal terms, namely as the violent, purposeful destruction of the communicative realm of the lifeworld. The notion of the lifeworld's colonisation is thus no longer grounded in a teleological account of societal functional differentiation but is rather conceived horizontally in communicative terms as a form of distorted communication.

Importantly, in conceiving traumatic status subordination as distorted communication, I also expand Habermas's own conceptions of distorted communication (as either deception, self-deception or functionally differentiated systemic colonisation). While deception – or concealed strategic action – entails a form of distorted communication for Habermas in that one actor is acting strategically unbeknownst to his or her conversation partner(s), who believe(s) they are acting communicatively (Habermas, 1984: 333, 2001a: 152; Susen, 2009: 104). Self-deception is an extension of this phenomenon in that now the person who is acting instrumentally (rather than communicatively) mistakenly believes that he or she is acting communicatively. They are acting instrumentally even unbeknownst to themselves. The last form of distorted communication Habermas accounts for is systemically distorted communication, which plays the most prominent role in his philosophical system. Systematically distorted communication occurs when the calculative logic of the systems of politics and the economy – which have become functionally differentiated with the growth of modernity – encroaches into the lifeworld and ends up undermining the lifeworld's communicative functioning. This latter conception is based on Habermas's diachronic account of modernity (Habermas, 1979, 1987b), which holds that as societies develop, they undergo functional differentiation and aspects previously determined by tradition are opened up for critical questioning. Hence, Habermas argues, in modernity, communicative action increasingly takes on the role of social coordination (Habermas, 1984). Yet the trouble is that its radical emancipatory potential is foreshortened by the other form of rationality that also increased in modernity, namely instrumental reason – thus leading to distortions in communication as the lifeworld becomes colonised.

Not only is this latter form of distortion part of the theory of modernity that I plainly reject, but I propose that traumatic status subordination entails another kind of distorted communication than the three conceptions outlined by Habermas. While traumatic status subordination may of course comprise acts of deception, by and large both victim and perpetrator are profoundly *aware* of the pain and injustice that is being inflicted. Furthermore, traumatic status subordination entails less a communicative distortion caused by the calculative rationale of anonymous functionally differentiated systems (though it may do), than a violence directly imposed by particular agent instrumentally geared towards the pursuit of power. Traumatic status subordination is thus rather a form of distorted communication in that in the *infliction* of violence the perpetrator adopts a violent instrumental attitude towards the victim, wherein the latter's intersubjective parity is violently betrayed through a status reduction (imposed through the gravest forms of misrecognition and maldistribution). Rather than being treated as an intersubjective peer, the victim suffers violent reification, wherein the victim becomes reduced to an object to be violently worked upon – symbolically and/or materially. Of course, traumatic status subordination's effects entail a form of distorted communication also, in that the free flow of debate, interpretation and meaning-making has been curtailed as the victim has been forcefully silenced.

Hence, traumatic status subordination is a highly effective tool of repression precisely because it directly betrays a fundamental counterfactual presupposition necessary for the well-functioning of the lifeworld. Indeed, in light of traumatic violence, the lifeworld collapses. Now of course, Habermas has famously argued that the collapse of the lifeworld is an impossibility since in rational debate one cannot possibly question every single held assumption. Here, he explained that the lifeworld is not an entity set in stone, but that it usually adapts as segments (or previously held assumptions) become problematised in light of new information and/or alternative perspectives (Habermas, 1987b: 122–123). And so, the lifeworld's symbolic reservoir of taken-for-granted norms and presuppositions simply changes and alters as we journey through life. And indeed, Habermas might very well be correct to point out that it is a practical impossibility to challenge the lifeworld's *every single assumption*. However, what he fails to recognise here is that some assumptions might be more fundamental to the lifeworld's functioning than others – that there hence might be an (implicit) hierarchy of importance. So, for instance the counterfactual presupposition of enjoying equal existential intersubjective parity is more important to the lifeworld's functioning than, for instance, the held assumption that one drinks coffee after dinner. And so, while it would be a practical impossibility to challenge every single minute detail of the lifeworld's background assumptions, if a foundational presupposition is violently challenged, the lifeworld might very well malfunction to the point of its collapse – at least that is how it is experienced in traumatic status subordination. This oversight possibly arises due to Habermas's normative philosophical focus on the processes of rational debate as such. The ways in which extreme violence – such as that of traumatisation – challenge the lifeworld is thereby overlooked.

One might wonder here, though, whether this means that the lifeworld always necessarily collapses in light of traumatic status subordination. After all, might there not be such a thing as a failed attempt at traumatic status subordination, wherein the perpetrator seeks to establish an overwhelming violent power relation consisting of symbolic and material violence and yet fails to break the lifeworld as such? Indeed, one such example that comes to mind is the practice of Sumud in Palestine, which is a form of community resistance in light of the continuing colonisation of the land and the extreme forms of everyday violence and torture (Meari, 2015). The difference here is that regardless of, and indeed in light of, the violent imposition of, symbolic and material force, the pain and suffering of a particular group (in this case the Palestinians) is intersubjectively recognised and held in a shared space, and becomes integrated into a new framework of meaning and identity. This points to the fact that the effects of the perpetrator's attempt to impose traumatic status subordination might be overcome, or ameliorated, through continued intersubjective recognition of the victim's equal worth by others. It may be compartmentalised as the recognition of intersubjective parity continues in other spheres of life, such as the private and social spheres (of family, school, work, friendship, etc.). Indeed, it is through the continued recognition of the victim's existential intersubjective parity by social others that may repair some of the intersubjective damage inflicted, and pull the victim out his or her atomisation and reintegrate him or her in a social community, with an adjusted lifeworld. Reintegration should here hence not so much be understood as the cognitive reintegration of an unusual experience into a coherent pattern of memory or narrative of the self but rather as an intersubjective repair of the violent betrayal of intersubjective parity.[10] And so, while the lifeworld is (temporarily) damaged ceases to function, the length and depth of this impairment may be lessened through the restoration of intersubjective parity by social others.[11] It is also within the context of such a supportive intersubjective context – which may differ in size and contest (ranging from say one's family to fellow activists in a global social movement) – that the victim regains the possibility of voice and seeks ways of addressing the violence inflicted. Unfortunately, however, as we will see in chapter 2 and especially chapter 3, such avenues for social repair were violently destroyed by the counter-revolution's careful manipulation inwards of the frustration that resulted from traumatic status subordination in the political public sphere into society. The result was that activists suffered traumatic status subordination at the hands of the military and Brotherhood leadership not only in the political public sphere but also in their social spheres as ordinary civilians – friends, neighbours, acquaintances, relatives – started to inflict grave (and indeed deadly) violence on each other. It was this purposeful redirection of traumatic status subordination inwards into society that inhibited intersubjective repair and thus put the final nail in the revolution's coffin.

The advantage of exploring traumatisation through a particularly Habermasian/Fraserian critical theoretical lens is that it not only highlights the purposive rationality of trauma but also that the analysis of trauma is liberated from the cognitive confines of an introspective, detached philosophy of the subject and firmly placed within the intersubjective context of socio-normative righteousness. This intersubjective reconceptualisation of trauma resolves the difficulties that have haunted trauma studies since the inception of PTSD in the 1980s: it avoids the tautological reasoning and dubious causal relation underlying PTSD, solves its dubious causal relation and undoes trauma studies' category mistake by locating it firmly in the sphere of socio-normative claims (or rather, (in)justice). For in the critical theoretical conception of trauma proposed here, trauma's aetiology is no longer included in its own definition as it was in the cognitivist concept of trauma as PTSD. That is, trauma's definition no longer includes both the causal event and its effect. Rather, its cause is the infliction of violence (which may be both incidental and structural) in the strategic pursuit of power, and its effects are the victim's incapacitation. Perceived in this manner, trauma is hence no longer determined through a positivist lens of detached observation using nosological diagnostic criteria. Rather than belonging to the realm of (medical) facts – or, of constative truth claims – trauma is instead firmly situated in the realm of socio-normative claims of righteousness: it is a matter of (in)justice.

This means that a Habermasian/Fraserian-inspired conception of trauma is now able to account for its normative orientation. Since its inception trauma studies is motivated by a distinctly political aim: namely the pursuit of justice for trauma victims. However, locked within a solipsist, introspective perspective of mental and medical cognitivism, trauma studies was unable to philosophically ground this normative claim. Regarding trauma from an intersubjective, critical theoretical perspective, however, means that we are finally able to account for its political normative orientation. Trauma is now no longer located in the realm of objective medical facts, or the realm of constative speech, but is rather conceived as a severe violation of intersubjective parity and is thus located in the realm of intersubjectively constituted social-normative righteousness. Trauma, in other words, is above all about justice:

it entails the injustice of not being treated and regarded as an equal peer. Hence trauma studies is motivated by the pursuit of justice: the undoing of intersubjective imparity. Of course, as such this is nothing new: from its very inception trauma studies has been motivated by such political goals (rooted as its origins were in the pursuit of justice for Vietnam War veterans (Alford, 2016)). However, as the object of trauma was confined to the cognitive realm and constative speech, trauma studies lacked the thin normative grounding and the proper analytical tools for its social and political critique. Its political pursuit of justice was rather hidden under, or added onto, a medicalised discourse of impaired cognition. Yet, the critical theoretical conception of traumatic status subordination provides us with a thin normative basis – namely the presupposition of intersubjective parity – for political critique, and thus an analytical lens through which we can assess the occurrences and divergent manifestations of (traumatic) status subordination in both violent structures and violent events.

Some might wonder whether the undoing of trauma's category mistake – or, relocation of trauma away from the realm of objective medical facts into the realm of intersubjective norms – will not lead to a decline in the perceived seriousness of trauma's subjective impacts. After all, does the labelling of trauma as a medical condition not add weight to its perceived severity? Is it not simply taken to be more serious because it is labelled as a medical impairment? Here, I would highlight that critical theoretical analysis in no way undercuts or diminishes the severity of the deep existential impact of traumatisation. Indeed, one of the strengths of a Habermasian/Fraserian-inspired conception of traumatic status subordination is that the lifeworld's collapse includes an account of how it distorts our sense of self. Yet, it enables us to perceive the deep subjective existential effects of traumatisation while placing these in intersubjective relation to a broader social and political context. Or rather, it enables us to see traumatisation for what it truly is: a deprivation of intersubjective parity and the destruction of agency in the world. Employing a critical theoretical lens thus means that trauma may now be conceptually located within the power relations of injustice wherein it is constituted.

Indeed, understanding trauma's (intersubjective) causality – namely the violation of intersubjective equality in the pursuit of power – enables us to grasp its effects of incapacitation but also to work towards its undoing. In this sense, a radically intersubjective conception of trauma thus advances trauma studies' potential of critique. It thereby progresses along the lines outlined by Latin American psychologist Ignacio Martín-Baró, who reflecting on the concrete dynamics of social, political and economic repression, insisted that we should not merely provide 'an account of what *has been done*, but what *needs to be done*' (Martín-Baró, 1994: 7). This, he explained (before being liquidated by a

El Salvadorian firing squat), requires a new psychological praxis that is geared towards 'breaking the chains of personal oppression as much as the chains of social oppression' (Martín-Baró, 1994: 7). Indeed, such a new psychological practice, he remarked, must promote 'a critical consciousness of the objective and subjective roots of social alienation' (Martín-Baró, 1996: 42).

And it is also in this sense that a Habermasian theory of trauma offers a fruitful avenue since it directly encourages us to adopt a combined first- and third-person perspective. It is not enough to merely look at the subjective experience of trauma but rather we have to place these within their intersubjective context – thus requiring us to both reconstruct the subjective phenomenological experiences of trauma (using the first-person perspective) with an account of its social and political constitution (thus requiring a third-person perspective). Needless to say, any such analysis is always necessarily fallible and subject to verification in debate with all those affected. Hence, this book has no higher ambitions than to merely provide a stepping stone towards opening up such debates to try and understand the dynamics and manifestations of counter-revolutionary trauma in Egypt and how these have shifted the structures of possibility. Or rather, the ways in which trauma has been a constitutive part of the counter-revolutionary violent domination – domination, which as Martín-Baró explains, becomes internalised in our understanding of ourselves and gives rise to a fatalistic idea of an unchangeable social and political reality of alienation that serves the dominating elite (Martín-Baró, 1994: 42).

CONCLUSION

The outline of a critical theoretical conception of trauma in this chapter sets the stage for the exploration of traumatic status subordination in counter-revolutionary Egypt. Hence, Part 2 will elaborate on the mechanisms through which the military and the Muslim Brotherhood have subjected Egyptian activists to the traumatic violation of intersubjective parity. Here, we will see that both the military and the Brotherhood leadership consistently used a tripartite structure of traumatic status subordination, comprising grave direct physical force, the procedural colonisation of the public sphere and neoliberal economic marginalisation to destroy the potential of revolutionary becoming. The infliction of grave physical violence incapacitated activists: it ruptured their lifeworlds and threw them into a disabling state of existential shock and atomised disorientation. The procedural colonisation of the public sphere – which included the military's strategic co-option of the Muslim Brotherhood, the holding of early parliamentary and presidential elections, implementation of constitutional amendments, steering the constitutional drafting process and the implementation of repressive laws – in the meantime deprived activists of the possibility to manifest themselves politically. Hence, using the rhetoric of quick, orderly transitions, built around the notion of establishing a procedural democracy, the military purposefully betrayed the intersubjective parity of activists and deprived them of a political voice – ultimately accumulating in deep political demoralisation. At the same time, the continuation and indeed acceleration of neoliberal economics further marginalised Egyptian protesters as ordinary Egyptians fell into economic precarity and poverty, the blame of which was carefully laid at the revolutionary door by the counter-revolution, while the military further enriched itself.

It was thus through this tripartite imposition that, as Part 3 explains, the social symbolic realm of the revolutionary lifeworld was systematically crushed. In light of the experiences of extreme violence – as well as the accumulation of violent experiences in a context of counter-revolutionary instrumental colonisation of the political and economic spheres – activists experienced a deep sense of disorientation as meaning – and the potentiality of meaning – appeared to evaporate into thin air, leaving them hanging in a state of existential despair. As that Part explains, it was particularly the accumulative burden of death and the destruction of (the particularity) of life in the context of a violent political impasse created by the counter-revolution that broke the symbolic order of the revolutionary lifeworld. Rather than potentiality of meaningful change, meaning now evaporated altogether, leaving nothing but a meaningless abyss – a deep existential nihilism – in its wake.

Before turning into demoralisation, this nihilistic despair, I then explain, resulted in frustration, anger and aggression which was then carefully directed inwards by the military so as to rupture intersubjective parity in the social sphere. This not only meant that the violent violations of intersubjective parity in the political sphere remained unrecognised but also disrupted the potential of creative collective becoming. That is, the potential of a new prefigurative reality based on intersubjective parity was violently foreclosed, as violence started to pervade everyday life as civilians (friends, relatives, neighbours and acquaintances) now fought each other to the point of serious injury and even death. As death was normalised even further and the potentiality of creative collective became destroyed, the nihilistic abyss grew ever wider as the revolutionary lifeworld truly collapsed – in the end, leaving nothing in its wake but demoralised atomisation: a depoliticised retreat into a speechless state of nothingness. That is, though multilevelled traumatic status subordination, the military had destroyed not only the intentional object of revolutionary politics but rather its very potentiality: it put the revolutionary genie back into the authoritarian bottle. No longer able to perceive any possibility of meaningful change, demoralisation was completed and activists withdrew from all political and often even social relations. And it is of course here that the counter-revolutionary military wanted to have activists: into a state of nothingness where the potentiality of meaningful change had been purposefully destroyed.

As these chapters will indicate, the critical theoretical perspective on trauma as outlined in this chapter is fruitful since it avoids all those pitfalls associated with a philosophy of the subject as well as trauma's tenacious problem of causality. Rather, by locating trauma firmly in the realm of (impaired) intersubjective relations, trauma studies is freed from its cognitive reductionism, and all its associated aporias – such as a detached universalist projection of PTSD, the individualisation of traumatic stress (and the problem of double injury), the inability of trauma studies to account for its own normative claims, the reliance on tautological reasoning and trauma studies' category mistake. Instead, trauma now appears for what it truly is: the violent betrayal of the counterfactual presupposition of intersubjective equality we have as human beings in relation to each other. Instead, traumatic status subordination violently destroys this presupposition through the infliction of symbolic violence (wherein the victim suffers misrecognition as an unequal peer) and maldistribution (through which inferiority may be materially manifested upon the victim). Conceived in this way, we can thus clearly perceive trauma as a matter of utmost importance for the study of (in)justice. And Habermas's theory of the lifeworld's colonisation (1979, 2001a) is extremely useful here since this injustice is not only instrumentally inflicted in the pursuit of power but also its incapacitating and alienating effects may indeed be explained with reference to the speechlessness and incapacitation that the lifeworld's collapse evokes. A critical theoretical conception, I argue, thus enables us to perceive more clearly the mechanisms through which trauma as a status subordination is inflicted (using the philosophy of Nancy Fraser (2003)), the deep alienating effects it has (drawing on the work by Rahel Jaeggi (2014)) and the purposive rationale it serves (through Habermas's theory of colonisation). Indeed, it enables us to carry out multi-layered analyses wherein the instantaneous fragmentation of the lifeworld through violent events intersects with the accumulative build-up of the lifeworld's destruction through structural violence. For indeed, it is often through a toxic mix of grave physical violence and structural marginalisation and violence that the victim is incapacitated – rendered speechless and disoriented.

NOTES

1. On this point, chapter 3 of Being and Time 'The Worldliness of the World' is particularly instructive (Heidegger, 2010: 63–86), and Heideggerian trauma theory clearly starts from this conception of the worldliness of Being.

2. For an interesting overview of how Heidegger's concept of death in this sense differs from Sartre and Levinas, see Crépon (2013).

3. This relationlessness thus brings us back to Rahel Jaeggi's conceptualisation of alienation as being constituted by a sense of relationlessness to the world, wherein one is unable to manifest oneself (Jaeggi, 2014).

4. Which connects to Matthew Ratcliffe's insights on Feelings of Being – and how the underlying structures of our existential being may be shifted from possibility towards impossibility (Ratcliffe, 2008, 2014).

5. Grounded as his work is in his theory of formal pragmatics, his theory of discourse ethics is based on radical reciprocity between participants in communicative relations – who are then able to take the perspective of the other.

6. Indeed, it was also on this basis that I argued Habermas's account of social evolution and modernity is in fact directly contraposed to his theory of communication – and may only be offered by him as an equal participant in debate rather than in the role of an analytical theorists. We should thus incorporate a hierarchical analytical distinction between Habermas's theory of communication and his social and political critique. Whereas in the former he reconstructs the patterns of argumentation as a philosopher, the latter prescribes a more substantive account that may only be subjected to debate as a participant within a particular context (Boon, 2009).

7. This instrumentality has also been noted by Paul D. Kenny with regards to the case of torture, whose purpose it is to establish a relation of domination (Kenny, 2010). A Habermasian perception of trauma thus philosophically expands this view beyond the case of torture and grounds its effects in the destruction of the lifeworld's interpretative horizon.

8. Here, he argues that (in the West), processes of modernisation have resulted in the rationalisation of the lifeworld as more topics (including those of faith and religion) have become opened up for communicative deliberation. Yet the paradox of modernisation is that precisely as these topics have become opened up the communicative realm has also become encroached on, halted and distorted by the instrumental rational drive for economic and administrative power (Habermas, 1979, 1984, 1987b).

9. This resulted in a deep theoretical contradiction between his theory's thin deontological universalist claims and its grounding in a Westocentric, particularist historiography, which accumulated in thick prescriptive accounts of European identity despite his calls for a thin European constitutional patriotism. Hence, I clearly disagree with Peter Verovsek's claims (2021) that Habermas has managed this universality and particularity well. While he has managed this well in this theory of communication itself, he has failed to analytically distinguish between his role as a philosopher and a participant in debate (Boon, 2009).

10. Hence, this conceptualisation differs from that of Janof-Bulman, whose cognitivist understanding I also previously adopted in my own work (Janoff-Bulman, 1992; Matthies-Boon, 2017).

11. On the importance of social repair in face of trauma, also see Gutlove and Thompson 2004; Ajdukovic, 2007a, 2007b; Woodside et al., 2007; Hutchison and Bleiker, 2008.

Part 2

COUNTER-REVOLUTIONARY TRAUMA IN EGYPT

INFLICTING TRAUMATIC STATUS SUBORDINATION

INTRODUCTION: POLITICAL TRAUMA IN EGYPT

Part 1 outlined a critical theoretical understanding of trauma as broken *inter*-subjectivity, rather than impaired subjectivity. It also explained that the problem with cognitive accounts, wherein trauma is regarded as a broken form of intrapsychic subjectivity, is that they remained wedded to the philosophy of the subject. This adherence to a philosophy of the subject ensnared trauma studies in a number of problems. These included the projection of a particular (Westocentric) conception of trauma as universally valid,[1] the overemphasis on trauma as a shocking (extraordinary) external event (as opposed to a structural experience of violence that persists in much of the world, notably the Global South)[2] and a depoliticised individualisation of trauma. The latter resulted in the problem of a 'double injury', wherein the victim not only suffered an injustice but is now also told there is something wrong with his or her mind or brain (or subjectivity) that he or she should fix.

In addition to these problems, we also saw that so long as trauma studies continues to be bound to the philosophy of the subject, the status of trauma's causality also remained unresolved. The fact that trauma includes its aetiology in its own definition not only gives rise to tautological reasoning (in that it entails both the traumatic event and its effects) but also means that the diagnosis of trauma relies on an interpretative moment, which transcends the bounds of symptomatic nosology (the observations of symptoms). Trauma studies then tried to solve this dilemma by taking recourse to neuroscience, which (as we noted in Part 1 (chapter 1)) merely reproduced the already held psychological assumptions. For, the fMRI scans used by trauma studies were too imprecise to ascribe the particular the brain functions to the amygdala and hippocampus in the way trauma scholars did. More importantly, it only gave us correlations rather than causal explanations (Kihlstrom, 2006, 2010; Alford, 2016). Hence, it did not resolve the fact that trauma relied on an interpretative moment that cannot be ascertained through the observation of symptoms.

Trauma studies, I argue, committed a simple category mistake that it remained bound by ever since. For, appealing as this might be, trauma can in fact not be validated with reference to the realm of objective truth (or medical facts), but rather entails a socio-normative claim of justice. Crucially, this does not mean that the experience of trauma is not extremely debilitating, and that the infliction of trauma is an issue of serious concern indeed. That is, the experience of trauma is real, and people who suffer trauma should be taken seriously. Rather, all I am arguing (in a Habermasian fashion) is that trauma's validity claims are located in the realm of socio-normative justice, and its claims are validated through a process of intersubjective meaning-making rather than the monological or solipsist observations of truth by the detached gaze of the atomised individual.

Hence, I thus propose a modified conception of trauma, wherein trauma is not regarded as broken subjectivity but as impaired *inter*subjectivity. As this book explains, trauma entails the violent betrayal of the counterfactual presupposition of being an equal peer in relation to another (group or individual). This counterfactual presupposition is necessary for the well-founded meaning-making in the world and a healthy functioning of the lifeworld, through which we orient ourselves in the world.

In trauma, the functioning of the lifeworld breaks down as the victim (either a group or an individual) suffers the infliction of traumatic status subordination. In traumatic status subordination, a victim (either a group or individual) is subjected to the gravest forms of misrecognition (perception and treatment of the other as of unworthy or inferior status) equal human being as such) and maldistribution (the infliction of material powerlessness) to the point of being rendered speechless.[3] This traumatic subjectification thus operates according to two (often intertwined) dynamics: one is the deprivation of the material resources necessary to speak back at its infliction and the other is the imposition of such norm transgressing violence that the lifeworld's taken-for-granted assumptions come crashing down, leaving one in a profound state of helpless disorientation and alienation. Now, while all forms of status subordination are unjust, they are only traumatic when one (temporarily) loses the capacity to speak back at the injustices inflicted.

Importantly, traumatic status subordination may be inflicted through both violent events (such as torture or killings) and structural violence (such as violent marginalisation and excruciating poverty). Indeed, often incidental and structural violence beget each other and constitute a toxic mix through which the lifeworld ruptures and breaks down – leaving one in an incapacitated state of atomised, speechless disorientation.

Now, while an adaptation of Fraser's philosophical framework (Fraser and Honneth, 2003; Fraser, 2014), and particularly her concept of status subordination, enables us to perceive the *mechanisms* through which trauma is imposed, it is Habermas's philosophy that helps us clarify its underlying *instrumental rationale* (Habermas, 1979, 1987b; Matthies-Boon and Head, 2018). For, human-induced trauma is most often inflicted in the instrumental pursuit of power. This pursuit of power which may vary in scope from the direct power over the victim to broader political and economic power. In fact, often (and certainly in the case of post-revolutionary Egypt) traumatic status subordination comprises both, as broader political and economic power is pursued through the direct manifestation of violent violence over individual bodies or groups of people. Trauma is thus a tool of (political) repression par excellence. Indeed, in all its shapes and forms, trauma is always already political[4] as it entails the imposition of a violent power relation over another.

As I will explain here, in Part 2, in Egypt, activists suffered a multi-layered imposition of traumatic status subordination that originated in the political sphere and was turned inwards into society by counter-revolutionary actors (primarily the military but also its temporary subsidiary the Muslim Brotherhood) and had profoundly incapacitating existential effects. While Part 3 addresses the existential effects of traumatic status subordination and trauma's societal turn inwards, this Part will focus particularly on ways in which intersubjective imparity was violently inflicted by political actors (and particularly the military but also its temporary subsidiary the Muslim Brotherhood) in the political public sphere.

Admittedly, such violent intersubjective imparity is of course not new in Egypt, but rather has typified Egypt's colonial and authoritarian rule.[5] Patterns of maldistribution and misrecognition were violently inflicted by the British colonial rule, not least in terms of the restructuring of the economy, the colonial surveillance state, the violent infliction of racist status subordination and draconian laws (some of which remain in effect until this day). However, this book will have to restrict itself to post-liberation Egypt, which commenced in 1952 with the Free Officer's coup that overthrew British colonial rule. After a brief period of rule by Mohamed Naguib, Abdel Nasser rose to power as Egypt's authoritarian ruler. Interestingly, however, during Nasser's authoritarian socialist rule, there was a certain trade-off between misrecognition and maldistribution. That is to say, there was certain compensation for the blatant lack of political freedoms through the provision of socio-economic goods and services. And so, while Egyptians were deprived of essential political freedoms – such as establishing a political party and engaging in public political debate – under Nasser's authoritarianism, they enjoyed relatively fairer forms of distribution.

However, this trade-off ceased to exist after Anwar Sadat's neoliberalisation of the Egyptian economy in the 1970s. And so, as well as violent misrecognition and security state abuse, Egyptians now also suffered grave socio-economic maldistribution – the grievances of which were again violently repressed through the intensification of securitisation. This toxic cycle of misrecognition and maldistribution continued under Hosni Mubarak's rule and constituted traumatic status subordination. This violent form of intersubjective imparity notably accelerated when the Nazif government intensified the programme of neoliberalisation in 2004 (Joya, 2011, 2020; Tansel, 2019). Crippled both by economic uncertainty and (the imminent threat of) physical violence, Egyptians suffered traumatic alienation wherein many interviewees lived atomised lives characterised by social and political estrangement, deeply fearful of raising their voice. Mubarak, who outwardly portrayed himself as a great democratiser of the Middle East, had rendered them speechless (Davidson, 2000; Kandil, 2013).

It was precisely deprived existential mode of being in the world, wherein the potentiality of change had been seemingly destroyed, that altered with the 2011 revolution. After having experimented with social movements such as Kifaya and the Free Palestine Movement in the early 2000s (El Mahdi, 2009), Egyptians ventured out onto the streets on Egypt's national police day – 25 January 2011 – and started a revolutionary uprising that eventually culminated in the overthrow of Hosni Mubarak. Importantly, during these eighteen revolutionary days, a prefigurative public sphere emerged (van de Sande, 2013), wherein the counterfactual presupposition of intersubjective parity was instantiated with all its transformative effects. Egyptians were pulled out of their atomised shells and engaged in collective creative self-becoming, as they raised their voices against the decades of traumatic injustice that Mubarak (and his predecessors) inflicted on them. As intersubjective parity was actualised in the revolutionary prefigurative public sphere, the existential structures of experience moved away from *im*possibility towards *possibility*, away from a deprivation of hope towards the hope of potential meaningful change.

Yet, this transformation also posed a great potential challenge to the political and economic interests of the Egyptian military, which after having ousted Mubarak, sought to protect its own instrumental interests (El-Menawy, 2012; Kandil, 2013; Abul-Magd, 2018). In order to curb this potential threat to their interests, the military resorted to the infliction of multilevelled traumatic status subordination in the political sphere. Traumatic status subordination was inflicted through a threefold violent dynamic, namely, the infliction of overwhelming physical force, the political procedural monopolisation of the formal public sphere and economic marginalisation through neoliberal rationalism. While the events of overwhelming physical force left activists in a state of speechless disorientation and existential isolation, political proceduralism ensured that activists were violently excluded from the formal political terrain and economic neoliberalism threw them ever deeper into a state of economic precarity and marginalisation. It was in this manner that Egyptians were violently excluded from the political terrain, incapacitated from creative political self-manifestation and rendered speechless.

This tripartite structure of traumatic status subordination remained remarkably stable throughout Egypt's successive counter-revolutionary regimes, with a notable intensification under Abdel Fattah el Sisi's rule. El Sisi sought to fully annihilate the potential of creative revolutionary becoming through the infliction of a politics of death, the procedural colonisation and repressive juridification[6] of the political sphere (rendering it entirely under the military state's control), the prisonification of Egyptian society and the acceleration of neoliberal economic rationalism (now entirely controlled by and beneficial to the Egyptian military). The point of all this traumatic violence is quite simple: to protect his own and the military's economic and political interests. Through the imposition of traumatic status subordination activists lost the capacity to intersubjectively manifest themselves in the world and found themselves existentially lost in a disabling state of disoriented alienation and speechlessness. They had been rendered mute.

And so, while Part 2 of this monograph illustrates the mechanisms through which Egyptian activists were violently excluded from the political public sphere through the systematic infliction of traumatic status subordination, Part 3 clarifies its underlying purpose. Importantly, the purpose was not merely to destroy the intentional *object* of revolutionary politics but rather to destroy the existential *potentiality* of revolutionary becoming. The purpose was hence to alter activists' mode of being in the world, from one of the revolutionary openness to one of the deprivation (wherein the potential of change could no longer be imagined). The aim thus ran deeper than the mere elimination of revolutionary politics from the political public sphere: the aim was to destroy activists' lifeworld's horizon and fling them into an atomised state of demoralised despair, wherein they would find themselves politically incapacitated. Their existential mode of being in the world became typified by a demoralised sense of impossibility and depoliticised atomisation.

Of course, Egypt's counter-revolutionary actors will probably not have *conceptually* thought through the depoliticising, atomising nature of trauma as such. Nor is it likely that they would have contemplated the nature of trauma, let alone traumatic status subordination, as such. Rather, for them, traumatic status subordination was a strategic tool of repression that was, to use Heideggerian language here, 'ready-to-hand'. They were well versed in the strategic employment of traumatic violence as they were practically deeply familiar with its particular effectiveness. And so, my argument is that, knowing its depoliticising, atomising and alienating effects, they employed traumatic status subordination to quell the revolutionary potential and pursue their political and neoliberal economic interests. They used traumatic violence as an effective and practical political tool that breaks intersubjective, revolutionary and self-becoming. Hence, while they might not have sat down and thought about it, they knew – like most authoritarian and repressive actors – that traumatic violence breaks social trust and ruptures communicative relations to such an extent that people withdraw 'into a protective envelope, a place of mute, aching loneliness, in which the traumatic experience is treated as a solitary burden' (Erikson, 1995: 195). For, it is precisely this where the Egyptian military and powerful elites wanted Egyptian citizens to be: muted, inward-focused, atomised, silenced, disorientated, fragmented and, above all, depoliticised. The reconstructive analyses presented here aims to elucidate how this strategic employment of this destructive counter-revolutionary tool exactly worked, so that we may hopefully arrive at a more comprehensive understanding of how revolutionary potentiality was crushed in Egypt.

NOTES

1. (Summerfield, 1995; Craps, 2014).

2. (Leys, 2000; Radstone, 2007; Eagle and Kaminer, 2013; Stevens et al., 2013; Straker, 2013).

3. As explained in chapter 1, here I expand Nancy Fraser's own understandings of these concepts somewhat. See Fraser and Honneth (2003).

4. Importantly, intersubjective imparity was also the characteristic trait of British colonial rule in Egypt, wherein the supposed superiority of the civilised colonizer was violently imprinted on the inferior 'native brute'. It only remodelled Egypt's economic structures for British purposes, thus inflicting grave maldistribution upon Egypt's population but also subjected Egyptians to the gravest forms of misrecognition – wherein their worthlessness was deeply and violently impressed upon them. It was for instance also the British that imposed repressive surveillance systems such as the City Eye project (Ismail, 2006) that formed the foundation for Egypt's later surveillance state. However, unfortunately, a more detailed discussion of traumatic status subordination during the time of Egypt's colonialism goes beyond the scope of this book at this moment in time and so the books narrative commences after this period. Yet, the reader should be aware that it foundations are much earlier. Also see (Badrawi, 2013).

5. 'Juridification' is a term I deliberately borrow from Habermas's philosophy, which described the encroachment of legal bureaucracy onto the communicative realm of the lifeworld (Habermas, 1984).

6. Political is here understood as both 'political' and 'Political'. That is, it may comprise the everyday political relations between people in the social sphere as well as the realm of formal politics. Indeed, more often than not these are intrinsically connected. And so, according to this understanding, the traumatic status subordination inflicted on a child in the case of child abuse is political in that entails a power relation which may or may not be related to patterns of maldistribution and misrecognition in the wider formal political terrain. However, as this book indicates, trauma may also be directly inflicted by political actors in the formal political public sphere.

Chapter 3

A Legacy of Traumatic Status Subordination in Egypt

From Nasser to Mubarak

Traumatic status subordination is not a new phenomenon in Egypt; indeed arguably it has characterised Egypt's all political regimes both during and after British colonial rule.[1] While a discussion of violent intersubjective parity during the time of British colonialism goes beyond the possible scope of this book, it is worth pointing out here that this historical period in Egypt is characterised by severe economic maldistribution and misrecognition The British not only radically restructured the Egyptian economy so that it would benefit the British motherland, as part of the colonial 'project' they also setting up far-reaching surveillance mechanisms such as the City Eye project (Ismail, 2006), which relied heavily on local informers and mailboxes on the street corners through which suspicious behaviour could be reported. They also inflicted horrific forms of racist discrimination and imposed draconian laws on the population, some of which remain in effect until this day. Indeed, the very principle of British colonialism of course relies on a presupposition of fundamental intersubjective *im*parity wherein the superior 'civility' of the British coloniser is violently impressed upon the native inferior, and is thus inherently unjust.

With the Free Officer's coup in 1952, however, British rule was upended as King Farouk's reign was overthrown (Kandil, 2013). After a year-long internal political dispute between Mohamed Naguib and Abdel Nasser, it was Nasser who reigned supreme and gained control over all Egypt's state organs. Under Nasser's socialist Arab nationalist rule, practices of socio-economic maldistribution relatively improved. Nasser reformed landownership laws so that it was no longer dictated by and restricted to big landlords: fellahin now also received a piece of agricultural land (300 feddans) whose rents were not only capped but also inheritable, Nasser also provided free public education and guaranteed employment within the Egyptian state for graduates

(Goldberg and Beinin, 1982; Amin, 2011; Bush, 2011; Kandil, 2013: 21; Joya, 2020). Furthermore, his welfare packages also included subsidised foods, fixed low prices and the establishment of a minimum wage. And, as Galal Amin reminds us, in Nasser's time 'Egyptian goods were produced solely for the Egyptian people', which decreased the space for (corrupt) speculative financial practices that became prominent with the influx of imports under Sadat and Mubarak (Amin, 2011: 32).

Yet, this relative improvement of maldistribution under Nasser came at a price: the price of civic political liberties. And so, the price of fairer distribution was misrecognition – wherein the presupposition of intersubjective parity was gravely violated. Nasser's authoritarian rule left no political leeway for citizens and political movements alike. Among the latter were also the Muslim Brotherhood, whose mass mobilisation Nasser had in fact relied on during the Officer's Coup. Probably fearing their mass mobilising potential after his rise to power, Nasser quickly turned against them and imprisoned most of the Brotherhood's leaders and prominent supporters (Kandil, 2013: 48). His regime subjected them to the most horrific forms of torture and banned them in 1954. This was of course after Nasser prohibited the formation of any other political parties than the Arab Socialist Union in 1953 (Kandil, 2013: 70). Nasser thus fervently consolidated foundations of the current authoritarian Egyptian state: he filled all important state functions with army officials and expanded the Egyptian intelligence services so that it now comprised the State Security Investigation Service, the Military Intelligence Directory and the Presidential Bureau of Intelligence (Kandil, 2013). These security branches spied not only on the Egyptian population but also on each other and reported back to the president. Egypt's security state was thus a tool of severe repression, primarily driven by the instrumental purpose of coup-proofing (or rather, maintaining political and economic power). Having risen to power by (military) popular dissent himself, Nasser was aware of the potential of mass mobilisation in overthrowing political leaders and thus did not condone any dissent, and his torturous prison cells are a notorious illustration of his violent violation of intersubjective parity. Subjecting dissenters (and anyone that the regime did not like) to the gravest forms of torture, including that with chains, ropes and dogs, Nasser inflicted traumatic status subordination on the Egyptian populace as he firmly consolidated his authoritarian rule.

Yet, within the Egyptian imaginary, Nasser holds an ambiguous position: while on the one hand he was the torturous Egyptian autocrat, he is also frequently remembered as the great nationalist anti-colonial (and later anti-capitalist or socialist) liberator or equaliser. After all, while Nasser subjected Egyptians to the gravest forms of misrecognition, he had not only ousted the British colonial ruler, for the majority of the population the socio-economic situation markedly improved.

MALDISTRIBUTION: NEOLIBERAL ECONOMICS

This notably changed when, after Nasser's death, Anwar Sadat took office. After an initial period of hesitation between 1971 and 1972, Sadat pursued an openly pro-Western, pro-capitalist agenda wherein he firmly placed himself in the American, Western sphere of influence – having used the 1973 war as a strategic entry point (Kandil, 2013; Joya, 2020; Stacher, 2020). This war not only sent a clear political message to the West (and particularly the United States) that Egypt is a regional power to be reckoned with but also managed to marginalise and discredit the more Soviet-oriented military leaders critical of such a capitalist economic turn (Kandil, 2013).

Even before the war, Sadat had made his intentions clear as he started to encourage public–private partnerships and established economic free zones. He also encouraged businessmen who had fled from Nasser's socialist Egypt to return to Egypt, as he introduced a range of economic measures under the banner of 'infitah' (the opening) (Weinbaum, 1985). The social, political and economic consequences of 'infitah' are complex: not only did the influx of cheap imported goods overwhelm (and destroy) Egypt's productive industries, it also encouraged a speculative financial system rooted in luxury real estate and luxury products (Mitchell, 2002). It increased the gap between the rich and the poor and gave rise to the formation of a corrupted, crony business-cum-political elite – wherein wealthy and successful businessmen became powerful players within the political regime, while the majority of Egyptians saw their livelihoods dwindle and struggled to survive.

Egyptians were thus subjected to grave forms of maldistribution that deeply violated the presupposition of intersubjective imparity. These matters came to a head in 1977 when the Soviet Union was unwilling to postpone debt payments and Sadat applied for a loan with the IMF, whose conditions included the termination of subsidies on essential goods – such as flower, bread, oil and sugar – that people relied upon for their livelihoods. The announcement of these subsidy cuts resulted in the notorious bread riots, wherein people went onto the Egyptian streets shouting slogans such as 'where is my bread' and particularly targeting shops selling luxury goods (Weinbaum, 1985; Mitchell, 2002; Joya, 2011, 2020).[2] Eventually, the army was ushered in to quell the protests, and Sadat was forced to insist he would not immediately lift these subsidies.

Nevertheless, Egypt's economic neoliberalisation was firmly consolidated by Anwar Sadat in the 1978 Camp David Accords and continued by Hosni Mubarak after he succeeded Anwar Sadat upon his assassination in October 1981.[3] While Mubarak initially insisted on a 'productive infitah',[4] it soon became apparent that he pursued exactly the same speculative neoliberal economic policies as his predecessor. The Egyptian economy became increasingly centred around volatile tourism industries, speculative housing, the importation of luxury goods and remittances from migrants working in the Gulf. When the oil prices crashed in 1986, the remittances of Gulf workers stopped flowing into Egypt, the Egyptian state was unable to pay all its external debt – and the United States withheld its annual support, thereby forcing Egypt not only to declare bankruptcy in 1989 but also to agree to an Economic Restructuring and Structural Adjustment Programme (ERSAP) deal of the IMF (Amin, 2011; Mossallem, 2017). This deal deepened the neoliberalisation of the economy even further. It imposed a programme of economic liberalisation on Egypt, which included the deregulation of the market and an overall state withdrawal from public assets. It hence also included the privatisation of state companies, including profit-making ones.

The IMF ERSAP deal particularly benefitted Egypt's crony business elite closely affiliated to the inner political inner elite: they were not only able to purchase state companies for extremely low prices (using corrupt mechanisms of allocation) but also gained significant political purchasing power on the political elite themselves (Adly, 2010, 2020; Soliman, 2011). Moreover, as Samer Soliman explained, the reduction in social welfare spending did not lead to a decrease in state spending as such, but rather its redirection away from essential social services towards logistical support for speculative, entrepreneurial projects (such as holiday villas for the super-rich on the North Sea coast) (Soliman, 2011). And so, in lieu of the IMF's programme, state spending was thus redirected away from the poor and disenfranchised towards the rich business elite whom the Mubarak family co-opted so as to ascertain their power (Adly, 2010, 2020; Soliman, 2011).

Hence, such neoliberal acceleration increased the gap between the rich elite and the poor majority and intensified the process of maldistribution (Amin, 2011). While the inner circles of the political-cum-business elite bathed in wealth, the majority of Egyptians were condemned to the brutal struggle for life itself as labour conditions, housing, food supplies and health and social services deteriorated to the extent of near-nonexistence. Particularly catastrophic was the liberalisation of agricultural rents, which forced many Egyptians to migrate to the cities, where they were forced to live in informal housing (or slums) without essential facilities. They were then also condemned to seeking employment in the informal economic sectors, with terrible, precarious and frequently abusive labour conditions. At the same time, schools, social services and public hospitals were structurally underfunded, and employees were unable to survive on the meagre wages they received. As this young doctor describes, this raised profoundly difficult ethical dilemmas:

> The basic rule is that I am a doctor and my salary is very low and I could not just hold one job, work in one place. [. . .] I was feeling it was worsening. Yaeny

... what I mean with worsening is that you cannot provide a good service, you are all the time trying not to be corrupted and not to harm the patient, you try this as much as you can. You have a lot ... you have certain choices, either you work in governmental places and earn nothing or you work in private places and take money from the patients, or you work in touristic places and you also take money from the patients. All the time, there is no rule that doctors should work independently. You should find your way, that you are not following anything but your conscience. It was not easy for me to do this and it was not easy for me to get money, to get so little. So, I decided to stay at home or just work for a governmental place without doing any other private work. But definitely, financially it was a very bad time. (Interview 32)

In face of such economic precarity, many workers resorted to working multiple jobs and accepting extra payments for additional services to make ends meet, which led to a normalisation of corruption throughout Egyptian society. For example, school teachers unable to live off their salaries, sometimes failed students so as to earn some extra income through after-school tutoring. Or administrators at the Mugammah would ask for extra tipping just to process a passport that needs renewing. As Galal Amin explained, not only did these extra payments become regarded as part of monthly salaries, they also became normalised, regarded as requisite fees by those paying them (Amin, 2011: 43). If we add to this

> the government's insouciance toward any complaints of corruption, the rarity of any complaints reaching the courts and the disdain with which those in power hold any court injunction that may be handed down if an infraction actually reaches the court – [. . .] you have what is called the 'institutionalization of corruption: corruption has itself become the law that cannot be broken' (Amin, 2011: 43).

At the root of this lies severe maldistribution, which not only creates networks of dependency and normalises systems of corruption but also equates the essential state services with mediocrity. As this young activist remarks:

> Nothing really works in this country. It is already corrupted and it is drowning in ... I would not say all the country is, but it is drowning in corruption but almost every single aspect of this country is drowning in mediocrity which I believe is an even bigger problem. (Interview 1)

MISRECOGNITION: SECURITY STATE VIOLENCE

Now, in contrast to the popular myth that economic liberalisation leads to democratisation, economic liberalisation has instead further consolidated authoritarian misrecognition in Egypt. Rather, economic maldistribution further compounded misrecognition as the presupposition of intersubjective parity was now systematically violated in Egypt. For, as Eberhard Kienle explains, economic liberalisation directly contributed to 'political deliberalisation', which is not a 'blocked transition to democracy' but rather an 'immediate corollary of reforms that were meant to enhance property rights, increase private sector growth, and otherwise liberalize the economy' after the consolidation of the IMF deal in 1991 (Kienle, 1998: 221). And so, instrumentally employing a rhetorical veneer of liberalism that would particularly appease Western donors and international institutions, Mubarak's regime ensured that National Democratic Party (NDP) fully monopolised the political public sphere: it always stood unopposed[5] in elections through electoral rigging, the adjustment of constituent boundaries and the intimidation, harassment and incarceration of political opponents (Kienle, 1998, 2000). The NDP was also careful in ensuring that no other spaces for meaningful creative collective becoming existed and thus also colonised other political arenas such as the syndicates or trade unions. They amended the electoral eligibility of these organisations, imposed NDP loyalists as leaders and incorporated trade union activism under the Egyptian Trade Union Federation, which stifled dissent and protected the interests of the regime rather than its workers (Kienle, 1998, 2000; Beinin, 2011).

Of crucial importance here was of course the state of emergency law, which had been in effect since Sadat's assassination in 1981 until 2011. This law provided police and security agencies with powers to prohibit demonstrations, censor newspapers, monitor personal communications, detain people at will, hold prisoners indefinitely without charge and send defendants before special military courts to which there is no appeal (el Dawla, 2009). Through this law, the security forces reigned with increasing impunity while at the same time penal codes were adjusted so as to apply 'stiffer penalties for belonging to [or advocating for] organizations considered to be undermining social peace or the rule of law' and 'prison terms were replaced with forced labour, temporary sentences with life sentences and life sentences with the death penalty' (Kienle, 1998: 221–222). As the vacuous, all encompassing, term of terrorism[6] was introduced into the penal code, harsh repressive measures were inflicted on the Muslim Brotherhood and human rights organisations, 'which the regime repeatedly lumped together with "terrorist organizations"' (Kienle, 1998: 229). As the neoliberalisation of the economy accelerated from the 1990s onwards, repressive violence at the hands of the security state also increased as the 'respect of law enforcement agencies for the life, personal freedom and physical integrity of citizens generally' declined. Citizens were not only referred more frequently to military courts, but torture, death sentences and imprisonment also increased (Kienle, 1998: 222).

For, the civic security forces, comprised of the Central Security Forces (the police and the Ministry of Interior), had not only expanded in terms of organisational structure and remit under Sadat and Mubarak but also reigned with increased impunity. The relation between the Egyptian military and civic security forces is a complex one, but while the civic security forces (and particularly the Ministry of Interior) became crucial in everyday policing and security, the military was increasingly relegated to the security of external borders and economic activities (resulting in what Robert Springborg calls 'Military Inc') (Marroushi, 2011). Indeed, while the military's assets are shrouded in mystery, it is a fact that the military, using free conscripted labour and enjoying other exclusive privileges such as cheap or free ground, became a dominant actor on the Egyptian economic landscape. This 'economisation' of the military was furthermore a direct deliberate attempt at coup-proofing that started with Sadat after he was confronted with his dependency on military power during the 1977 bread riots and continued during Mubarak's rule (Kandil, 2013). The point was to decrease the military's security role, in return for monetary and economic privileges, while increasing the policing role of the civic security forces, which posed less of a danger in terms of being coup-ready.

And so, it was at the hands of the police and civic security apparatus that Egyptians suffered the greatest violations of intersubjective parity: they were subjected to daily abuses as these security forces reigned with increasing impunity. As Aida Seif El Dawla writes, there arose a state of 'lawlessness [wherein] security forces act with impunity, with the result that ill treatment and torture of ordinary Egyptians has become a systematic, daily practice' (el Dawla, 2009: 120). Indeed, the caseworkers in the Nadeem Centre for the Rehabilitation of Victims of Torture, where she works, noted that the torture of Egyptians for petty offences had gone through the roof – though official reporting was of course compromised due to fear of harassment and retaliation by these very same security forces (el Dawla, 2009: 122). And as El Dawla writes:

> Police also use torture to solicit confessions from suspects, from members of suspects' families or from neighbours; to complement stories they have obtained from third parties; to force people from their land or homes; or simply to teach respect for authority. Commonly used torture methods include electric shocks, *falaka* (beating the feet), whipping, suspension in painful positions, solitary confinement, rape and sexual abuse, death threats and attacks on relatives. In addition, the El Nadim Center has recently documented several cases of people being drowned or thrown off police buildings. (el Dawla, 2009: 123)

It was the lower social classes who found themselves particular (though not solely) vulnerable to this abuse. Lacking a higher social status and influential regime connections that could shield or protect them from these systems of abuse somewhat, they often found themselves vulnerable to the whims of the security apparatus. The civic security services then strategically used this vulnerability to create (a violent) dependency upon these very institutions that repressed them in the first place. So, for example, microbus drivers that refused to be co-opted into the security apparatus as informers would suddenly have their licences revoked or would be forced to drive less profitable routes (Ismail, 2006). And so, lower-class people were often not only more susceptible to security state abuse but also especially vulnerable to becoming incorporated into the very system that violated their intersubjective parity to begin with.

DESTROYING POTENTIALITY: TRAUMATIC ALIENATION

This recruitment of informers served a particularly important function in Mubarak's authoritarian repression: not only were they the tentacles through which the repressive surveillance state ventured deep into society, they also ensured that intersubjective parity was violently betrayed not just in the political sphere but the social sphere as well. It thereby markedly inhibited the potential of creative collective creative becoming, as intersubjective relations were mired in fear suspicion. As this young doctor remarks,

> there was a lot of fear, and you cannot express yourself because you fear everyone around you. You know that we have a very strong intelligence security and you are expecting all the time that you speak that this guy or this woman is going to inform about you – and stuff like this. So, we were suspicious, we were all the time trying to be on the fence, not taking one side. (Interview 32)

As social relations were marked by fear and distrust, activists experienced a deep sense of alienated atomisation: they felt alone in the world as meaningful relations with other people (wherein they were able to freely engage in creative self-manifestation) were violently inhibited. Hence, a deep sense of alienation descended over them, particularly strengthened by the NDP's complete colonisation of the political and economic spheres. It resulted in a great sense of depoliticised individualisation and apathetic demoralisation, as the impossibility of meaningful social and political change was imprinted upon them. As this same young man explained, during the time of Mubarak's rule, people would not talk of politics. Instead, they would merely focus on the trivial aspects of their atomised individualised existence:

Before the revolution, you . . . even did not dare to speak about politics. You only spoke about politics like a meaningless thing for any people. You spoke about it as a meaningless thing for any people. They speak about they know the results and nothing is going to change, and people were more easy about what is going on, yaeny. They would never express their true feelings about what is happening, just accepting what is happening, and they know what will happen and they know that the regime is much much stronger than them to change anything so when they spoke about politics it does not really matter to them. They are not interested in expressing their own personal opinions or fight based on their believes, no not at all. It was actually very peaceful when speaking about politics, because there was no speech about politics in general. Yaeny, people preferred to speak about football, about private things, about the female and sex but not about politics in general. (Interview 32)

Hence, in light of the violent misrecognition and crippling maldistribution suffered under Mubarak, Egyptians suffered a deep sense of depoliticisation. In this context, they were unable to make a meaningful social and political changes due to their violent exclusion from Egypt's political sphere, It is thus not surprising that they experienced a profound sense of estrangement. Many interviewees expressed an overwhelming sense of relationlessness, as they were unable to appropriate their surroundings and speak back at the injustices inflicted. In Jaeggi's terms, they thus suffered a profound, and I would argue traumatic, sense of alienation wherein the meaninglessness of the world was violently imprinted on them, as the potentiality of change had been structurally removed from their lifeworld's horizon. Sinking into a state of atomised demoralisation, they felt estranged from themselves, from the world and from social others. Unable to manifest themselves in the world, they could no longer find their place in it. The world, their lives, appeared utterly alien devoid of meaning's potentiality, as the possibility of creative collective self-becoming had been violently destroyed. Having been thrown into a state of incapacitated atomisation, they felt detached and estranged from others and the country they live in. Suffering a violent rupture of intersubjective parity, there was nothing they could do to exert any influence on their social and political surroundings:

All the time I was feeling that I have no meaning to live in this country, I have no role I mean. I did not belong to it. Things happen and my opinion does not matter to anyone. Whatever you think and whatever you believe, no one cares about it. It does not matter. Things just go as the security and the politicians want it to go. And for sure this feeling makes you feel as if you are a foreigner in this country. Although you were born in this country, you at the same time find yourself totally separated from it. You are not integrated. I attempted many times to be a bit more integrated but it was whatever, it gave me the feeling that what I am doing is nothing. (Interview 32)

NOTES

1. On the dynamics of what I refer to as maldistribution and misrecognition in colonial Egypt see Whidden (2017).

2. The similarity between these slogans in 1977 and the call for 'bread, freedom and social justice' in 2011 is striking – and points to the grave socio-economic grievances, resulting from severe maldistribution, that also underpinned both these protests (Ismail, 2006; Joya, 2011, 2017a, 2017b, 2020).

3. The dominant narrative is that Sadat was killed by an Islamist, though as Kandil point out there are also indications that the assassin had links to the air force – and may have been motivated by internal military disputes (Kandil, 2013: 402).

4. See Strohmayer (2007).

5. As Rebab el Mahdi writes: "The ruling party/organisation has had various names – al-Hay'aat al-Tahrir (Liberation Agency), al-Ittihad al-Qawmi (the National Union), al-Ittihad al-Ishtiraqi (the Socialist Union) and most recently al-Hizb al-Watani al-Dimuqrati (the National Democratic Party, NDP). The last emerged in 1976 as one of a series of organisations within a notionally multiparty system. In fact it inherited all the powers of the earlier monoliths. Each of Egypt's three long-term presidents has come from the inner circles of the party, which continues to control what Brownlee (Brownlee, 2007: 3) calls 'one of the oldest authoritarian regimes in the developing world'" (El Mahdi, 2009: 88).

6. The vague term of 'terrorism' applied particularly harsh measures against those who 'provided force or even the threat of force [. . .] to disrupt public order, [. . .] actually or potentially harmed individuals, or damaged the environment, financial assets, transport or communications, or which [physically occupied] sites and places, or obstructed the application of the law' (Kienle, 1998: 222).

Chapter 4

Revolutionary Becoming

The Politics of Prefigurative Intersubjective Parity

REVOLUTIONARY PRECURSOR: KIFAYA

Prior to the eighteen days revolution of 2011, there had been the formative experiences of the Pro-Intifada mobilisations in 2001 and the anti-Iraq War demonstrations in 2003, which culminated in the Kifaya (Enough) movement in 2004. The Kifaya movement fervently opposed the possible prospect of Gamal Mubarak acceding his father's position: Gamal Mubarak, having worked as an investment banker in London, and being at the top of Egypt's corrupted business-cum-political elite, avidly pursued further economic neoliberalisation. As he was being prepared for accession, Kifaya arose and demanded an end to both '"repressive despotism" pervading all aspects of the Egyptian political system', systemic corruption and the 'squandering of the wealth of the nation' by Mubarak's elite (El Mahdi, 2009: 90). Importantly, Kifaya was a horizontal, diversified, collaborative protest movement whose modes of organisation expanded upon such earlier models of contestation in 2001 and 2003 (El Mahdi, 2009: 93). This horizontal organisational structure directly challenged the regime's violent infliction of status subordination, as it prefiguratively instantiated intersubjective parity, albeit on a relatively small scale.

Unsurprisingly, these small gatherings and protests were heavily securitised by Mubarak security state. As this young woman recalls:

> I was 18 years old and it was my first protest ever, it was a protest against 'tawreed', against the succession from Hosni to Gamal Mubarak, so before Mubarak stepped down yaeny. There was like a . . . bad . . . . If you think it is bad now, it was really bad then there was like 200 people crammed in one apartment we got masalan about and we got some security downstairs and we got the plainclothes

men everywhere and then I was like going there you know, it was my first protest and I was very excited and then there was like 'wherever you going?'. 'Ah, my university is close to here, I have nothing to do with this'. I called my dad 'can you come and pick me up'? I was so scared. (Interview 30)

Though the activities of Kifaya remained relatively small scale and soon dwindled, they nevertheless had an important influence on other protests that followed. Rebab El Mahdi argues that they also had a spillover effect on the later Judges Club protests (consisting of judges who urged for judiciary independence) and the workers' protests, such as those in Mahalla al Kubra (El Mahdi, 2009). As she explains, 'Although the democracy movement cannot claim direct links to workers' activities through organisational coalitions, overlapping constituencies or shared personnel, the rise of the workers' movement cannot be dissociated from its influence' (El Mahdi, 2009: 101). It was out of this workers movement that the 6 April Movement arose in 2008, which later also played an important collectivising role in the 2011 uprising, as it unified a diverse body of people – notably, Islamists, Copts, socialists and liberals and others – under the same organisational umbrella. Again, in doing so, it prefiguratively showed that intersubjective parity is possible. But of course, as always, the state responded with violence to these mobilisations:

> Obviously, repression was very high. It was like very limited – if you get a demonstration of 200 people then they have to break it up and everyone is arrested and everyone is beaten up and we run away and were chased away. Obviously back then it was so small that the state was not actually threatened. (Interview 19)

Yet, one of the characteristics of Mubarak's rule was that it allowed small, heavily securitised and controlled pockets of dissent, since this provided the veneer of relative political liberalism which his regime needed for external political relations with Western governments and institutions. But of course, any potential meaningful change was kept firmly in check. These contestations hence never led to any meaningful transformation, and thus were unable to overcome the deep seated forms of alienation. And so, as this young man explained, while joining Kifaya enabled a certain level of relationality to others, it was too small to be truly meaningful:

> My fear started to decrease when I started to hear other people criticise what is happening, and see that what is happening is totally unacceptable. I started to feel more free. I started to feel that there is something happening. That there is a power, that there are other people thinking, that there is something wrong happening in this country. But all the time I had the feeling that it was a minority,

it was not a majority. I always had this feeling . . . [. . .]. people say that we are a pharaonic country, and it was always like that. We never chose our ruler, we never shared our politics, all the time the Egyptians are not included in the equation. So yes, yaeny joining this organisation and speaking with these people makes me a little calmer, give me a little comfort but I still could not find a space for myself. I still did not believe that this minority is going to make any change. Ehmm because it was not represented at my street, it was not represented at my normal life, that is it. (Interview 32)

EGYPT'S 2011 REVOLUTION: POLITICS OF INTERSUBJECTIVE PARITY

Nevertheless, as one interviewee put it, these 'flirtations with the idea of challenging Mubarak' (interview 19) proved to be an inspiration for the later horizontal nature of Egypt's revolutionary mobilisation in 2011. They were small scale experiments in the prefigurative formation of intersubjective parity that would later come into fruition during the eighteen days' revolution, which started on the day of the National Celebration of the Police on 25 January 2011. Inspired by protests that ousted Ben Ali in Tunisia a month earlier, and engrieved by the brutal murder of Khaled Said in Alexandria six months[1] previously, Egyptians gathered on Egypt's streets and notably Tahrir Square to protest police abuse, including torture and random arrests. As the mobilisation momentum grew, the demands were expanded to include socio-economic equality and political freedoms, and were encapsulated in one of the most prominent slogans 'bread, freedom and social justice'. Notably, the Egyptian word for 'bread' refers to both the food product and to life as such. They were literally calling for a dignified life. A life without political repression (misrecognition) and excruciating poverty (maldistribution). They were calling for a life without traumatic status subordination. A life characterised by intersubjective parity: wherein their lives would mean something, wherein they would be valued as equal partners in relation to each other, wherein meaningful change was a possibility.

This call for intersubjective parity was of course not limited to discursive slogans, but was rather also prefiguratively materialised in Egypt's revolutionary public sphere (van de Sande, 2013). Though many interviewees were initially cautious and even scared of joining, as they were fearful of Mubarak's security state, once the mobilisation momentum grew, it was like all the chains that Mubarak had put on them were being thrown off. A new prefigurative social reality was created, wherein every single person was respected as an equal member in relation to others. The barriers of atomising separation that Mubarak had erected in order to protect his own political and economic interests were being undone. All those participating were regarded and treated as equal peers as intersubjective parity was prefiguratively actualised: one's worth (or equal status) in the eyes of the other no longer depended on one's socio-economic background, religious or political affiliations. Rather, revolutionary mobilisation (temporarily) levelled the painful inequalities and divisions created by Mubarak's repressive regime. A counterfactual, idealised state of intersubjective parity materialised in the Egypt's revolutionary squares and streets. Herein, new communicative relations were established, and the potential of creative, collective self-becoming unfolded:

> What happened in the 18 days of the uprising. You see the Salafist person sit next to the most liberal person. You know, I don't know if that was, I don't know if that would ever happen again. But it was very heart-warming. You see the poor classes with the crème de la crème and you see them sitting together enjoying a civil conversation and it was beautiful and so simple. Because it was something beyond it. I think we need to restore that you know something that actually brings us all together. You know, we need to attach to the human values. You know the stuff that was long forgotten you know. So, I think the only way to a happier Egypt is finding means to reinstall these values to all of us I guess. (Interview 10)

Through the establishment of the revolutionary public sphere, participants challenged the decades-long inflicted traumatic status subordination as they overcame fear, broke down social divisions and engaged in creative collective self-becoming: they manifested themselves fervently in this world – as they refused to be treated like inferior human beings by Mubarak's regime.

Faced with this challenge of revolutionary becoming, Mubarak resorted to two tactics that he knew best: the infliction of direct physical force, which was accompanied by what I call 'conspirational victim blaming'. This term requires some explanation. Conceived intersubjectively, victim blaming has less to do with the subject's stabilisation of inner cognitive thought patterns (Janoff-Bulman, 1992) than the politically convenient redirection of responsibility away from the violent perpetrator towards the weak, the subordinate and the victim. Indeed, the violent logic of victim blaming holds that the victim's actions supposedly not only triggered but also justified the perpetrator's violent response.[2] Victim blaming is hence a political tool par excellence: it entails both the normalisation of violence (through its justification) and the disempowerment of the victim through his or her social segregation (by means of insisting that his or her behaviour falls outside the spectrum of socially acceptable behaviour and thus triggered the violence). This redirection of blame towards the victim ensures that identification with the victim's suffering is forfeited, and that instead, they suffer a form of social isolation

– or, social death (which may vary in depth or scope). In contexts of traumatic status subordination, victim blaming is thus a tool to ensure the victim does not regain the power to speak back at the injustice inflicted, but rather finds the perpetrator's intersubjective imparity perpetuated in his or her social surroundings as he or she experiences a form of relationlessness.

While all forms of victim blaming entail an asymmetrical power relation, in authoritarian contexts, victim blaming often takes a conspirational form. In conspirational victim blaming, the violence inflicted on the victim is justified through a discourse centred around the existential threat the victim supposedly poses to the state or nation (either in terms of its national security or its moral compass). Importantly, such conspirational victim blaming is an essential part of the machination of the authoritarian regime used as it is for 'mobilizing masses, reinforcing incumbent structures of power and authority, and assuring the loyalty of the people' through the active construction of an in- and out-group (Giry and Gürpınar, 2020: 318). Conspirational victim blaming hence serves a fourfold purpose: first, it helps boost allegiances to authoritarian structures of power through the creation of a Manichean dualism between insiders and outsiders (who may also be cast as 'internal enemies'). Second, it redirects responsibility for social, economic and political problems (as well as its resulting anger and frustration) away from the state institutions towards these (often invisible) 'Others'. Third, it deliberately creates social tension, discord and violence through the reproduction of stereotypes (Giry and Gürpınar, 2020: 318–319), which destroys people's reciprocal communicative relations and ruptures the potential of collective creative becoming. Hence, lastly, in doing so, conspirational victim blaming seeks to extend and perpetuates the violence of intersubjective imparity in the political realm into the social sphere, where the victim is ostracised and silenced. This means not only that the violent injustice suffered by the victim remains unrecognised or is disregarded but also that the victim lacks the necessary social support to speak back at the inflicted injustices. Instead of speaking back, he or she now often spends the limited energy he or she has on 'combatting' social others (rather than say fighting the perpetrator or perpetrating institutions). Needless to say, conspirational victim blaming is profoundly anti-Habermasian: its goal is to destroy intersubjective manifestation in the public sphere through the social atomisation of the victim while bolstering authoritarian power. Importantly, conspirational victim blaming is thus not deaf to the victim's cries and whimpering, but entails a destructive logic that rather rejoices in it. The victim's suffering is needed as the perverse justification of the state's own strength and forms a focal point around which the (revolutionary) potential of intersubjective parity is deliberately undone.

Now, while this repressive tactic would become extremely powerful again in the later post-revolutionary years – particularly after political frustration and impotence had been manipulated inwards into society by the Egyptian military and its associated businessmen. During Mubarak's final eighteen days, conspirational victim blaming no longer did the (dictatorial) trick: in light of newly formed revolutionary creative becoming, it lost its hold over people. And so, while Mubarak portrayed the revolutionaries in his televised speeches as internal enemies 'who sought to spread chaos and violence, confrontation and to violate the constitutional legitimacy and to attack it' (Mubarak, 2011), many Egyptians no longer believed this rhetoric. What was important in undoing the 'magic power' of conspirational victim blaming was the fact that revolutionary mobilisation affected not just one group or section within Egypt's population, but had spread across the different segments within Egyptian society. People from all walks of lives saw with their own eyes what was happening on the streets and squares of Egypt, which stood in clear contrast to Mubarak's narrative of conspirational victim blaming.

The other strategic tool Mubarak of course employed was direct physical force. This commenced directly on the evening of 25 January itself, when in light of the newly erupting mobilisation, the security forces responded with heavy gunfire, teargas, water cannons and rubber bullets. Such security state violence continued over the next few days as the Central Security Forces brutally cracked down on protesters: they ripped tents apart (and set them ablaze), teargassed, shot, tortured and maimed activists, while Mubarak at the same time banned protests on 26th of January and cut off the internet and telecommunications for five days in a desperate effort to stop the announced million-man march planned after Friday midday prayers. However, activists explained that in the formative process of new creative and revolutionary self-becoming, Mubarak's clear instrumental efforts to break up the prefigurative revolutionary public sphere that was being formed had the opposite effect: Egyptians across all sections of society became even more outraged. For them, Mubarak only provided them with more proof that he was a dictator they needed to get rid of.

Hence, on Friday the 28th of January, the Day of Fury, protesters violently clashed with Central Security Forces as they stood their ground, fighting off Mubarak's repressive police force. As Neil Ketchley describes, hordes of protesters tried to descend to Tahrir Square 'from Cairo's different neighbourhoods and popular quarters' and 'a pitched battle was fought on the Kasr el-Nil Bridge as CSF troops blocked protestors advancing from Giza to downtown Cairo and the road to Tahrir' (Ketchley, 2017: 46). This battle 'lasted most of the afternoon and culminated in the bottom-up defeat of the CSF, but only after protesters endured armoured vans ploughing indiscriminately into their ranks and seemingly endless volleys of tear gas, water cannon, and shotgun pellets' (Ketchley, 2017: 46). On this very same day, protesters managed to enter and raid the NDP offices located next to Tahrir and attacked four prisons on the outskirts of Cairo, resulting in the release of some prisoners.³ For protesters, the 28th of January constituted nothing less than 'Egypt's Bastille Day, a transformative event that imposed a new reality on the ground. "Revolution" emerged as the new interpretive framework that informed the language and praxis of claim-making' (Ryzova, 2020: 280). Indeed, the 28th considerably changed the set up of Egypt's political scene. Around evening-time the CSF forces had to acknowledge defeat and retreated from the streets. This meant that Mubarak was, for the first time in his rule, forced to enrol the armed forces onto Egypt's streets and squares to protect vital institutions (Ryzova, 2020: 280). This was significant not only because the CFS retreated, but also because with this retreat Mubarak was suddenly reliant on the military as the main protector of his regime. Like Sadat before him, Mubarak had always sought to coup-proof his regime through a stronger reliance on the civic security forces rather than the army. Mubarak had purposefully bolstered the internal security role of the police and the CSF, while relogating the military's security role to external borders and encouraging the direction of the military into economic activities. Yet, with the retreat of the CSF, he was nothing but an emperor without any clothes. Without the military's support, Mubarak proved powerless.

In the days that followed, a precarious stand-off took place between the army and the people, since it was not yet certain how the military would respond (whether they would side with the protestors or support Mubarak despite their disagreements with him and particularly his son's possible accession). As Neil Ketchley describes, during this time, protesters engaged in repertoires of fraternisation with military officers and soldiers in an attempt to win them over to their side (Ketchley, 2017: 50). Finally, on 31 January 2011, the military issued a statement saying that they would not engage in violent action against the protesters. This military refusal to intervene was the final nail in the coffin of Mubarak's rule and was motivated by the military's disgruntlement over Gamal Mubarak's possible accession (rather than say identification with revolutionary collective transformation) (Kandil, 2013: 222). Gamal Mubarak, a civilian without military connections like his father, had made it abundantly clear that he would prioritise the new neoliberal political-cum-business class over the military elite and threaten their economic privileges should he take over presidency. This was hence their 'once in a lifetime' opportunity to turn the course of events in their own favour.

And so, this turn of events forced Mubarak to issue his second televised speech on the evening of 1 February, wherein he attempted to appease the protestors by stating that he would not put himself forward as a presidential candidate in the forthcoming elections in September 2011. Any disagreement between protesters about whether to give Mubarak the benefit of the doubt that emerged out of this was quickly resolved with the

Camel Battle that occurred the next day: wherein Mubarak's informal thugs (baltagiyya) descended onto Tahrir Square, beating protesters with wooden and metal batons while riding horses and camels. In light of such violence, interviewees remarked that consensus was quickly reached among protesters: Mubarak has to go.

Mubarak at the same time, of course, sought to stop revolutionary collective becoming through typical dictatorial carrot-and-stick methods: while imposing the severest forms of brutal violence (meant to frighten revolutionaries back into submission), he also sought to placate demonstrators through concessions. So, over the next couple of days, Mubarak and his second man Omar Suleiman also promised: 1) a safe exit with no reprisals for protesters that stopped demonstrating immediately, 2) a 15 per cent pay increase for government employees, 3) the freeing of political prisoners, 4) constitutional amendments and 5) the possible lifting of the emergency law (Naylor, 2011). At the same time, they of course continued the conspirational victim blaming narrative frame wherein they cast blame for Egypt's revolutionary 'chaos' on the Muslim Brotherhood (which initially hesitated to take part in the revolution but was now a full participating member).

Trying to walk a (dictatorial) tight rope here between appeasement and threat, on the 10th of February Mubarak issued his last televised speech, wherein he portrayed himself as the father of the nation, who had heard the protesters' claims and promised constitutional amendments, but that it was time for protesters to leave the streets since Egypt can no longer descend down this path of chaos for economic reasons (Mubarak, 2011). He also reiterated the military sacrifices he supposedly made for Egypt and stated that he would not part with Egypt.

Yet, it was clear that Egypt was parting with him. For, the following day, Omar Suleiman issued a televised statement on national television wherein he transferred all political power away from Hosni Mubarak to the Supreme Council of Armed Forces (SCAF). And so, Mubarak was forced to step down and had to leave his presidential palace. Rather tellingly, as the news reached his wife Suzanne, she was reportedly prostrating on the floor, sobbing and clinging onto her possessions as she was forced to leave the presidential palace (El-Menawy, 2012). Upon this news, Egypt's squares and streets erupted in jubilation and celebration, and many activists stated that the moment they received this news was the happiest moment in their lives:

> Definitely after falling of Mubarak [. . .], it was the most happy. It was full of joy, but I had the feeling that there was something totally new, that we are together. The feeling was amazing. And you have the great hopes, and the great dreams. We can do whatever we want. And my eyes start to shine again, now I feel that I have a role in this country. I can do something. Really, at this moment

I start to feel that I love this country. This was my happiest moment, definitely. (Interview 32)

Though not all interviewees had anticipated this televised moment to be so significant, as this young man's story indicates:

I heard that Mubarak would say some speech, and I thought that oh no the speech will say the same bullshit. So I will not listen and I will be at home. So just when I went home, to just take a shower, I heard on television the speech that he resigned . . . ohhhhh noooo, nooo nooo, I was not in the square! [laughs]. So I went back again. So I change my clothes very fast, and I just ran to find a taxi and I told him I will give you LE100 to get me into the square in 10 minutes. Then I found a lot of people celebrating, I am so happy I did stuff I did not imagine I would do. And this time, I had never drunk before, at this point I just drank alcohol with my friends to celebrate. I danced, although I did not dance again as I did not know how to dance. I did a lot of crazy things there. I got a tattoo, a lot of crazy stuff that I would never imagine that I would do. And the tattoo said Fuck to Mubarak. And we say some. . . . You know and this time the media say that we are sissy boys so we make a proverb at this time: 'we the sissy boys kicked Mubarak's arse'. (Interview 12)

While perhaps Mubarak's disposal was influenced by the military's refusal to support the dictator who was standing on his last legs, many interviewees experienced the moment that Mubarak resigned as a validation, or proof, of their newly discovered sense of agency. And indeed, without their collective uprising, Mubarak might have ruled for another decade. Hence, interviewees experienced an overwhelmingly sense of joyful empowerment, rooted in the (hopeful) belief that together, ordinary Egyptians could make a new Egypt. Their lifeworld's horizon had thus shifted away from one broken by the weight of violent intersubjective imparity towards one full of possibility. Suddenly, they perceived futures different to bleak dystopias imprinted into them by Mubarak. They publicly spoke out against injustice and even cleaned the streets as they took ownership over their lives, their environment and each other. They felt alive and in this world, no longer alienated and no longer living lives that were 'dead of themselves' (interview 32). Rather, as they engaged in collective mobilisation and established a revolutionary prefigurative sphere wherein intersubjective parity was actualised their lifeworld was full of potentiality as they experienced a new sense of (hopeful) Egyptian identity:

It was the first time I felt Egyptian in this country, that I come from this country. I will change, I can change and everything will go well and everybody will change, and everything is going to be good, we will get the rights for people, we will help the poor, this kind of stuff. (Interview 12)

Definitely after falling of Mubarak [. . .], it was the most happy. It was full of joy, but I had the feeling that there was something totally new, that we are together. The feeling was amazing. And you have the great hopes, and the great dreams. We can do whatever we want. And my eyes start to shine again, now I feel that I have a role in this country. I can do something. Really, at this moment I start to feel that I love this country. This was my happiest moment, definitely. (Interview 32)

Hence, through the establishment of the prefigurative revolutionary public sphere, wherein each of the participants was regarded and treated as an equal peer, Egyptians overcame Mubarak's violent social divisions wherein they were atomised from each other. In the revolutionary public sphere, they were no longer felt alienated from each other and they were able to raise a loud collective voice against the injustices inflicted by Mubarak through creative collective becoming. And so, after decades of traumatic status subordination, consisting of the gravest forms of misrecognition and maldistribution, their voices were loud and clear: they were able to speak back both verbally and physically as they manifested themselves collectively in the world against all the abuse they had suffered. So, with the inauguration of a prefigurative revolutionary intersubjective parity, it was not only that they were pulled out of their atomised individualisation but rather also their muted *depoliticisation*. As this interviewee remarked:

Somehow the uprising gave me the strength to speak up about what I want and decide to do what. Somehow the uprising, I got to know many people through this, I got to know people who actually share my dreams and my you know hopes for Egypt. And where I can actually share like you know and like enjoy an intellectual conversation with without being afraid. Like I know that I'm not alone. Which was really refreshing. You got to know that we actually . . . we're quite plenty of people with you know who actually want to be happy and independent. Who think of a different future and who would want to work on it. [. . .] The uprising gave you, gave you that, it gave you you know like you know. It opened your eyes to the many, many different people I never saw before. Who actually wanted to make a difference. Which is brilliant in itself. (Interview 10)

Hence, it was not only that they established relations with people they had been previously separated from, but rather that after decades of political apathy and alienation, they were being *politicised*: they could manifest themselves intersubjectively in the world. They thus developed a deep sense of political agency, as for instance this young woman explained:

In terms of political activism, I never demonstrated or protested before 25 January 2011. After all, for 30 years we did not see any change and I did not think that change would be possible. They made us feel that food and working three jobs a day just to get by was more important than protesting and democracy. (Interview 38)

This view was corroborated by nearly all other interviewees, except a handful who were previously active in Kifaya or a political party, and even those experienced a deep intensification of their politicisation. Yet, most interviewees' stories mirrored this young man's experience, who 'was not activist before the revolution', but 'now, the life in Egypt and political life in Egypt is my main point' (Interview 3). What changed was that the process of creative collective mobilisation, and the creation of revolutionary intersubjective parity, shifted the existential structure of experience from one wherein they could only see, feel and smell impossibility, towards one wherein the future was brimming with potentiality and one wherein they no longer regarded themselves as weak or inferior. Rather, they were strong:

And I didn't believe in people much. Now I actually believe in people and myself much more. Before that I didn't believe in our strength as people, or my strength as an individual. I didn't know how strong I was or nor did I know how strong people could be. So, I think the uprising tested that. (Interview 10)

As they gained this deep sense of agency, a strong belief arose that things were going to be different – that they were not going to be pressured into submission (or status subordination) again:

After the Mubarak stepping down even during the military junta. You know I think Egypt will never be the same and I said like Egyptian will not remain silent again even with all the circumstances. So, I had the feeling that you know – khalas – Egypt was going to be different. (Interview 9)

Hence, to be extra clear here, it was not just that they were hopeful of the future as such but rather that they were *politically* hopeful of a future devoid of (traumatic) status subordination:

I had a very weird feeling I never felt this in my life. I had this massive gratitude for the Egyptian people, and I really appreciated how we can get together and protect each other against anything that might harm us, all of us, not to protect individual property no it was all of us trying to protect ourselves from thieves, thugs, from criminals, whatever [. . .] The feeling I remember quite well is feeling safe, very safe when I see a popular committee which is a checkpoint done by the people and controlled by the people, local residents of the neighbourhood, compared to when I see a military. that the revolution had brought up all the good things in the Egyptian people together on the surface you know. And we managed to utilise these good things collectively together to do something good, and together with the massive mobilisation of the people in Tahrir square it was good. The whole environment made me feel very happy and very hopeful, and I really believe that our dream will be reached. . . . That all that we want will be achieved, that people will not live in poverty anymore. People will not take police brutality anymore. That people will not take the marginalisation and injustice anymore. That the streets will be clean, you know [laughs]. We were all like this. We would be a society that respects minorities, that respects everybody. . . . That we would be pioneers in whatever. You know, our economy would be great, we would be pioneers in scientific research, you know [laughs loudly]. It is like the feeling that you get when you see your own people, you see the good side, the very good side. [. . .] It is going to be great, and be going to build the future of this country altogether so I should be contributing somehow. (Interview 17)

And it was precisely this renewed political consciousness grounded in a new prefigurative relation of intersubjective parity that worried the military as soon as it had ousted Mubarak. For central to this new radical consciousness were the demands of ending both misrecognition and maldistribution. Egyptians insisted on being treated with dignity, namely as an equal human beings. This radical equality directly challenged the economic and political interests of SCAF, which sought to increase both its influence over the economic and the political sphere as soon as it took over as an interim government. It was thus clear to the military that in order to safeguard its political and economic power, it had to break precisely this newly formed *will* to transformative change. It was not only a matter of removing revolutionary politics from the political public sphere but rather ensuring the *potentiality* would never occur again. It thus had to shift the underlying unitary structures of possible existence away from an openness to the world, from a readiness to collectively manifest in the world, to a deprived one wherein the world appeared without potential and devoid of meaning. Hence, the military was in this for the longer haul. Having the institutional and material resources at its disposal, it remained in the driving seat of Egypt's post-revolutionary political landscape which it carefully redirected towards its own strategic interests, eventually culminating in the rise of Abdel Fatah el Sisi's power in 2013.

NOTES

1. Khaled Said, a young man with a middle-class background, had been brutally murdered by Egypt's police when he had visited an internet café. A Facebook page

'We are all Khaled Said' was erected by Wael Ghoneim and others, which helped to bring attention to the case. Said's death became a focal point of Egyptian revolutionary mobilisation, spurred on also by the events in Tunisia following Mohamed Bouazizi's self-immolation when he put himself on fire in response to the confiscation of his goods and his suffer humiliation.

2. It is thus a clear case of adding insult to injury as described by Nancy Fraser: the victim not only suffers an injustice but is also made responsible for that injustice perceived in this light, victim blaming is not so much merely a case of stabilising the internal cognitive patterns of one's assumptive world as Janoff-Bulman suggests (1992), but rather deeply political in nature. It constitutes an intersubjective power relation wherein one attempts to uphold one's moral or normative intersubjective superiority over another – either directly as the perpetrator or through the (implicit) identification with the powerful perpetrator. Of course victim blaming as a deliberate tactic might fail. The victim might not only refuse and fight such subordination, it might also result in the opposite effect: social others identify with the victim rather than the perpetrator. However, often such tactics result in the division of the public sphere (along the lines of perpetrator or victim allegiance) and thus results in social and political polarisation, and a decline of unity – which serves the repressive authoritarian well.

3. Though the raids were organised by the protesters, there is speculation as to whether the retreatist response by the police and security officers was a deliberate response to spread chaos on the streets.

Chapter 5

Supreme Council of Armed Forces
The Politics of Traumatic Status Subordination

As soon as the Supreme Council of Armed Forces (SCAF) took over as the interim governing actor in Egypt, it inflicted traumatic status subordination in the political sphere using a threefold tactic: the procedural colonisation of the political public realm, the exercise of direct (lethal) force and the monopolisation of the economic sphere using neoliberal economic rationalism. While the deployment of physical force was in a sense blatant for all to see, its political procedural and neoliberal economic colonisation were part of what Habermas calls 'concealed strategic actions', which constitute instrumental orientations that are not open to public deliberation and which occur behind the backs of those affected (Habermas, 1984: 333). One such concealed strategic action was the military's co-option of the systemic opposition, the Muslim Brotherhood, in its transitional roadmap. In this roadmap, 'orderly politics' of established political actors replaced the 'disorderly politics' of the revolutionary streets. It thus entailed the counter-revolutionary restriction of the political terrain to formal procedural electoral politics. By occupying this formal political space, Egypt's counter-revolutionary actors also ensured that revolutionary politics would never be able to manifest itself in this terrain. The point was to thwart the potential of revolutionary political becoming through the structural marginalisation and exclusion of the revolutionary opposition, as well as the usurping of any political energy into electoral affairs (also see Stacher, 2020). At the same time, SCAF also strategically implemented a range of constitutional amendments which not only shielded the military's political and economic interests from public oversight but also ensured that the military remained at the steering wheel of Egypt's post-revolutionary constitutional process.

In addition to such a political procedural colonisation of the public sphere, the military directly inflicted grave physical violence, which included the gravest violations of intersubjective parity, such as the maiming, killing and torture (including sexual torture) of protesters. The purpose of such violence was twofold: the immediate physical or material removal of protesters from sites of demonstrations and the breakdown of protesters' lifeworlds with incapacitating effects. When the violent betrayal of intersubjective parity is so grave, it constitutes traumatic status subordination, the lifeworld's functioning as a shared symbolic realm breaks down. One experiences not only severe disorientation (as the grid of meaning-making collapses under one's feet, exposing a gaping hole of nihilistic nothingness) but one is also thrown into debilitating isolation (as the ability to maintain meaningful intersubjective relations is ruptured). This isolation was then furthermore aggravated through the accompaniment of conspirational victim blaming, wherein the infliction of violence was justified through the redirection of blame onto the victim (now representing so-called 'unknown third parties'), which increased social tension and thus deepened the obstruction of creative collective self-manifestation. The point was to tear communicative relationality apart, thereby obstructing the very potential of revolutionary becoming as such.

At the same time, the military fervently pursued its economic interests and monopolised the economic sphere through a militarised neoliberal economic rationalism. Taken together, the purposive rationality of these concealed strategic actions comes clearly into view: while the counter-revolutionary's procedural colonisation of the political public sphere resulted in a deep sense of political defeatism (namely a horizon without other political possibilities), the infliction of grave physical violence plunged activists into a disoriented atomisation and neoliberal economic rationalism increased economic maldistribution, which, through greater economic precarity, cultivated the desire for a supposed 'to return to stability' amongst the populace, thereby rupturing revolutionary solidarity ever deeper and marginalising revolutionary activists ever further.

POLITICAL PROCEDURALISM: COLONISING THE POLITICAL PUBLIC SPHERE

Upon the removal of Hosni Mubarak, SCAF took over as the governing party that would lead Egypt through this phase of post-revolutionary transition. From the very inception of their rule, SCAF insisted that with their takeover the disorderly time of revolutionary politics was over, as it was now time to return to procedural formal politics.

Importantly, there is nothing wrong with political proceduralism as such, so long as the formal political procedural institutions are inclusive of and responsive to the plurality of voices in the political public sphere. Indeed, this is the basis of Jurgen Habermas's deliberative model of legal discourse ethics, wherein the points and issues emerging in a free flow of communication in the informal public spheres (namely the realms of private and social relations) are then taken up by social movements (such as not only political parties but also anti-oppositional revolutionary forces such as the Socialist Alliance) who then feed these public opinion formations into the formal arena of political decision-making, where they take the form of will formation and gain an institutional binding force (or rather, communicative power) (Habermas, 1996). The free flow of communication and deliberation in the informal sphere and the inclusive nature of the formal sphere are thus prerequisites of a legitimate political and legal order. This conception hence depends on the existence of an open, deliberative public sphere.

Yet, it is precisely this inclusivity that the Egyptian military purposefully and systematically sought to destroy. As it did so, it not only created a politically unjust order but also directly destroyed the public and private autonomy of Egyptian citizens. As Habermas has extensively shown, private and public autonomy are co-original: because we are intersubjectively constituted linguistic animals, the very attribution of individual rights depends on public autonomy (the deliberative coming to an agreement on a particular individual right) grounded in public participation rights – that themselves beget the notion of individual rights (intersubjectively conceived not merely as negative liberties but also rights that ensure the capacity for equal participation) (Habermas, 1996). Hence, political legitimacy is based on a deliberative model that guarantees such co-originality of public and private autonomy through an open, non-exclusionary model of deliberation. Thus, a violent counter-revolutionary structural violation of participation in an inclusive public sphere directly affects and destroys both our public and private ability to manifest ourselves in the world. The violent instrumental violation of the communicative realm directly destroys the functioning of the lifeworld. The gravest violations of intersubjective parity destroy the lifeworld foundational assumptions of meaning-making, which results in the incapacitating effects of both disorientation and isolation. And this was precisely the purpose of the military, because disorientation and isolation destroy the potentiality of revolutionary becoming.

Now, under SCAF, as well as the other successive post-revolutionary regimes, one of the tools employed was the violent reduction of politics to the formal politics of the counter-revolutionary status quo. That is, SCAF strategically pursued a path of *orderly* political proceduralism, which it dichotomously opposed to the supposed the *disorderly* masses and chaos of the street (Stacher, 2020). Hence, urging that with the disposal of Hosni Mubarak, the aims of the revolution had been achieved and that it was now time to leave the Egyptian streets, the army insisted on the importance of an orderly path of transition. This transition entailed the reduction of politics to formal political actors and procedural electoralism – wherein the strategic co-option of the conservative Muslim Brotherhood served the purpose of consolidating this path – while SCAF also implemented constitutional amendments that would be instrumental in the protection of its own political and economic interests. Putting it in stronger Habermasian terms, SCAF pursued a path of concealed strategic actions wherein its actions were guided by a purposive rational, instrumental rationale that is not open for debate among those affected. That is, it did not openly declare to the Egyptian public that it would be instrumentally pursuing its interests, but did so through backhand deals and concealment.

The primary concealment was its co-option of the Brotherhood during the spring of 2011. The Brotherhood was part of what Joshua Stacher (2020) calls the systematic revolutionary opposition, which – in opposition to the anti-systemic revolution – deemed the revolution complete with the removal of Hosni Mubarak. The Brotherhood, a rather conservative political group, thus believed in the necessity of returning to an orderly status quo, characterised by formal procedural politics and neoliberal economics. Hence, in contrast to the anti-systemic opposition[1] which sought to achieve progressive economics and an inclusive political public sphere, the Brotherhood found a natural ideological and strategic ally in the military with whom it could have a (temporary) mutually beneficial relationship (Roll, 2015; Stacher, 2020). The Brotherhood thus agreed to a backhand deal wherein the military promised speedy elections in return for keeping some of the military affairs (such as its direct political affairs and economic budget) away from public parliamentary oversight (Stacher, 2020). The Brotherhood would be the guaranteed winner of these elections, since new revolutionary actors would neither have the time nor the organisational experience or the capacity to pose a real challenge to the Islamists (Khalifa, 2015: 125). Hence, perhaps also rather dazzled by the prospect of attaining direct political power after decades of struggle, the Brotherhood fully supported the military's transitional roadmap and its insistence it was time to get back to 'business as normal'. Many revolutionaries experienced this backhand deal, which was solidified in September 2011, as a profound betrayal of the revolutionary goals of 'bread, freedom and social justice'. And they were correct: the instrumental orientation of both the military and the Brotherhood fundamentally violated the principle of intersubjective parity in an inclusive political public sphere, wherein all affected would be heard. Instead, the Brotherhood and military's orientation was purely purposive rational, geared as they were towards advancing their own political and economic interests (Stacher, 2020: 27)

And so, by the summer of 2011, the Brotherhood and the military staunchly supported the transitional roadmap and insisted on holding early parliamentary elections as soon as possible. This aggravated the gap between activists who supported a 'constitution first' approach and those who insisted on an 'election first' approach (el Amrani, 2011; Khalifa, 2015: 82–84). While the former, represented by the anti-systemic opposition, demanded a civilian interim government (wherein all factions within Egyptian society would be represented) should draw up a constitution in order to avoid an exclusive constitutional framework. The systemic opposition insisted that it was urgent to hold immediate parliamentary elections, the winners of which would then write the new Egyptian constitution. Unfortunately, the latter won. This is unfortunate since it not only violated the discourse ethical norm of an inclusive constitutional founding moment (wherein intersubjective parity is guaranteed) but also splintered revolutionary unity and redirected revolutionary transformative political energy into formal electoral processes.

As we will see later, not only did the constitutional drafting process (and its results) one-sidedly reflect both the Brotherhood and the military's interests, it also tore the potential of inclusive creative collective becoming apart. This became particularly apparent during the six-day street battle of Mohamed Mahmoud, wherein anti-systematic revolutionaries battled Egypt's security forces and the military's exclusionary roadmap of orderly transition, and the Brotherhood withdrew its support from the streets.[2] That is, while having partaken in the rather more orderly demonstration[3] that took place the day before, as soon as the security state attacked the protesters that remained at the sit-in the Brotherhood issued a statement demanding its supporters withdraw from the streets. They issued this demand at a time when hundreds of activists were being injured and forty people were killed. This was interpreted by most activists as the ultimate betrayal of their ideals of the revolution. In the words of this young man:

> Actually, it made me a natural enemy of the Brotherhood. I will never forget and tolerate what the Brotherhood did at that moment. I don't have any ideology. I don't have any problem with anyone. But the Brotherhood created a natural enemy for them out of the conflict. I can tolerate the police as we expected this of them but never the Brotherhood, because at this point in time they uncovered us – not only this, they did not only remain silent they incited against us, and they used to find excuses for the police's doing. They expressed their support for the police, saying that the country should carry on, and be stable and stuff like that. (Interview 7)

The military's strategic co-option of the Brotherhood fragmented the political terrain and facilitated political polarisation as the Brotherhood now betrayed intersubjective parity in the strategic pursuit of its own (short-term) political interests. The primary interest of the Brotherhood was of course holding early parliamentary elections. During the bloodbath of Mohamed Mahmoud, the head of SCAF, Tantawi, announced that these would go ahead as planned regardless of the violence on Egypt's streets, and he also installed a new government headed by Kamal Ganzouri after Essam Sharaf (who had been rather more supportive of the revolution) resigned in light of the violence inflicted by the state security apparatus during Mohamed Mahmoud (Khalifa, 2015: 97). And so, in December 2011 and January 2012, parliamentary elections were held wherein the Islamists were the overwhelming winners – with the Brotherhood achieving 46 percent and the Salafist Nour party achieving 25 per cent of the votes (54 percent of the eligible voter turnout) (EISA, 2013).

The speedy electoral process, we have to understand, is a primary way of excluding anti-systematic revolutionary voices from having a say in Egypt's formal political processes and installing a conservative political actor in Egypt's political driving seat which would pose less of a challenge to the military's fundamental political and economic interests (Stacher, 2020). Indeed, as Stacher points out (2020), the recourse to elections was itself a counter-revolutionary attempt to depoliticise Egypt's newly politicised public sphere: its aim was to redirect revolutionary energy into electoral processes and drive a wedge between the wider Egyptian public (who increasingly longed for stability) and the protesters on the streets (who demanded deeper political transformation). The point was to break intersubjective unity. Hence, between 2011 and 2020, Egypt has had three constitutional referendums, four rounds of presidential elections, two rounds of parliamentary elections and one round of Shura Council elections – none of which had resulted in radical social, political or economic change and only deepened the counter-revolutionary political status quo.

Electoral politics thereby also deepened an existential sense of political defeatism in activists and was thus an essential tool in shifting the revolutionary sense of possibility towards an overwhelming belief in the *im*possibility of change. Hence, rather than facilitating deliberative democratic participation, elections were employed as a counter-revolutionary tool to halt creative collective self-manifestation in the world. Hence, for many interviewees, the term 'elections' became equated with a deep sense of depression and hopelessness as they were typified by political manipulation and a counter-revolutionary colonisation of the political public sphere. As this interviewee commented:

> When the elections had started, my happiness stopped because I was cutting through all the trees. Yaeny, after people start to go from the street. I was the participating in the marches all the time. The happiest times were in the demonstrations and in the matches, but when people started to be political, and be

asked to go to the election box and make his choice, it was a very sad moment for me as the politicians were trying to direct people. And they are using misusing words, misusing people's religion and misusing people's dreams and misusing people's needs. And they are trying to direct them and get them away from what they really need. (Interview 32)

Elections were rather used to advance an exclusionary political status quo, wherein misrecognition and maldistribution would continue unabated. And thus, interviewees increasingly reported that elections invoked a deep sense of depression in them, because, as this young man remarked: 'I did not believe in the political process at all, because this was not the political process I wanted for my country. Not the political options that I hoped for' (Interview 7).

It was not only parliamentary elections that evoked such a depression but also particularly the presidential elections whose first round started on the 23rd of May, and whose second round was held on the 16th and 17th of June 2011. Within the presidential elections, the revolutionary vote was divided among Hamdeen Sabahi and Abdel Moneim Abdel Fotouh, a former Brotherhood candidate with progressive economic ideas, while the remainder of the vote was predominantly split between Mohamed Morsi and Ahmed Shafiq.[4]

Morsi was the Brotherhood leadership's second choice, earning himself the less gracious nickname of 'spare tire' as he was put forward after the Brotherhood's first choice business tycoon Khairat al Shater was dismissed on the grounds of his former imprisonment under Hosni Mubarak's regime. First, Morsi's presidential candidacy – and that of Al Shater before him – violated the Brotherhood's earlier promise, when it enlisted itself for parliamentary elections, that it would not yield a presidential candidate so as to not monopolise political power. It came in direct response to rumours that the newly elected parliament would be disbanded on the basis of a technicality (namely that candidates ran on collective and individual tickets simultaneously), which eventually occurred two days before the final round of presidential elections, on 14 June 2011 (Khalifa, 2015: 117). Hence, the Brotherhood's putting forth of a presidential candidate was a strategic attempt to try and salvage its newly found political power in light of the impending parliamentary dismissal.

The other remaining candidate, Ahmed Shafiq, had not only been the minister of aviation during Mubarak's regime but had also been appointed prime minister on the 29th of January 2011, after Ahmed Nazif had been forced to resign, by Mubarak himself. Ahmed Shafiq was hence part of Mubarak's regime, and someone who demonstrators had protested against on 25 February when SCAF had ordered a cabinet reshuffle on the 22nd of February (which had left most of the ancient regime ministers in place). Shafiq had been forced to resign on 3 March 2011, due to ensuing protests (after which Essam Sharaf had been installed as Egypt's prime minister). Yet, with the presidential run-off, there was now a real prospect that he would become Egypt's first elected, post-revolutionary president. Importantly, Ahmed Shafiq had publicly stated his firm opposition to the revolution (and was openly anti-Islamist).

Hence, the military's transitional roadmap of speedy elections thus not only sidelined revolutionary activists from the formal political terrain, but also resulted in two highly conservative presidential candidates who would not address the systematic forms of misrecognition and maldistribution that Egyptians had suffered at the hands of the Egyptian state. Rather, for many interviewees, the electoral process and its outcome constituted nothing less than a counter-revolutionary slap in the face. This young woman described it as one of the worst moments she has ever experienced:

> One of the worst days since January 25, was the day they announced the Shafiq and Morsi thing. I was working from home that day [. . .] I am sitting at home, I have this tiny room you know, it used to be the balcony [. . .] so I am sitting in this tiny little room and usually, I have a high blood pressure problem you know, seriously in a day like this usually my blood pressure skyrockets. . . . But yeah, I'm sitting there and my blood pressure gets high, and I'm getting ready anxious and we do this thing where we do every bit separately so I am sitting there writing and publishing and then sharing. Because that is my job you know I write down and then I publish, and then I share on Facebook and twitter so that people actually read it, you know. And then I do another city like Fayoum, and it is all Morsi and Shafiq, and my blood pressure is like, it is rising very gradually and my mum and my relatives are sitting outside and watching the news and stuff, and I am sitting there writing like crazy, like really fast really fast really fast. And that my nose starts bleeding because my blood pressure is way too high, and I start crying and became hysterical, and my mum came into the room and was like you okay? And I was like 'What the fuck, I hate this country, I cannot believe they voted for Morsi and Shafiq. I hate this country. The fuckers' I was really angry. Yeah, it was like a mixture of blood coming out of my nose and like tears and like hysterical cries and it was probably the worst day during the last three years. It was the worst day. I felt like khalas it was done like. How could they choose these terrible terrible candidates? I was devastated. (Interview 30)

Apart from the Islamist interviewees, all activists commented on the deep sense of betrayal and desperation they felt during these presidential elections: they felt not only that the revolution had been stolen from them but more importantly that the revolution as such was finished now that there only remained two political players on the formal political field – both of which were conservative and destructive to revolutionary aspirations of radical change. SCAF's speedy electoral process, rather than facilitating a responsive deliberative political order representative of the diverse voices within Egypt, instead operated as a counter-revolutionary tool: to silence oppositional dissent (through its exclusion from the political public sphere) while also undermining activists' belief in the potentiality of revolutionary change.

Constitutional Amendments

This procedural electoral process of exclusion was moreover complemented by SCAF's constitutional amendments, where it not only sidelined revolutionary voices but also instrumentally advanced and solidified its own political and economic interests. This commenced as soon as Mubarak was disposed and SCAF assigned a constitutional committee of jurists and legal experts charged the possible amendments of the 1971 constitution. Reflecting its strong preference for the conservative Brotherhood as a temporary ally in Egypt's post-revolutionary process, the committee was heavily tilted 'in favour of the Islamists at expense of other political factions' (Khalifa, 2015: 73). While prominent social democratic or other revolutionary scholars were excluded, it included the prominent Islamist legal scholar Tareq Al Bishry and lawyer and former Islamist MP Sobhi Saleh, and on 9 February 2011 proposed changes to nine articles of the Egyptian constitution. These amendments 'included new term limits on the presidency, change the criteria of eligibility for presidential elections, ensure stronger judicial oversight of the polling process and constrain the authorities' power to sustain emergency law' by restricting its duration to six months after which its continuation would have to be put to a public referendum (Khalifa, 2015: 73). Moreover, adopting an 'elections first' approach, it also stated that after parliamentary and Shura Council elections elected members of both houses must select a Constitutional Assembly of hundred members which would be tasked with drafting a new constitution. Presidential elections will follow, and the elected president will have to present the draft constitution to a referendum within one year (Khalifa, 2015: 77).

Now, these amendments were put to a popular referendum on the 19th of March 2011, where 41 per cent of the eligible electorate (18 million) voted with 71 per cent in favour of these amendments. As Kristen A. Stilt remarks, the referendum was beneficial to SCAF since it enabled it publicly present itself as different than Mubarak by the sheer virtue of intending to amend the constitution, while the voting process itself provided (implicit) legitimatisation of SCAF's (Stilt, 2012: 10–11). However, on the 30th of March, SCAF surprised everyone by unilaterally deciding to supersede the 1971 constitution with a constitutional declaration consisting of nothing less than sixty-three articles. This declaration had not been subjected to deliberative debate in any form whatsoever, and thus violated any democratic norms of constitutional founding. Indeed, it was not even clear who had drafted this piece of legislation. Rather, 'it was presented as a sort of offering by the military, which obviated a wider public debate over its content' (Khalifa, 2015: 78), and it was 'procedurally and substantively confusing' (Stilt, 2012: 11), for while the 19th of March referendum abided by the 1971 constitution, SCAF now:

> Put together a document that better suited its changing goals and essentially abrogated the constitution whose procedures it had asserted were necessary to follow in the referendum process. In doing so, SCAF transitioned from presenting itself as a caretaker of the revolution and the constitution to taking control of the process and creating its own constitution, one that, unlike the 1971 text or its final set of amendments as adopted in the referendum, made SCAF a constitutional actor with broad powers. In the process, SCAF left most of the 1971 constitution on the drafting room floor, such that many issues are simply not provided for in the declaration, with the result that SCAF has significant power and discretion. (Stilt, 2012: 12)

These amendments directly served SCAF's political interests in a fourfold manner. First, by implicitly annulling the constitution and leaving many gaps in the constitutional declaration, SCAF created a legal vacuum which left many institutions on unstable ground as to what legal ground they were operating on. This uncertainty provided fertile terrain for SCAF to emerge as the most powerful political broker in the field. Second, Article 56 gave SCAF 'wide legislative and executive powers [. . .] in the transitional period' through which it was able to 'substitute itself for the will of the Egyptian people, including adopting other Constitutional Declarations' (ICJ, 2012: 2). Third, SCAF also prolonged its transitional role by stipulating that it would remain in effect 'until elections for both houses of parliament and for president have been completed and they have all assumed their duties' (Stilt, 2012: 14). Hence, any delay in presidential elections would now also mean a prolonged rule of SCAF. And lastly, within this declaration SCAF unilaterally amended the constitutional drafting process: it stipulated that a committee would need to be formed immediately after parliamentary elections and the constitution must be presented to a public referendum within fifteen days of its completion (Ahram Online, 2012). It did not specify who the representing actor is. It could even be SCAF itself. At the same time, SCAF also strategically paved the way for its political accomplice the Brotherhood leadership by removing Article 5 of the 2007 constitution that stated that political activities or parties' 'religious frame of reference' was prohibited.

And then, as a cherry on top of SCAF's counter-revolutionary cake, the military council introduced the notorious Selmy document which announced a range of 'supra-constitutional principles' that would *not* be amendable by the elected Constitutional Assembly. This document not only assigned the military as the custodian of Egyptian constitutional legitimacy, it also stipulated that any legislation pertaining to the military and the military's defence budget would be a matter for the military only and thus not subject to parliamentary or civil overview (Khalifa, 2015: 94). Moreover, the document also limited the power of the People's Assembly to appoint the members of the Constitutional Assembly by stating eighty out of a hundred had to be non-partisan individuals representing all of Egyptian society – and then stipulated exactly where these members had to be drawn from (Teti and Gervasio, 2011; Trager, 2016). And, importantly, the document significantly restricted the deliberative power of the constitution-writing body by stipulating that the new constitution could not contravene SCAF's 30th of March declaration (Trager, 2016: 122). SCAF's dubious 30th of March declaration thereby gained an essential legal status that would restrict the scope of the actual constitution itself. Moreover, if the constitution-writing assembly would fail to produce a new constitutional draft within six months of its appointment then SCAF would have the power to dissolve the assembly and appoint a new one, essentially keeping SCAF at the steering wheel of Egypt's post-revolutionary constitutional process.

Even the Brotherhood found this objectionable and joined a protest on the 18th of November which included a broad variety of Egypt's political forces, including the liberal, social democratic and socialist oppositions. Perhaps fearful of losing their closest ally (the Brotherhood) in the political procedural process, the military then quickly announced that these amendments were no longer binding, but merely advisory. It 'also revised the rules to say that the only role of the armed forces was protecting the country and 'preserving its unity', rather than the broader writ to guard Egypt's 'constitutional legitimacy' and now placed the military under civilian government as it should, 'like other state institutions [. . .] abide by the constitutional and legislative regulations' (Kirkpatrick and Stack, 2011). And so, the Brotherhood crawled back into the military's counter-revolutionary bed and announced that its members should withdraw from the streets of Egypt, leaving anti-systematic protesters to battle the security forces by themselves during the six-day battle of Mohamed Mahmoud. After which the parliamentary elections were held a few days later, wherein the Islamists (both the Brotherhood and the Salafists) gained an overwhelming majority.

Yet, despite its reduction to an advisory status, SCAF's Selmy document remained a direct assault on Egypt's inclusive democratic transitional processes and served to ensure that SCAF not only remained in control of the post-revolutionary process but also its economic assets. Thus, when the newly formed (Islamist-dominated) People's Assembly elected a Constitutional Assembly it was found to be unconstitutional by the Supreme Administrative Court in April 2012 because its composition (which included members of parliament) contravened the guidelines stipulated in the Selmy document (ICJ, 2012: 15). A later judicial ruling stated that members of parliament could be elected but not elect themselves.

Moreover, on the 5th of June 2012, SCAF set an ultimatum that gave the Islamist parliament and political leaders forty-eight hours to agree on a hundred-member committee and threatened that upon failure to do so that SCAF would write its own interim charter (Khalifa, 2015: 117). And so, a second Constitutional Assembly was formed on 7 June 2012, whereby thirty-nine seats went to members of parliament, nine to legal experts, one to the armed forces, one to the police and one to justice ministry respectively, thirteen to the unions, twenty-one figures to public figures, five to Al Azhar and four to the Coptic Church. It was obvious that the Islamist-dominated parliament maintained a clear majority in the assembly, much to the dislike of the liberal, socialist and secular political opposition (Tarek and Maher, 2012).

This was, however, a rather short-lived agreement since, on the 14th of June, the Supreme Constitutional Court (SCC) issued a decision wherein it declared that the parliamentary elections had been unconstitutional and parliament was thus abruptly disbanded the following day (Al-Ali et al., 2012).

The dissolvement of parliament also raised questions about the legal status of this newly formed Constitutional Assembly, which after all had been assembled by the now disbanded parliament. As we will see in chapter 6, this legal ambiguity of the Assembly's status resulted in a longlasting court case with the Supreme Administrative Court that was eventually referred to the Constitutional Court. Then, in autumn 2012, Morsi not only found himself under immense pressure to finish a constitutional draft before a decision of the court on the legality of the Constitutional Assembly as such, but SCAF could also still veto any clause which meant that this clause would need to be referred to the SCC for deliberation (and Assembly might be disbanded in the meantime). And if the SCC would disband the Constitutional Assembly then SCAF would get to appoint another Constitutional Assembly. When around November 2012, rumours emerged that the SCC would soon issue a verdict on the legality of the Constitutional Assembly, Morsi issued a constitutional declaration wherein he sought to immunise his decisions against all legal challenge. However, instead of bolstering his political power, Morsi was not only forced to withdraw this declaration soon after, it also served to further rupture revolutionary unity as it set in motion violent social polarisation that further undermined revolutionary unity. Rather, what became abundantly clear was that the military had set the parameters of the constitutional drafting process in such a way that it remained in full control of Egypt's post-revolutionary trajectory. In doing so, it of course directly contravened the principles of a democratic, inclusive constitutional founding moment wherein all voices would be heard and represented. Rather, SCAF merely used the constitutional process as a means to maintain the political and economic privileges it had just gained when Mubarak was overthrown. In other words, the constitutional drafting process was colonised by the military's instrumental pursuits and founded on the principle of intersubjective *im*parity rather than parity.

And so, on the last day of the presidential elections, the 17th of June 2012, SCAF also issued a constitutional declaration wherein it protected its own political and economic interests directly. It imposed a full separation between the civilian authorities and the military, as it withdrew any civilian oversight over any military-related affairs. Moreover, it curtailed the power of a civilian government to declare war: it stipulated that the incoming president would need the approval of SCAF – rather than parliament – to declare war. This declaration cemented 'parliament's dissolution by conferring legislative power, in the absence of a sitting parliament, to the SCAF' (Al-Ali et al., 2012: 13) – and that this may be conferred back to parliament only after a constitution has been approved. Hence, on the evening of the presidential elections, SCAF had appropriated all legislative powers, thereby creating great uncertainty as to what political powers the incumbent president would actually have, particularly in the absence of a parliament and a constitution and while the constitutional drafting process remained controlled by the military. Hence, SCAF set the stage for a great political saga, whereby the backhand deal struck with the military would eventually devour the Muslim Brotherhood itself, leaving one victorious political player on the political stage: the Egyptian military.

Repressive Juridification

SCAF's manipulation of Egypt's post-revolutionary process, including its procedural colonisation of the political public sphere and its self-serving constitutional amendments went hand in hand with repressive juridification of the political public sphere. 'Juridification' is a term employed by Jurgen Habermas in his *Theory of Communicative Action* Vol 2 and describes the increasing encroachment of legal bureaucracy, as a systemic mechanism, into the communicative, symbolic realm of the lifeworld (Habermas, 1987b). He particularly focuses on the development of the Western welfare state and outlines how law increasingly attained a socio-normative regulatory function – which he argued undermined the communicative structures of the lifeworld. Later, in his book

Between Facts and Norms (Habermas, 1996), Habermas changes his mind somewhat and argues that in an increasingly plural and diverse world, law ought to take on a socio-normative function of binding communities together, so long as its formation and executive power is discursively rooted in a deliberative model wherein the formal sphere of law is responsive to the plurality of voices in the informal public sphere. I employ the term 'repressive juridification' in the Egyptian counter-revolutionary context to refer to the implementation of law as an instrumental means to restrict the public sphere and destroy the communicative realm of the lifeworld, resulting in disorientation and isolation. Hence, repressive juridification is a violation of a Habermasian legal discourse ethics. In his legal discourse ethics, the counterfactual presupposition of intersubjective parity is the foundation upon which individuals and groups are able to see themselves as the authors and subjects of the law. Rather, in repressive juridification, they are subjected to the harsh punitive character of law: they are not only unable to see themselves as authors of these laws, but it is an instrumental means to erode any sense of legal and political self-becoming.

Throughout their interim rule, SCAF inflicted such repressive juridification on the Egyptian populace through the imposition of several highly repressive laws. The purpose of these laws was to close Egypt's (revolutionary) public space and marginalise (or re-atomise) protesters. Hence, the day after Mubarak's ouster, the military promised to lift the state of emergency *if protesters would leave the streets* (thereby making clear they wanted the disorderly politics of the streets to disappear). Yet, SCAF *not* only maintained the state of emergency law until after the protests at the Israeli embassy in September 2011 but in fact expanded the existing law to include a wide range of vaguely worded threats to national security, such as 'spreading false news'. While in 2010, Mubarak had restricted the law to terrorism (in practice broadly interpreted) and drug-related crimes, SCAF reverted the law back to its original scope: it now covered 'offences that include disturbing traffic, blocking roads, broadcasting rumours, possessing and trading in weapons, and 'assault on freedom to work' (Amnesty International, 2011). As Amnesty stated: 'These changes are a major threat to the rights to freedom of expression, association and assembly, and the right to strike' (Amnesty International, 2011). These were thus a direct attempt at closing public sphere, and the possibility of creative collective self-becoming.

Moreover, on 1 March, SCAF had already amended Egypt's penal code on thuggery, which was defined as 'displaying force of threatening to use force against a victim' with the 'intention to intimidate or cause harm to his or her property' 'in order to send civilians and protestors to military trials' (Taylor, 2011). As Eric Trager explains:

> Although this amendment was widely supported in the aftermath of the Tahrir Square revolt, during which pro-Mubarak thugs violently terrorized the public,

'thuggery' has since been interpreted much more broadly to include breaking curfews, possessing illegal weapons, destroying public property, theft, assault, or threatening violence – in short, a wide variety of activities that grant the military maximum discretion for locking up civilians. (Trager, 2011)

Moreover, SCAF used this law to send more than 12,000 civilians to military courts during the first seven months of its rule (Daily News Egypt, 2011) – where they lacked access to counsel and were tried in collective groups and subjected to long prison sentences. In comparison, Mubarak had 'only' sent 2000 civilians to military trials during his 30 year rule (Daily News Egypt, 2011). Furthermore 'the military has not been shy about its rationale for resorting to military trials, frequently telling the families of those arrested that its goal is to 'terrorize the nation back into submission' (Trager, 2011).

DIRECT PHYSICAL FORCE: DISORIENTATION AND ISOLATION

Yet, such submission would be hard to achieve without the infliction of direct physical force that SCAF resorted to as soon as it took over as Egypt's interim government. The first grave incident occurred within merely one week of Mubarak's ouster. On 25 February 2011, SCAF cracked down with brute physical force on protesters who had gathered to object to SCAF's cabinet reformation that had occurred on 22 February 2011 (wherein many of Mubarak's cronies would retain powerful ministerial positions in crucial areas such as defence, tourism, finance, interior and justice). Early in the morning,[5] 'soldiers and security officers stepped into the square to beat protesters, using stun guns and batons, and to tear down their tents' (Khalifa, 2015: 75). The message of the army was clear, the time of 'revolution' was over, and 'there would be limits to their tolerance of dissent' (Khalifa, 2015: 75). Later on this same day, the military issued a statement on Facebook wherein it apologised and stated it had not given orders to hurt any Egyptian national. Yet, when this protest continued it cracked down with extreme force two weeks later. On the 9th of March, Egyptian soldiers and plain-clothed 'baltagiyya' destroyed the tents and beat protesters to a pulp, before sending them to military courts. They also detained protesters inside the museum and its gardens and subjected them to torture (Human Rights Watch, 2011). One of interviewees was among those tortured at the Egyptian museum, and describes his ordeal as follows:

> I was arrested and tortured by the army on 9 March 2011. In the Tantawi period, and it was like a punishment for Mubarak and especially for the songs I used in the square. It was a horrible day for me but at the same time, it was really very

important day and it was a days with experience for me. What happened is that they arrested about 200, about 20 girls and 180 men and tortured us in front of the Egyptian museum outside the garden and the torturing takes about 5 hours. They treated me very specially, because they knew me when I was arrested and they take all of them after torturing to the jail but for me they left me in the end of the 5 hours because my case, my situation was very bad, and I could not move. They put me in a taxi and left me. They tortured all of us but for me, the case was completely different. After 10 minutes, they started smashing my head on a column, then they take off my clothes except underwear and then tied a rope on my leg and they pull me to inside the garden and they started the torturing by wooden sticks, metal sticks. Some officers jumping a lot on my back on my head, and in the end they electrocuted me, they burnt me – and they cut my hair with broken glass. And during the torturing they try and use words to break your spirit and to break you inside. I was lucky too, because I was from the first group who realised that the military is not completely good. They have no mercy, they don't know this word. And I realised that they are really a part of Mubarak. And there were some friends with me, K., was also tortured very badly at the same time and when they took the rest to the jail where they tortured A.S. and they cut his hair also, and A.I. he is a painter, and a lot of other protestors. (Interview 36)

Importantly, torture in the Egyptian counter-revolution has nothing to do with interrogatory practice, which is still the common frame of reference through which torture is often viewed in academic literature and public debate. Rather, the purpose of torture is to punish, to silence, to mute protesters, to render them into a state of speechless alienation through the infliction of overwhelming violence. For, torture entails the subjection to a violent asymmetrical power relation: wherein the perpetrator's omnipotent malevolent will renders one helpless. In torture, the perpetrator violates the victim's intersubjective parity in the gravest manner and directly annihilates the victim's agency in the world. In torture, one has no agency, no voice. The victim is rendered helpless, reduced by the perpetrator to mere flesh, an object upon which the torturer may act as he or she pleases. Hence, in torture, it is not only the experience of the (threat of) excruciating pain and death that is so destructive, but particularly that this occurs due to the malevolent *volition* of another human being, in the face of which we are helpless. It is this deep violation of intersubjective parity that, as Jean Améry famously noted, 'part of our life ends and it can never be revived again' (Améry, 1980: 29). Through its fundamental rupture of intersubjective parity, torture shatters our faith in others, selves and the surrounding world. It exposes our radical intersubjective constitution, and its existential fragility, precisely at the moment of its violent destruction. In torture, we thus experience a breakdown of a shared symbolic order which destroys one's creative (collective) self-becoming not only at the moment of its infliction (the moment of our deepest helplessness) but also in the longer term. This is why torture is so destructive – and effective – as a tool of demobilisation: in its deep violation of intersubjective parity, it ruptures the shared interpretative horizon upon which our shared linguistic order is based. It thus entails an experience that cannot be expressed or made sense of through this shared symbolic order, leaving many victims disoriented, isolated, atomised, alienated and *speechless*. As this young man, tortured at the museum expressed it:

> You cannot describe what you lived in these moments. You cannot put it in words. You live in different world than other people. Once you have experienced what I have experienced, you have experienced the worst and you live with death inside of you every day. (Interview 36)

Torture destroys one's communicative relationality with other human beings. And so, the political, social and personal repercussions of torture are grave: it throws one into a deep state of disorientation and existential isolation, which destroys creative collective self-becoming and renders one mute. Torture was thus inflicted with the aim of silencing Egypt's revolutionary public sphere because it is a highly effective tool in demobilisation and incapacitation.

Yet, this young man who was tortured on the 9 March 2011 regarded himself as one of the 'first group who realised that the military is not completely good. They have no mercy; they don't know this word. [. . .] they are really a part of Mubarak' (interview 36). For most interviewees, the this realisation came with the Maspero massacre in October 2011. This was when they stopped believing the military benevolent intentions: that it would act in the interests of the revolution in any way. The Maspero massacre occurred during a demonstration organised by Coptic Christians who protested the demolition of a church in Aswan (Upper Egypt) and the leniency of the interim government towards sectarian violence. As protesters marched from the Shubra area towards the television station, they were suddenly attacked by the Egyptian military. An immensely chaotic situation emerged as teargas covered the entire area, while soldiers were firing wildly and armoured personnel carriers literally into the crowds. These vehicles zigzagged across the street, running over people who were desperately trying to flee this chaotic situation, leaving nearly 200 people injured and over 30 died (Mosireen, 2011). One of those who died was Mina Daniel, a Coptic revolutionary protester who gained an iconic status as a revolutionary martyr. This young woman, who herself did not partake in the demonstration, witnessed the chaotic events unfolding:

> Maspero was a great shock because it was very unexpected. It was so shocking and you know it was unexpected. I was in the square, as first I was at home

and then I saw the clashes on TV but I did not know what was happening and I lived in downtown back then. Now I don't anymore. So I went to the streets on them while in Tahrir Square in Abdel Moneim Riad I saw huge trucks . . . . It was a huge truck it was like a. . . . I don't know what it was. There were some police cars, and then there is this vehicle. . . . I cannot remember what it was but anyway, I saw driving really fast and then moving on the side, like over the sidewalk and then threatening to override people right in front of me [. . .] . . . That was really scary. So I was not in the demo but I was around the clashes and we started to slowly realise what was happening and then this guy started fighting with me and chasing me and I don't know. . . . There were police or security people. I don't know. We don't know. You know they pretend that they are civilians and then they talk to you and stuff. (Interview 23)

The violence inflicted by the military at Maspero was horrific: people were run over by trucks, their heads were split in two, their bodies crushed and malformed to death, and sometimes even severed. Interviewees present at the scene expressed being utterly shocked by the deformed bodies and body parts they saw lying around. They also struggled to grasp that the military would respond with such a level of violence at what had been a peaceful demonstration. They were overwhelmed and felt utterly disorientated, unable to make sense of the events that were unfolding in front of their eyes.

Many also relayed that they found it shocking to discover that at the same time that the military was inflicting this violence, it adopted a frame of conspirational victim blaming on state television wherein it described the massacre as a battle of the Egyptian army versus dark, unknown forces. The military thus called upon '"all honourable citizens" to assist the army' against these 'Copts [who] had put Egyptian soldiers in peril' (Khalifa, 2014). The point of the Maspero massacre was hence not only to violently indicate the military would no longer tolerate processes of politicisation (including street protests) of any type and impose an overwhelmingly violent power relation, it also used these events to ignite a social divisions through the frame of conspirational victim blaming. That is, it deliberately sought to sow the seeds of social distrust, which breaks the potential intersubjective parity and thus collective self-manifestation. It purposefully tried to re-atomise Egyptians. The point was to break intersubjective relations, to throw activists in a state of disorientation and isolation, destroy the potential of creative collective becoming and establish a power relation wherein the military would reign supreme.

Hence, on 12 October 2011, generals Mahmoud Hegazy and Adel Emara not only absconded the military from any wrongdoing during the Maspero events, they also blamed the victims directly. Turning perpetrator–victim relations on its head, they insisted that the soldiers had been the victims at the hands of the rioting, unruly Copts – who had pulled 300 soldiers from their trucks. According to the same (conspirational victim blaming) narrative, the zigzagging military vehicles were not deliberately driving into people, but rather soldiers desperately trying to flee the scene. The generals even asked the Egyptian public to imagine these poor soldiers, as their sons, who run away from this violence in fear of their lives (Khalifa, 2015: 92). This public statement was a clear manipulative effort to 'discount and discredit the testimonies by witnesses, videos and autopsies that confirmed that many were crushed to death by army vehicles, while others died of bullet wounds' (Khalifa, 2015: 92). And as Amnesty International rightly remarked, even if one would adopt the military's narrative, and assume that 'the military police and other security forces were not acting under orders, it raises questions about their ability to police demonstrations in the first place' (Khalifa, 2015: 93). But, of course, official media outlets would never raise such critical questions.

While the violent imposition of protesters' death by the military started with Maspero, it reached its peak during the Mohammed Mahmoud Street battle which occurred in November 2011. During the Mohammed Mahmoud Street battle, young (largely male) protesters fought Egypt's security forces for 6 consecutive days, resulting in 40 killed and over 400 injured. It started during the early hours of 19 November, directly after a mass demonstration entitled 'The Day of the One Demand' which was held on Tahrir Square on 18 November. This protest had joined an earlier smaller protest by the families of martyrs. While this sit-in by the families of the martyrs demanded accountability and compensation for those killed during the eighteen days, the larger demonstration was organised by an alliance of revolutionary activists comprising Salafists, Liberals, Socialists and Brotherhood supporters who also were outraged by the 'Selmy document'. This document not only gave the military control over the constitutional drafting process but also shielded its political and economic affairs from parliamentary oversight. Protesters were thus angry about this document since it jeopardised the transition from military to civilian rule.

Two important points have to be made here about the nature of this mass protest: first, it constituted a cross-sectional alliance, which arguably reminded the military that the revolutionary genie was not back in the authoritarian bottle yet as it indicated that the potential of revolutionary creative becoming was still very much alive. And secondly, it was a direct affront to the military's political and economic interests as it demanded civilian transparent rule. Hence, in the early hours of the morning on 19th November, Egypt's security forces violently attacked the square from the direction of the Ministry of Interior. This young man vividly recalled how the violence started:

> It was exactly during sunset prayers, during Maghreb prayers when the military parachuting sections attacked Tahrir Square from all directions. Because usually

they attack from one direction, so you retreat. And this time I saw them attacking from Mohamed Mahmoud and Qasr al Aini, I thought this was the direction, which was two which was unusual, and I started retreating to the parallel street to Mohamed Mahmoud which is I think Tahrir Street and I found them attacking too and I looked to A.M. (friend) and they were attacking from that direction too and I found them attacking from all the different directions, it was about maximum 15 minutes before the square was closed except for Abd Moneim Riadh direction, so we were retreating but many people could not. And they did not understand the dynamics of retreating because retreating is an experience I learnt. You should run back in a way, what you look at and things like this. So I have seen many people being shot at, and seen them dragging the bodies and collecting them and throwing them in the garbage. I have seen them using fire, fire machines, burning the tents. And I thought I would be shot at and that was scary . . . but I still did not leave. At a certain point you stick. Nowadays I when I look back, I wonder why did I not just run away and go home. I just could not. Yeah, that was scary. Especially when I saw the videos after Mohamed Mahmoud, the ones that were taken from a distance, like from a rooftop. When you are in the middle you don't see everything but you see fire, someone putting fire to a tent, you hear live ammunition from everywhere and people bleeding and running behind you, in front of you and then you are not shot. It is a strange feeling that you are not dead. You always wonder why am I not dead. (Interview 25)

What ensued was nothing less than a bloodbath. Upon hearing the news of this violent closure of the sit-in, hundreds of young men and women made their way back to the side street of Tahrir, Mohammed Mahmoud, where Egypt's security forces responded with a ferocity not seen before: they killed, tortured, maimed and teargassed protesters for six consecutive days. Interviewees relayed that the overwhelming violence that surrounded them flung them into an eerie, disoriented, dreamlike state wherein the world appeared surreal – steeped as it was in violence, death and blood. As this young man then continued:

I felt like I don't exist, like I am dreaming that something was making me stick and refusing to leave although I was scared. But I just could not leave. So, I remember very well zoning out, watching the first life bullets in my life flying over my head and I did not run, I did not move, I was just frozen watching this. Ehm . . . I was watching people bleeding and maybe some of them looked already dead. I did not engage with this, that I was very close, very close to the front line, and I refuse to leave and this feeling of being out of place in this feeling of like dreaming, and this is not real, it was over after two of three hours. And then I started realising that this is where I am, and I am not leaving and I am here not to necessarily engage in violence because I did not actually believe in throwing a stone after the military and the police but I really wanted first to understand what the dynamics of violence are. I don't know why, but ehm. . . .And also trying to help, like seeing these people bleeding was really breaking my heart and I was like carrying, carrying them . . . brigading, organising the spaces for the ambulances to run and the motorcycle ambulances making . . . like yeah, with the people carrying and trying to help as much as I can. (Interview 25)

Interviewees commented on the relentless stream of dead or half-dead people they were carrying away from the frontlines: 'I have seen a lot of dead bodies. Yeah that was actually the most violence experience I have been through. I carried a lot of dead and injured people' (interview 25). All of the twenty-two interviewees present at Mohammed Mahmoud shared personal stories of extreme violence they endured. For instance, a girl described how she was physically harassed by informal security officers, who tried to grope her from behind. A doctor relayed how he blacked out after being shot and teargassed at the frontline, only to be dragged back and treated by the very same 'kids' he had been training in the field hospital just half an hour earlier. Several young male interviewees explained that they were shot by 'khartoush' in their hands, eyes and back. Indeed snipers positioned at rooftops which aimed at protesters' eyes were rife. And one of the interviewees narrated how he lost his second eye in these battles, after he lost the first one on the 28th of January. His blindness, so horrifically inflicted by Egypt's security state. gained him an iconic status among the revolutionary opposition. Another protester relayed how he was taken to the Ministry of Interior after he walked away from the battle with injuries to his head, and was tortured and detained for a month, with no medical aid in sight of course. And all of them commented on the dead bodies lying in the streets, or how the dead and injured were carried in away on motorcycles that now functioned as improvised ambulances.

In addition to being shot, or seeing others killed right before them, they were also teargassed. Since teargas is classified as a tool for non-lethal crowd dispersal, its existential impact on those 'being teargassed' is often underestimated. And the literature on teargas in Egypt suggests that protesters got addicted to the smell of teargas as such (Schielke, 2011). What such accounts overlook is the fact that teargas is an effective tool for demobilisation and the violent closure of political public space: it (temporarily) physically incapacitates a person while throwing them in a deep sense of disorientation. As Part 3 outlines in more detail, teargas is a useful tool of repression and demobilisation since in the process of being teargassed, one temporarily loses one's grip on the world. Interviewees relayed not only that they could not see anymore, but rather also that felt as if they were choking to death – and so it was extremely distressing. For most interviewees, the process of being teargassed was hence far removed from the romantic vision of the brave revolutionary protester. Rather, it was a frightful existential experience wherein they thought they were going to die. Teargas for many interviewees constituted nothing less than a near-death experience: 'Teargassed "you feel like you're going to die [. . .]. Teargas is really bad in that sense. Like if I don't get out of here I am going to die" (interview 19). It comprises:

> A physical reaction in the sense that I am going to cough my lungs. Pain. It's like sheer pain. And it's weird, because it is like pain and then you black out, so you cannot see. In particular moments when it's really heavy tear gas and you're caught up in it, suddenly everything is black, but it is like you can see for one second every two seconds. And that sense of panic obviously just accelerates. With pain and with the knowledge that actually you can't get out of here. It's going to take me a while; there a lot of people, and I cannot go – I am talking about the couple of incidents when I could not easily run and it increases the panic, because you feel like I'm going to be stuck here, I am going to die. And then you start thinking about everything they told you about teargas it creates panic, so don't panic. Obviously, you cannot not panic. How do you not panic? (Interview 19)

This sense of deep disorientation and the feeling of choking to death indicates why teargas is such a powerful tool. In the deployment of teargas, the victim is drawn inward, deeply into his or her own body due to the experience of overwhelming pain, while at the same time, one loses a sense of disorientation in the world. Many activists commented that they were fearful they could not quickly escape the crowd, that they were going to die. One is thus physically and existentially thrown into a state of incapacitating disorientation, through the imposition of a gravely violent power relation.

Moreover, the disorientation that results from teargas occurs at the moment of its infliction but may have long after-effects. This was certainly the case with teargas during Mohammed Mahmoud, the gravity of which many interviewees believed was worsened through an additional toxic or neurological incapacitating component in the gas, which left them in existential agony for hours and sometimes even for days after these violent battles. In the words of this young female protester:

> I felt like it was not normal teargas I felt like . . bass . . . I . . . A lot of people actually reported that it was nerve gas yaeny, and so my mother [who was also present] started hallucinating, yeah . . . and I was actually quite, I do know, I went into a like into this mood of like hysteria, even though nothing really happened to me. [. . .]. We think, we think that it was not just teargas but that it had some nerve-shit you know. Because there was a lot of other, a

lot of my friends also reported the same thing. They were saying that 'Oh you know after I got home, I was like crying hysterically and stuff'. Yeah, yeah. (Interview 30)

Yet, what also aggravated these experiences of violence was that increasingly they were suffering such violence alone. SCAF's procedural transitional roadmap and conspirational victim blaming was increasingly successful in rupturing solidarity and intersubjective unity. And so, while on the few streets surrounding Mohammed Mahmoud there was still revolutionary unity amongst the young protesters as such, increasingly societal and political support started to wane. A major moment of such marginalisation was of course when the Brotherhood officially withdrew its support for the Mohammed Mahmoud protests in light of its own political interests which it pursued through co-option by the military's. The fact that the Brotherhood thus urged its members not to participate in the protests, precisely at the moment that so many were dying on the streets of Cairo was interpreted as an ultimate revolutionary betrayal and created a violent division between the anti-systemic revolutionary forces and the Brotherhood:

> I saw people being shot. They were being shot for no reason. And the brotherhood, [. . .] they remained silent. Actually, it made me a natural enemy of the Brotherhood. I will never forget and tolerate what the Brotherhood did at that moment. I don't have any ideology. I don't have any problem with anyone. But the Brotherhood created a natural enemy for them out of the conflict. I can tolerate the police as we expected this of them but never the Brotherhood, because at this point in time they uncovered us – not only this, they did not only remain silent they incited against us, and they used to find excuses for the police's doing. They expressed their support for the police, saying that the country should carry on, and be stable and stuff like that. (Interview 7)

Importantly, this sense of betrayal was also felt inside the Brotherhood itself, with some of its (particularly younger) Brotherhood members rebelling against their won leadership. They joined the protests regardless of their leadership's demand not to do so. As this young Brother remarked: 'I felt it was my duty to go to help the people who were at the sit-ins, they were our partners in the revolution and I felt that the Islamists betrayed the movement' (interview 40). However, such defiance of the leadership position was relatively small scale.

Revolutionary unitary was not only fractured by the political retreat of the Brotherhood but also by the broader decline of social support for the street protest in light of SCAF's 'orderly path of transition'. Since the military is largely regarded as a heroic national institution of liberation, 'a large segment of Egyptians were prepared to take the military's word that it was committed to hand power over to civilians eventually' (Khalifa, 2015: 71), despite the fact that is actions indicated otherwise. With the demand that 'Mubarak has to leave' fulfilled, the military thus presented itself as the national guardian of the revolution, which stood in direct opposition to the 'immoral' rabble-rousers that refused to leave the streets and wanted to throw Egypt into chaos, instability and disorder. Hence, SCAF issued a statement that the dispersal of the sit-in on the 10th was 'in the public's interest, aiming to benefit citizens and lighten traffic congestion' (Khalifa, 2015: 95). General Mohsen Al Fangari also directly demonised the protesters as lawless rioters who sought to spread chaos and cause the downfall of the state in a televised phone call. He also warned that 'if security is not applied, we will implement the rule of law. Anyone who does wrong will pay for it' (Khalifa, 2015: 95). The trouble was that this conspirational victim blaming started to have more effect, since it was only a section of the population (notably, though of course not exclusively, the young) that were on the streets of Mohamed Mahmoud. Many of their relatives and friends only saw these events evolve on television, and thus often failed to rectify the televised accounts with the experience on the streets. This left many interviewees feeling increasingly isolated, as this young woman remarked:

> And the fact that so many people have died in front of my eyes and justly and that I would go home and look to the media, when my parents meet some of their bourgeois friends and I would hear from them 'ah those thugs what do they want, where is the legitimacy, blablabla. The police is defending itself. The police is descending the Ministry of Interior', and all of that stuff that used to be said back then. So just being in there in morning and all day, perhaps until 10 or 11 PM, in that context and then going home to this completely different context, I was quite afraid from the notion that people have no idea whatsoever what is going on. [. . .] I see that there is a big divergence between what people think that is happening and what is really happening on the streets. But this was broken somehow with the 18 days of the revolution where the same kids who were called thugs and baddies and so on were all of the sudden the great kids of the revolution and the youth and blablabla. (Interview 28)

And thus, unlike the revolutionary days, the conspirational victim blaming narrative gained an increasing hold. As this young man explained a deep rift started to occur between those who experienced Mohammed Mahmoud and those who did not: 'Those who see what's happening are different from those who are just hearing the stories. I could actually make this the slogan of the revolution: those who see are different than those who hear' (interview 16). This was especially hard, he explained, in light of the death and destruction activists experienced during Mohammed Mahmoud, 'There were people that we lose and we couldn't help them. People at home just say: may he rest in peace, but I witnessed this' (interview 16). The existential impacts of the direct physical force inflicted, wherein intersubjective parity was so gravely betrayed, were being compounded through the purposeful, counter-revolutionary tearing apart of intersubjective relations. It meant that activists suffered an increasing misrecognition in the social sphere of the violent injustices (or intersubjective imparity) they suffered at the hands of Egypt's security forces in the political sphere. They found themselves increasingly isolated, marginalised and indeed ostracised.

This disruption of intersubjective relations is not accidental of course, but rather constituted the core of the counter-revolutionary project. Hence, in the months that followed, SCAF continued to inflict grave (deadly) direct physical force, while also intensifying conspirational victim blaming and fuelling social discord. So, when protesters gathered to stop the newly formed Al Ganzouri cabinet[6] from meeting, the military regime responded with deadly force: security forces not only kidnapped, beat and shot protesters but also threw concrete blocks from rooftops on top of demonstrations in the violent attempt to close down Egypt's public space. Interviewees narrated that, in face of such an overwhelming deadly violence, they experienced a deep sense of estranged detachment from the world, which they also often described as a profound state of shock. While, there was still solidarity and intersubjective parity among protesters in the streets, the social environment around them started to change: many activists commented that friends and relatives not present at the scenes of conflict where now starting to agree with the military's narrative of the need for an orderly transition and increasingly adopted its frame of conspirational victim blaming. Ganzouri also intensified this narrative frame: he denied that the security forces had shot at protesters and blamed riotous 'third parties' for spreading chaos instead. He even went so far as to argue that 'the government was for "the salvation of the revolution" and that protesters outside the Cabinet Building were "anti-revolution"' (Jumet, 2018: 138). The blame for a lack of revolutionary process was hence carefully redirected away from the counter-revolutionary actors, towards the revolutionaries, thereby seeking to justify the violent intersubjective imparity inflicted.

Yet, the violent event with the greatest existential impact on some interviewees during the SCAF period was the Port Said massacre which occurred on 1 February 2012. This massacre took place on the first anniversary of the legendary Camel Battle, wherein Mubarak's state hired thugs had hit and beaten protesters while riding camels and horses (Ashraf, 2021), after a football match between Al Ahly (from Cairo) and Al Masry (from Port Said) in the city Port Said. At the end of the game, Al Masry fans ran across the field and attacked Al Ahly fans as lights were turned off and the doors remained shut. The result was a stampede wherein 74 young men were killed and more than 1,000 were injured, as the police stood by, watched and refused to open the doors. Many activists, including many interviewees, interpreted this massacre as being orchestrated by the Egyptian security forces in violent retribution for the intense anti-SCAF battles fought by the young Al Ahly supporters. These supporters were the frontliners, the hard core of the revolutionary fighters, who fought the fiercest battles against Egypt's security state, also during the Mohammed Mahmoud Street battle just a few months earlier. With Port Said, seventy-four of these young men were killed. They were the ones who shouted the loudest and fought the hardest against SCAF's rule. They were the life and blood (quite literally) of Egypt's revolutionary creative becoming, and thus constituted the greatest challenge for Egypt's counter-revolutionary actors, most notably the military and its security state. These young men were not going to be depoliticised anytime soon. Hence, playing on existing tensions between Al Masry and Port Said, the Ultras fans were subjected to violent traumatic status subordination during the massacre wherein they were annihilated, injured and thrown into disorienting grief, as the police stood by and watched.

The Port Said massacre was furthermore instrumentally useful for the military regime in that it tore intersubjective relations ever deeper as it increased existing social tensions between the cities of Port Said and Cairo. That is, the deflection of political violence away from the state as the perpetrator to other civilians (in this case football supporters) not only conveniently redirected attention away from the military regime itself but also led to cycles of revenge wherein unitary revolutionary action crumbled ever further. This social discord continued well after 2017, when the courts sentenced twenty-one individuals from Port Said to death, imprisoned five persons for life and sent twenty-two persons to prison (serving terms between two and fifteen years) over the Port Said massacre. Indeed, while the courts sent ordinary Al Masry fans, who very likely had nothing to do with the events, to prison (or indeed, their deaths), no single security officials were held accountable (Piazzese, 2015). The sentencing sparked off riots in Port Said which left 30 dead and 250 injured, as citizens in Port Said fought the police while also trying to raid the prisons to release the condemned. At the same time, however, in Cairo, Al Ahly fans publicly celebrated this sentencing, including the imposed death sentences.

Hence, the Port Said massacre, not only delivered an incapacitating blow to the Ultras but also directly undermined the potential of revolutionary social unity by initiating a cycle of polarised social violence and revenge (CBC, 2013). Revenge, as discussed in more detail in Part 3, entails the attempt to regain intersubjective power after one (believes to have) suffered a grave violation of intersubjective parity. Revenge may be directed to the perpetrator but when that is difficult or impossible is often redirected towards those who come to represent the perpetrator – thereby frequently unleashing a vicious cycle wherein communicative relations are perpetually distorted by violence and distrust. And so, the fostering of an inward cycle of social revenge is a useful counter-revolutionary tool in that it not only directs attention away from the military as the main perpetrator of violence but precisely undermines the potential of transformative revolutionary politics. The ensuing social chaos and discord also enabled the military regime to position itself as the harbinger of stability and security, directly emphasising its transitional roadmap. In the words of Tantawi: 'We will get through this stage. Egypt will be stable. We have a roadmap to transfer power to elected civilians. If anyone is plotting instability in Egypt they will not succeed. Everyone will get what they deserve' (Al Jazeera, 2012).

NEOLIBERAL ECONOMIC RATIONALISM

Yet, of course, this roadmap was strategically geared towards not only safeguarding the political interests of the military but also reinforcing its economic gains. While the military's economic consolidation only becomes properly visible during Abdel Fattah el Sisi's rule after 2013, its foundations were already laid during SCAF's transition period. SCAF, from the moment it took office, pursued a policy of 'plus ça change, plus c'est la même chose'. That is, it adopted exactly the same path of neoliberal economics as Mubarak, the only difference being that it was now the Egyptian military (rather than the Gamal Mubarak's newly emerging business class) that was in the driver's seat.

Of course, any discussion on the military's economic undertakings is seriously hampered by the fact that its holdings and economic affairs are not only shrouded in mystery but also immunised from public scrutiny (Marshall and Stacher, 2012). Yet, we do know that the Egyptian military already had a huge stake in the pre-revolutionary period, with its businesses being widely dispersed in Egyptian society and its factories covering everything from daily household goods to key assets in the petroleum, maritime, construction and renewable energy industries (Marshall and Stacher, 2012). Some of its companies are organised under the umbrellas of the Arab Organisation for Industrialisation, the National Services Projects Organisation (NSPO) and the Ministry of Military Production, but there is a vast network of companies and private–public partnerships that fall outside of these umbrellas (Marshall and Stacher, 2012; Harding, 2016). Not only has the officer's class since the 1990s been increasingly 'entrepreneurialised' (Abul-Magd, 2018), the military has also been a key player in attracting foreign investors – particularly through collaborative projects that 'bring [. . .] in Gulf conglomerates, as well as Western and Asian multinationals, as partners' (Marshall and Stacher, 2012).

Located as many of these projects are in the immensely lucrative areas of maritime, petroleum, construction and renewable energy (among other sectors), they reaped considerable economic benefits for the military's officers' elite.

The trouble was that Gamal Mubarak's possible accession had put these privileges at risk, as he clearly favoured the new civic business-cum-political elite and had indicated he would seek to expand their economic privileges into the terrains until then dominated by the military. Hence, after disposal of Mubarak, and the eradication of this particular threat, SCAF did not radically overhaul Egypt's economy nor did it pursue a nationalist protectionist economic policy (as often presupposed), but rather it simply continued the neoliberal path it had always already been on. The primary advantage for the military now was that, with Mubarak and his sons out of the way, it's significant competitors were eliminated from the economic terrain. It was thus merely a case of redirecting Egypt's neoliberal policies so that the military was now its primary beneficiary.

Yet, in order to be such a beneficiary, the military needed political unrest – and particularly the politicised challenge to their economic gains – to end. Hence, from the moment it took over power, SCAF insisted that protesters needed to leave the streets so as to 'stabilize the economy'. During SCAF's rule the financial situation of Egypt deteriorated as both tourism and foreign investors largely stayed away, foreign reserves plummeted and unemployment rose (Global Post, 2011), throwing more people into abject poverty. However, rather than using this moment as an opportunity to re-evaluate Egypt's neoliberal economic policies and address its structural problem of grave maldistribution, Egypt's economic woes were only used by the military to stigmatise protesters, fragment social unity and close the newly politicised public terrain. Hence, rather than adjusting a neoliberal economic system so dependent on speculative and volatile industries such as the luxury housing market and tourism, SCAF instead blamed the disorderly politics of the street and insisted that it was time for 'everyone to go back to work' and follow the military's orderly transitional roadmap. Thus, adopting the familiar frame of conspirational victim blaming, SCAF stated that while the initial aims of the revolution had been noble, it was now being corrupted by 'third parties' keen on destroying Egypt's prosperity. Hence, it was supposedly high time to 'get back to business' and let the army prevent Egypt from falling into chaos.

In reality of course, this roadmap worked to deprive Egyptians of their political voice and throw them into an incapacitating sense of isolation, while protecting the military's own political and economic interests. Unfortunately, the military's narrative fell into fertile soil, since the declining economic situation aggravated the existential anxieties of many ordinary Egyptians, who were already living on the brink of poverty and were now sinking ever deeper into a struggle for survival. And so, fed up with protests and chaos, many ordinary Egyptians accepted the military's narrative of the need for stability and security. This not only left the structural underlying problems of neoliberal maldistribution unaddressed but also resulted in a (gradual) decline of support for revolutionary action and transformation, which undermined the potential of creative collective becoming wherein traumatic status subordination would be undone.

At the same time, the military adopted a clear neoliberal line of economic development, wherein it toed the line of international financial institutions: it 'issued tranches of dollar-denominated treasury bills to guard against inflation and reassure investors' and refused to raise the ceiling of debt for increased social spending (Marshall and Stacher, 2012). Hence, regardless of outspoken public opposition to such deals, SCAF accepted the IMF's deal consisting of a $3.2 billion IMF loan facility in December 2011 and also appointed Hazem Beblawi as the minister of finance. Beblawi was notorious for being a strong 'advocate of free-market liberalism and the "rationalizing" of state subsidies on staples' (Marshall and Stacher, 2012). At the same time, the military 'dragged its feet on draft laws setting minimum and maximum wages and legalising independent labor unions' (Marshall and Stacher, 2012), while also fervently cracking down on labour strikes and protests that emerged across Egypt's factories. During these clampdowns, they even directly employed the military police as workers protested against corruption, bad working conditions and mismanagement (Abul-Magd, 2012). The military labelled any such unrest as 'fi'awi – as divisive and parochial (Marshall and Stacher, 2012) and thus – again – decisively bad for the economy. As Zeina Abul-Magd explains:

> The military accused the striking workers of stalling the wheel of production and harming the national economy. In reality, the actions mainly threatened the military's immediate economic interests. The largest labor strikes targeted entities run by retired generals, either in the public sector or in enterprises owned by the military. (Abul-Magd, 2012)

The generals also went to great length to ensure that those foreign investors, who cooperated with the military, were not deterred by political unrest, and it even protected these investors' access to their assets with armed forces personnel (Marshall and Stacher, 2012). Moreover, it pursued a 'showy but highly selective anti-corruption campaign' that targeted big NDP businessmen like Ahmed Ezz while 'civilian businessmen with strong links to military companies were passed over by prosecutors – another signal to politicians to accept the military's role in the economy or be shut out completely' (Marshall and Stacher, 2012). In all these developments, it was clear that SCAF favoured political players who view Egypt's interests as synonymous with those of the military's economic planners. Importantly, in its instrumental pursuit of its own economic interests that SCAF not only left military-friendly businessmen unscathed but also co-opted the Brotherhood in its transition plan (Marshall and Stacher, 2012). For, despite the rise of tensions between the military and Brotherhood, the Brotherhood's economic agenda (which was also based on neoliberal principles) would leave the military's economic interests intact. Yet, as we will see in chapter 8 (Part 2), these economic interests only came into full fruition after the Brotherhood had been eliminated from the political field, under the rule of Abdel Fattah El Sisi who consolidated the military's economic enterprise.

NOTES

1. Note that *throughout* the book, I employ a distinction between the systematic and anti-systematic opposition in this book, which is directly borrowed from Joshua Stacher's excellent book *Watermelon Democracy* (2020). Stacher describes the differences as follows: 'The latter reject the formal politics of an autocratic regime, as they feel entering into politics with an autocratic state that defines what is legal dilutes the ability to push for any measures beyond incremental change. They therefore remain outside of formal politics, such as elections, and instead have a proclivity for street protests. Systemic opposition groups, by contrast, participate in formal politics and mostly adhere to a regime's rules. Scholars that work on the region have noticed this trend of an obedient opposition for decades' (Stacher, 2020: 27). Hence, while the latter refers to the revolutionary opposition, the former refers to organisations such as the Muslim Brotherhood.

2. For an excellent account of this street battle and its pertinence, see Ryzova (2020).

3. This demonstration was organised against the Selmy document wherein the military shielded its economic interests and political affairs from oversight, and crossed political divides as the Brotherhood, as well as the liberal and social political parties took part.

4. The other presidential candidates were Amr Moussa (a former minister of foreign affairs and aviation minister under Mubarak), Abdel Moneim Abdel Fotouh (a leftist moderate member of the Muslim Brotherhood who had been expelled from the Brotherhood when he had decided to put forth his candidacy) and Hamdeen Sabahi (a socialist). Morsi achieved 24.78 per cent, Ahmed Shafik 23.6 per cent, Hamdeen 20.72 per cent, Abdel Moneim Abdel Fotouh 17.47 per cent and Amr Moussa 11.13 per cent. As many commentators have remarked, would the revolutionary vote not have been split between Hamdeen and Fotouh, they would have had a good chance of winning the elections.

5. The military often attacked sit-ins or gatherings in the early hours of the morning when numbers dwindled.

6. El Ganzouri had been appointed as the new prime minister by SCAF after Essam Sharaf had resigned in opposition to the violence inflicted by security forces during Mohammed Mahmoud and was tasked with forming a new government.

Chapter 6

Mohammed Morsi

The Politics of Traumatic Status Subordination

When Morsi was inaugurated as Egypt's president, SCAF had carefully delimited the parameters of his presidency, effectively rendering him rather more powerless than the Brotherhood had perhaps anticipated or hoped. Morsi was effectively a president without a parliament, without a constitution, without a clear delineation of his legislative powers and with an economy in tatters, and the military was clearly controlling the Egypt's post-revolutionary process from behind the scenes. It not only clearly directed the constitutional drafting process in such a way that its own political and economic interests would remain protected, but also effectively retained more power over the drafting process than the new incumbent president.

And so, as soon as Morsi attained office, the honeymoon of mutual convenience soured, and the Brotherhood engaged in a variety of different strategic efforts to ascertain its political power over the military. This was a battle the Brotherhood eventually lost, as it culminated in Morsi's disposal by the military in July 2013. It not only lost this battle because the military and its cooption of the remnants of the Mubarak proved a more powerful force, but also because in its attempt to attain political power the Brotherhood inflicted the tripartite structure of traumatic status subordination onto ordinary civilians which alienated them even further. Of course, this alienation was effectively manipulated by the military and resulted in a downwards spiral of social polarisation and hatred. While chapter 10 will discuss this downward spiral of social revenge, this chapter is concerned with the mechanisms of traumatic status subordination Morsi inflicted in his one year rule. This chapter argues that Morsi imposed traumatic status subordination through procedural colonisation (including repressive juridification of the public sohere), the infliction of grave physical violence (including the demonisation of protestors) and the continuation of economic neoliberalisation. Morsi sought to attain political power procedurally, in that he not only insisted on the legitimacy of the speedy elections vis-à-vis street politics, but also sought to reinstate of parliament, while retiring Tantawi and Annan (in exchange for legal immunity) and sack of the general prosecutor. When these attempts however backfired, the Brotherhood president stepped up the repressive juridification of Egypt's public sphere (notably through the presidential declaration in November 2012 but also the Protest Law and NGO law) and started to employ direct physical force. In the absence of control over the security forces, this violence was carried out by Brotherhood supporters themselves, thus setting in motion a vicious spiral of civilian onto civilian violence. At the same time, the Brotherhood leadership also continued the same neoliberal economic policies of Mubarak and SCAF before them, thus also leaving the issue of maldistribution unresolved and repeating the pattern of economic marginalisation. In these strategic attempts to assert their political power, the Brotherhood colonised the political public sphere and engaged in instrumental action that brutally violated the foundational presupposition of intersubjective parity. As they were geared towards gaining their own political power, they violently excluded, marginalised and silenced alternative political voices, voices that they had once united with (albeit perhaps initially hesitantly) in the revolutionary public sphere. And so, the sad irony is that, Morsi ended up continuing the very same mechanisms of traumatic status subordination that SCAF, and indeed Mubarak, had inflicted before him.

The result was a further disintegration of the potential of intersubjective revolutionary becoming, as Egypt's social and political spheres sank ever deeper in into a downward spiral of traumatic status subordination. Moreover, the emerging social violence and chaos (wherein frustration was directed inwards as civilians fought civilians) established fertile ground for the military – and particularly Abdel Fattah El Sisi – to rise like a phoenix from the ashes under the pretext of saving national stability and security, which will be discussed in chapter 8.

POLITICAL PROCEDURALISM: MORSI'S STRUGGLE FOR POWER

With no constitution, no parliament and with many of the presidential legislative powers transferred to the military (in the June 2012 declaration), Morsi was upon his inauguration arguably one of the most powerless presidents in recent Egyptian history. Hence, one of the first things the Brotherhood president did was to try and reinstall parliament, which had been disbanded by the SCC in April 2012. On the 8th of July, Morsi called on the People's Assembly to reconvene, in clear defiance of SCAF's military decree and the

SCC. While Brotherhood supporters regarded this as a democratic move, as the motive was above all one geared by instrumental rational considerations: 'The precise decision by the president, however, could be attributed to his desire for the support of the Islamist dominated parliament and to examine the extent and boundaries of his authority in the early stages of his presidency' (Khalifa, 2015: 133). And so, on the 10th of July, the parliament met, and a vote for appealing the parliament's dissolution was passed.

Yet, while Morsi's supporters interpreted this as a reinforcement of civilian democratic authority (strictly procedurally interpreted), many of the secular opponents interpreted this as a direct and authoritarian affront to the rule of law, thus deepening tensions within Egypt's post-revolutionary political landscape (Khalifa, 2015: 133). In any case, Morsi's attempt to regain parliamentary political power turned out to be short-lived as the Supreme Constitutional Court (SCC) immediately overturned Morsi's decision. It stated that the president was in violation of the court's ruling and 'threatened the president with the equivalent of contempt of court if he continued to dismiss its decisions' (Khalifa, 2015: 133). On the 11th of July, Morsi declared that he would comply with the ruling and promised that he would seek out a dialogue with Egypt's political forces and the judiciary to try and solve the issue of the dissolved parliament (Khalifa, 2015: 134). The military generals in the meantime showed who is really in control and issued a statement saying that the Egyptian military would not allow Egypt to fall into the hands of a certain group. This clearly referred to the Brotherhood but did not name it explicitly. And so, less than a few weeks into Morsi's presidency, the cooperative honeymoon between the Brotherhood and the military appeared to be truly over, as the previously happy partners now appeared at loggerheads.

Just a few weeks later, Morsi again tried to indicate his political power as he sent the head and deputy head of SCAF, Field Marshall Tantawi and Lieutenant General Sami Hafez Anan, into retirement. While Morsi's supporters exclaimed this to be an audacious move and victory of a civilian president over the armed forces, anti-systemic revolutionary activists were outraged that Morsi had awarded them with the Medal of the Nile and other accolades, which rendered them immune to any legal prosecution (Ahram Online, 2012a). This included any crimes committed under SCAF's interim rule, such as the killing, maiming and torturing of protesters. Oppositional activists thus interpreted this not so much as an audacious move but rather as a strategic appeasement, wherein the generals were pardoned for their crimes in the Brotherhood's instrumental pursuit of greater political power. For Morsi also used this opportunity to overturn the military's June declaration, thereby reappropriating the military's legislative powers. Lastly, he instilled some 'new blood' into the military's higher echelons through the appointment of the youngest member of SCAF, the chief of military intelligence,

Abdel Fattah El Sisi as the minister of defence. His choice for Sisi was based on the presumption that Sisi's conservative religious orientation would make him more sympathetic to the Brotherhood and the president. This calculation will cost him – and indeed the entirety of Egypt – dearly one year later.

At the same time, Morsi also tried to gain political procedural ground over the judiciary. When, on the 10th of October, all twenty-four defendants charged with killing protesters in the Camel Battle were dismissed by the court (sparking strong condemnation and protests across Egypt), Morsi sacked the general prosecutor Abdel Meguid Mahmoud and appointed him as the envoy to the Vatican instead (Reuters, 2012). Perhaps this was an attempt to appease the revolutionary opposition, which interpreted the court's dismissal as a strategic conspiracy between the Brotherhood and the ancient regime of Mubarak, and perhaps it was Morsi's attempt to test the waters of his judicial power. Either way, it was not very successful, since 'Egyptian law afforded immunity to the prosecutor general from expulsion by the president, so Abdel Meguid Mahmoud refused to comply, citing the law' (Khalifa, 2015: 140). Morsi was ultimately forced to back down on his decision to sack Mahmoud in order to avoid a complete showdown with the judiciary, again emphasising his relative weakness as a president. Nevertheless, many interviewees interpreted this attempted sacking of the prosecutor general as a direct affront to judicial independence and interpreted this as an attempted takeover of the legal and political realm by a particular group (the Brotherhood). This view was furthermore confirmed when the Judges Club issued a strong condemnation of what is also regarded as a presidential infringement on the judiciary independence (Khalifa, 2015: 141).

This view was reinforced in November 2012, when Morsi issued a presidential declaration wherein, he sought to immunise his decisions, laws and decrees from legal challenge and called for a referendum on what most in the political opposition regarded as an overly Islamist constitutional draft (Teti et al., 2012).[2] The political context for this controversial presidential decree is as follows: on the 23rd of October, the issue of the legality of the Constitutional Assembly was referred by Egypt's Administrative Court to Egypt's Supreme Constitutional Court (SCC). With this referral, the Brotherhood-dominated Constitutional Assembly found itself in a difficult situation: if the Constitutional Assembly finishes a draft before the court verdict, it would render a possible dissolution moot. Yet, SCAF could still veto any clause, which the assembly could then overturn but the matter would have to be referred to the SCC for deliberation, which means the Constitutional Assembly would probably run out of time (Selim, 2015). Yet if the Constitutional Assembly does not finish the drafting of the constitution in time and the Supreme Court dissolves the Constitutional Assembly in its verdict, SCAF would get to appoint another assembly. Initially, the Supreme Administrative Court postponed its decision to 9 October, after which the hearing was adjourned to 16 October, for it then to be referred to the SCC on the 23rd of October instead. Around the middle of November, rumours started to emerge that the SCC would issue a verdict. It is in light of this daunting prospect that the Brotherhood president issued his presidential decree (Khalifa, 2015: 145). While his supporters heralded this as an audacious move by a civilian, procedurally elected, president against Egypt's deep state, his critics were furious that this would render him immune against legal challenge since it constituted a deeply authoritarian, anti-democratic move. After all, even his predecessor Mubarak had always at least kept a *veneer* of legality and the theoretical possibility of legal challenge – no matter how unrealistic in practice. Hence, for many of Morsi's opponents, the presidential declaration was the straw that broke the camel's back. It was experienced as the ultimate betrayal of the revolutionary goals of justice, equality and transparency, since Morsi was merely interested in the strategic pursuit of the Brotherhood's political interests, rather than advancing intersubjective equality for all.

Moreover, Morsi betrayed intersubjective parity not only through his strategic procedural tactics but also through the bias towards substantive Islamist content wherein other opinions were forcibly excluded from the public terrain. For instance, not only was the Constitutional Assembly comprised of Islamists (since all non-Brotherhood members had withdrawn due to blatant disregard for their opinions) but the Brotherhood's constitution also prioritised substantive (yet vaguely worded) Islamist cultural and social values (such as the 'traditional family'). These 'values' not only left large legal loopholes in the constitution drafted under Morsi's rule but also severely undermined the protection of individual human rights. Or, to put it in stronger Habermasian terms, since the exercise of public autonomy in a deliberative public sphere where all affected are heard and treated as equal partners in debate was damaged, private autonomy was under threat. Indeed, the Brotherhood's constitution was so badly drafted that the liberal opposition leader Mohamed El Baradei scathingly remarked it was nothing but a document belonging to the dustbin of history (El-Dabh, 2012).

Yet, the draft was eventually approved in December 2012 through a constitutional referendum, wherein 63.8 per cent of the 32.9 per cent eligible votes were in favour of its adoption. This approval was not so much based on a principled agreement on the statutes of the constitution (indeed many voters remain illiterate and there were no serious attempts to engage them in a deliberative debate over its content) but rather on the lack of other viable political options and the increasing desire among many Egyptians for the country to move out of a political impasse. This constitutional referendum clearly violated the foundational principles of discursive legal legitimacy, for as Jurgen Habermas reminds us: 'Only those statues may claim legitimacy that can meet with the assent of all citizens in a discursive process of legislation' since it is essential for the formation of legitimate legal norms is that 'legal associates [...] recognize one another as free and equal members of an association they have joined voluntarily' (Habermas, 1996: 110). Both of these conditions were deeply violated by the Brotherhood's constitutional process, which continued to adopt an instrumental orientation in the constitutional drafting process that violated what ought to be an inclusive, intersubjective deliberative establishment of legal norms).

And so, while blatantly disregarding the *substantive* norms of deliberative democratic proceduralism, the Brotherhood took (strategic) recourse to formal democratic proceduralism as it sought to rhetorically justify its political power and political decisions (which, again, were based on instrumental rather than deliberative considerations). That is, while violently repressing and disregarding the plurality of views, the Brotherhood stated that both the president and the constitution were 'legitimate' since they had followed formal procedural rules. Hence, like SCAF before them and Sisi after them, they took strategic recourse to formal electoralism as a way to rhetorically justify their deeply exclusive politics wherein the plurality of discursive voices was violently excluded from public debate. The upshot of the Brotherhood's violent marginalisation of diversity in its instrumental pursuit of political power was the increasing perception that the Brotherhood did not seek to represent or include all Egyptians in democratic debate, but rather that they were hijacking the revolutionary moment for their own 'sectarian' gain.

This view was further reinforced in the later spring of 2013, when the perception arose that the Brotherhood was interested in monopolising not only the formal political realm as such but also Egyptian society as such. Several incidents affirmed this belief, most notably the appointment of Alaa Abdel-Aziz as the culture minister in May 2013, who was rumoured to have plans to radically overhaul Egypt's culture industry – including removal of Ines Abdel-Dayem as the opera chair (Saad et al., 2013). This sparked a range of protests by artists, writers and performers, including public ballet performances outside the Opera House. This appointment came just under a month after the Brotherhood's announcement that it would reduce alcohol consumption (Doss, 2013) in Egypt (through a ban on alcoholic products) and after its earlier statements that it would ban bikinis in tourism resorts (Michael, 2011). It also came after Morsi's concerted effort to take legal measures against media critical of the Brotherhood president, including the removal of media licences and the arrest of the ever so popular satirist Bassem Youssef. Furthermore, during his rule, Morsi also allegedly sought to implement a protest law, wherein the assembly of people would be strictly controlled by the Egyptian state, as well as a new NGO law that gave the government a vast array of power to repress and close such organisations (Human Rights Watch, 2013a). Morsi hence not only continued SCAF's repressive juridification of the public sphere, thereby structurally violating the principle of intersubjective parity, but also did so under an Islamist cultural veneer. As this interviewee remarked:

> Morsi and his Muslim Brothers, they dominated all the political scene. They wanted to have, they wanted to dominate all positions in the state. They wanted to they didn't really believe in pluralism. Political pluralism. They didn't even believe in dialogue – a real national dialogue with the opposition. Although we really don't have any opposition. I don't like to say that they are a sham opposition, but some of them are a sham opposition. You know many of them. So, but even Morsi certainly didn't pay attention to the opposition and he continued to fulfil the Muslim Brotherhood and their plan of dominating and Ikhwanizing the society and government. [. . .] Ikhwanizing is really different from Islamizing the society. Because you know Islamisation is even it is a noble idea than Ikhwanizing the society. That's an evil idea. (Interview 9)

DIRECT PHYSICAL FORCE: TURNING VIOLENCE INWARDS

Needless to say, such instrumental attempts to colonise the political public sphere could not depend on formal proceduralism and the repressive juridification alone but also required a physical show of force. The trouble for the Brotherhood, however, was that, unlike SCAF before them, Morsi lacked sufficient power over the Egyptian security forces, which proved largely unwilling to adhere to the demands of an Islamist president. And so, the closure of political public space through physical force was mostly carried out by Brotherhood supporters themselves, thereby unleashing a downward spiral of civilian onto civilian violence that would come to characterise Morsi's rule. The first of these incidents took place in October 2012, when Morsi attempted to sack the prosecutor general. In show of support for their president, Brotherhood supporters took to the streets, but this gathering coincided with a protest by the oppositional activists who protested against the lack of political and economic progress during Morsi's hundred days.[3] In their strategic attempt to violently silence the opposition, Brotherhood supporters physically attacked the other protesters, ransacking the stage and destroying the sound installation – thereby unleashing civilian onto civilian clashes that lasted for several hours and resulted in 110 injuries. While this was a relatively small-scale event, in comparison with what was still to come, it commenced a dynamic wherein civilians fought civilians.

However, it was in the aftermath of the presidential declaration that we see a real turning point in the nature of violence in Egypt. This was the presidential decree wherein Morsi attempted to immunise his decisions against legal challenge. Protesting Morsi's immunisation, revolutionary activists commenced a sit-in just outside the presidential palace in the area of Heliopolis in December 2012. However, rather than de-escalating the situation, the Brotherhood drove buses full of their supporters to the site of the sit-in. This unleashed an extremely violent battle wherein 10 people died and 748 were injured as the police stood by and watched the scene unfold. These clashes marked a radical change in Egypt's post-revolutionary violence: people were now no longer fighting Egypt's security state as such but rather each other as violence turned inwards into society. Many interviewees thus relayed experiencing a deep sense of shock as the people they once loved and socialised with were now the ones with whom they were engaged in such ferocious violence. As this person remarked:

> I'm always used to conflict and violence from the police, from the army, but what I saw around the palace in December 2012 was traumatic, shocking, so ehm . . . I mean I. . . . It is very hard to see one of your friends, or those who used to be your friends, like . . . I won't say that they are shooting us or anything like that because very few number of them were using weapons, but almost every one of them was throwing stones, being violent with us . . . so imagine that anyone of them could be your friend [. . .], your neighbour, your brother even. And what made me more shocked that I . . . I always used to be a pacifist, peaceful . . . I did not like violence or conflict or anything like that but that day I was shocked even by my reaction to that. After the Islamists were attacking us, I started attacking back, throwing stones back and I was shocked at my reaction afterwards. I went back home, wondering how I did that. How everything turns me into this, into this violent person, so ehm. That was kind of the turning point for me. (Interview 1)

After the presidential clashes, violence was no longer contained to just clashes but rather increasingly spread into the daily fabric of everyday life itself. The violent infliction of intersubjective imparity thus became part of the social realm as friends, colleagues, acquaintances and loved ones now openly fought each other on the street, at cafés and in their homes. Hence, interviewees were no longer only subjected to traumatic status subordination at the hands of Egypt's authoritarian state but rather suffered multilevelled traumatic status subordination as their intersubjective parity was violently violated in the social realm too, leaving them in a deep state of disorientation and isolation (see Part 3). As their relations of trust severed and became marked by radical unsafety and violence, activists lost their ability to manifest in and make sense of the world, throwing them ever deeper into a state of depoliticised alienation.

Hence, the inward turn of violence during Morsi's rule had a deep counter-revolutionary effect: it severed intersubjective relations it destroyed the potential of revolutionary collective becoming. It served the counter-revolutionary goals of (seemingly) destroying the challenge to the Brotherhood rule in the short-term, but ended up fundamentally undermining relations of trust (through a downward spiral of ever more violent polarisation), which hampered the possibility of a revolutionary uprising in the longer term – and thus directly served the interests of the military. What the Brotherhood perhaps underestimated is that these violations of intersubjective parity did not so much protect as undermine their rule in the longer term: it precisely ended up feeding the grievances that the military-cum-business elite later capitalised on when it moved towards ousting Mohammed Morsi from his presidential office.

The primary grievances against the Brotherhood included the strategic (authoritarian) colonisation of the public sphere, its 'Ikhwanisation' of society, and also that in its instrumental political orientation it resorted to both conspirational victim blaming and ever-increasing violence. For, frustrated by the limitations to their political power (and particularly the obstacles put in place by both the military and the judiciary), the Brotherhood increasingly adopted a frame of conspirational victim blaming wherein they regarded *all* oppositional voices as instruments of the deep state (including those who had in fact always fervently objected to any cooperation with the military). The Brotherhood, hence, not only rhetorically demonised oppositional protesters as immoral thugs, prostitutes and infidels but also directly encouraged their civilian supporters to inflict physical violence on them.

And so, in the spring of 2013, polarised violence spiralled out of control, with violent battles of all sorts of shapes and sizes occurring anywhere at any time between the Brotherhood and oppositional protesters often occurring weekly. Activists were disturbed not only by the levels of grave violence inflicted from both sides but also how hatred and a desire for the actual annihilation of the Other became a prominent feature of everyday life, setting in motion bloody cycles of revenge.

A notable example of such violence were the Moqattam clashes which took place outside the Brotherhood headquarters in that area in March 2013. On the 22nd of March, anti-Brotherhood protesters marched onto the headquarters in protest to a female demonstrator being beaten by Brotherhood supporters during a smaller demonstration one week earlier – and to object to the fact that the Brotherhood 'undemocratically dominated the political sphere in post-revolution Egypt' (El-Dabh, 2013). During this march, violent clashes unfolded wherein the Brotherhood captured and tortured its opponents inside a mosque. They captured the well-known labour activist Kamal Khalil who

> saw for himself a number of demonstrators who had been stripped of their clothes and savagely flogged until most of them lost consciousness. The Brothers were

> using a large whip to beat their victims. Kamal questioned the owner of the whip who turned to him with pride and said: 'I've been soaking this whip in oil for a long time. One hit from this takes off the skin.' (Al Aswany, 2015: 400)

This event marked the beginning of the 'public' manifestation of torture under the Muslim Brotherhood, wherein torture was no longer confined to police cells and military detention places but was carried out by Muslim Brother vigilantes in public spaces including mosques and street corners (Al-Aswany, 2013; al Nadeem, 2013). This 'normalisation' of torture had a deeply shattering effect on activists. As this interviewee narrated:

> It was a bit of shock, because we were used to the policemen doing torture, the army doing torture . . . the politicians doing torture like military police also for intelligence or whatever but for normal people like here in the streets torturing people who they think are thugs or whatever, different from them, dehumanising people by other people is really shocking. (Interview 22)

The manifestation of torture by civilians not only subjected the victim to incapacitating traumatic status subordination during the moment of its infliction but was itself part of the wider infliction of polarised political violence in the social sphere. As chapter 10 (Part 3) explains in more detail, as social relations became increasingly mired in everyday, unpredictable, random violence, many experienced a deep and overwhelming state of existential anxiety and alienation. Not only did they, in the face of such pervasive intersubjective imparity, experience a deep sense of alienation (as in Rahel Jaeggi's sense of the inability to manifest oneself in the world (Jaeggi, 2014)), which now appears to stand over and above them but also a deep existential fear as no place was safe from violence and chaos. Hence, the inward societal turn of violence under Morsi created the conditions (or, experience of 'chaos') wherein a possible return of the military became increasingly acceptable and the experiment with Brotherhood 'civilian' rule was regarded as a failure.

Morsi, activists agreed, had been a phenomenal failure – with many even referring to him as an idiot or even an imbecile that they were embarrassed having to listen to him. As this young man commented:

> Morsi was phenomenal. [. . .] I think history will stop in front of Morsi in terms of the comic material and the satire material that he provided for the Egyptian society. He was a very fertile ground for satire and [. . .] I think Morsi left a heritage behind him in that we can still continue to laugh about him and these things. (Interview 24)

NEOLIBERAL ECONOMIC RATIONALISM

Perceptions of Morsi's incompetency were also reinforced by the lack of economic progress during his rule. In fact, as this interviewee put it:

> It is worse, it is even worse. Salaries is not that good, life is more expensive, life is more expensive, everything is more expensive and people are suffering more and more. You don't talk about it in Cairo, you just go to one of the villages, you go there they really suffer. And I know some families who live there a month without . . . they are Egyptians who are hungry. . . . And they don't care about revolution or who gets the presidency or not, so all these people died for nothing and all these people will die also for nothing. And this gets me like no hope. I feel there is no hope. (Interview 3)

Indeed, under Morsi Egyptians suffered a further economic decline, wherein many saw their livelihoods disappear into thin air and found themselves sinking into ever greater poverty. Egypt was suffering such a rapid economic downturn that fears were emerging it would suffer the same economic crisis that Egypt experienced in the 1970s and 1980s, when Mubarak eventually had to declare bankruptcy (Mahmoud, 2013) Under Morsi, Egypt experienced a decline 'in GDP growth, a reduction in foreign reserves and a sharp increase in unemployment' (Financial Post, 2013), while inflation skyrocketed and Egyptians experienced grave shortages of essential goods and services (notably including fuel and electricity) which resulted in a black-market surge (Hanke, 2013).

Perhaps this is not altogether surprising given the fact that, like SCAF before him, Morsi basically continued Mubarak's path of neoliberal economics, albeit this time with an Islamist veneer. The Brotherhood were not principled objectors to neoliberal economics as such, nor did they advocate structural redistribution inequality as such. Hence, rather than seeking an economic overhaul or re-evaluating Egypt's grave maldistribution as such, they merely advocated a form of 'pious neoliberalism'. They believed that the problem in Egypt's economic model lay not in its systematic inequality but in its corruption, which could be rectified through the adoption of an Islamic pious attitude. And so, they advocated pious neoliberalism wherein religious practices are reframed so as 'to depict economic rationality, productivity and privatization as part of what it meant to be religious' (Gamal, 2019: 3).

An important figure in the formulation of this economic vision was of course Khairat al Shater, a famous Brotherhood business tycoon (who had in fact also been the Brotherhood's first choice as a presidential candidate).

Al Shater was the mastermind behind the Brotherhood's economic vision (the 'Renaissance Project') and played a crucial role in ousting more left-wing Brotherhood figures such as Abdel Moneim Abdel Fotouh from the Brotherhood (Howeidy, 2012). Wealthy businessmen, such as Khairat al Shater and Hassan Malak, were not only formative in the development of the Brotherhood's neoliberal outlook but also well integrated with the networks of the upper-class business elite in Egypt that included Mubarak's cronies (Roll, 2013: 14). They not only sought to appease relations with Mubarak's business elite before Morsi's election but also attempted to align their interests with that of this business elite during his rule (or vice versa).

Morsi's government thus emphasised the need to attract foreign investors, lower subsidies on essential goods and increase the free market's hand by further privatisation of key strategic and public sectors (Gamal, 2019: 4). Moreover, Morsi set up the Egyptian Business Development Association (EBDA) which actively tried to persuade Mubarak's businessmen that had fled Egypt due to corruption charges to return (Gamal, 2019: 4). A key role in these negotiations with 'members of the business elite under suspicion of corruption or already facing prosecution' (Roll, 2013: 17) and the presidency was also played by the Tawasul (intercession) employers committee which was set up by Morsi in July 2012. This committee led negotiations with notorious figures such as Hussein Salem and Rashid Mohammed Rashid, the trade and industry minister under Mubarak's Nazif government.

Moreover, while the Brotherhood previously criticised the IMF as 'selling Egypt and its Egypt's wealth' (Gamal, 2019: 4), Morsi's government now actively

> adopted pillars of the neoliberal approach. It prioritized economic growth and slashing public debt. It resumed negotiations with the IMF over a recue loan and agreed to an austerity package that included raising the price of energy and public services. In March 2012, the Brotherhood's parliamentarians met with an IMF delegation and supported a loan deal. (Gamal, 2019: 4)

Similarly, while in 2004 it had opposed the Qualified Industrialised Zones agreement with the United States and Israel, wherein 11 per cent of all Egypt's exports would have to be produced in Israel, once in power the Brotherhood not only supported it but even travelled to Washington to try and expand it (Gamal, 2019: 4). This cosying up to the international financial order and Mubarak's business elite was regarded by activists as yet another indication of deep revolutionary betrayal. They fundamentally betrayed the calls for a systematic overhaul of Egypt's economic system, so that the problem of maldistribution may be addressed. Instead, economically, Morsi gave Egyptians more of the same, because as this your person remarked:

> They [the Brotherhood] basically understood that the Mubarak regime is still powerful, they still have a lot of money, and networks of power and circles of power. So instead of trying to unite, with like you know the youth groups to try and dismantle the Mubarak regime, they decided to unite with the Mubarak regime to dismantle the youth groups and the revolutionaries. (Interview 8)

The trouble for the Brotherhood was that the appeasement of Mubarak's business elite was at best only partially successful because most businessmen remained deeply suspicious of the Islamist current and founded their own secular 'liberal' political organisations instead,[4] while it increased revolutionary grievances against Morsi's rule.

Such grievances were furthermore aggravated when the Brotherhood violently cracked down on the workers' movements and labour strikes – the latter of which had in fact doubled during Morsi's rule. Morsi's government took a 'tough stand on those who "obstruct the wheels of production." In the months following Morsi's appointment, riot police broke up labor protests and arrested local strike organisers, while public sector employees found engaging in collective actions were fired, transferred or referred to disciplinary hearings' (McGrath, 2013). Moreover, instead of fostering independent labour unions (essential as they are to substantive democratisation), Morsi ensured that he 'acquired direct influence on the leadership appointments in the state-controlled Egyptian Trade Union Federation (ETUF)' (Roll, 2013). For activists, this repression of the workers' movement also constituted yet another layer in the betrayal of intersubjective parity, as the ideal of equal redistribution was exchanged for the Brotherhood's pursuit of political and economic power.

And so, the Brotherhood's adoption of both an instrumental political and neoliberal economic vision violently betrayed intersubjective parity and ended up feeding its own demise as grievances increased. As this interviewee put it, it led to the perception that 'Egypt used to be a corrupt state under Mubarak, and under SCAF it became a soft state and under Morsi it became a collapsed or a failed state' (interview 7). And in any case, as we will see, with the continuation of multilevelled traumatic status subordination that encompassed the tripartite mechanisms of political colonisation, physical violence and neoliberal marginalisation, the Brotherhood not only aided the undoing of revolutionary unity and solidarity but also created fertile soil for the primary counter-revolutionary actor, the military, to return to Egypt's political scene as the saviour of national stability and security.

NOTES

1. Private correspondence with interviewee 27, June 2020
2. On the internal debates on this controversial declaration inside the Brotherhood as well as political parties, see Khalifa (2015: 145–147).
3. At the start of his rule, Morsi had promised significant improvements in the first 100 days – which given the deep structural problems Egypt was facing was of course bound to fail and result in great disappointment (el Sharnouby, 2012).
4. A notable example here is the Free Egypt movement of business tycoon Naguib Sawaris.

Chapter 7

The Military's Deadly Return

TAMAROD AND THE 30 JUNE PROTESTS

As the previous chapters explained, the Brotherhood had hesitantly joined the revolutionary upheaval, and was always part of what Joshua Stacher calls the systemic opposition rather than the anti-systemic revolutionary opposition (Stacher, 2020). Hence, the revolution above all offered the Brotherhood with a golden opportunity to finally achieve its long desired goal of actual political power. And so, in this strategic pursuit of political and economic power, the Brotherhood not only entered into a counter-revolutionary marriage of convenience with the military but when this relationship soured during Morsi's rule also repeated the tripartite structure of traumatic status subordination. It not only adopted an increasingly suspicious viewpoint, wherein all opposition including the anti-systemic ones were regarded as part of the deep state, but also attempted to colonise the political sphere, inflicted grave physical violence and pursued its own agenda of Islamist neoliberalisation. With this continuation of traumatic status subordination, and the military hiding in the background waiting to jump on the opportunity to regain political power. the seeds of Morsi's destruction were laid.

The start of Morsi's actual undoing may be traced back to the Tamarod campaign which arose in the spring of 2013. Tamarod was initially a grassroots petition movement that called for early elections and was founded by five activists from the earlier Kifaya movement (and led by Mahmoud Badr, Moheb Doss, Walid el Masry, Mohammed Abdel Aziz and Hassan Shahin) (Jumet, 2018: 181). It expressed dissatisfaction with Morsi's government, demanded Morsi's resignation and called for early presidential elections through a signature campaign that the organisers claimed reached 15 million signatures.

What was unknown to many at the time, however, was that this grassroots campaign had soon been infiltrated and co-opted by the military and the security apparatus. The Ministry of Interior not only actively helped to collect signatures, it also provided tactical and logistical advice for the protests that Tamarod organised on the 30th of June 2013. It also 'helped' drafting its televised statements, wherein Tamarod's call for a peaceful democratic transition was suddenly replaced by 'a request for the army to step in to protect the people from terrorists and chaos' (Jumet, 2018: 187). As the other organisers began to attend frequent meetings with Sisi and the Ministry of Interior, Ahmed Doss came to realise that 'army and security officials slowly but steadily began exerting an influence over Tamarod, seizing upon the group's reputation as a grassroots revolutionary movement to carry out their own schemes for Egypt' (Jumet, 2018: 187; Frenkel and Atef, 2014). Later, rapports also emerged that elite businessmen from Mubarak's era in fact funded the initiative – with Naguib Sawaris (the owner of Orascom) transferring nothing less than $28 million to the campaign (Jumet, 2018: 187). Hence, while Tamarod outwardly appeared as a grassroots movement led by the people (and may have indeed started as such), it was in fact deeply infiltrated by the feloul (Mubarak regime supporters) and Egypt's security apparatus, who were 'hoping to regain power through an overthrow of the Islamist government' (Jumet, 2018: 187).

Egypt's security apparatus, working in tandem with Mubarak's business elite, manipulated and capitalised on increased grievances, polarisation and the 'sectarian chaos' that had increased during Morsi's one-year rule. The business elite employed its media outlets to step up a violent anti-Brotherhood rhetoric, wherein the Brotherhood were depicted not only as sheep and religious idiots but also as 'terrorists belonging to a foreign entity' (which was mostly a reference to Hamas). Yet, Brotherhood for its part also increased polarisation through the demonisation of all protesters. It invited hateful religious sheikhs to its talk show programmes, while its supporters formed sectarian lynch mobs that attacked other religious minorities (predominantly Shia and Christian civilians) whom they accused of working with the deep state.

This deeply polarised 'chaotic' political climate provided the perfect setting wherein the military could put itself forward as the necessary saviour of national unity and security. And so, on the 23rd of June, Sisi warned that if matters would not be resolved, the army would interfere – since 'the armed forces have the obligation to intervene to stop Egypt from plunging into a dark tunnel of conflict and infighting' (al Arabiya, 2013). Morsi, unwilling to budge, dismissed calls for an early presidential election and adopted a conspirational frame of reference: he blamed protesters for harming the Egyptian economy, argued thugs were spreading chaos in the streets and stated 'unknown enemies' were harming the path of constitutional legitimacy he was not willing to deviate from this (Khalifa, 2015: 166; Jumet, 2018: 191). Indeed, on the 2nd of July, he issued a speech wherein he reiterated the 'legitimacy' of his own position fifty-seven times – therein always relying on a technocratic understanding of formal democratic procedures rather than a substantive notion of an inclusive deliberative democracy, characterised by plurality, diversity and intersubjective parity.

Hence, on the 30th of June, millions of Egyptians protested against Morsi and the army eventually disposed Morsi on the 3rd of July, placing him under house arrest. Most interviewees were deeply ambivalent about the 30 June protests. While they were happy that it meant an end to Brotherhood rule, which had betrayed the primary revolutionary goals, they were also deeply concerned about the prospect of a military takeover. As this person commented:

> I was extremely happy, I was super happy with what happened on June 30th, I was with the Itehedya, the sit ins for 4 days I had my tent, going to work and afterwards I used to sit with my friends because we were working. I was very with what happened [. . .] But to be honest, [. . .] I don't want to be ruled by generals at the end of the day. And enough generals in our life! Enough generals, it is too much. It is getting on my nerves. How come the spokesperson for the Egyptian football federation is a general? Why? Why on earth? So, enough generals and enough sheikhs. We don't want sheikhs or generals. Khalas, we want normal people to govern and rule the country. (Interview 11)

However, interviewees experienced a marked difference between the uprising in January 2011 and 30 June: while the former offered a critique of the Mubarak regime in the pursuit of collective ideals of social and political justice, the 30th of June only offered a negative critique. As this person continued:

> A lot of times . . . I am afraid . . . there are two types of fear for me. I mean more than two types, but I'll tell you about two and one of them is the fear of being killed or harmed and there is a fear of being defeated. Fear of being harmed is . . . there a lot and fear of friends being harmed is a lot. People go out and you don't know. . . . But there is a fear I have been experiencing as well. . . . The death of the revolution. That's a bigger fear for me. That June 30th overrides January 25th. And it's not any jealousy or anything. June 30th is certainly the biggest protest that I've ever seen personally and I've been to a lot of big protest. I am not contending that but they called *against* Morsi, they didn't call *for* anything. And January 25th for me is all about calls for freedom, for all these . . . chants that we had. So, I fear that all our accomplishments are rolled back already public space has been taken away from us, I fear that you know. . . .

> That's currently my biggest fear. There is not June 30th revolution for me – it's a protest, it's just protesting something. And that's it. What else do you want? Really June 30th is fine you got what you wanted. I didn't get what I wanted from January 25th. (Interview 11)

For indeed, while the 25th of January revolutionary uprising was premised on the pursuit of achieving intersubjective parity – through an end of misrecognition and maldistribution – by the time the 30 of June came, all such ideals appeared to have disappeared. The protest was merely against Morsi's rule and the Brotherhood but arguably failed to articulate more positive goals. And so, unfortunately, this interviewee's worries were warranted.

THE RABAA MASSACRE

Initially, after the 30th June protests, the Egyptian military created an inclusive, democratic image of itself as it created an interim government led by the Head of the Constitutional Court (Adly Mansour) and entailing representatives from all parts of Egyptian society (including the Coptic Church, Al Azhar, the liberal, social democratic and Salafist political parties). However, the military's violent, self-interested instrumentalist orientation soon violently cracked through the veneer of democratic civility with the massacres at Ennahda and Rabaa squares on 14 August 2013. Brotherhood supporters had staged a sit-in on these squares in support of Morsi's 'legitimacy' since the 2nd of July 2013. Then, in the early morning of 14 August 2013, the military and Egyptian security forces descended onto the squares, closed off the exits and fired on everyone and everything inside. In this frenzied attack, they threw teargas into the area, bulldozed the tents and shot at anyone inside the camps, as well as those trying to flee. They ended up killing more than thousand people and wounding thousands more (HRW, 2014). Interviewees present at this bloody scene, described their harrowing experience as follows:

> They were . . . they corned us in a place, just a square just like this. In this place there were many corners, five corners and if I walk in any place I will be shot – by a sniper. We were in a real battle – noises of explosions and ehm . . . bullets are everywhere . . . and each minute, every minute I see a dead people and people are trying to get it to be healed and solved . . . Ehm, that was for maybe 8 hours or so. . . . They shot us not only by sniper, but they used, if you know – that is a gun by a military carting, a huge gun, that is a big gun. And they shot us from helicopters and there is a video that show the helicopter, the apache, I don't know what it is and it is shooting us. They were . . . when they met us, we hear them telling us 'you serve the Syrian people and we are Egyptian' they were telling them that you are terrorists that you are Syrian people you are not

Egyptian. That we have different agendas. So they were so angry of us. And we saw one of them that is not even holding a gun. And another person, his face is not hidden, so they know we are not holding guns. They know we are not holding anything. But they are filled up with anger of us, so they killed us with all of this ugliness. (Interview 15)

Interviewees present at Rabaa and Ennahda described the most horrific scenes, wherein loved ones and friends were shot right before their eyes, and corpses were gathered at nearby mosques which soon overflowed. One young woman narrated how relatives desperate to find their deceased loved ones in a nearby mosque had to wade through soggy carpets filled with a mixture of water and blood, as blocks of ice had been put on top of the bodies in the attempt to keep the process of decay at bay. It was round 40 degrees Celsius outside, and she described how the stench and sights of these places continue to haunt her to this day. Hence, those who attended Rabaa or Ennahda and experienced the massacre firsthand were left in a deep state of disorientation: they were subjected to such overwhelming deadly violence that many struggled to make sense of the world around them (also see chapter 10).

Moreover, even those who did not attend were greatly affected. Within a context of increasing (violent) political polarisation, revolutionary activists who did not affiliate themselves with the Brotherhood (and were in fact often deeply opposed to them) nevertheless also experienced a deep sense of estrangement, albeit a slightly different one perhaps. Critical of the Brotherhood's policies during Morsi's rule, wherein their own intersubjective parity had been systematically violated, they were reluctant to accept what they regarded as the Brotherhood's purposeful construction of a victim status. Yet at the same time, there was no doubt that the Brotherhood had just been subject to one of the greatest massacres in recent Egyptian history – and indeed that this massive infliction of death appeared to be celebrated by many people around them. Many interviewees struggled to make sense of this and found that it not only alienated them politically but also resulted in the severance of intersubjective relations, as trust had been fundamentally betrayed by the Brotherhood, the military and those who celebrated death.

Furthermore, politically, Rabaa and Ennahda are a prime example of the military's violent concealed strategic action, as the massacres served a four-fold counter-revolutionary purpose. First, through these mass annihilations, the military not only asserted an overwhelming (deadly) power relation over the Muslim Brotherhood but in doing so ruptured the potentiality of mass protest. That is, the military violently showed not only that it is the superior, most powerful, actor on Egypt's political scene, but also that it was willing to inflict mass murder on those who posed an obstacle to its economic and political interests. The military subjected the Brotherhood leadership and its supporters to a horrific form of traumatic status subordination as it violently, indeed murderously, manifested its annihilating will to power. It thereby not only eradicated the Brotherhood from the political public sphere but also sent out a clear signal to all those who might consider objecting to the military's rule: it was no longer afraid to use deadly force on a scale unseen before. As one young woman later explained, the massive infliction of death was the final nail in the coffin of revolutionary protest. Not only would the military no longer hesitate to impose mass murder on any group that protested, but these mass killings themselves directly followed Sisi's call for Egyptian people to enter onto the streets to legitimise the fight against terrorism on 24 July 2013 (Kingsley, 2013). It thus directly 'associated street protest with death and mass murder' in all possible ways.[1] The Rabaa massacre thus managed to do nothing less than to turn the revolutionary idealism of the 25th of January directly on its head: while during the eighteen days protest stood for the prefigurative manifestation of intersubjective parity, with Rabaa it became synonymous with the greatest infliction of intersubjective imparity: the mass murder of life.

Second, in the heat of counter-revolutionary polarisation between the Brotherhood and the military, the voices of those who identified with neither (and instead sought revolutionary transformation) were completely marginalised from the public terrain. With Rabaa, the political playing field was solidified as a dichotomous battlefield between two major political actors, the Brotherhood and the military. And so, any protest or demonstration that did occur remained strictly bound to this dichotomy (consisting of either pro-military or Brotherhood supporters), and further marginalised alternative (revolutionary) voices. Hence, within Egypt's post-Rabaa political reality, those who were neither in favour of the military nor the Brotherhood were ever deeper alienated as they identified neither with the military nor with the Brotherhood and its supporters. As this activist put it: 'The two big elephants are fighting, and we are grass that is being trampled' (interview 38). Or, as this young man remarked:

> I don't believe in any side right now. I'm fed up. I feel like all sides are . . . Because political actions only works or demonstration only work if you have an extreme – meaning wise. [. . .] I'm not Ikhwani, I'm not going to protest. Even though I think you might be on the right on some things. But you already alienated the middle. The middle is always alienated. Why? Because political action and political – unfortunately the middle always stands there waiting for which side to grab it. Extremes grab it. [. . .] I'm not gonna protest for a military protest according to the military. No way. I'm not going to support for the Ikhwanian either. No way. Because that's an extreme and that's an extreme. (Interview 2)

Squeezed between these two violent polar opposites, activists were unable to manifest themselves in the public sphere at the very moment they saw their revolutionary ideals being destroyed through counter-revolutionary purposeful action. Being speechless and alienated, many started to withdraw from political activities, the political sphere and even political conversations (see chapter 10). They cut themselves off not only from their political engagements but also from their friends, relatives and loved ones as conversations frequently ended up in political arguments and physical fights. Exasperated and experiencing a deep sense of demoralisation, they retreated into their own protective (depoliticised) atomised shells – trying to cut themselves off (at least for as much as possible) from the violent cacophony of noise around them.

Activists were not the only ones who retreated from the public terrain, so did political actors such as Mohamed El Baradei and Ziad Bahaa El Din. While El Baradei, Egypt's vice president, resigned as soon as he heard about the massacre,[2] Ziad Bahaa El Din resigned a few months later publicly citing the completion of his part in the new constitutional drafting[3] while internal circles knew this decision to have been made much earlier (interview 27). They both left in protest to the Rabaa massacre and the direction of political developments the military was pursuing in Egypt. For, the Rabaa massacre was a concealed strategic action par excellence as the military did not even inform the government in advance of its intended actions. The vice president was at this stage still seeking political and diplomatic ways out of the impasse with the Brotherhood. Knowing about these diplomatic efforts, General Abdel Fattah El Sisi nevertheless ignored them, went behind the government's back and inflicted one of the greatest mass killings in Egyptian history. Sisi thereby inaugurated his politics of death (see chapter 8), through which he not only inflicted grave political injury on the Brotherhood but also instrumentally ousted his political opponents from Egypt's formal public sphere. With his opponents out of the way, Sisi was able to put forward the (populist) claim that in the absence of political alternatives, he was left with no choice but to respond to the call of the people. He thus put himself forward for presidential elections in January 2014.

And lastly, the Rabaa massacre resulted in a wave of Islamist retributive violence, as Egypt became locked in a downward spiral of increased violent polarisation and destructive cycles of revenge. Revenge entails the attempt to regain intersubjective power vis-à-vis another (individual or group) using violent means after one suffered status subordination (wherein one's powerlessness was reinforced)[4]. Revenge may directly target the perpetrator but also be redirected elsewhere – onto subjects taken to represent the perpetrator or those associated with the perpetrator. Importantly, revenge is thus both the outcome and the continuation of a distorted mode of communicative action typified by status subordination. Hence, after Rabaa, what we see is a flurry of Islamist retributive violence directed not only at both the institutions of Egypt's security state (such as police stations and military camps) but also those the Islamists deemed to be colluding with the military (such as Christians and other minority groups). This cycle of revenge was fed by a dichotomous Islamist understanding of the political situation, wherein events were interpreted as constituting a battle between the religious 'good' and the infidel 'evil'. And so, in light of such overwhelming (deadly) status subordination, collective rage was turned into revenge directed at those deemed complicit with the military or security forces.

They also explained that the military's incarceration of the Brotherhood leadership intensified this wave of violence: the upper echelons of the Brotherhood now largely lost control over a section of the younger Brotherhood generation who increasingly resorted to more radical Islamist groups (such as Al Beit al Ansar Maqdis, which later joined ISIS) in an effort of post-Rabaa meaning-making. It was of course not only the leadership but also Brotherhood supporters (and indeed those merely present at the Rabaa and Ennahda sit-ins) who found themselves flung into Egypt's prisons. This incarceration, often accompanied by torture, abuse, medical negligence and terrible prison conditions, had a deeply radicalising effect on many of those prisoners. As this young Brother explained: 'Let me tell you that those who get imprisoned comes out knowing he is more stronger and has more energy to go after his rights and had a belief in the cause' (interview 20). Or, as this other young Brother stated:

> With Rabaa, you are building the terrorists, these people, after all this oppression, of course you can see people who are killing others because of all this oppression we have seen. So I'm afraid, for a long time with this oppression actually we can see the real terrorist. (Interview 15)

And so, the trouble is that Rabaa reified a violent, oppositional interpretative framework and thus directly contributed to a violent intensification of social and political polarisation, wherein one side 'glorifies the army as the fighter, the warrior against terrorism' and the other side 'glorifies the brotherhood as victims of the coup' (Interview 35). Such violent polarisation of the political public sphere not only structurally marginalises alternative, revolutionary, voices from the public terrain, it also constitutes the 'violent chaos' and social-political discord that Sisi's regime is premised upon. It was against the backdrop of precisely this increased Islamist political violence that Sisi was able to project himself as the 'saviour of the nation' and claim the necessity of his extremely violent repressive measures.

This construction of Sisi as the 'saviour of the nation' was aided by a Sisi-mania that swept through the country wherein a personalist, populist cult was carefully manufactured around the figure of El Sisi himself (France24, 2013). Shops sold Sisi jewellery, Sisi t-shirts, Sisi chocolates and biscuits, Sisi perfume, Sisi underwear and even fake Sisi id-cards which stated that his profession was 'the saviour of Egypt' and listed his address as 'the presidential office' (Jumet, 2018). Hence, post-Rabaa, an El Sisi's 'cult' following was created which included numerous billboards and posters with his image; military-themed weddings; El Sisi portraits; military cups, flags and pins; portrayals of El Sisi as a superhero; and the likening of El Sisi to a Prophet of God (Kurzman, 2014). In a typical populist fashion, Sisi was simultaneously depicted as a God-like masculine hero who would save the nation from Islamist violence, as well as an ordinary man of piety who is one with ordinary Egyptians. As this Sisi hype got hold of the public sphere, the streets and residential apartment buildings were plastered with posters of Sisi next to a lion, and pro-military songs such as 'Teslem al Ayadi' (May those hands be safe) rung from every street corner, as it had by now become a popular mobile phone ringtone (Jumet, 2018). Unsurprisingly, within this setting, most revolutionary interviewees whom neither identified with the military nor with the Brotherhood experienced a deep sense of demoralised alienation, wherein all hope for meaningful change had dissipated into thin air. Unable to alter or influence the social and political reality around them, they increasingly withdrew into their private, depoliticised, atomising shell of social isolation (see Part 3).

NOTES

1. Interview in Berlin with Egyptian exile, March 2019.
2. Reuters (2016).
3. Ahram Online (2014b).
4. Also see chapter 10.

Chapter 8

Abdel Fattah El Sisi

The Politics of Traumatic Status Subordination

Sisi's authoritarian rule violated intersubjective parity so gravely that it destroyed the *possibility* of creative or revolutionary aspirations. As this interviewee noted:

> My life in Egypt is on hold. Sisi put a suffocating blanket over us. We cannot breath, we cannot see. I feel disorientated. There is no direction, no purpose. Nothing. I don't know what to do. Why should I live? I mean, I cannot live. My life is on pause, I am not living and I am not dead. I am in between. I am nowhere. I have no life. My life has been put on pauze . . . muted. . . . But, for how long do I have to wait? There is no end in sight. We have lost not only the revolution but our lives. There is no life in Egypt, only death – or, this Zombie like state. And people accept this, this is the new normal. And often I think that I am the one insane. I need to get out. I need to be able to breath and see.[1]

Unfortunately, this young person will not be able to leave Egypt anytime soon, due to the travel restrictions Sisi's regime imposed on him informally (thus also outside the bounds of any legal challenge). Should this person go to the airport to try and leave the country, the risk would be incarceration in Egypt's expanding prison complex (which includes one directly underneath the airport in Cairo) and being subjected to the life-destroying, grinding mill of Egypt's corrupted judicial system, and Sisi's expanding prison complex.

Yet, these words provide a clear illustration of the deep existential impacts of Sisi's authoritarian rule, wherein the structural, deep and relentless violation of intersubjective parity destroyed the potential of (collective) self-manifestation in the world. Under Sisi's rule, traumatic status subordination became so complete, so totalising, that many were left in a continuous state of traumatic alienation and disorientation. Unable to speak back at the injustices inflicted, the potential of meaning-making evaporated as their lifeworlds collapsed. When the counterfactual presupposition of intersubjective parity is so fundamentally and systematically betrayed, the lifeworld's symbolic order comes crushing down, giving rise to great existential disorientation, distress and alienation (or, the aforementioned zombie-like state). As a result, many interviewees experienced a depoliticised apathy, or rather, a demoralised retreat of hopelessness as Sisi's rise to power progressed.

Now, importantly, some of the materials discussed in this chapter on Sisi clearly transcend the timeline of the interviews. While the interviews were conducted between October 2013 and February 2014, which was the time Sisi started to rise to power, this chapter will discuss Sisi's repressive measures up to 2021. This move is, however, warranted as it indicates that the reality many activists believed to be transpiring in 2013/2014 turned out to be even worse.

For, it was under Sisi's rule that counter-revolutionary traumatic status subordination was completed. Sisi inflicted traumatic status subordination in exactly the same manner as Mubarak, SCAF and Morsi before him: namely through a tripartite structure of violence consisting of (1) formal political proceduralism (including both electorialism and repressive juridification), (2) the infliction of grave physical violence and (3) the intensification of neoliberal economic rationalism. The main difference between Sisi's regime and his predecessors was that he was able to enforce these measures much more forcefully due to his unriddled access to the security state apparatuses and due to the fragmented nature of Egypt's social and political spheres. And so, whereas SCAF was still hindered by the presence of revolutionary potentiality (since the memory of revolutionary pre-figuration was still fresh and (limited) forms of solidarity still spanned across social divisions) and Morsi was powerless due to his lack of access to (and control over) Egypt's security state, Sisi faced neither of these obstacles. Rather, the former minister of defense rose to power after the potential of social unity had already been successfully destroyed through counter-revolutionary violence. Hence, the path was clear for Sisi's unbridled infliction of traumatic status subordination that left activists in a total demoralised state. Not only had meaning, and the potential of meaning evaporated, under Sisi's rule they were literally continuously tinkering on the edge of (non)existence through his politics of death and the prisonification of society. Sisi thus basically completed the counter-revolutionary project of the re-atomisation of social and political life.

POLITICAL PROCEDURALISM: SISI'S COLONISATION OF THE POLITICAL PUBLIC SPHERE

The first tool through which Sisi imposed traumatic status subordination was the formal procedural colonisation of the political public sphere, wherein the intersubjective parity of Egyptian activists and others was structurally violated as they were marginalised, excluded and muted. As Joshua Stacher explains, Sisi pursued political formalism as a way not to increase public deliberation but rather instrumentally to expand his own and the military's political power over the public terrain (Stacher, 2020). The military's power was firstly greatly expanded through the new constitution that was drafted by a newly appointed committee set up by the post-Rabaa interim government – which was passed into law in January 2014 as it received 98 per cent of the vote (with a voter turn out of less than 39 per cent). In this constitution, the military was 'no longer treated as part of the executive branch of government but rather a branch unto itself' (Brown and Dunne, 2013). It provided the military with 'jurisdiction whenever they wish, such as in any area military officials declared a "military zone", and stipulated that the military will directly *appoint* the defence minister for at least the next two presidential terms' (Brown, 2013). Similarly, the constitution also rewarded the judiciary (which had been sympathetic to the military and its removal of the Brotherhood) with increasing autonomy: 'judicial bodies receive their budgets in a lump sum, the judicial council selects the prosecutor general, and each judicial body is granted autonomy' (Brown and Dunne, 2013). Yet, at the same time, the constitution directly restricted participation in the political public sphere by banning political activity that was based on religion. It also left the sequencing, structure and timing of parliamentary and presidential elections unclear (Brown and Dunne, 2013). It thereby conveniently opened the way for Sisi to put himself forward as a presidential candidate, which he did (after supposed hesitation) in March 2014.

In March 2014, Sisi resigned from the new military post he had been awarded in January and declared himself a candidate for the presidential elections that would take place 26–28 May 2014. In true populist fashion, Sisi claimed that, after a period of great hesitancy, he decided to listen to the people's demands and put himself forth as a presidential candidate. Yet the public terrain was carefully cleared of all political opponents as one presidential candidate withdrew from the electoral process after the other: while Khaled Ali cited moral reasons such as undue military interference in electoral politics, Ahmed Shafiq withdrew due to the likelihood of the electoral process displaying unethical behaviour (Ahram Online, 2014c). At the same time, Ayman Nour withdrew because, he stated, the situation resembled that of Mubarak (Gamal, 2014), while Amr Moussa retreated from the presidential race since he claimed to have seen that 'the people want Sisi' (Egypt Independent, 2014), and former SCAF general Sami Annan pulled out in order to ensure unity within the country as well as the military (Ahram Online, 2014a). Hence, two candidates remained in the 2014 presidential elections: Abdel Fattah El Sisi and the socialist Hamdeen Sabbahi. Sabbahi never formed a serious threat to Sisi's presidential race because he lacked

Sisi's connections to Mubarak's business elite. Hence, Sisi won the elections with 97 per cent of the votes (of a 47 percent voter turnout) and was inaugurated as Egypt's new president on 8 June 2014.

Yet, even after extending the elections with an extra day and cajoling voters to the polling booths, the turnout is still much lower than the 80 per cent Sisi had called for in the run-up to the elections. This might very well suggest that in the absence of meaningful political alternatives, military's depoliticisation campaign might have proven to be more successful than the construction of Sisi's own popularity. Or rather, 'Sisi's popularity may not be as universal as his allies claim' (Kingsley, 2014). In any case, the pressured resignations, the public praise of El Sisi as 'the chosen one' as well as the reports of large-scale rigging (wherein votes were likely exaggerated in favour of El Sisi) are all indicators of the ways in which electoral politics was instrumentally deployed to shrink Egypt's public political space (Sanyal, 2015: 284). That is, rather than being used to expand deliberative politics, formal electoral proceduralism was instead used to close Egypt's public space: it was reduced to an instrumental means of power.

Or rather, putting it in stronger Habermasian terms, it was a primary tool for the refeudalisation of Egypt's political public sphere (Habermas, 1991). In refeudalisation, political authority is merely displayed in front of the masses, who no longer play a constitutive but are reduced to passive spectators of the political scene that is unfolding in front of them (Habermas, 1992). Refeudalisation thus breaches intersubjective parity through the closure of political space and the exclusion of those affected and thus results in political alienation (understood as the inability to manifest oneself in the world (Jaeggi, 2014)).

This closure of the political public sphere continued unabated under Sisi's rise to power, as indicated by the 2015 parliamentary elections (which was held in two phases between 17 October and 2 December). As Serap Gur explains, these 'elections were dominated by two main groups: pro-regime supporters, and supporters of the Mubarak regime', which came together in the pro-Sisi coalition of 'For the Love of Egypt' (Gur, 2016: 462). In the absence of any meaningful choice, voter turnout reached a new low: a mere 28.3 per cent. Rather, with the procedural shrinkage of political space, and the structural violation of intersubjective parity, the political apathy that held sway under Mubarak was back in full swing. As Ahmed Moustafa, interviewed by *The Guardian* newspaper, stated, 'It's not going to matter. It's just for show, to show that we are a democracy, and we have elections' (Agence France-Press, 2015). Hazem Hosny remarked in the same newspaper: 'This parliament will be a parliament of the president. It's really a parliament . . . to keep things as they are, to give an image of democracy' (Agence France-Press, 2015). Again, formal electoralism was employed as a political instrument for the display of political power and to cast a veneer of supposed 'legitimacy' over Sisi's instrumental pursuit of his own political and economic power.² Again, elections were part of Sisi's refeudalisation of Egypt's public sphere, wherein the 'lord' merely displayed his power in front of the people. It deeply betrayed the necessity of intersubjective parity in the political sphere, as all Sisi's political opponents were structurally marginalised and violently subordinated.

This violent subordination only intensified as Sisi's rule progressed. For instance, in 2018, those that dared to put themselves forward as candidates in the presidential elections suffered direct physical violence and intimidation, which left all candidates (apart from Sisi himself) to withdraw from the electoral race. Ahmed Shafiq announced he would no longer run as a candidate since he was 'the wrong person for the job'. Notably, this was after he was captured by the Sisi-supporting government of the United Arab Emirates and flown back to Egypt, where he first disappeared before making this televised address (BBC News, 2018). Similarly, Mohamed Anwar Sadat (the nephew of Egypt's former president) withdrew his presidential campaign citing a climate of fear (Michaelson, 2018). Khaled Ali pulled out after the large-scale arrests and abuse of his supporters under so-called terrorism charges. And even Sami Annan, the military's former military chief of staff, was arrested three days after the announcement of his candidacy on the charges of inciting against the military and committing forgery and kept under house arrest (CBC News, 2018). A few days later, Sami Annan's aide Hisham Genena was also attacked and wounded by unidentified men outside his home on the outskirts of Cairo after appearing on television in favour of Annan (Reuters, 2018). And so, in the face of all this intimidation, Sisi would be the only presidential candidate left. That is, until Moussa Mustafa Moussa put himself forward as a contender at the very last minute (possibly to avoid the embarrassment of one candidate election). Moussa, however, presented himself as pro-Sisi and directly urged people to vote for Sisi in the presidential elections (Lotfi, 2018). Sisi employed the electoral process as merely an instrumental tool of displaying power, as a tool for the refeudalisation of the public sphere, wherein intersubjective parity was violently crushed and the communicative rational potential of deliberative politics undone. For him, formal procedural elections were nothing but a counter-revolutionary means to exclude alternative political voices from Egypt's political public sphere. It was a means to colonise the political public sphere and extend Sisi's authority.

This extension of repressive political power became especially apparent in the constitutional referendum, which took place from 20 to 22 April 2019. Firstly, within the context of this constitutional referendum, the Egyptian authorities arrested and detained over 160 perceived dissidents, threatened oppositional figures and blocked approximately 34,000 websites in order to curtail access to the 'Batel' (Void) campaign, which was critical of the proposed constitutional amendments. Secondly, the proposed amendments significantly expanded Sisi's formal political powers. It extended his presidential term from four to six years, thereby retrospectively adding another four years to his time in office. Furthermore, the amendments installed him as the head of the Supreme Council for Judicial Bodies and Authorities, which supervises and may intervene in the judiciary's affairs (including promotions and appointments). Sisi thus gained de facto control over the judiciary's composition. He also attained the power to appoint the chief justice of the SCC, the leader and members of the Commissioners Authority, the public prosecutor and and other positions (Human Rights Watch, 2020a). Notably, these amendments came after Sisi had already given himself the authority to choose the chief justice of the Court of Cassation, Egypt's highest appellate court, the heads of the Supreme Judicial Council (which was replaced by the above-mentioned Supreme Council for Judicial Bodies and Authorities) and the State Council which contains the country's Supreme Administrative Court, The State Lawsuits Authority and the Administrative Prosecution Authority (Human Rights Watch, 2019). In other words, Sisi thus directly destroyed any semblance of judicial independence and expanded his direct political control over this sector. He thereby directly contravened the 'fundamental rule of law principles concerning the separation of powers, the independence of the judiciary, and the right to a fair trial by a competent, independent, and impartial tribunal' (Human Rights Watch, 2019). To make matters even worse, Article 200 also tasks the military with the responsibility to protect constitution, democracy and the pillars of the state, which means that the 'military's position above the state by giving it legal means to intervene against elected governments and enhanced powers to prosecute its political opponents' (Mandour, 2019a). And so, under Sisi, formal political procedures of elections, constitutional drafting and constitutional amendments were employed not to safeguard the inclusivity of the political public sphere but rather to *close* Egypt's political public space. Through such formal means, Sisi closed Egypt's political space by systematically violated intersubjective parity and expanded his own and the military's political power.

REPRESSIVE JURIDIFICATION OF THE PUBLIC SPHERE

Similarly, to SCAF and Morsi before him, Sisi's procedural colonisation of the political public sphere was also advanced through the repressive juridification of the public sphere, which ensured that alternative voices were muted and that the potential for creative collective self-becoming was stilted. Through the banning of social and political movements, the imposition of Protest, Assembly and Anti-Terror legislation and the reinstatement of the state of emergency, Sisi violently closed Egypt's political space. Using these legal tools, he further subjected Egyptians to traumatic status subordination, wherein they would be left speechless in face of the intersubjective parity inflicted.

The first signs of such repressive juridification occurred immediately in the aftermath of Rabaa when the interim government banned not only 'vigilante groups' on the 19th of August but also explicitly prohibited the Muslim Brotherhoods existence on the 23rd of September. And on 25 December 2013, the Brotherhood was moreover declared a terrorist organisation. Following this declaration, clashes broke out wherein 5 people died and 295 were violently arrested (many of whom were subjected to serious maltreatment and tortured). Then on the 28th of April, Sisi's interim government also banned the revolutionary 6th April movement, which was an amalgamation of Muslim brothers, liberals, social democrats and others, on the spurious basis of 'espionage' and their alleged 'defaming the image of the state' (Kholaif, 2014). And as if his malicious intentions were not made clear enough during the mass killings of Rabaa and Ennahda, in the run up to the 2014 elections, Sisi also publicly vowed to finish off the Brotherhood should he be elected (Alkhshali, 2014).

Prior to this, Adly Mansour had also signed the Protest Law of 2013 into effect, which gave the Ministry of Interior 'wide discretionary powers over protests and lay[ed] out broad circumstances in which demonstrators can be found to violate the law' (Amnesty International, 2013). It not only stipulated that the Ministry of Interior has to be informed three days in advance of any protest, it also gave the Ministry of Interior the right to stop, delay, ban or move any protest as well as use excessive force in the dispersal of protests. Moreover, it greatly expanded these rights by stipulating that Egypt's security forces may legally use shotguns and rubber bullets not only in the protection of human life, as stipulated by international law, but also in the safeguarding of property and money, which, as Amnesty pointed out, is in direct violation of international law (Amnesty International, 2013).

Importantly, however, the legal foundation of this repressive Protest Law was the 'Assembly Law' (law 10/1914) which dated back to British colonial times. The Assembly Law was imposed by the Brits as a means of 'collective punishment and cordoning off the public sphere' (Hussin, 2017: 1). It 'consisted of five articles that criminalized any assembly of five or more persons if the public authorities deemed the assembly liable to disturb the peace' and imposed a prison sentence of up to two years upon such assemblies (Hussin, 2017: 3). The law was deeply draconian: the Brits regarded any assembly, even in the absence of a crime, as a direct disturbance of public peace (a concept which remained notoriously ill-defined). The law stipulated that the security forces were allowed to fire at protesters after just one oral warning, using small gauge shotguns, live ammunition arms and rapid-fire weapons. Furthermore, it 'upheld the notion of collective responsibility, [and] paved the way for collective mass sentencing' (Hussin, 2017: 31). While this law was repealed by the Egyptian parliament in 1928, it nevertheless continues to be in force until this day, and provided the foundation upon which Sisi pursued his wave of mass arrests and collective punishment in his instrumental pursuit of the violent closure of political public space. As the CIHRS writes, 'It is the Assembly Law then, rather than the Protest Law, which provides the basis for collectively punishing participation in a demonstration', while the Protest Law made it a separate crime to undertake 'a demonstration without a permit' (Hussin, 2017: 49). Hence, the '"assembly" is the first and principal charge brought against protestors; other crimes following from the Protest Law, including participation in an unlicensed demonstration, follow and are considered the purpose of the gathering' (Hussin, 2017: 49). The upshot of this was that the courts imposed the penalties set forth in the Assembly Law because they are more severe: while the Protest Law carried a fine, the Assembly Law prescribed a fine or a prison sentence (Hussin, 2017: 49). And so, the 2013 Protest Law should be regarded as an addendum (or expansion with further crimes) to this initial repressive law that originated in British colonial times.

Then two years later, on 15 August 2015, Sisi further compounded Egypt's repressive juridification of the public sphere through the ratification of a new Anti-Terror Law (El-Sadany, 2015). This law was one of the 175 laws and decrees that Sisi singlehandedly ratified in the absence of a sitting parliament. This law vaguely defined terrorism as that which:

> Disturb[s] public order, endanger[s] the safety, interests, or security of the community; harm[s] individuals and terrorizing them; jeopardize[es] their lives, freedoms, public or private rights, or security, or other freedoms and rights guaranteed by the Constitution and the law; harms national unity, social peace, or national security or damages the environment, natural resources, antiquities, money, buildings, or public or private properties or occupies or seizes them; prevents or impedes public authorities, agencies or judicial bodies, government offices or local units, houses of worship, hospitals, institutions, institutes, diplomatic and consular missions, or regional and international organizations and bodies in Egypt from carrying out their work or exercising all or some of their activities, or resists them or disables the enforcement of any of the provisions of the Constitution, laws, or regulations. (EgyptSource, 2015)

Significantly, this law now cast terrorism so widely that it basically encompassed not only any type of public dissent or civic disobedience but also any form of critique. This law made it explicitly illegal to *dissent from the government's message* on issues of terrorism and national security (Human Rights Watch, 2015). Such diversions were made just as punishable as the acts of terrorism (as vaguely defined) itself. Hence, it was not only the right to assembly that was destroyed through the Assembly and Protest Laws but the freedom of expression was also directly curtailed by the Anti-Terror Law. After all, Article 35 stated that 'anyone who publishes or even promotes "untrue" news about acts of terrorism or news that contradicts official Defence Ministry statements about counterterrorism operations can be punished by a fine of 200,000–500,000 Egyptian pounds (US$25,000–$64,000)' (Human Rights Watch, 2015). And anyone who publishes this as part of their profession (such as journalists) may not only be barred from their profession for up to a year but also serve a minimum prison sentence with hard labour of five years if such information was published on a website (EgyptSource, 2015; Human Rights Watch, 2015). How this exactly pertained to personal or business-related websites was conveniently left undefined and open to the interpretation of the courts (which as we have already seen fall under the control of El Sisi himself). And lastly, this 2015 Anti-Terror Law also provided the president with the power to impose a six-month curfew and evacuations in defined areas and eliminated any legal time limit for the prosecution of terrorist crimes. The Anti-Terror Law was thus a means through which Sisi violently repressed any actions that might challenge his political interests (and pervasive injustice in Egypt), through the prohibition to disrupt general order or harm national unity.

Moreover, in March 2020, Abdel Fattah El Sisi further intensified his anti-terror legislation by designating any act that includes 'raising funds, collecting, possessing, supplying or transferring of funds or other financial assets, weapons, explosives, equipment, data, information, or other materials that can help in the activities of any terrorist individual, group or entity operating inside or outside the country' as a terrorist act (Ahram Online, 2020). Particularly the vaguely worded concepts of 'information' and 'other materials' now meant that anything and everything could be classified as an act of terrorism. At the same time, the punishment for such 'violations' also notably increased as the amendments stipulated 'life sentences and capital punishments for those accused of financing terrorist-designated groups' (al Masry Al Youm, 2020).

These amendments to the Anti-Terror Law of course come after Sisi reinstated the state of emergency in the aftermath of the two attacks on churches in Alexandria and Tanta in April 2017, wherein forty-five people were killed and more than a hundred were injured (Saker, 2017). This state of emergency is valid for three months but has been renewed continually until 2022, when Sisi under pressure from the Biden administration has stated he would stop the state of emergency (after having enshrined most of its principles into

Basic Law) (Reuters, 2021). Under the state of emergency, citizens may be tried under emergency courts for violating military orders (such as the above-mentioned curfew) without the right to appeal. The president is also granted the right to monitor electronic messaging, newspapers and any other form of expression (and has the right to censor these outlets or close them). The president furthermore has the right to impose curfews on (or close) public transportation, shops and street vendors. And though legally the president has no right to forcibly arrest any citizen, we see that hundreds of thousands of Egyptians have been arbitrarily detained, arrested, disappeared and undergone extrajudicial killing under the banner of so-called terrorism charges.

Such repressive juridification of the public sphere hence comprised nothing less than the purposeful infliction, by Abdel Fattah El Sisi, of traumatic status subordination: it was a means to impose an overwhelming power relation wherein the intersubjective parity of Egyptian citizens was systematically and gravely violated, and their capacity to speak back at the injustice fundamentally destroyed. For, the banning of political movements, the Anti-Protest Law, Assembly Law, Anti-Terror Law and the reinstated state of emergency meant that Egyptians were now left unable to protest, speak out and stray from the government's message, at least not without serious risk to physical abuse, torture, incarceration and even death. These laws were hence instrumental tools employed in the strategic attempt to put the revolutionary genie back in the authoritarian bottle. The aim was to destroy the potential of collective intersubjective becoming and self-manifestation in the world and thereby mute any potential challenge to the military's political and economic interests.

Indeed, the purpose was to ensure that only one voice would be heard in Egypt's political public sphere, namely that of El Sisi (and those that publicly agreed with him). Hence, in addition to the above-mentioned repressive laws, Sisi also ratified new media regulations and ensured that the entirety of the Egyptian media would fall directly under his control through a shift in media ownership. In December 2016, Sisi installed a new media bill which created the Supreme Council for the Administration of the Media (al Jazeera, 2016). The chairman of this council, appointed by the president himself, would lead a committee that was tasked with the revoking of licences and fining or suspending media outlets not deemed to be in line with the government's message (and would thus break licence terms). This new media legislation thereby directly facilitated the executive branch's control over the media and ensured the reduction of critical voices in the political public sphere (Al Jazeera, 2016).

Additionally, the Egyptian government launched a new TV network DMC which became 'the mouthpiece of the intelligence services' (RSF, 2017) and replaced existing owners of media outlets with businessmen connected to

Sisi's inner circles before taking direct control over the media industry itself. A particular case in point here is Ahmed Abu Hashima, a business tycoon in the steel industry who was an outspoken supporter of Sisi and maintained close links with the Egyptian intelligence services. Hashima became the owner of four newspapers (*Sout Al Omma, Ain, Dot Masr* and *Al Youm al Sabea*) as well as the CBC, Al Nahar and ONTV television channels in 2016, the latter of which had once been a critical voice in post-revolutionary Egypt but now adopted the military's counter-revolutionary narrative.[3] However, after the protests in June 2017 over Sisi's transferal of sovereignty over the islands of Tiran and Sanafir to Saudi Arabia, Sisi's General Intelligence Service quickly sidelined these businessmen, including Ahmed Abu Hashima, and took direct control over media ownership by 'buying out' the shares of these businessmen. This included a 'deal' that these businessmen themselves had no effective say in. Sisi's regime had basically decided that it was best for Egypt's security apparatus to have 'complete control of media by buying up outlets, rather than making do with the cooperation of their owners' (Baghat, 2017). In this context, the editor of Youm al Sabea even stated that '"President Sisi is the newspaper's new owner" and that it could therefore not continue to employ critical journalists' (RSF, 2017).

Of course, it was not just traditional media that suffered from Sisi's repression. Rather, in the instrumental pursuit of colonising Egypt's public sphere, Sisi's regime has also blocked access to (alternative) media content on a large scale. In 2017, the Egyptian authorities blocked sixty websites under terrorism charges and the supposed spreading of false news. This included not only websites such as Aljazeera Arabic and English but also Human Rights Watch as well as Mada Masr (the only remaining independent outlet with high quality, investigative journalism in Egypt). Since then, the blocking of websites and news outlets accelerated, with Sisi's government blocking more than six hundred websites on supposed terrorism charges between 2017 and 2019. This included the attempted blocking of BBC and the Huffington Post on terrorism charges (Freedom House, 2021). During the controversial constitutional referendum in 2019, the Egyptian state not only blocked the Batel (void) website that opposed Sisi's constitutional amendments but also filtered 34,000 website domains as a means of denying people access to dissenting information.

This blocking was furthermore written into law, when the Supreme Council for Media Regulations issued a set of draconian by-laws that legalised the council's power to license, block or halt the activity of any website, regardless of the content it offers (Mamdouh, 2018). It also imposed stiff fees for the creation of press-related website (LE100,000), television station or channel (LE2,5 million) as well as any personal or business-related website (up to LE50,000) (Mamdouh, 2018). It furthermore stipulated that any personal or business-related social media profiles, YouTube channels or Twitter accounts with more than 5,000 followers could now fall under the government's professional media regulation (which among other things prohibited 'insulting state institutions', 'generalization' and 'harming state interests') (Mamdouh, 2018; Human Rights Watch, 2020b).

The point of these by-laws was clearly to mute political plurality in Egypt's public sphere. However, arguably, it was as much about the repression of alternative voices as it was about the form: namely the destruction of communicative relations between people, thereby deepening their social isolation and individualised atomisation (which again inhibits the potential of creative collective becoming, and thus the challenge to the military's interests). This was clearly illustrated by the fact these by-laws directly targeted private social media content as well as destroyed VPN networks and blocked private communication technology such as WhatsApp, Signal and Wire.

Moreover, the Egyptian authorities not only blocked private messaging and communication apps but also started a campaign of intimidation using new technologies. The Ministry of Communication and Information Technology deliberately targeted activists, journalists, lawyers, academics and anyone they deemed to be critical of the government's official line. Sisi's regime hacked their phones and installed malicious spyware that would not only reveal their location (even if they had turned off their location tracking) but also provided access to emails, apps and all other mediated correspondence (Bergman and Walsh, 2019). Similarly, the Egyptian government engaged in a large-scale attempt to gain access to activists' Gmail accounts, using OAuth tokens by third-party apps (Cimpanu, 2019). The instrumental rationality underlying these hacks was the strategic pursuit of information relevant for Sisi's repressive intelligence services but also to impose fear, suspicion and distrust which would make people think twice about what they communicate and to whom even in their private and personal correspondence and interaction. The point was to install fear and distrust, which ruptures intersubjective relationality, and thus further erases the potentiality of revolutionary becoming that might challenge the strategic interests of Sisi's military elite.

DIRECT PHYSICAL FORCE

However, the colonisation of the public sphere could not succeed if it occurred by political proceduralism and repressive juridification alone. Rather, underlying these tactics is a direct threat and manifestation of grave physical violence, which reached its pinnacle under the repressive semi-totalitarian regime of Abdel Fattah El Sisi. Indeed, Sisi's rule has been characterised not only by the expansive and intense physical crackdown on any form of protest or dissent but also by the purposeful blurring of the existential boundaries between existence and non-existence. Through the violent imposition of what I call a politics of death, a prisonification of society and enforced disappearances, Sisi intentionally placed Egyptians on the existential edge of being and non-being as such. Through the relentless violent confrontation with the potential of non-being as such, Sisi thereby imposed such a grave form of traumatic status subordination that the symbolic realm of the lifeworld ruptured from underneath activists' feet, giving rise to a deep existential crisis wherein ordinary meaning-making no longer makes sense and the structures of possibility are closed (see Part 3). Hence, the purpose extends beyond the removal of the intentional object (namely revolutionary politics) to the destruction of the underlying existential structures of possible existence. The underlying instrumental purpose is to break the potential of an intersubjective (revolutionary) 'being-with' others.

First, Sisi (like SCAF and Morsi before him) inflicted death and violent status subordination through the physical crackdown on protests, demonstrations and gatherings. Having made his repressive and deadly intentions particularly clear during the massacres of Rabaa and Ennahda, Sisi adopted a stance of non-tolerance on public gatherings, demonstrations and protests. In the aftermath of Morsi's disposal, his regime thus frequently clashed with Brotherhood protesters, including the students against the Coup who organised sit-ins and rallies at Egypt's institutions of higher education (notably Al Azhar, Cairo University, Ain Shams University and Alexandria University). Initially, these groups consisted primarily of Brotherhood supporters that protested against Morsi's disposal and the Rabaa massacre, but soon its composition widened to include liberals, leftists, socialists and its claims were expanded to a more extensive denunciation of the military's violent crackdown on all sectors of society (Hamzawy, 2017). The state's crackdown was extremely violent: students were killed on and off campus (by both Egypt's security apparatus as well as private security firms hired by Universities and facilitated by the state). They were also detained, tortured and forcibly disappeared. For instance, in the year 2013–2014 alone, 1,677 student protests occurred on university campuses during which security forces killed 14 students and arrested hundreds (Hamzawy, 2017). Additionally, students suffered punitive measures imposed by their own university leaderships (which were sympathetic to Sisi's repressive regime), such as referrals to disciplinary boards, dismissals without litigation and prohibitions to take exams (thus halting their educational progress and professional development). Moreover, on 8 October 2015, the Ministry of Higher Education issued a decree that stipulated that students with disciplinary records, with a criminal record and associated with 'terrorist organisations' are not entitled to participation in student elections (Hamzawy, 2017). The ministry thus clearly used anti-terror legislation to mute student's critical voices while universities at the same increasingly deployed private security firms on their campuses, which were tasked with maintaining social order and control.

Making liberal use of the Anti-Terror, Protest and Assembly Laws, Sisi's security apparatus violently repressed any emerging protest or dissent in Egypt's public sphere. And so, while small-to-middle-range protests were organised on a near bi-weekly basis in the first few years of Sisi's rule (particularly by Brotherhood-affiliated groups), Sisi consistently responded with violent and deadly repression. Between 2013 and 2014, at least 3,143 people were killed in political violence in Egypt, which includes 228 students and 871 deaths at Rabaa (Dunne and Williamson, 2014). Notably, the anniversaries of the 25th revolution were particularly violent and tense events, wherein security forces killed 64 people in 2014 and 18 in 2015, while arresting more than a 1,000 and 516, respectively, and wounding hundreds of protesters (Ashraf, 2014; Human Rights Watch, 2016a). The violent crackdown on protesters, however, reached a particular momentum in April 2016, when a demonstration erupted in downtown Cairo in light of Sisi's decision to transfer the sovereignty of the islands of Tiran and Sanafir to Saudi Arabia (Fahim, 2016), during which the security state arrested 1,227 people in a ten-day time span (from 15 till 25 April 2016) (Dawoud, 2016). While the majority of people were released shortly after, the courts had sentenced 152 people to prison terms of two to five years with hard labour for participating in protests without the prior approval of the Ministry of Interior, and 585 other individuals (including children) were charged with terrorism-related offences (including the spreading of false news, harming the unity of the state, the obstruction of traffic, the threatening of public order and 'instigation' against the government) (Human Rights Watch, 2016b). During these arrests, many were assaulted, tortured and suffered enforced disappearance at the hands of the NSA. Moreover, 'in response to the media and public outcry, President Abdel Fattah El Sisi made it clear in televised speeches that there was no room for dissenting voices, warning: "don't listen to anyone [in the media] but me" (24 February 2016) or "don't talk about this subject [the issue of Tiran and Sanafir] again" (13 April 2016)' (Amnesty International, 2020).

Similarly, when in September 2019, former contractor Mohamed Ali released a series of videos from exile in Spain wherein he accused El Sisi of corruption, relatively small-scale (but nevertheless brave and significant) protests occurred across Egypt, particularly (though not exclusively) among the younger generation. The Egyptian state, however, responded with an iron fist: it closed down the entire area of downtown Cairo, checking the mobile phones of passers-by for any social media accounts that would hold any 'crime of unauthorized assembly' or contain any information or links to persons deemed critical of the Egyptian state. It also arrested more than 4,000 people during this crackdown, including 111 children, many of whom have been subjected to enforced disappearance for periods ranging between two and ten days, and sixty-nine of whom are facing 'charges of participating in a terrorist group, helping it in achieving its objectives, broadcasting and disseminating false news, misusing social media, and participating in an unlicensed demonstration in connection with Case 1338 of 2019' (Amnesty International, 2019; ECRF, 2020).

During this particular crackdown, the Egyptian state also detained a number of foreign nationals, namely, two Jordanians, a Dutch tourist, a Palestinian and an American student who had also been threatened with torture. The targeting of foreigners was not new as such. After all, the Egyptian state had already tortured Cambridge PhD student Giulio Regeni to death after security officials had captured him on the 25th of January 2016, when he was on his way to meet a friend in downtown Cairo. Yet, the scale of these foreign arrests, the victims of which were paraded on national television and provided 'live confessions of foreign meddling', was a new development. It was geared both at instilling fear of 'foreign' or 'third-party' interference in these protests, while simultaneously sending out the message that even the previously relatively privileged foreigners are no longer safe under Sisi's regime of fear. The message was clear: no one is safe, not even foreigners, children or random passers-by.

Indeed, Amnesty International documented the arrest of random passers-by, entirely unrelated to the protests, including 'the arrest of five children, three of them were buying school stationery and uniforms from downtown Cairo at the time; and two were returning home from school in Suez' (Amnesty International, 2019). This violent treatment of children is not an isolated affair specific to this particular crackdown but rather has been endemic to the military's repressive force: in 2011 SCAF captured and tortured children before sending them to military trials (AFP, 2012), and Sisi's NSA has detained, waterboarded, tortured and disappeared children both before and after this particular crackdown in September 2019 (ECRF, 2020). Often parents are not only denied access to their children or knowledge of their whereabouts, they are also frequently threatened with the same fate as their children when they come looking for them.

Enforced disappearances – including that of children as young as newborns and one-year-olds[4] – particularly increased in Egypt (both in number and duration) after Major-General Magdy Abdel-Ghaffar was appointed by Sisi as the new minister of interior in March 2015. The ECRF has documented 2,273 cases of enforced disappearance under Sisi's rule – though the actual number is likely to be much higher due to obvious difficulties in the monitoring and documentation of these cases (ECRF, 2020). Amnesty International stated that local NGOs estimate that three to four people go missing every day (Amnesty, 2016a). Enforced disappearance constitutes one of the gravest betrayals of intersubjective parity, and clearest manifestations of traumatic status subordination. For, in the act of enforced disappearance, the subordinated subject's very existence is thrown into jeopardy. Not only are those who disappear often subjected to torture, and thus left at the behest of the malevolent perpetrator with no help in sight as their agency is robbed from them, their *legal* existence as a person is also directly thrown into jeopardy. To put it in stronger Arendtian terms, enforced disappearance purposefully destroys the right to have rights (Arendt, 2017 [1951]). One has moved from a realm of wherein one's existence as a person was recognised on paper at least, to one wherein one's very existence if negated at its fundamental core. One has disappeared: erased, evaporated and vanished from the face of the earth. In enforced disappearance, often accompanied by the experience of torture, one is left entirely at the behest of one's captor in utter helplessness as one loses any influence over one's surroundings. Rather, in enforced disappearance the line between existence and non-existence is purposefully blurred: it is precisely this state of existential precarity that enables the perpetrator to manifest his power with such a violent blow. No one knows where you are, no one will come to your aid. You are alone, atomised, and utterly subjectified: the security state may exercise complete control over your body which has become objectified as pure flesh. In enforced disappearance, one's fate dangles by a thin thread from the hands of perpetrator, without help or support in sight. Enforced disappearance is thus one of the deepest, most fundamental, betrayal of intersubjective parity, wherein traumatic alienation and existential helplessness are violently bestowed upon the victims – as well as his or her relatives.

Indeed, enforced disappearance leaves not only the victim, but also his or her loved ones (who are unable to locate the victim, or change the circumstances) hanging in an alienated state of existential powerlessness. Families and loved ones desperately searching for the disappeared are not only often left helpless in the face of authorities unwilling to share information, but the ECRF (2020) has noted that enforced disappearances also put families and loved ones of victims under great financial strain.[5] Moreover, relatives and loved ones are frequently subjected to threats by the security forces when they make enquiries and may even co-disappear with the victim. Often, a victim's apartment is stormed in the middle of the night and family members frequently co-disappear with the victim on the sheer account of being present at the time of arrest. Life, Sisi's regime makes abundantly clear, is disposable, so one person more or less does not make a difference. One such notable case was that of Islam Khalil, whose brother and father disappeared with him, but while his brother was released a few days later and his father 12 days later, Islam disappeared for 122 days, until he suddenly reappeared at a court in

Alexandria on September 2015, and was finally released on 31 August 2016. Families might also be summoned to the NSA headquarters, where they are threatened 'with the fate of their forcibly disappeared relatives, explicitly saying: 'If you do not stop talking, you will never see him again'' (ECRF, 2020). Indeed, the NSA also arrested family members, and 'interrogated them for hours on end' when they enquired about their loved ones, with some families being 'forced to change their place of residence due to the constant threats' (ECRF, 2020). One such case is Ibrahim Metwally, a lawyer, who disappeared on 10 September 2017 as he was on his way to meet the United Nations Team on Enforced and Involuntary Disappearances to discuss the case of his son Amr Metwally, who had disappeared since 8 July 2013. After suffering serious abuse and medical neglect during his detention, Ibrahim Metwally gained a release order on 14 October 2019, only to disappear again. He remains forcibly disappeared to this day. Ibrahim Metwally is not the only lawyer subjected to this fate, the ECRF has documented forty-eight cases of lawyers who have been forcibly disappeared in connection with their work (ECRF, 2020).

Nor is Ibrahim Metwally the only person to suffer what the ECRF calls 'rotation detention' (and rotation disappearance) – whereby individuals ordered for release are subjected to re-detention on a different case or subjected to another episode of enforced disappearance (ECRF, 2020). Often this happens in the transition from the prison to the police station, from where they are supposed to be released: they simply never arrive or do they ever leave the station. Hence, for many relatives and friends whose loved one is ordered for release, the prisoner's ride to the police station is the most frightening one: as the prisoner verges on the boundary between release and disappearance, or existence and non-existence.

Furthermore, such rotation detention and rotation disappearance are an endemic feature of what I call the prisonification of society under El Sisi (MENA Rights Group, 2021) wherein the brutal punitive prison system (directly controlled by Egypt's NSA) is not only intensified inside Egypt's prisons but rather also extends far beyond its physical prison walls. The boundaries of the prison itself are purposefully blurred in order to achieve a continuous traumatic status subordination; wherein Egyptian citizens are robbed of both their capacity to speak back at the injustices inflicted and their ability to form intersubjective relations that would enable creative (collective) becoming. The prisonification of Egyptian society thus imposes a way of being in the world wherein one experiences the continuous, lingering pressure of (potential, reoccurring, random) imprisonment. In this sense, prisonification is of course closely connected to Foucault's notion of a disciplinary society (Foucault, 1995), but explicitly refers to the deep existential weight of the always immanent threat of direct physical incarceration and how this particular threat deeply ruptures one's being in the world. For, under Sisi's rule, the inside and outside boundaries of prison have been deliberately obscured: not only does one lack freedom when outside prison (as one can be taken and re-taken by Egypt's NSA at any time), but the NSA often imposes illegal reporting duties on those who have been released from prison, including overnight prison stays. The frequency of these (often illegally imposed) 'reporting duties' differ, seemingly randomly, per case. While some have to rapport a few times a week and others had to spend every night at the police station, for an unspecified duration of time. Such was the case with famous activist Alaa Abdel Fattah who was illegally forced to spend every night in solitary confinement at the police station after he was released from prison. The existential and practical burden this poses on 'ex'-detainees should not be underestimated: not only do they experience the practical stress of making it back to the police station on time (despite of Cairo's traffic) but continuously returning to the NSA or prison (every day) also means that the threat of re-detention relentlessly hangs over one's heads like the sword of Damocles. The prisoner in this sense finds himself in an existential no-man's-land: one is not in prison and not outside it, but in between, constantly returning. And so, the released person is not truly freed and not really imprisoned. Rather in this ambiguity, he or she remains trapped in the chains of the Egyptian NSA, not only through surveillance but rather also through direct physical contact. And so, Egyptian citizens are not even afforded the existential freedom of release, but instead experience continuing pressure, which directly compromises the possibility of rebuilding of intersubjective relations. Sisi's prisonification of society purposefully leaves them in purgatory: neither free nor imprisoned, many are left in between and experienced a deep level of existential stuckness. This betweenness not only keeps one bound to the prison system but also disables a temporal articulation of intersubjective meaning-making. That is, in light of such existential insecurity, a clear articulation of the past, present and future is inhibited, meaning the lifeworld's background as a grid of orientation ruptures and one experiences a deep sense of disorientation and atomisation.

Moreover, imprisonment (as well as enforced disappearances) not only shatter one's being in the world and the potential to establish fruitful intersubjective relations through the ever-immanent possibility of (a return to) physical incarceration (or disappearance) but through the sheer fact of social fear. Many of those who are released from prison experience grave social isolation – indeed, a form of social death – after their release, since friends, relatives and loved ones are often afraid that any association with the ex-prisoner might be sufficient reason for the authorities to detain them too. This again clearly highlights the instrumental rationale underlying Sisi's prisonification of Egyptian society: namely the violent rupture of intersubjective self-becoming and the violent silencing atomisation of society.

And of course, often the sword of Damocles does come down, with many finding themselves returning to Egypt's prison system on the most spurious of charges (MENA Rights Group, 2021),[6] as well as having family or those (vaguely) related to the prisoner being detained. One such person was Alaa Abdel Fattah who was kidnapped and tortured when he was supposed to be released from Dokki station on one of the mornings of many of his overnight stays. His detention was then soon followed by that of his sister Sanaa who was kidnapped from the public prosecutors' office on 20 June 2020 when her family tried to rapport a beating they received from an anonymous group of 'people' when they tried to get a sign of life from Alaa inside the prison. While Sanaa has thankfully been released from her unjust imprisonment, Alaa has been sentenced to 5 years in prison in a trial deeply marred by outrageous injustice. Meanwhile, Alaa has also been directly subject to Sisi's politics of vengeance, as he has been denied visits, clean clothes, books and access to the prison library and radio, as well as recreational time outside of his cell and is currently on hunger strike (BBC News, 2021). Alaa is currently on a hunger strike, and withholds water and food, as he is denied consular access to the British Embassy. Alaa holds dual Egyptian – British citizenship.

This prisonification of Egypt's society of course is grounded in the material production of prisons, which under Sisi has grown exponentially. Since 2011 revolution, thirty-eight new prisons have been built in Egypt. To put this prison building boom into perspective somewhat, prior to the January 2011 revolution the number of prisons Egypt housed was forty-three. Out of the thirty-eight newly built prisons, two were built by SCAF and one under Mohamed Morsi, leaving Sisi as the master prison-builder. Sisi's prison building particularly accelerated in 2016, after the Tiran and Sanafir protests, when Sisi built nineteen prisons in just one year. It is this growth of prisons that facilitated, or literally, made 'room for everyone' (ANHRI, 2016; El-Fekki, 2016). Under Sisi's rule alone, at least 63.032 individuals have been arrested and incarcerated in Egypt's jails, including 691 women and 1,161 minors (AOHRUK, 2019). However, this number is likely to be a gross underestimate with local NGOs unofficially stating that the estimated number of arrests comes closer to at least triple that amount, namely approximately 180,000 arrests. The vast majority of these people have been 'detained without trial or sentenced to prison terms or to death after often grossly unfair trials' involving not only corrupt judges but also collective sentencing (Amnesty International, 2016b). The counter-revolutionary purpose of this prisonification of Egyptian society was of course to subject Egyptians to traumatic status subordination, namely a deeply violent power relation wherein the intersubjective equality of the victim is betrayed to such an extent that he or she loses her bearing in the world and the potential challenge to the military's interests is stifled.

This prisonification hence also coincided with, and was part, of the acceleration of the politics of death under Sisi. Since Sisi commenced his rule, death sentences have been imposed and carried out ever more frequently. For instance, Reprieve confirmed that while the Egyptian state has handed down 2,595 death sentences between 2011 and 2018, 2,433 (including 11 children) of these occurred after Sisi's takeover of power (Reprieve, 2019). From of these 2,433 death sentences, 1,884 were handed down in mass trials of 15 people or more. Moreover, while Egypt's post-revolutionary government carried out 1 death sentence between 2011 and 2013, Sisi has executed 144 people between July 2013 and September 2018 (Reprieve, 2019).

This stark increase in death penalties, particularly after 2017, is the direct result of Sisi's reforms of the Court of Cassation wherein he not only accelerated the process of death sentences but also took away the right to appeal (Magdi, 2019). However, as Maged Mandour explains, since public state-sanctioned executions pose the potential of a social backlash, the Egyptian state has increasingly resorted to extrajudicial killings as a way of 'silencing' their political opponents (Mandour, 2019b). The Egyptian security forces found extrajudicial killings a much more expedient manner of executing political opponents (particularly the Muslim Brotherhood) because it is free of judicial oversight (Magdi, 2019). And so, the Arab Organisation of Human Rights confirms that at least 3,185 citizens have been killed by Egypt's security apparatus since 3 July 2013, 2,194 of which have been killed in protests and gatherings (AOHRUK, 2019). The exact numbers are however difficult to verify, and the Nadeem Centre of the Rehabilitation of Victims of Violence and Torture writes that in 2015 alone 'the number of killings "connected to contact with the security forces" reached 474. Some of these were killed in shootouts, including innocent bystanders, whilst 175 the result of the direct execution of suspects and 137 deaths were inflicted inside detention centers' (Mandour, 2019b). The official narrative around these deaths is often remarkably similar: those killed (including the previously disappeared) were nearly always casualties in a shootout between terrorist militants and the security forces. Yet, witness accounts often 'suggest victims died from close range execution and were moved after death' as well as bore clear marks of extreme torture (Mandour, 2019b).

Additionally, prisons became an important place of death, with the AOHRUK confirming that from the 766 individuals that died in detention centres since 2013, 122 died under torture inflicted on them by the security state, 91 persons died due to corrupt prison administration, 37 due to overcrowding and bad detention conditions and 516 due to deliberate medical negligence (AOHRUK, 2019). Such bad detention conditions, at least for those not affiliated with Mubarak's ancient regime, include overcrowded cells (with prisons operating at 207 per cent of their capacity), lack of mattresses and blankets, poor hygiene and sanitation (including buckets as a toilet, water leakages and vermin) and absence of appropriate ventilation or warmth (leading many prisoners to suffer – and die of – extreme heat in the summer and cold in the winter). In addition, prisoners have insufficient access to fresh air and exercise. They also suffer from a shortage of food and nutrition as well as clean water. Prison authorities, moreover, often deny them family visits, thereby deliberately withholding them from essential goods such as food, clothing and safe water (Amnesty International, 2021: 17). Hence, many are left to suffer (and die) cold, hunger and indeed disease.

With regard to the latter, many have suffered from medical negligence inside Egypt's prisons as they suffered the deliberate withholding of appropriate medical care, including access to doctors and medication. Medical negligence entails a deeply punitive, highly destructive power relation, wherein the victim's health, well-being and continued corporal existence are made entirely dependent on the malevolent (and random) will of the other (the prison guards, prison authorities and prison doctors, if there are any). Like in torture, the prisoner is bereft of his or her agency, of his or her ability to influence the world, and is instead treated as worthless and left entirely at the behest of the authorities. Medical negligence is thus yet another manifestation of traumatic status subordination under Sisi which violently violates the intersubjective parity of the prisoner (whose existence is treated in this abusive power relation as inferior, worthless and indeed disposable). The victim thus suffers the gravest form of misrecognition of his or her equality as a human being through the deliberate withholding of medical resources. Unable to speak back or alter his or her situation, the prisoner's very existence hangs on a thin thread, and not infrequently results in physical death.

The most famous cases of medical negligence of course include former president Mohamed Morsi, video maker Shady Habash, human rights activist (and co-founder of the Social Democratic Party) Zyad El-Elaimy and former presidential candidate Abdel Moneim Abdel Fotouh. Morsi was held in solitary confinement for six years. During this period, he was only allowed three family visits and denied all access to medical care or his lawyers. Eventually, he died on 17 June 2017, after he collapsed in a courtroom during one of his hearings (Raghavan and Mahfouz, 2019). The Special Rapporteur on extrajudicial, summary or arbitrary executions found that Mohamed Morsi's death was intentional and amounted to a state-sanctioned arbitrary killing (al Jazeera, 2019). Shady Habash was also denied appropriate healthcare after he had accidentally consumed pure alcohol and suffered alcohol poisoning, while Zyad El-Elaimy was systematically denied treatment and medication for his sarcoidosis, asthma, hypertension and type 2 diabetes in prison which directly put his life in danger. At the same time, Abdel Moneim Abdel Fotouh has been deliberately denied medical healthcare after his fourth stroke during his incarceration and denied access to medication for his hernia. As the CIHRS writes: 'The medical neglect of Aboul-Fotouh is a shamefully evident example of indirect torture in Egyptian prisons, constituting yet another attempt to intimidate Egyptian activists and dissidents.' It is, the organisation concludes, 'a prolonged death sentence as a form of retaliation' (CIHRS, 2018). Such fate not only befalls well-known political actors or artists but maybe inflicted upon anyone who enters through Egypt's prison doors. Most of these are ordinary people who remain largely anonymous to the outside world, and who are left to die in Egypt cells, having suffered a lack of access to medical professionals, medication, humane prison conditions and having endured solitary confinement.

Indeed, solitary confinement is a frequently used method of punishment in Sisi's prisons, and though the state authorities can inflict it on anyone, it has particularly been inflicted on 'detainees and prisoners with a political profile' (Amnesty International, 2018: 15). Under the pretext of terrorism and national security, the Egyptian NSA subjects activists of all variations to random, prolonged and extensive periods of solitary confinement. Often these isolation cells are not bigger than 1 metre by 1.80 metres, and contain nothing but a bucket as a toilet (Amnesty International, 2018: 38). Though international law stipulates solitary confinement may not be inflicted for a longer period than fifteen days and must be subject to independent review, under Sisi there is no such review and the Prison Law has been amended in 2015 so that prison wardens themselves may impose a period of solitary confinement for thirty days, while the assistant minister of interior for prison affairs can now order solitary confinement for up to six months (Amnesty International, 2018). In reality, however, prisoners may not only be subjected to solitary confinements for weeks or months but even years. During these times, they are entirely cut off not only from their fellow prisoners but also their relatives and loved ones, as they are most frequently denied any such visits when in isolation. Solitary confinement entails nothing less than, as Lisa Guenther has aptly remarked, the machinery of living death (Guenther, 2013). In solitary confinement, the prisoner suffers a form of social death as they are 'deprived of the network of social relations, particularly kinship relations that would otherwise support, protect and give meaning to one's precarious life as an individual' (Guenther, 2013: xxi). In solitary confinement, one is purposefully atomised, cut off from intersubjective relations (from where we derive meaning-making and find our bearing in the world) and the ability to maintain meaningful relations to others, the world and thereby the self. One is literally thrown into a decapacitating state of atomised isolation. The punitive measure of solitary confinement is thus yet another way in which Sisi's security regime imposed traumatic status subordination, wherein intersubjective relationality was deliberately destroyed.

NEOLIBERAL ECONOMIC RATIONALISM

Sisi's political procedural colonisation of the public sphere and measures of punitive physical violence were compounded by an intensification of maldistribution under Sisi, wherein the vast majority of Egyptians increasingly suffered from marginalisation as the state accelerated its neoliberal economic politics that only served the military-business elite. During Sisi's rule, the military not only tightened its grip over the political arena (including the judiciary and legislative branches) but also instrumentally expanded its influence over economic activities. This 'dual capture of the political and economic spheres by the military marked a new era, where the military, instead of business elites, captured both spheres' (Khalil and Dill, 2019: 12). Sisi strategically utilised his newly founded violent domination over the political terrain to consolidate the military's economic empire (which then itself further supported its political domination). After Sisi took political power, the army capitalised on its privileges to exploit its substantial mandates and capabilities into pure economic profit (Marshall and Stacher, 2012). And so, while under Mubarak and Morsi, neoliberalism comprised a reallocation of public funds towards enterprise and privatisation (which benefitted the business-cum-political elite), now its main beneficiaries were military enterprises. These military enterprises left some space for the big business tycoons through direct military cooperation, since they did not pose a political threat to Sisi's regime. For instance, the Sawiris family, despite all tensions with the El Sisi regime, continued to implement public works projects, while Ahmed Ezz was released from prison and continued to manage his economic empire (Adly, 2017: 21). Yet, ultimately, the military held the economic strings firmly in its own hands: it was up to the military to decide not only which projects it would be implementing and which are left to the private sector but also who would get to participate in commercial activities in Egypt and in what form (Khalil and Dill, 2019).

Particularly instrumental here were the new tax and economic reform laws Sisi's administration passed on the first day of Sisi's grandiose Sharm el Sheikh conference organised in March 2015. This conference was instrumentally geared towards attracting direct foreign investment and to appealing to international financial institutions through the intensification of neoliberal economic reforms (Khalil and Dill, 2019). These economic reforms particularly served the interests of the military, which consolidated its economic power through alliances with (opportunistic) private enterprises. Sisi's new economic reform laws 'privileged the military exclusively', as it 'dismantled the tender and bids law, enabling the military to gain full control over state business contracts, privatisation decisions, procurement processes and all sales concerning public enterprises' (Marshall, 2015; Marshall in Khalil and

Dill, 2019). Military businesses were moreover shielded 'from the duties and regulations on procurement that are imposed on civilian businesses' (Mandour, 2020). The military furthermore enjoyed 'tax exemptions on profits generated from military owned hotels, sales of basic foods and custom duties' (Mandour, 2020).

At the same time, Sisi's tax and deregulatory investment reforms directly appealed to foreign direct investors and Egypt's business elite as it 'sliced taxes on higher incomes and corporate profits from 30% to 22%. making it one of the lowest in the region' (Khalil and Dill, 2019: 11; also see Mandour, 2020a). The administration also nullified the 'capital gains tax after various objections and protests by stock market investors, and assert[ed] the liberalisation of the energy sector and the subsequent shrinking of the subsidy system, including the energy subsidy' (Khalil and Dill, 2019: 11). Sisi also 'advertised several tax exemptions in new special economic zones, ended the judicial oversight over state contracts with private businesses and thus ensured 'investor protection' even from the judicial system in Egypt' (Khalil and Dill, 2019: 11).

In addition to attracting foreign direct investment, the conference was also Sisi's opportunity to explicitly promote his big projects, including the expansion of the Suez Canal, a project which was launched on 4 August 2014 and clearly dominated by the military:

> The army supervised the planning and execution of the mega project, after mobilising 400 private companies, 25,000 workers, and raising US$8 billion to fund the expansion, 80% of which was funded by Egyptians investing in state-issued bonds [. . .] In one year, the military showcased its efficiency, finishing a new 35-km channel – an extension of the original canal by 37 km, thus delivering on their nationalistic discourse of building a new canal for Egyptians. (Tasch in Khalil and Dill, 2019: 14)

Importantly, the Suez Canal project served both Sisi's economic and political ends: it put money in the coffers of the military and expanded its economic influence, while also boosting public and international legitimation of Sisi's regime. Internationally, it sent out a strong political and economic message that the military was 'the' partner to do business with since it delivers results (Tasch, 2015), while domestically, the Suez Canal project appealed to (nostalgic) nationalist sentiments centred around Nasser's 'golden days' and a 'strong Egypt'. Importantly, this legitimation is of course not based on the public use of reason in debate but rather functions as a display of public legitimation *in front of* the public. It is thus itself part and parcel of the refeudalisation of Egypt's public sphere and domination of the political realm by the Egyptian military. Moreover, while the Suez project was directly financially beneficial to the military, its national economic benefits are dubious, not least because of its huge costs, its delayed revenues and the overall decline in global shipping (Malsin, 2021).

Another big project Sisi embarked on was Sisi's New Administrative Capital, which he initiated on 13 March 2015. This project clearly aimed not only at increasing the military's political and economic capital but rather also insulating the government in a new clean city (largely run by renewable energies) from the 'dirt' of its own people. The purpose was to 'isolate most Egyptians from their centers of government in an effort to fortify the regime against any social pressures' (Mandour, 2021). Or rather, to manifest concretely the division between the 'haves' and 'have-nots', between the gated elite and the ordinary people living in squalor, so vividly depicted in Ahmed Khaled Towfik's novel 'Utopia' (Tawfik, 2011).

And here too, the military clearly took 'the lead in procurement, planning and execution, marginalising the majority of local businesses, but including large business tycoons' (Khalil and Dill, 2019). As Khalil and Dill write:

> The New Administrative Capital for Urban Development (NCUD) is the holding company in charge of planning and executing the vision of a new capital. The holding company is co-owned by the state's New Urban Development Communities Authority (49% of shares) and the military's National Service Projects Organization and the Armed Forces National Lands Projects Agency (51% of shares) (State Information Service, n.d.). While the military is taking the lead in land distribution and procurements, it opens the space for large local private businesses, such as Hassan Allam, Orascom Construction Industries, Concord, Talaat Mostafa Group, Arab Contractors and Petrojet to execute particular plans in the new capital, including residential neighbourhoods, which remain unaffordable to the majority of Egyptians. (Khalil and Dill, 2019: 12)

These mega projects were thus directly advantageous to the military's and its affiliated business elite, while smaller local civic companies have found themselves struggling to compete. The army profited not only from its tax exemptions, economic privileges and free conscript labour but also from the state's large-scale investments into these projects, namely at least $200 billion between 2014 and 2019 (Mandour, 2020). Most of this investment was financed through domestic and international loans. And so, while these projects were publicly pitched as serving social welfare goals of 'education, health and housing', the reality is that it derailed 'public funds from much-needed social and welfare spending, by investing heavily in infrastructure that benefits a narrow segment of society and creates only short-term employment' (Khalil and Dill, 2019: 13).

The financing of these mega projects also resulted in huge levels of external debt – with loans from Saudi Arabia and the United Arab Emirates in 2015, as well as the IMF and World Bank – all of whom attached conditions of economic 'liberalisation' to their loans (Mandour, 2020b). Such economic liberalisation did not imply the emancipation of the economic terrain from military domination but rather entailed the standard neoliberal reforms of regressive taxation, the slashing of the state's public spending and floating the Egyptian currency on the stock market, which would directly negatively affect the livelihoods of ordinary Egyptians. These loans not only bolstered the autocratic nature of Sisi's repressive state (by transferring accountability from the Egyptian public towards both domestic and international creditors), but it also increased the gap between rich and poor (Mandour, 2020b).

Living costs for ordinary Egyptians skyrocketed as inflation soared and subsidies on essential goods such as basic foods and energy were cut. In 2017, food prices rose with a 33 per cent inflation in 2017 and continuously with 14–15 per cent ever since (Reuters, 2019). And so, poverty – already a problem in Egypt – increased even further under Sisi, with many struggling to feed their families and make ends meet (Mahmoud, 2017a):

> In 2019, the Egyptian Central Agency for Public Mobilization and Statistics reported a spike in poverty rates, from 27.8 percent in 2015 to 32.5 percent in 2018. The World Bank also reported a similar pattern, observing an increasing from 22.7 million people living in poverty in 2012 to 32.5 million in 2017. In other words, 9.8 million Egyptians fell into poverty in the span of five years. (Mandour, 2020b)

Moreover, the average levels of expenditure among ordinary Egyptians decreased by 9.7 per cent in 2019, and the trend continued in 2020 when the Egyptian state cut social spending even further, despite COVID-19 (Mahmoud, 2017a; Mandour, 2020b). The authorities reduced bread subsidies and further increased the price of metro tickets by scrapping the lowest fee of LE3 and raising prices to LE7 and LE10. To put the price hike somewhat into perspective, in 2014 the price of a metro ticket was still LE1. Price hikes like these directly affect the incomes and livelihoods of the poor and lower middle classes, whose mobility was now often restricted to that which could be travelled by foot or bicycle, thereby impacting their employment and employment opportunities. In other words, neoliberal measures like these directly facilitate and aggravate, socio-economic segregation.

Hence, while Sisi's military was enriching itself, it asked ordinary citizens to bear the burden. It even did so explicitly, with Sisi's government stating that people ought to be patient and 'understanding' in the context of a deteriorating economy. General Mohamed Mansour even went so far as to ask

Egyptians to 'go hungry' and 'sacrifice their dinners' for the sake of Egypt's prosperity (Mahmoud, 2017). Strikingly, Sisi's neoliberalisation of the economy is not only shrouded in a discourse of (supposed) nationalist development but especially that of sacrifice, wherein the burden of responsibility is purposefully shifted away from the rich to the poor. For instance, at the time the $12 billion IMF loan was agreed (with its associated cuts to social welfare), Sisi asked ordinary Egyptians to step in and sacrifice any spare coins they might have for a housing developmental project (owned and controlled by the military) (Middle East Eye, 2016). They were asked to put the money into a fund entitled Tahya Misr (Long live Egypt)[7], which was especially set up for businessmen and citizens to contribute to the alleviation of poverty through 'out of their own pocket' contributions. Such programmes aimed at poverty alleviation through voluntaristic charity donations that smoothly fit the neoliberal imaginary wherein the state outsources socio-economic responsibility towards private citizens and third-party actors. This withdrawal of state support and responsibility places the greatest burden of responsibility on the weakest, the lower socio-economic classes, which are then frequently faulted for 'not making it' in the capitalist world through a reference to character traits (such as being lazy, unsophisticated, etc.). And so, while avidly pursuing the further neoliberalisation of Egypt's economy, Sisi asked private Egyptian citizens to showcase their national pride and strength through monetary contributions to this fund, whose resources were supposed to be used for social housing, infrastructure and social service projects for the poor (Khalil and Dill, 2). Not only is this fund run by the president himself without any form of accountability, but it has (unsurprisingly) also been accused of corruption and mishandling. Those who led investigations into these practices have since been imprisoned, and are languishing, in Sisi's jails.

And so, under Sisi's dictatorial rule, the gravest forms of misrecognition in Egypt's political public sphere were compounded by the most serious forms of maldistribution in the economic realm, culminating in a total violation of intersubjective parity. Egyptians hence suffered the greatest violations of justice in both the political realm (where they were shot, tortured, forcibly disappeared and structurally marginalised) and the economic realms (where they were thrown into (or kept in) struggles for economic survival, financial precarity and life-threatening poverty). The purpose of such grave patterns of maldistribution is not only to assert the overwhelming superiority of the military through subjectification but rather to destroy the capacity to speak back at the injustices in the first place. The impact of (material) poverty and economic inequality are deeply existential: impoverisation systematically erodes one's agency in the world, one's the ability to manifest oneself in equal relation to others. Economic deprivation results in high levels of stress and anxiety, deteriorates physical health, restricts social mobility and socially isolates. Indeed, poverty is not only a 'material disadvantage' but a 'shameful corrosive relation, characterised by a lack of voice, disrespect, humiliation and reduced dignity and self-esteem' as people are thrown into a struggle for existence (Jo, 2013: 516). In addition to its physical and material manifestations, the attributes of poverty also include 'shame, stigma, powerlessness and disrespect' which are 'socially induced and social relational in nature' (Jo, 2013: 517). Shame, like all these emotions, is not atomistic but deeply intersubjective: it entails an assessment of one's compliance with perceived *social* standards, values or norms which 'determines whether or not a person should be ashamed, in the eyes both of others and the self' (Jo, 2013: 519). Shame's close relation to self-esteem hence 'stems from the link between the self and the others that award value and recognition upon the self' (Jo, 2013: 519). While this relation between shame and poverty is deeply rooted and arguably universal (though contextual), it is particularly strong in classist societies such as that of Egypt, where one's socio-economic standing directly influences one's level of social esteem and respect (including one's marital, educational and other material possibilities as well as the relative possibility to avoid of police brutality, which remains organised along classist lines) (Ismail, 2006). The point here is that Sisi's crippling poverty and maldistribution are a traumatic violation of intersubjective parity: it results in a lack of voice and an inability to participate in sociopolitical life (Lister, 2004). Poverty thus constitutes a power relation wherein a deep sense of existential inferiority is violently impressed upon the victim through material status subordination. Poverty cripples agency (one's ability to shape or influence the surrounding world) and gives rise to a deep sense of alienation from both the self and others, with isolatory and atomising effects (see Jo, 2013).

Hence, Sisi's policies have not been merely unjust but deeply traumatic: it combined the most violent forms of misrecognition with the gravest forms of maldistribution in a deliberate attempt to rob Egyptians of their voice altogether, of their potential for creative collective becoming. The systematic violation of intersubjective parity (through political procedural marginalisation and repression, the infliction of the gravest direct physical violence, including the prisonification of Egyptian society and the avid pursuit of a politics of death) and crippling economic maldistribution has deep existential effects. As Part 3 will outline further, it destroys the communicative realm of the lifeworld, it leaves people in an existentially agonising state of demoralised disorientation, alienation and atomisation.

Yet, the uncomfortable truth for any such authoritarian (or semi-totalitarian) ruler such as Abdel Fatah El Sisi is that while such purposeful, multi-layered destruction of the potential for creative collective becoming is extremely effective as counter-revolutionary tool for depoliticisation, it can never be totally complete. That is, even in the face of total annihilation, there may still be small signs (or small pockets) of resistance. We have seen this in the case of Ahmed Mohi (Middle East Eye, 2019), the lone protester who took to Tahrir Square carrying a handwritten sign saying 'leave ya Sisi' while realising horrific consequences would be bestowed upon him. Or, one can think of the protests that emerged after Mohammed Ali's videos from Spain. And so, even as multilevelled traumatic status subordinations erodes the potentiality of transformative collective resistance, of voice and collective self-manifestation, there nevertheless always remains a potential (no matter how small) that people will stand up or voice critique in either overt or covert ways. For instance, jokes – including social media memes – are often used as a way of voicing critique, or highlighting the absurdity of authoritarian rule. Other small instances of protests have included the toy (consisting of two balls on a set of string) which was renamed by Egyptian children as 'Sisi's balls' – resulting in absurd scenes of the police chasing children through small Egypt's alleyways trying to confiscate these toys (Mahmoud, 2017b). The trouble, however, is that in the context of such comprehensive and systematic traumatic status subordination, instances of resistance or critique remain relatively limited in scope and influence and are directly followed by brutal regime violence. However, as repression is never complete, it also means that regimes such as that of El Sisi have to go ever deeper and further in the purposeful annihilation of intersubjective potential, and in that sense, while they use the words of security and stability in rhetorical abundance, they are fundamentally based insecurity and instability.

CONCLUSION

Part 2 of this monograph explored the mechanisms through which SCAF, Morsi and Sisi have inflicted multilevelled traumatic status subordination upon Egyptian activists. We have seen that there has been a remarkable consistency throughout SCAF, Morsi and indeed Sisi, with all three post-revolutionary regimes inflicting grave physical violence, colonising the political sphere procedurally (including through the usage of repressive juridification of public space) and the perpetuation of economic neoliberalisation that resulted in marginalisation. While physical violence resulted in grave existential disorientation, procedural colonisation gave rise to political voicelessness which was aggravated by increasing economic deprivation. As we have seen in this particular chapter, it was the regime of Abdel Fattah El Sisi that accelerated and intensified these processes, through nothing less than a politics of death and a prisonification of Egyptian society. The point of this was to bring Egyptians on the brink of existential non-existence through the violent disposability and worthlessness of life – through the traumatic violation of intersubjective parity – since it is through such a shift in the underlying structures of experience that the possibility of imagination and potentiality is destroyed and the military's assets are thus retained. Hence, the infliction of such a multilevelled traumatic status subordination follows a purposive rationality and accumulates in the destruction of revolutionaries' lifeworlds. And it is the phenomenological experience of this that the next part will discuss in more detail from a first-person phenomenological perspective.

NOTES

1. Interviewee 17, private conversation, 24 June 2020.
2. Also see Stacher (2020).
3. It had even hosted Bassem Youssef's popular satirical show, wherein politicians and political affairs were discussed and ridiculed.
4. The enforced disappearance of children is part of a pattern that the ECRF has documented (ECRF, 2020) with at least 123 children having been subjected to enforced disappearance, even including newborn babies or children younger than one year. Often these smaller children have been co-disappeared with (one of their) parents. For instance, the one-year-old Al Baraa Omar Abdel Hamid Abu Al-Naja was taken with his parents from the Alexandria governate on 9 March 2019, and they have not appeared since. Other children have been enforcably disappeared without their parents. For instance, twelve-year-old Abdullah Boumediene Nasr El Din was arrested from his home in Al Arish on 31 December 2017 and 'remained in enforced disappearance for a full six months inside the headquarters of Military Brigade 101 until he was brought before the prosecution on June 2, 2018, on charges of joining a terrorist group and helping to plant fireworks' (ECRF, 2020). The Abbasiya juvenile court the ordered his release, after which he was transferred to Azbakeya Department and then to the second section of the Arish Police station – where he disappeared again.
5. They might lose a significant portion of their livelihood or have to spend a large amount of their (already meagre) income on trying to trace their loved one, thus throwing many in a state of (abject) poverty wherein their very existence is threatened.
6. Important to note: not only does that Sisi's executive (security) branch have ultimate control over the judicial system's composition, the juridical branch facilitates the NSA's repressive tactics. It does so not only through regime friendly judges such as Hassan Farid who willingly turn a blind eye to claims of torture or issuing collective rulings on cases entirely unrelated to each other but also through the near automatic renewal of pretrial detention, which not only often occurs in absentia but also frequently bypasses the legal maximum of two years.
7. This is a rather cynical name, given Sisi's earlier mentioned explicit politics of death, to which Sisi's economic neoliberalisation with its systematic deprivation of the lower socio-economic classes directly contributes.

Part 3

BREAKING THE REVOLUTIONARY LIFEWORLD AND POTENTIAL OF CREATIVE BECOMING

INTRODUCTION

Part 1 of this monograph developed a critical theoretical conception of trauma wherein trauma is no longer regarded as a cognitive impairment, or impaired subjectivity, but rather as broken *inter*subjectivity. That is, trauma became conceived as a violent (instrumentally purposeful) betrayal of the counterfactual presupposition of existential intersubjective parity and was inflicted through traumatic status subordination. Traumatic status subordination consists of a violent power relation wherein the victim is subjected to grave symbolic and material violence: the misrecognition of being an equal human being in relation to another and the maldistribution of material resources so this power relation may be manifested.[1] Shining a Habermasian light on trauma not only revealed its underlying purposive rationality[2] – namely, that it is imposed in the instrumental pursuit of political and economic power – but also that its instrumental destruction of intersubjective parity destroys the functioning of the lifeworld. Trauma thus constitutes a violent form of the lifeworld's colonisation and has deeply distortive effects: as the lifeworld's horizon of interpretation disappears from underneath one's feet, the victim experiences a grave sense of incapacitating alienation[3] – a relation of relationlessness to the world, others the self. Or rather, with the crumbling of the lifeworld's symbolic order, the victim is thrown into a nihilist abyss, unable to grasp or make sense of the world, as the potentiality of meaning has evaporated. Hence, the result of the violent infliction of traumatic status subordination is that the victim is unable to manifest him-, her- or themselves in the world. Rather, one is muted, disoriented and (re)atomised.

Hence, Part 2 of this book, through a descriptive account of the political developments in post-revolutionary Egypt, relayed the mechanisms through which Egypt's counter-revolution imposed traumatic status subordination on activists in Egypt. Journeying through Egypt's post-revolutionary developments, it became strikingly apparent that the Egyptian military and its temporary subsidiary of the Muslim Brotherhood have consistently and relentlessly subjected Egyptian activists to a tripartite betrayal of intersubjective parity – consisting of grave physical violence, the procedural colonisation of the public sphere and the continuation (and indeed acceleration) of neoliberal economics. Physical violence was inflicted not only as a means of reducing the number of demonstrators on the streets but also as a way of imposing a superior power relation and throwing activists into a state of agencylessness, disorientation and atomisation. Or rather, the point of physical violence was not only to kill and severely injure critical agents on the street but rather in doing so break activists' agency in the world: to rupture their capacity for (collective) self-manifestation and revolutionary becoming. At the same time, the military and the Brotherhood also avidly pursued a procedural colonisation of the political public sphere, through the instrumental insistence on speedy elections, an orderly transition, self-serving constitutional amendments, repressive laws and steering the constitutional drafting process. Using such means of political repression, revolutionaries were increasingly violently marginalised from the political public sphere, which was increasingly submitted directly under the control of military. Indeed, especially after Morsi's disposal in the summer of 2013 and Abdel Fattah El Sisi's rise to power, we see the intensification of such a political colonisation: using political procedural means both the political and juridical spheres now directly fell under Sisi's totalising control, and Sisi avidly pursued both a prisonification of Egyptian society and a politics of death. Sisi procedurally colonised the political public sphere to such an extent that at the slightest incline, the slightest aberration from the regime's narrative and viewpoint, one could be subjected to rape, torture, enforced disappearance, rotation detention and increasingly also extrajudicial killings. Activists' ability to manifest themselves politically in the public sphere (and thus assert their political agency) was hereby systematically and violently crushed. At the same time, neoliberal economics deeply betrayed intersubjective parity by increasing economic precarity and the impoverisation of Egyptians and activists alike, all the while the military enriched itself and submitted all economic resources under its control. As we have seen, both the political stalemate and the economic decline were then strategically deployed by the military to turn frustration inwards: that is, the blame for such increased precarity was deflected away from the continuation of neoliberal politics towards the supposed disorder caused by the revolution itself – and particularly those who were still protesting on Egypt's streets.

While the previous part thus provided this overview of Egypt's post-revolutionary developments, and therein paid particular attention to the *mechanisms* of traumatic status subordination, Part 3 particularly focuses on the subjective *existential impacts* of such deep violations of intersubjective parity. And so, while there will be some overlap in terms of content between the former and current parts, Part 2 really emphasised Egypt's social and political developments from a third-person analytical perspective, whereas this part concentrates on how these violations were phenomenologically experienced by activists and thus emphasises its existential impact from an (intersubjective) first-person perspective.[4] What we see here is that a new prefigurative lifeworld was created in the eighteen days of the revolution: a new revolutionary symbolic order, wherein intersubjective parity was (albeit precariously and temporarily) established.[5] During this time, the potentiality of meaningful change (wherein intersubjective parity (namely the value of each individual life) would continue to be established) burst out into Egypt's streets and squares with a transformative force. Suddenly all things deemed eternally impossible were possible. And it was precisely this potentiality, this possibility of change, that the counter-revolution sought to systematically destroy through the infliction of a tripartite structure of traumatic status subordination (as outlined in Part 2). This part explores the phenomenological effects of this tripartite of traumatic status subordination.

Chapter 9 relays how the symbolic order of activists' lifeworlds was eroded by the counter-revolution through the infliction of deadly physical violence in the context of the counter-revolutionary colonisation of the public sphere. It narrates how those who were subjected to of grave deadly violence, including such as torture, killings near-death (including teargas), experienced deep sense of relationlessness to the world as the symbolic order of the lifeworld collapsed. As the lifeworld collapsed in face of such grave intersubjective imparity, they experienced a profound disorientation, which they also referred to as a sense of deadness or deadly life as it left them in a state of nihilistic existential isolation. This chapter not only relays witness testimonies of such experiences, but also explains how the revolution and the clashes that followed it should also be interpreted as a form of 'Being-Against-Death', wherein they actively fought against death and a deadly life while facing the possibility of immanent death itself. Now, the trouble is that in the context of counter-revolutionary colonisation, which eradicated the possibility of creative revolutionary becoming, it became increasingly impossible for revolutionaries to ascribe meaning to the martyrs death. The upshot of this is that it was not only the incidents of grave violence that ruptured their lifeworlds, but the accumulative burden of death and violence weighed so heavily on them that it drove them into a nihilistic abyss. Burdened by so much death and bloodshed, they were plunged into a state of 'Being-Towards-Loss' wherein grief for the lost revolution intertwined with grief for lost lives, and impressed the meaninglessness of existence onto them. Deprived of the potentiality of meaningful change, the structures of counter-revolutionary violence were furthermore internalised as a personal failure, thus flinging them into debilitating bouts of what I call 'powerless guilt' and depression (the latter of which itself was interpreted as a betrayal and deep personal failure).

Unsurprisingly, both the lack of revolutionary progress and the experience of excruciating powerless guilt resulted in deep feelings of anger and frustration. As chapter 10 then explains, this anger and frustration, which resulted from both the disposability of life and the seeming inalterability of politics, was then redirected inwards into society by the military and counter-revolutionary elite, by the counter-revolution. Here, it ruptured the potential of intersubjective parity ever further and deeper. It meant that the violent imposition of multi-layered traumatic status subordination now extended from the political sphere to the social and private spheres as vicious cycles of revenge were unleashed. Revenge is the strategic attempt to regain status when one's intersubjective party has been violently damaged and one has experienced a state of inferiority. Revenge is often directed at the perpetrator, but may also be redirected elsewhere, and is thus an essential part of the victim-turns perpetrator dynamic. What we see is that in 2013, such cycles of revenge were deliberately fuelled by the military but the Brotherhood leadership also fuelled these vicious cycles through its uncompromising stance. Eventually, this of course accumulated in the Rabaa massacre and the celebration of death that followed in its wake. These cycles of revenge and Egypt's increasing social polarisation sense of demoralisation. As Matthew Ratcliffe explained in his excellent work on depression, demoralisation entails a state on depression wherein the lifeworld's horizon has become deprived not only of meaning as such but of the very potentiality to have meaning (Ratcliffe, 2014). And it is of course precisely this erosion not only of the object of revolutionary politics but rather the potentiality of its being that the Egyptian military sought to achieve when it started to impose multilevelled traumatic status subordination onto Egyptian activists.

INTERREGNUM: PREFIGURATIVE INTERSUBJECTIVE PARITY IN EGYPT'S REVOLUTIONARY PUBLIC SPHERE

Yet, in order to understand this deprivation of meaning, we must first quickly note how the revolution, and revolutionary actions entailed nothing less than a lived embodied experience of full potentiality, of the possibility of meaning.

Breaking the Revolutionary Lifeworld and Potential

For many interviewees it heralded the possibility of ending a deadly life or a life characterised by systematic humiliation and poverty.

After all, as described in chapter 3, under Mubarak's authoritarian rule, Egyptians were systematically subjected to the gravest forms of status subordination: they were unable to influence or contribute to the political public sphere as this was entirely colonised by Mubarak and his business-cum-political elites. They also suffered the gravest forms of misrecognition (including torture, maiming, serious forms of physical abuse and random humiliations) at the hands of Mubarak's security state. All the while, serious maldistribution resulting from Mubarak's neoliberal economic policies threw ordinary Egyptians deeper into existential precarity and poverty. Due to these systematic and violent betrayals of their intersubjective parity, activists experienced deep forms of alienation during Mubarak's rule: they described feeling estranged from the world, from people around them and from themselves. They explained that during Mubarak's rule, they did not feel alive but rather more zombie-like – cut off from others and the world, as the world offered no possibility of (meaningful) change.

And so, when the revolution erupted in January 2011, this was a truly transformative experience. Though many described being initially hesitant to join the uprising (as they were still fearful of Egypt's security apparatus and particularly informers) when they gradually overcome their fear as more and more people ventured onto the streets, the result was deeply transformative. Though the eighteen days were marked by violence, in that protestors were forced to fight off Mubarak's security state and informal thugs, they discovered a new way of being in the world: one wherein social relations were no longer marked by inherent distrust but were rather united in solidarity against the violence of the Mubarak regime. Many could not believe what was happening in front of their eyes. They experienced a new way of being in the world, one wherein the lifeworld's horizon was brimming with future potentiality. It was the dawn of a new era, based on the possibility of hope, of meaningful change, of a different kind of life. As this young man explains, the eighteen days brought a deep inner will to change into the open, into Egypt's streets and squares:

> I was so high and yet I was so scared, I will never forget my feelings the first time I hear in the square people shouting 'ishab urid isqat al nizam'. It was like all my inside was shaking. I was not feeling like myself. It was so strong, so clear, so loud. Really felt that something new happened. And yaeny, suddenly I did not see the same people. I was seeing a new Egypt. Suddenly I feel new hope coming. Suddenly I feel like . . . a massive strong inside me, a massive power, willing of change. (Interview 32)

Mubarak's violent repressive walls of divisive atomisation that had for so long separated them came crumbling down, and a prefigurative reality of intersubjective parity was established in Egypt's revolutionary public sphere. Egyptians from all walks of life, from all sections of society, came together as equal peers, and thereby established a new sense of 'humanity' (interview 10). As this young woman describes:

> What happened in the 18 days of the uprising. You see the Salafist person sit next to the most liberal person. You know, I don't know if that was, I don't know if that would ever happen again. But it was very heart-warming. You see the poor classes with the crème de la crème and you see them sitting together enjoying a civil conversation and it was beautiful and so simple. Because it was something beyond it. (Interview 10)

The revolution thus marked a deep existential shift of the structure of experience as such: it enabled them to see the *possibility* of change. Whereas under Mubarak, the very perception of such a possibility had been foreclosed, it now opened up before them as they engaged in creative (revolutionary) self-becoming in Egypt's public sphere. As one interviewee commented: 'Everything we believed in, all that we thought was reality, had vanished' (interview 38). Rather, in their prefigurative coming together, the possibility of creative collective becoming was opened up right before them. Suddenly, there was the possibility of hope, real hope based on the concrete actions and manifestation of people who come together in full intersubjective parity:

> The revolution had brought up all the good things in the Egyptian people together on the surface you know. [. . .] The whole environment made me feel very happy and very hopeful, and I really believe that our dream will be reached. . . . That all that we want will be achieved, that people will not live in poverty anymore. People will not take police brutality anymore. That people will not take the marginalization and injustice anymore. That the streets will be clean, you know [laughs]. We were all like this. We would be a society that respects minorities, that respects everybody. . . . That we would be pioneers in whatever. You know, our economy would be great, we would be pioneers in scientific research, you know [laughs loudly]. It is like the feeling that you get when you see your own people, you see the good side, the very good side. [. . .] We are going to build the future of this country altogether so I should be contributing somehow. (Interview 17)

The revolution thus pulled Egyptians out of their depoliticised atomisation that had been so violently imposed by the Mubarak regime, and in doing so it constituted 'nothing less than the rebirth of hope for those who had lost it' (interview 11). This hope encompassed a profound politicisation of ordinary Egyptians, which were now pulled out of the political apathy that had been violently imprinted in them by Mubarak's colonisation of the political sphere (which had made any meaningful change impossible), they now suddenly found a voice and they were shouting loud and clear on Egypt's streets and public spaces. They were finally speaking back at all the suffering and injustice that they endured under Mubarak, whose regime had consistently and violently violated their human dignity. As this young man remarked,

> During the 28th, I was violent during that day though. Yaeny, I think it was the first day for me to shout 'ishab urid' for example, and I did not have fear seeing other people been shot and have then been thrown with teargas and bullets around you. Seeing how they insist to continue. They want to go, they keep going and they are so strong, just catching the tear gas and throwing it back to the police. I was one of them, yaeny. I was totally with them. And I was feeling a huge anger inside me, a huge anger inside me. All this time I did not . . . yaeny, it was not anger against the poor policeman or the poor soldier who did not understand anything but I was throwing my stone at all the depression I had suffered through my life. Towards all, yaeny, all unappreciation, a lack of dignity. (Interview 32)

In speaking back, the revolutionary uprising entailed a direct confrontation with the indignity suffered during Mubarak's rule, as indicated by the centrality of the call for dignity in the revolutionary slogans. They demanded to be treated as an equal human being, a human being of worth, of value, a human being no longer disposable either through poverty or security state abuse. Pulled out of their atomising isolation, they were politicised and they spoke out against violent abuse in political chants, slogans and direct physical revolutionary action. As this young woman remarked:

> Somehow the uprising gave me the strength to speak up about what I want and decide to do what. Somehow the uprising, I got to know many people through this, I got to know people who actually share my dreams and my you know hopes for Egypt. And where I can actually share like you know and like enjoy an intellectual conversation with without being afraid. Like I know that I'm not alone. Which was really refreshing. You got to know that we actually . . . we're quite plenty of people with you know who actually want to be happy and independent. Who think of a different future and who would want to work on it. (Interview 10)

Being able to creatively manifest themselves in the world for the first time in their lives, politics burst into their lives 'like a train hitting a wall' (as one young woman put it) (interview 39). Of course, from the moment the uprising started Mubarak sought to quell it, using both rhetorical appeals (notably his speeches) and direct physical violence. But the revolutionary genie – full with potentiality – refused to go back into the bottle. And Mubarak's efforts fell on infertile grounds. And so, on the eighteenth day, with a firm push behind the scenes by the Egyptian military (which simply used the revolutionary momentum to get rid of Mubarak and his sons), Mubarak was forced to resign. For most interviewees, the moment that Mubarak resigned was the happiest in their lives. Though, as this young man's testimony indicates, not all were lucky enough to be in Tahrir Square at the moment the resignation was announced:

> For about two or three days I did not take a shower would change my clothes, so I wanted to go and have a shower and change my clothes. I heard that Mubarak would say some speech, and I thought that oh no the speech will say the same bullshit. So I will not listen and I will be at home. So just when I went home, to just take a shower, I heard on television the speech that he resigned. . . . ohhhhh noooo, nooo nooo, I was not in the square! [laughs]. So I went back again. So I change my clothes very fast, and I just ran to find a taxi and I told him I will give you LE100 to get me into the square in 10 minutes. When I found a lot of people celebrating, I am so happy I did stuff I did not imagine I would do. And this time, I had never drunk before, at this point I just drank alcohol with my friends to celebrate. I danced, although I did not dance again as I did not know how to dance. I did a lot of crazy things there. I got a tattoo, a lot of crazy stuff that I would never imagine that I would do. And the tattoo said Fuck to Mubarak. And we say some . . . You know and this time the media say that we are sissy boys so we make a proverb at this time: we the sissy boys kicked Mubarak's arse. (Interview 12)

The eruption of joy and elation upon Mubarak's resignation was real, with many interviewees feeling immensely empowered:

> Hosni Mubarak was of course like the monster. When you are playing games there are like different levels, and Hosni Mubarak was like the last level. We are facing now the dragons. So we toppled Hosni Mubarak just by demonstrating people – and wow, I was over the moon. (Interview 7)

Yet others explained that while they felt immensely relieved and happy with Mubarak's resignation and celebrated, they also felt a little trepidation about what was possibly to come:

When Mubarak resigned, I felt that we succeeded somehow because this was our you know. . . . This was our tangible demand because our demands are basically dignity, freedom, bread which means like ending poverty. But above all we wanted Mubarak to step down and this was the only tangible demand, and he did. So we felt very happy because we are successful. Our voice was heard, and they did that through people's means, through activism and protesting actually works And at last finally we got our demand fulfilled but this was like a minor feeling in comparison to the big feeling which is the stronger feeling basically we don't want the military to take over. . . . But not actually, you know this is what I felt, right away . . . Of course I celebrated. I did not celebrate in Tahrir Square. But of course, the streets were all filled with celebrations and I went to the streets, but I had this very annoying feeling that no I don't want the military too. Simple as that. (Interview 17)

Unfortunately, as we noted in Part 2, this interviewee's apprehension turned out to be warranted. For, as soon as Mubarak was ousted, the Supreme Council of Armed Forces immediately set out to destroy the revolution's transformative potential. It embarked on a tripartite infliction of traumatic status subordination, using grave and deadly physical force, the procedural colonisation of the political public sphere and the continuation of neoliberal economics (now with the military rather than Mubarak's politico-cum-business elite as the primary beneficiary) (Adly, 2017, 2020). It was in this manner that the military sought to curtail the *potentiality* of revolutionary hope – to destroy the revolutionary sense of a future 'as a dimension in which significant possibilities can be actualized' (Ratcliffe, 2014: 110). For, in order to protect its newly acquired political and economic gains and interests, it had to re-atomise Egyptians and shift the existential structures of possibility back to a state of impossibility. It had to break the symbolic order of the revolutionary lifeworld: thereby destroying the potential of creative self-becoming. It is this existential rupture of the potentiality of meaning, of creative self manifestation, that the next two chapters will explore in detail through a first person phenomenological account that draws on activists' testimonies.

NOTES

1. As we have seen, this conceptualisation draws heavily from Nancy Fraser's philosophy and particularly her account of misrecognition, including the concepts of status subordination and participation parity (Fraser and Honneth, 2003; Fraser, 2014).

2. This conceptualisation is based on a horizontal, purely communicative theoretical, reading of Habermas's colonisation thesis (Habermas, 1979, 1987b). For more details, see chapter 2.

3. My understanding of alienation is directly based on Rahel Jeggi's excellent account (Jaeggi, 2014).

4. This book hereby clearly continues the Habermasian reconstructive tradition wherein the participant's perspective is combined with a social and political analyses conducted from a third person's perspective.

5. On the prefigurative nature of the eighteen days, see van de Sande (2013).

Chapter 9

Breaking the Lifeworld

On the Existential Burden of Violence and Death

While Part 2 discussed the mechanisms through which the Egyptian counter-revolution inflicted traumatic status subordination upon activists, Part 3 explores the deep existential impacts that this infliction of multilevelled traumatic status subordination has had on activists. It will thus examine the ways in which the infliction of such violence destroyed the existential register of possible experience away from one brimming with (revolutionary) potentiality towards one of demoralisation. As part of this endeavour, this chapter will focus on the ways in which the imposition of grave deadly violence in a context of counter-revolutionary colonisation and neoliberal acceleration tore activists' lifeworlds apart. Direct experiences of overwhelming violence, such as torture, killings and near-death (including being teargassed), destroyed their orientation in the world. It flung them into a deep existential disorientation wherein the world they inhabited no longer made sense. Interviewees experienced severe forms of alienation, estrangement and numbing as the unitary structure of the lifeworld through which meaning may be derived was broken. Many also described this as a form of 'deadness' or 'deadly life', wherein they experienced great difficulty in re-engaging with the world after it had appeared utterly surreal. That interviewees would experience such deep existential estrangement is not surprising since, as Heideggerian trauma theory (Bracken, 2002b, Stolorow, 2007, 2011) and the work of Gill Howie (2006) remind us, the confrontation with death gives rise to an existential shock wherein life suddenly appeared deprived of meaning, purpose and orientation. The confrontation with death unhinges our intersubjective relations to the world, others and our selves, and particularly so in a context wherein these deaths were also the result of the malevolent will of another.

Importantly, what weighed heavily on them was not only the direct experience of brutal force, but rather also the accumulation of deadly violence in a context of counter-revolutionary colonisation which enforced a deep sense of political hopelessness. Death, as Sartre reminds us, is never rally our own since, even if we try and ascribe meaning to it (by dying for a particular cause). at the moment of its occurrence we are disposed of ourselves (Sartre, 1956). This means that others basically become the carriers of the meaning of our deaths. Death is thus fully intersubjective. As this chapter illustrates, revolutionaries felt a deep responsibility to provide meaning to the deaths of martyrs, through a (Levinasian) remembrance of their individual particularity and the continuation of the revolutionary path. However, since the process of revolutionary becoming was violently sabotaged by Egypt's counter-revolution's colonisation of the public sphere, the burden of accumulative death flung them into a 'Being-towards-Loss', wherein grief for the lost lives intertwined with grief for the revolution. As a result, interviewees not only found themselves gazing into a nihilistic abyss of enforced meaninglessness, but also experienced a profound level of, what I call, powerless existential guilt wherein the structures of violence became internalised as a deep (crippling) sense of personal failure. They thus experienced a deep state of depression, wherein the world was deprived of the potential of signification. Yet, the trouble is that from within the spectrum of powerless guilt, even this depression was itself interpreted as a form of failure – or, betrayal of the revolution. What we thus see is that the violent infliction of multilevelled traumatic status subordination not only flung them into a state of disorientation, but rather also reimposed a deadly life on them, a life deprived of potentiality and creative collective self-becoming.

LIVING DEATH: EXPERIENCE TORTURE

The Egyptian military sought to break the symbolic order of the lifeworld through the infliction of grave deadly violence in the context of counter-revolutionary colonisation and neoliberal acceleration. It was through this tripartite mechanism that it sought not only to contain but rather destroy Egypt's revolutionary potentiality, and reinforce a deadly life depraved of the possibility of meaningful change on activists. One of the tools it employed to reinforce this deadly life was torture, which four of the interviewees directly endured when they were detained by SCAF's rule while many others also had family or friends who were tortured at the hands of the military or Brotherhood. The very principle of torture is the brutal eradication of intersubjective parity. In torture, the perpetrator seeks nothing less than the violent erosion of the victim's sense of belonging to humanity and the manifestation of the perpetrator's power. In torture, one is entirely subject to the malevolent will of the all-powerful other without any help in sight. Rather, the victim is subjected to the most violent of power relations, wherein he or she is entirely at the behest of the violent perpetrator, who may do as he or she pleases. Herein, the victim, is reduced to a mere object, mere flesh. He or she is not only confronted the impending possibility of death but rather also that the inflicted misery it is the result of another's violent *volition,* in the face of which one is utterly helpless. It is this helpless subordination that makes torture so destructive. Hence, when tortured, Jean Améry famously noted, a 'part of our life ends and it can never be revived again' (Améry, 1980: 29). For, what happens in torture is that the symbolic realm of the lifeworld (the way we used to make sense of the world) collapses as our intersubjective existential equality is betrayed in a most fundamental way.

As this young man, who was tortured by the Egyptian military on the 9th of March when the military cleared a sit-in on Tahrir, narrated:

> What happened is that they arrested about 200, about 20 girls and 180 men and tortured us in front of the Egyptian museum outside the garden and the torturing takes about 5 hours. They treated me very specially, because they knew me when I was arrested and they take all of them after torturing to the jail but for me they left me in the end of the 5 hours because my case, my situation was very bad, and I could not move. They put me in a taxi and left me. They tortured all of us but for me, the case was completely different. After 10 minutes, they started smashing my head on a column, then they take off my clothes except underwear and then tied a rope on my leg and they pull me to inside the garden and they started the torturing by wooden sticks, metal sticks. Some officers jumping a lot on my back on my head, and in the end, they electrocuted me, they burnt me – and they cut my hair with broken glass. And during the torturing they try and use words to break your spirit and to break you inside. (Interview 36)

He explained that emotionally the experience left him emotionally numbed, even taking away feelings of fear:

> In the beginning of torturing [I experience fear] – maybe in the first hour, but during the rest I think I forget this especially because I thought they would kill me. And after torturing, not only for me but for all the real protestors, completely forget to be afraid because we faced death a lot and a lot. So, we are facing the bullets, the gas, the cars, their sticks, everything and we lost a lot of our friends, there is no fear now. (Interview 36)

During the interview it became apparent that this emotional numbing, and the inability to feel fear even in the face of death, should not necessarily be interpreted as a sign of revolutionary bravery. Rather, sadly, it constituted an impoverishment of the available emotional spectrum, a collapse of the lifeworld's horizon which was experienced as a form of inner death. As he described it:

> You cannot describe what you lived in these moments. You cannot put it in words. You live in different world than other people. Once you have experienced what I have experienced, you have experienced the worst and you live with death inside of you every day. (Interview 36)

Torture is experienced as a form of death since the world as we knew it, the way we made sense of it, of others and even of ourselves is destroyed. Hence, it is often experienced as a death of a previous self as well as a death of relations to others, as a social death. As meaning, and the potentiality of meaning, disappears in torture, it atomises, separates and divides: the victim doubles up inside him- or herself in a painful nihilistic retreat. The lifeworld collapses under the burden of sheer painful misery that is impossible to comprehend. Torture throws one into an existential prison of solitude, not only at the moment of its infliction but often also afterwards, as the story of this young man, tortured by Egypt's security forces during his detention after the Mohammed Mahmoud street battle indicates. He spoke quietly, his body softly shaking, as he explained how during his torture, they not only inflicted physical pain but also sought to break him psychologically through demeaning and mocking words. They sought to break his spirit, he explained. This experience of torture had left him profoundly alienated from himself and from others. Above all, he was fearful that he was now radiating negative energy to everyone and everywhere. In his words:

> If my past self of 2010 or 2011 met my present self right now I believe I would not have known me to be the same person. I mean, even my. . . . Even my looks changed from this. Everyone used to tell me how cheerful and positive I was and until two years ago really. Ehm . . . But now I feel like I am radiating negative energy to the people around me. Ehm . . . I have been mentally changed quite a lot. I don't think the same way. I don't look the same way. I actually have been, I left my family, about a year ago because I cannot live with anyone anymore. [. . .] . . . And I actually lost many of my friends. (Interview 1)

His lifeworld had come crushing down under the pressure of both his detention and torture: his notion of self and relation to others lay in tatters, and he struggled to engage with the world. He explained that he was continuously haunted by a deep sense of separation, an existential divide between his experience of the world and that of others. This sense of atomising, alienating separation is also acutely felt by this young man who suffered the torture of a sexual nature. As he relayed:

> When . . . eh . . . Israel attacked Gaza, so we went to protest and it was the second time I was put in jail because of protest. The army. . . . Get us under the bridge after they caught us, our eyes are covered, our hands are tied on our back . . . and . . . eh . . . yeany . . . It was the first time that I was feeling . . . [sighs . . . tears come from his eyes] . . . That someone can break me, I did not have this feeling before. I felt like I was nothing . . . eh . . . when we was with the prison of the army, they electrocuted us, they burnt us, hit us under our feet, and I was one of the last people who received the beating. . . . yeany . . . Some person, I did not meet him again, it was . . . eh . . . he . . . do you know the sound of a woman who is pregnant with a baby and gives birth and screams? He was screaming like her . . . because of . . . some son of a bitch . . . soldier . . . was fucking him. So like him . . . [breathing heavily and crying] . . . after the fourth day, or something like this, when they found that we did not do nothing they let us free. But . . . eh . . . Something inside of me was broken. (Interview 12)

In sexual torture, the existential weight of torture was compounded by its explicit societal stigmatisation, and especially so in Egypt where the impact of male anal rape is particularly severe due to Egypt's social and political context. There are two reasons for this. First, male rape is not only deeply stigmatised in society but its infliction itself is also steeped in a violent patriarchal logic. Security forces who inflict male rape in Egypt's places of detention employ a particularly violent patriarchal logic wherein the perpetrator is regarded as the 'active' party (the embodiment of active male strength), while the 'receiving party' is hollow (characterised as feminine weakness). Hence, the destructive logic of male rape comprises not only the horrific reduction to the flesh but also the supposed nullification of masculine strength and the imprinting of a gendered 'powerlessness' and 'weakness' upon the victims, which in a patriarchal society has grave impacts on one's social orientation and standing. The point is hence to render them inactive, isolated and passive, through their violent purposeful feminisation, and is thus part of the traumatic status subordination that is purposefully inflicted on them.

The second reason that male rape is particularly destructive is that it is not even formally recognised by Egyptian law.[1] In Egyptian law, rape is limited to the vaginal penetration of a woman by someone other than her husband. Thus, legally, anal, male-on-male (as well as domestic) rape does not exist. And so, any road towards accountability and reclaiming some intersubjective parity through the judicial system (however unlikely within Egypt's corrupted judicial system) is thereby foreclosed. This young man's horrific experience hence left him in a terrible existential state – it numbed his emotions entirely, thereby making death appear like an appealing option. In his words:

> Now my problem is that I don't feel at all, I don't feel death, I am not afraid. Right now I am not afraid to lose anybody. My family, my friends right now I don't have any feelings, I just don't care. I have never had this feeling before but now . . . just. . . . Like when I cross the street I don't look. I look sometimes to my destiny of dying. (Interview 12)

This desire for death was also shared by the young man tortured at the museum gardens, who admitted: 'I want to tell you . . . that I want to kill myself. The honest truth is that I have been thinking about killing myself' (interview 3). Death, and the existential state of nothingness, seemed like a profound relief to the continually suffering alienation and estrangement, to not feeling human anymore, to leading a deadly life.

BEING AGAINST DEATH: CLASHES AND THE POLITICS OF VIOLENCE, DEATH AND DISORIENTATION

It was of course also precisely such a deadly life that both the revolution and subsequent protests railed against. It was the demand to be treated as a human being of equal worth, the assertion that life was not disposable, that drove protesters to the streets and take a stance against both the Egyptian state's security apparatus and its economic maldistribution. Indeed, one may even regard not only the revolutionary uprising but also the protests and clashes that followed for years in its wake, as what Marc Crépon calls a 'Being-against-Death' (Crépon, 2013). Here, Crépon is critical of Heidegger's notion of Being-towards-Death, wherein the heroic sacrificial soldier's orientation towards death entails an embrace of his particular ontology. Instead, Crépon argues that soldiers at the front do not so much embrace death but rather united in a battle *against* death. As Crépon explains:

> They show a relation that consists specifically in coming together to oppose death with the greatest possible resistance, to effectively join forces against it (against hunger, against the cold, against illness, but also against enemy fire) through mutual assistance. One might call this relation 'being-against-death'. (Crépon, 2013: 23)

This being-against-death neither implies the 'refusal of death nor the attempt to escape it' (Crépon, 2013: 23), nor does it even negate a

'Being-towards-Death' as such but rather transforms its meaning away from an acceptance or resignation of death into a battle or a fight against death (in the full realisation that one might die during this battle). This is precisely what happened in the Egyptian revolution and clashes: activists and protesters united against the (deadly) traumatic status subordination the Egyptian state was trying to inflict. They fought against the death of poverty, the deaths by security state abuse and living a deadly life, in the full awareness in this struggle they might very well die. In the words of this young doctor:

> And for me.... The main reason for the display to in the revolution is that I feared that we don't have any value in this country. And our life is dead in itself. And I was participating from this point from this view. I was participating because I have a right and you should respect it, and I have something and you should appreciate it and I have a right in this country. My life should be respected through the very little things, when I get out of my home to go to work, I should be respected all over the way. I should not feel that I not worth anything in this country. One human life means a lot. We are not numbers, bass ... Yaeny.... Now when I'm thinking back, I appreciate how I did not die whilst participating in the revolution. I was so lucky. I was so lucky. I have no reason why I did not die. (Interview 32)

Egyptian revolutionaries thus did not deny death, nor did many of them indeed escape it. Rather, they were fully aware that in their engagement with revolutionary politics, street clashes, demonstrations and gatherings, they risked nothing less than their lives. As this young man explained:

> Anything will happen – even to the point of dying, and that if I or anyone go to protests, we must be aware of that we can die right away, and that we ourselves can only be responsible for our lives as the government does not care. No one cares about the lives of those who died. And so, when I go into the streets, I need to realise that I can die at any time. (Interview 39)

Indeed, quite a few interviewees started to make arrangements in light of the very real prospect that they might die. As this young person for instance remarked:

> I was worried because I used to see a lot of dead bodies and families come to identify them so I didn't want my family to go through that – to have come and identify me as a dead body. I used to write a friend's name and number on my arm. (Interview 16)

Nearly all interviewees also confirmed that it was precisely this display of selfless 'Being-against-Death' by the frontliners that earned them such a heroic status. These young men, frequently associated with football clubs such as Al Ahly, threw their bodies into the battles with Egypt's security apparatus with full force. They fought Mubarak's regime of death with a collective Being-against-Death: as the regime fired machine guns and other artillery, they threw stones, self-made Molotov cocktails, sticks and other improvised weapons. Hence, for most interviewees, revolutionary hope was embodied in this collective 'fight-against-death', in these frontline revolutionaries:

> Jikas friends is a whole generation of young determined activists. These guys give me complete hope. They're the ones front lining and take the risk and go out and scream against the military and against the brotherhood in the streets. [They] went in front of the Giza governorate [where there were] nearly thousand troops in black and a handful like 20 or 30 young activists, who didn't care and just showed it to them, you know, out on the street. [. . .] They give me complete hope because the revolution changed people which is . . . actually more monumental of a change than changing a regime I think. (Interview 11)

The point of these battles was perhaps not always to win but rather not to lose without putting up a good fight, without resistance, since it was through this resistance, this act of speaking out with their bodies, that they negated the regime's forceful imposition of intersubjective imparity. They said no, and meant no. No more abuse, no more corruption, no more military leaders, no more deadly lives and no more injustice. So, as one young man (part of the 6th April movement) explained, even when they knew the organised march was a trap, that they would lose the battle and indeed would lose many lives, they went nevertheless (interview 11). It was through putting up a fight that they reinscribed meaning to their actions, the protests, the revolution and indeed to themselves. The point was to not let injustice pass unnoticed but rather to put up a good fight against it, to 'stand one's ground' (interview 11). In this sense, clashes were indeed nothing less than a life-or-death battle: between a deadly life or a human life, between disposability and human dignity.

The trouble is of course that even so, even with protests and clashes being the site of collective 'Being-against-Death', it was nevertheless also the site of the overwhelming imposition of death, violence and bloodshed, which regardless of the fight of 'Being-against-Death' left a deep existential toll. Indeed, for many interviewees, the confrontation with so much death (and the distinct possibility of one's own death) still constituted a profound shock, wherein meaning evaporated as the lifeworld's symbolic realm lay in tatters. They were unable to make sense of it, as death – and especially so much of it – escaped comprehension. As Gillian Howie explained, no matter that we know it rationally, the confrontation with death nevertheless entails a surprise that gives rise to an existential crisis of meaning and purpose (Howie, 2016), and arguably even more so when (the threat of) death is due to another's malicious intent. The violent confrontation with death thus ruptures the lifeworld, the way we used to derive meaning from and in the world, the way we used to relate to ourselves and others. Rather, in the face of death, nothing makes sense anymore. Of course, it is also precisely for this reason, the violent imposition of death (or rather, murder) is so useful as an instrumental tool of repression: its purpose is not merely to (literally) reduce the number of bodies on the streets, but rather to destroy protesters' way of being in the world. The point is to incapacitate them, to deprive them of their agency.

Death, as Heidegger teaches us, is brutally atomising: in the face of death, we become painfully aware of our profound singularity (our 'ownmost') as our usual everyday way of making sense of the world collapses (Heidegger, 2010: 252). Rather, in the face of death, 'what one normally does' (or what Heidegger refers to as the 'They') falls away, and thrown back onto our particularity we can find no comfort in the world anymore. The way we used to make sense of the world, the everyday diversions of the 'They' proves to be profoundly inadequate and misleading. They provide no comfort as we confront the brutal reality of our ontological existence. For Heidegger of course, it was precisely in this way that death opened up the possibility of authentic being in the world, namely a being devoid of ordinary distractions and diversions, a way of being that is nonrelational and ownmost (Heidegger, 2010: 252). The trouble here is that Heidegger holds a particularly solipsist view of Being, which its focus on the singularity of the individual leads us directly back to the trappings of the philosophy of the subject. Nevertheless, his philosophy is immensely useful in that it reveals how in the face of death, the interpretative framework of the lifeworld dissipates and throws us into a state of atomisation as it severs intersubjective relations. And it is of course precisely this (re)atomisation that makes the violent imposition of death such a powerful tool of repression.

Moreover, Heidegger is also useful in that he points out that death takes away our future and thus erodes our common ways of making sense of the past and the present, leaving us standing in a (meaningless) present. This of course relates directly to experience of temporal stuckness that Heideggerian trauma theory so well describes: in trauma we experience a profound closure or rupture of potentiality. This is due to the way in which our meaning-making is inherently connected to the 'ecstasies of temporality' (Heidegger, 2010: 357): the manner in which our sense of past, present and future always refer to each other. Each dimension only makes sense in reference to the other, thereby 'constituting a meaningful whole in which all three are indissolubly united' (Stolorow, 2007: 19). And so, the way in which we normally make sense of our existence, the world and others is through temporal cross-referencing: it is through reference to a past that we can shape a present and project ourselves into the future. Hence, the imposition of death is a powerful political tool since it not only literally takes away the future but also collapses the horizon of future potentiality: we can no longer make sense of the present through the past, nor can we project ourselves into the future. Instead, we become 'freeze framed into a constant reliving of present' which contributes to the sense of alienation and estrangement from other human beings [. . .] since our ability of being-in-time with them (Stolorow, 2007: 55).

Hence, in the face of death protesters often experienced a deep, disorienting estrangement – an existential dreamlike surreality as the lifeworld's interpretive framework collapsed. For many, such a surreal disorientation occurred during the violence of clashes, as this young explained:

> So yeah, in the first . . . in my own case, in the first two or three hours, I felt like ehm . . . it was a strange psychological feeling. I felt like I don't exist, like I am dreaming that something was making me stick and refusing to leave although I was scared. But I just could not leave. So I remember very well zoning out, not move, I was just frozen watching this. Ehm . . . I was watching people bleeding and maybe some of them looked already dead. I did not engage with the idea that I was very close, very close to the front line, and I refuse to leave and this feeling of being out of place in this feeling of like dreaming, and this is not real, it was over after two of three hours. (Interview 25)

This young woman recalled her deep sense of disorientation, and above all her inability to make sense of her surroundings during the battle of Mohammed Mahmoud and the Cabinet clashes that followed. Reality, she explained, did not seem to be able to get through to her. In her own words:

> You see men dressed in like you know army from the roof top of the Cabinet buildings. And they're like throwing stuff, big concrete cement blocks, at you. And you see other people throwing stuff. And you see street kids, like, you know, taking out the steel from something and you don't know what they're about to do with it. I remember this day it was really, really, it was really I mean it didn't feel real. I was just blocked, and I was walking past all the beating. And like you know, my friend came and was like you know 'perhaps get outta here' and I just you know. I wasn't really aware of what was going on. I mean I was just walking past people beating each other, someone is just throwing something. You don't know. And you don't know what to do with it. You just, you know. You don't know how to react. Or if there's a reaction. [. . .] The amount of gasses you know. It was very hard to breath in and you see little girls protesting for the first time behind their parents back and they're trying to make their own decisions. And then you see you're out there. And you see like you

know, the soldiers are right here, the protestors are right here. They're swearing at each other. It's quite juvenile. You don't get what it is about, but you see a plate all of a sudden, you see a bomb being thrown there. You see people throw stones the other way. And it won't make sense and you get dizzy. It just doesn't make sense. (Interview 10)

Another young female activist also narrated that in the midst of the clashes' vertigo of violence she no longer felt human – and that in her case, it was the sight of blood that allowed emotions to return somewhat. In her own words:

You are just in a state of excitement, fear and helplessness shuwayya, yeah whenever you see blood it is just like 'oh you know' and you become human again because at that time you are not really human, you are just kind of like yeah yeany you are not really feeling anything. You are so high that you are not really human anymore. You are watching and you are seeing and you are laughing hysterically and it is being scared, being high on the experience yaeny. And then you see the blood and it is like 'oh shit call the ambulance' you know and then you are reminded that you actually have some feelings yaeny. (Interview 30)

Yet, for most interviewees, it was precisely the sight of blood and death that, rather than pulling them out of a numbed state, flung them right into it. For, the confrontation with death and (deadly) injuries left many feeling existentially paralysed – confronted as they were with a world that seemed surreal, a world wherein the fact of 'not having died' constituted nearly as much of an existential surprise as having nearly died:

You hear live ammunition from everywhere and people bleeding and running behind you, in front of you and then you are not shot. It is a strange feeling that you are not dead. You always wonder why am I not dead. (Interview 25)

They all described a deep sense of estrangement from the world, which they experienced as numbing.

Now it might be tempting to interpret such numbing in the 'traditional' manner of trauma studies: namely cognitively, as the overflowing of the processing capacities of the brain. The trouble with such an interpretation, however, is not only that it would bring us back to the philosophy of the subject, but also that it remains stuck at the philosophical level of intentionality, namely the object of one's *belief contents*. As explained earlier, intentionality refers to our mental directedness towards objects, subjects and affairs in the world: our ability to gain a cognitive understanding of and engage with others, things and the world around us.[2] Yet, what such intentional analyses overlook is the fact that such engagement with the world depends on the lifeworld's functioning as a background for orientation and meaning-making. As we already noted, in trauma, it is precisely this background that is ruptured: the violent betrayal of intersubjective parity undermines the lifeworld's fundamental presuppositions and throws us into a state of existential disorientation and nihilistic meaninglessness. The rupture of the lifeworld thus entails a breakdown of our underlying existential register which structures our possible engagement in the world in the first place.

Hence, numbing, I propose, ought not to be perceived as an overwhelming of the brain or mind by events that do not fit the structure of one's belief *contents* but rather as a break in the unitary phenomenological structure of experience, which runs deeper than the level of cognitive schemata of belief contents. When the unitary and integrative structure of the lifeworld is broken, one's sense of being or dwelling in the world becomes profoundly unhinged. One experiences a deep sense of alienation and estrangement from the world (and oneself): an existential uncanniness that is difficult to express in words. The world, as well as objects and people in it, appears in a fundamentally different light, as surreal. A common experience of lifeworld disruption is hence a deep uncanny feeling of numbing detachment wherein reality appears ghostly, surreal, unbelievable and unreachable (Ratcliffe, reference: p30). If possible, at all, it takes great effort to re-engage in the world. Of course, this was precisely the point of Egypt's counter-revolutionary violence: to fundamentally alter the existential structure of experience through traumatic status subordination, so that the potential for creative revolutionary self-becoming would be broken, and the military's strategic interests safeguarded.

This effort of re-engaging with the world was particularly hard in the context of near-death experiences, where a real rupture between the self and the world had taken place. For instance, this young man shared his near-death experience at the Cabinet clashes in December 2011. After having spent the whole day looking for his friend, whom he had presumed dead, he finally found his friend in a hospital, where it transpired, he had been tortured: his fingers were smashed and his back was broken. Since hospitals were an unsafe place for protesters (because they were frequently raided by Egyptian security forces, who either detained or shot people on the spot), he transported his friend to a field hospital near the Cabinet clashes. Then, at the end of this long day, at 4.00 am:

> I wanted to go home to take a shower and charge my phone and then go back. [. . .] at 4, I said I would go home and I would be back in an hour [. . .] So my friends were like okay we are going to come with you, and the whole streets were totally dark . . . Completely dark. So they were like okay we are going to come with you because if anything happens we need to be with you. They had

a shield that could cover us, a big one made of metal . . . and then they were like okay we will walk like this, behind this. And you know move really cautiously, and protected by this thingie. And then when we got to Tahrir, they were like 'ok it is fine. We are going to go back. It will be fine you take a taxi. Bye bye bye'. And then I remembered that I forgot something at the field hospital, my car keys. . . . My mum's car . . . So I was like okay I'm going to go back. Nothing happened so it should be fine. Eh . . . when I was on my way back, I was moving back carefully, moving back from tree to another tree, and you know to be hidden. And then from the building of the IDSP, the Cabinet basically, eh . . . I was right in front of it but it was from the other side, the very other end of the street . . . and it was really dark so it was very difficult to see . . . then suddenly right beside me 'peeeeew' [makes high tone noise] . . . a bullet . . . then I was really terrified . . . so I turned around, and I started running towards Tahrir. I don't care about the keys anymore, I started to run back. As I ran back there was 'tsktsktsktsktsktsk' [makes machine gun noise] following me, right beside me I was really terrified. . . . And when I arrived in Tahrir my body was really. . . . I could not even stand on my legs you know. I lost everything I had in my pockets as I just ran like a crazy person. I was completely traumatised. I went home in a taxi, and I just sat there like that [gives expression of someone gauntly staring into nowhere]. I was basically running, and right after me I could hear the sound of the bullets hitting the wall that I just passed by you know . . . peeeew, peeew, peeeew, peeew [makes sound of gunshots] stuff like that. So I went home, I was completely shocked and I just slept for an entire day. Everyone thought I was dead because I lost everything, and I was home. . . . There was no one at home. . . . All my friends and my family they thought I was dead. And so they did the same thing, they went to ask the guys 'what happened? He left and we did not hear about him afterwards? So he is probably'. . . . But I was really shocked and so when I was home I just slept for an entire day. (Interview 27)

While this young man slept that whole day, he explained that since that day, he had not been able to sleep properly as he was suffering from severe bouts of anxiety and a numbing sense of separation between himself and the world. He was also particularly worried about the reduction of his emotional spectrum, as he now appeared unable to feel at all, including the inability to mourn or care about the death of others (also see chapter 10). He felt numbed and actively wondered if, in light of the absence of such emotions, he could still be considered human as such.

This deep sense of alienation was shared by others who had near-death experiences, including some of those who believed they were going to die through teargas. The profound existential effects of teargas are often underestimated, perhaps because it is supposed to be a non-lethal weapon used for crowd dispersion without long-term impacts and perhaps because within

Egypt's post-revolutionary context (masculinised) narratives around teargas bravado have emerged.³ Yet, for many interviewees being teargassed constituted nothing less than direct confrontation with the imminent possibility of death. They explained that being teargassed evoked a great sense of existential disorientation, wherein they panicked, thinking they were going to choke to death on the spot. As this young man put it, when being teargassed 'you feel like you're going to die [. . .]. Teargas is really bad in that sense. Like if I don't get out of here I am going to die' (interview 19), Teargas, he explains, involves

> a physical reaction in the sense that I am going to cough my lungs. Pain. It's like sheer pain. And it's weird, because it is like pain and then you black out, so you cannot see. In particular moments, when it's really heavy tear gas, and you're caught up in it, suddenly everything is black, but it is like you can see for one second every two seconds. And that sense of panic obviously just accelerates. With pain and with the knowledge that actually you can't get out of here. It's going to take me a while; there a lot of people, and I cannot go. [. . .] It increases the panic, because you feel like I'm going to be stuck here, I am going to die. And then you start thinking that everything they told you about teargas it creates panic, so don't panic. Obviously, you cannot not panic. How do you not panic? So, it's a very – even though there have been times that I have been fired at, teargas for some reason always has been more painful and scarier. Sometimes. And then after 5 minutes you feel better and you feel like wow it's like nothing has happened. You feel like you're being cheated. And that's why teargas is a very effective weapon. I mean obviously if it's not abused it doesn't; it cannot kill you, when it is abused and it has killed a lot of people in Egypt. (Interview 19)

Interviewees also explained that the impacts of teargas were not merely instantaneous but rather longer term, with several activists explaining that since being teargassed they had difficulty breathing or had lasting eye pains. Others particularly commented on the longer term emotional or cognitive impacts of teargas, especially after the battles of Mohammed Mahmoud and the Cabinet clashes. Protesters suspected the security forces used an additional toxic, neurological component in the teargas employed during these clashes, with several interviewees remarked they felt hysterical, out of control or entered into a really dark feelings of depression. This young woman narrates her experience as follows:

> I was there with my grandma, my mum and my boyfriend, my ex-boyfriend, and they started, they started throwing teargas, and eh . . . my grandma passed out, and we were running and stuff and it was kind of, kind of stressful yaeny but then when I got home, that is the thing, I don't know how to prove this, but I felt like

it was not normal teargas I felt like . . . bass . . . I . . . A lot of people actually reported that it was nerve gas yaeny, and so my mother started hallucinating, yeah . . . and I was actually quite, I do know I went into a like into this mood of like hysteria, even though nothing really happened to me. We were fine. All that happened is that we got teargassed and people started running, and my grandma was there. . . . But my grandma is deaf you know so she can barely hear anything. She's not really deaf but she cannot really hear anything, all her senses are compromised because she is old. You know when you got this person that you want to take care of, and she is kind of like so slow and stuff, and I'm trying to get her into the car and stuff and full running and stuff you know. And when I got home it was not good for my nerves you know. We think, we think that it was not just teargas but that it had some nerve-shit you know. Because there was a lot of other, a lot of my friends also reported the same thing. They were saying that 'Oh you know after I got home I was like crying hysterically and stuff'. Yeah, yeah. And it was used again against . . . there was teargas at the end of 2012 that had the same effect on me, that I got really like dark thoughts afterwards. This was during the Palace clashes. Yeah but . . . It was like having a panic attack almost, where you feel very anxious and you cannot really breathe, you know. And you just get this really dark, you start to get this really dark thoughts you know of like helplessness and fear and must not cry you know. So that happened to me twice during the Mohamed Mahmoud clashes and last year. (Interview 30)

Hence, teargas does more than merely disperse crowds, it not only resulted in the deaths of protesters in Egypt, but rather it directly resulted in deep existential incapacitation. Being teargassed hence has a double impact: it entails a severe violation of intersubjective parity that crumbles the lifeworld and it worsens these effects through its physical effects of disorientation, blindness and physical incapacitation (which frequently result in existential panic and a fear of death). Teargas is thus a perfect tool for traumatic status subordination, wherein activists lost their bearing in the world as they had (temporarily) lost control over their body's physical orientation and manifestation in the world. As this young woman aptly commented, teargas hence instilled a sense of being at loss in the world:

I become at loss. I mean I just you know, it's the gas. I just stare in to nothing for a day or two and like you know. I go into the average depressed phase [. . .]. I wouldn't know what to think. I'll just, you know, be a typical little person at loss. Who does not understand what's going on, who has no energy to try to understand. (Interview 10)

She, like many others, felt disoriented – a deep uncanny sense of numbing alienation as she was no longer able to make sense of the world. She felt lost in the face of so much violence and death.

234   Chapter 9

MARTYRS, REVOLUTIONARY BETRAYAL AND THE BURDEN OF DEATH

This sense of being lost in the world was imprinted on activists not only in instances of violence but also through the accumulation of violence and death, particularly in light of ever-increasing and accelerating counter-revolutionary colonisation of the political public sphere. This toxic mix of overwhelming death (and a growing number of martyrs) and the increasing inability to affect any political change resulted in a profound feeling of hopelessness as they were unable to retrospectively ascribe meaning to these deaths. the result was that both the revolution and life itself were increasingly emptied from any meaning. Rather, a growing sense of nihilistic despair took hold, wherein interviewees experienced a build-up of aggression and hatred, which was then redirected inwards by the counter-revolution so as to erode intersubjective parity ever further and deeper (see chapter 10).

So how does this toxic mix of revolutionary death and procedural colonisation exactly work? In order to grasp this, we first need to note Sartre's argument that, in contrast to Heidegger's beliefs, our death is never really our own. That is, the peculiar thing about death is we can never truly own it because in the moment of our death we are disposed of ourselves. Hence, even when one tries to die a qualified death through the ascription of a certain meaning onto one's death (for instance, by dying for a political cause, such as the Egyptian revolution) one necessarily fails since upon death itself others become the holders of my death's meaning. Hence, rather than death being our own utmost potential of being, as Heidegger claims, it in fact abandons the totality of my existence to the judgement of others (Crépon, 2013: 36) And so, Sartre famously argued that 'to be dead is to be a prey for the living' (Sartre, 1956: 593; Crépon, 2013: 39), since 'in reality, the "justification" that would *redeem* me does not belong to me' (Crépon, 2013: 36). Death is thus intersubjective not only because it takes place in a social context but also because the burden of meaning-making is placed on the shoulders of others, the living, who through their actions and interpretations decide the fate of the dead (Crépon, 2013: 40). The living 'must assume a position in relation to the dead' and decide which of the dead do not 'shrivel up in its plenitude' (Crépon, 2013: 41).

Importantly, this election of the dead 'is not limited to a knowledge of history' but rather becomes an integral part of our own identity, of our own forward projection of our being in the world. As Crépon explains: 'I am not merely responsible for their survival, I am first and foremost, responsible for the Being that I choose, with them, to become' (Crépon, 2013: 41). Importantly, this 'choosing to become with them' is not merely a private or subjective relation one takes up to the dead but rather is also intersubjectively constituted through the public recognition of (and values ascribed to) these deaths in the social and political sphere. And so, the election of the dead remains a matter of social and political contestation, as it is part of 'that which divides what is shared' (Crépon, 2013: 41).

Now, the trouble in Egypt was that activists were not only subjected to the violent imposition of death and the existential shock thereof, but also that they became the carriers of meaning of martyrs' deaths in a context wherein the public sphere was violently colonised by the counter-revolution. In other words, they shouldered the meaning of these deaths in a situation wherein any sense of meaningful revolutionary projection (the ability to 'become' at all) was purposefully destroyed through the counter-revolution's infliction of multilevelled traumatic status subordination. The inability to ascribe meaning to these deaths through the continuation of revolutionary weighed heavily on interviewees' shoulders. It eventually compounded to such an extent that the revolutionary lifeworld crumbled into a nihilist abyss of nothingness, wherein both the meaning of the revolution and life itself dissipated. Now, importantly, this should not merely be interpreted cognitively as the inability to ascribe a positive outcome to the end result (namely revolutionary politics) but rather existentially as a foreclosing of possible becoming, which runs at the deeper level than philosophical intentionality as it affects the existential structures of possible existence. And so, the difficulty was that, in Egypt, it was precisely this underlying potential of revolutionary becoming and creative self-manifestation that was violently destroyed through traumatic status subordination.

Hence, the accumulative burden of death thus coincided with the erosion of the possibility of revolutionary becoming, thereby intertwining grief for the lives lost with a deep grief for a lost revolution. The severity and accumulation of grief overburdened their lifeworld's sense-making capacities to the point of its collapse, making them existentially tumble down a nihilistic, atomising hole wherein both the meaning of death and life were annihilated. As this young man's story indicates so well, interviewees felt deeply betrayed not only by the military and the Brotherhood who violently pursued their own instrumental interests but also by the ineffectiveness of other political actors (such as Hamdeen Sabbahi or Mohamed ElBaradei). Their ineffectiveness, in Egypt's counter-revolutionary context, further eroded their political hopes and deepened the existential burden of death:

> I was in the church crying when political figures in Egypt decided that they would not go to protest after the clashes in Itehedya, where almost 25 or 27 people died in one night – when the Muslim Brotherhood came and attacked the protesters in front of the palace. I was one of the people protesting there and

> I believed that we could not leave this place, that we have to protest. And we have to say our word, we have to make marches, not to just let it go but when the public figures in political life decided that 'we will not go there', we will go to Tahrir Square, and they just talk – and for me that is what they do, they just talk, they don't act. And when they do do action, the people who will pay for this action are people like me, on the street. So they did not get any interaction on their actions. So I get really angry, and I cried, and I felt like everything was crashing down on me. And I was so stressed – even my friend N. came to touch me and. . . . I did not want anyone to touch me. And I remember that . . . some of the people in the church told me that they thought they saw me crying because of someone died in your family. No, my friends died, but. . . . I believe in . . . sometimes that God can give you a brother, and he is not from your blood . . . but he can be a true brother that you can have. And I lost many. (Interview 3)

The political betrayal inflicted in the political terrain thus severely compounded the already debilitating impacts of the grief many activists experienced as they lost their loved ones, friends and family members to Egypt's counter-revolutionary violence. It was the overwhelming sense that, with the counter-revolutionary encroachment of the political change, meaningful change was being made impossible. Hence, as the counter-revolution progressed, activists increasingly experienced a deep alienation of the kind described by Rahel Jaeggi (2014), wherein the world came to stand over and above them, as the violent betrayal of intersubjective parity in the political terrain left them incapacitated, unable to influence or shape their surroundings. Interviewees thus felt deeply betrayed, they had been played for fools, as the military was steering the course of Egypt's post-revolutionary direction directly since Mubarak's ouster. Many remarked that they felt stupid for having ever believed in a revolutionary change in the first place. Some even commented that they regretted having participated in the revolution at all, since it had resulted in nothing but death and the destruction of hope. The revolution, they commented, was nothing but a political game wherein the revolutionaries had been at the losing end from the moment it commenced. As this young man noted, they had been naïve to believe in the possibility of political change:

> We have been used in January 2011, we were very happy and I don't know we were very naive, seriously. We were very happy, like we had a lot of expectations though things were really clear. The army was in power and the army was Mubarak's blablablabla, but we were very happy. And then we realised that we were used. And then a whole year of protest during the SCAF period, and then we try to work with the Muslim brotherhood in their first days, and then discovered we were being used. We were used by the Muslim Brotherhood to vote

against Shafik, and then . . . now June 30th, I am realise we were completely used. We never learn. I thought that actually . . . you know, then that the army yeah you know they are blablablablabla but I had hope that they had learnt and that they don't do this and this and that. And then: the same thing. Even worse. I mean, it is now even worse than before. So yeah I have a general state of depression. [. . .] . . . I am generally very depressed and even started to lose hope that some sort of reform can ever happen . . . eh . . . yeah. (Interview 27)

Hence, as the lifeworld's horizon of revolutionary possibility was systematically destroyed, interviewees suffered a debilitating loss of hope which flung many into a deep state of depression and anxiety. The more the counter-revolution progressed, the less hope they had about the potentiality of change and the heavier the burden of the dead weighed on their shoulders:

> You feel that you are nothing, and all these people who had died, they died for nothing and I knew some of them and he died for nothing, and no one even was remembered then because the last 3 years since the revolution we came to the point, to point zero, because nothing changed. (Interview 3)

For, with the possibility of a meaningful future increasingly destroyed, activists also lost the ability to effectively appropriate the deaths of the martyrs in an, intersubjectively constituted, forward projection of their own revolutionary identity. Rather, it now appeared that they faced nothing but a nihilistic abyss of destruction, wherein the meaning of death and life alike lay in tatters. They arrived back at point zero, with the difference being that now the martyrs' calls for justice and revolutionary progress continued to ring in their ears as a desperate plea for their deaths not to have been in vain.

Grief for the loss of loved ones, friends and others was thus compounded by a grief for a seemingly lost revolution. As Robert D. Stolorow remarks, grief is debilitating in that 'in loss, as possibility, all potentialities-for-Being in relation to a loved one are nullified. In that sense, Being-toward-loss is also a Being-toward-the-death of a part of oneself – toward existential death, as it were' (Stolorow, 2011a: 44–45). In grief, our lifeworld (temporarily) collapses – as we are pulled into a dark abyss of missing someone and of missing a part of our lives. The things we used to do no longer make sense, as Being-towards-Loss nullifies the significance of the everyday. As this story of a young photographer indicates, the loss of a loved one often entails the loss of (a meaningful) part of oneself:

> At the clashes of Madinat Nasr happened, my best friend, he is 17 and I feel like I am a brother to him, I love him so much. He was shot in his back . . . [deep breath] . . . Since this time, I . . . eh . . .I say fuck to Islam, fuck to Egypt, fuck to everything here. I will not care about anything. I will leave this Egypt, and

there is no way that I will come back. And I will not shoot any person again with photography because of my friend. . . . My friend asked me for a printer, his name is A. We make a deal, I will photograph him when he films, and he will photograph me. But . . . unfortunately we did not have the time to do this. It was the last photo I taken. . . . It was of him. And after he was shot, I did not have the feeling that I would want to photograph anyone again. Maybe I will photograph a building or something, but people I don't have the feeling to photograph anyone again. (Interview 12)

Yet Being-towards-Loss is compounded when this loss is the result of counter-revolutionary murder: wherein it is not a natural end of life, but the brutal hands of another that took our loved one. Murder aggravates the call for justice, the call not to disappear into the anonymous pit of the unknown, but to restore their face to remember them in their particularity as part of a forward projection of revolutionary becoming. However, with this forward projection being destroyed, the Levinasian sense of responsibility not to forget the martyrs' faces but to live up to their ethical demand weighed ever heavier on them. Levinas reminds us that it is not only through the face of the other that we engage in a process of self-becoming but also that since this face demands us not to harm or kill him it also reminds us of our own intersubjective vulnerability (Levinas, 2005; also see Burggraeve, 2003; Edelglass, 2006). For Levinas, the face of the other places a direct ethical responsibility on us, wherein we are called to safeguard the other's particularity, wherein we are reminded that he or she is unique, specific, singular and is both irreplaceable and not subsumable under abstracted categories, numbers or figures. Hence, to do right by the other is to do justice by his or her particularity and take up our ethical responsibility of the other's safekeeping. Of course, Levinas admits that we may choose to ignore our ethical responsibility, either through an attitude of denial, indifference or active justification of the harm done to another. However, in all these cases, the failure to prioritise this ethical relation constitutes a form of self-denial wherein a part of ourselves is silenced (Topolski, 2015: 152). And so, positive freedom for Levinas is based on the prioritisation of goodness, wherein we take up our ethical responsibility towards the other (Topolski, 2015: 152). The first act of goodness, according to Levinas, is the 'being capable of doing, of accepting responsibility for the other, of responding to his or her call or face' – and thus to 'apologise for the prioritization of our own self over the stranger, widow, the vulnerable' (Topolski, 2015: 140). Importantly, the other, for Levinas, elects us, places a demand upon us and while it particularizes us in that election, it also holds us hostage: its pointing finger persecutes us, haunts us. And hence, to do justice to the other is to be reminded of the responsibility we have towards the particularity of the (irreplaceable) other.

It is precisely this Levinasian sense of responsibility, the ethical demand by those particular others, that placed such a deep existential burden on activists. In the wake of the Egyptian state's violent subsumption and annihilation of particular lives, activists experienced a deep ethical demand not to forget their particularity but to remember them as full individuals in their particularity using songs, stories, slogans and Kazeboon showings:

> A very distinct memory I have of a Kazeboon showing on Karika's birthday – Karika is an Ahly fan who died in the cabinet clashes in December 2011 and Kazeboon were celebrating his birthday with his family right opposite his house . . . and his mother was there, his sister was there . . . and we were – we stared to screen a song written like played to his images in memory of him, a tribute song. It was very, very moving and throughout – I didn't know him personally, I got to know who he was and what Ultras did for him and basically Ultras chanting is what led to the Port Said massacre. So, as I was watching the video, it showed me what a wonderful person he is . . . he was learning drums, he was an engineer, he was tennis champion, he was a swimming champion and he was from a Middle-Class family. I mean he had . . . no reason to stand up to a brutal force, because he had a relatively good life. But he was doing it out of his own courageousness and his kindness and he was a person who had it all but chose to go on and protest you know . . . and as I see the statuses that he wrote, the last one he wrote Midan Tahrir and hearts next to it – he loved that symbol. And at that point – that moment is realising . . . we've lost a lot of really, really good people. It's just moments like these you know – it dawns upon you what you've lost and then you keep going and. . . . For him against the military that killed him. (Interview 11)

Indeed, it was through the active remembrance of their *particularity* that interviewees sought to resist the martyrs' annihilation into oblivion, their abstract reduction to numbers. As this young woman remarked: 'Martyrs, you know, are not just a number, rather their death directly affects their family and friends' (interview 38). Moreover, by actively recalling and remembering their specificity, they responded not only to the ethical call of the dead but also to the particularity of the living, including the martyrs' families, loved ones and friends. As this young man noted, 'The one who dies is not alone, he has his family, his girlfriend, his friends, he has like . . . he is surrounded by a large circle of people who really need him' (interview 31). And so, many interviewees experienced an extension of the ethical demand beyond the martyrs to their suffering families and loved ones, who were engrieved by their painful loss. For instance, one young man was enraged as to how the families of the seventy-four young men killed at the Port Said massacre had still not received answers. He explained how the weight of their parents' hopelessness on his shoulders, and how this ushered him to 'not stop mentioning these people's names as long as they did not get their rights, as long as there was no revolution in the justice system. As long as questions have remained unanswered, the painful memories cannot be closed' (interview 39). Indeed, many used this remembrance to propel the project of revolutionary becoming forward. To remember those who died in order to persist and continue their fight against death, so that these very deaths were not meaningless. In the words of this young doctor:

> These people [the martyrs] were believing in the revolution. [. . .] I believe that someone should pay the price, someone should continue and trying to change. I believe that this is our responsibility. I believe that this is our responsibility. . . . It is a message. It is message that you pay, and the price is blood. You pay by your blood, and the prize is the hope and the smiles on the faces of the little kids. Yaeny, you should continue . . . you should continue . . . [. . .] In the darkest moments when I feel that all the people have stopped thinking and that there is no hope, and then I feel that 'no, we have already paid the price'. People have paid the price, and they lost their life and they lost their eye for that. I should continue, because they were definitely better than me. (Interview 32)

Nearly all interviewees expressed a strong sense of having been elected by the martyrs, in that these martyrs placed a strong ethical demand on them to progress along the revolutionary path. But in a context wherein such propelling forward was purposefully obstructed and destroyed by counter-revolutionary violence by multilevelled traumatic status subordination, it aggravated their sense of impotence in the world:

> One human life means a lot. We are not numbers, bass . . . Yaeny . . . [. . .] And it tires me as a question, what should I do? Yaeny . . . how am I going to get justice for my friend and my relatives who have died? And what is their death mean for me? (Interview 32)

The trouble for many activists was that they felt the obligation to act, they recognised the call of ethical responsibility and that they were elected to respond in goodness. Yet, the counter-revolutionary situation they found themselves in made this impossible. Rather, their ability to act was severely hampered (and eventually destroyed) by the counter-revolution's multilevelled traumatic status subordination, which came down upon them like a ton of bricks, destroying their capacity to manifest themselves in the world. This resulted in an excruciating painful awareness of the particularity and irreplaceability of each martyr's life while at the same time being unable to live up to the calls these deaths placed upon them. The result was something akin to existential purgatory: they were persecuted by the particular faces of the dead and dying – who came to them in their dreams, nightmares and as they walked past particular places where these persons had died – while being stuck, unable to act upon the call of these deaths, unable to hold security state officials accountable for these murders and unable to augment the recognition and institutionalisation of intersubjective parity.

For many, this accumulated in a deep sense of survivors' guilt, wherein the loss of the other is not only experienced as a loss of (a part of) the self but also collapsed inwards into a deep sensation of existential guilt. For instance, one young woman narrated how when her brother found out one of his best friends died at a protest,

> Another young woman narrated feeling immense pain has her younger brother found out one of his female friends had been shot dead at a protest: 'he cried and cried and cried and then he went numb' . . . [. . .] And for days he just uttered the words 'why?' – randomly at any moment during the day. He just could not understand why she had to die and why he was still alive. (Interview 38)

And many interviewees narrated how the martyrs were definitely much better than they, more heroic, stronger and a better version of being a human as they had paid the highest price. Being unable to live up to these demands, some wondererd, perhaps they (the interviewees) did not deserve to live (interview 32). Hence, haunted by the faces of those who died and their suffering families, many interviewees experienced a deep sense of debilitating existential (survivor's) guilt. For, unable to give meaning to these deaths in forward revolutionary becoming (since the counter-revolution increasingly destroyed all pathways of meaningful change) ethical responsibility collapsed inwards, resulting in debilitating state of existential guilt and self-reproach. They experienced a profound sense of inferiority, wherein the structural destruction of progressive revolutionary change was often interpreted as a direct result of their personal failure. It was as if *they* had simply not been up to the job, even when the martyrs had paid the highest price. Surely this was a sign, they reasoned, that they had not been as strong as the martyrs. Hence, the externally imposed structural violence became internalised as subjective inadequacy or defectiveness, thereby further eroding the possibility of creative intersubjective becoming as it flung them into a state of deep depression.

Notably, only a few interviewees, such as this young legal scholar, experienced a more ambiguous, or conflicting, attitude towards the martyrs. On the one hand, he felt the strong ethical obligation to actively remember them and to respond to their ethical demand by continuing the process of revolutionary becoming. He relayed he constantly asked himself questions such as 'how would they feel about the anti-protest law?' or 'would they have been happy about the 3rd of July 2013?' (Interview 27). Yet, at the same time, he experienced a realisation that none of this mattered: 'They died, it does not matter, they are dead, just gone . . . no need to think of these memories, . . . [. . .] No, they are not anything, they are just dead, so why would we care about this?' (interview 27). This was then compounded by the fact the full realisation that he himself could have died, become a martyr, for absolutely *nothing*:

> I mean, there have been many cases in which I could have been one of them. For example, especially, December 5th, I was at the front line because I was really . . . I did not have any control over my nerves, I was really nervous. So, I was in the front-line throwing stones very passionately as I was attacking the Muslim Brotherhood and they had arms, so I could have been killed easily. That was not the only time, but of course also during the occupy Cabinet sit in and other clashes in front of the Muslim Brotherhood headquarters in April. A lot of incidents, so this sometimes comes to me. I remembered this and sometimes when it comes to mind, I say I could have been one of them so I should be loyal to them. And other times, it comes to me and I think 'oh my god, I could have been one of them. Thank God I did not die. I would have been dead for nothing, you know. I mean my life is . . . I can do a lot in my life, why would I die for this bullshit'. So, there are two conflicting persons within me, you know. (Interview 27)

As with most interviewees, it was the fact that these people had died for nothing that flung him into bouts of debilitating depression. As Ratcliffe explained (2014), depression entails deprivation of our mode of existence in the world, wherein our existential unitary structure becomes devoid not only of change but rather the very possibility of change. The world rather appears static and unchangeable, as the sufferer experiences a profound 'paralysis of hope' (Brampton in Ratcliffe, 2014: 46), a detachment from the world, a deep sense of overwhelming meaninglessness and, above all, the closure of possibility (namely the possibility of anything mattering at all) (Ratcliffe, 2014: 65). In depression, life is deprived of any meaning, potential and pleasure, thus also leading to the inability to feel joy. Rather, depression therefore 'involves a change in one's sense of belonging to the world' (Ratcliffe, 2014: 61), which is typified by an erasure of *all* practical significance. The world of the depressed is hence often experienced as colourless, oppressive, suffocating, solitary, inescapable and motionless (Ratcliffe, 2014: 76). Yet, for some interviewees, being depressed put them in another existential bind, since this depression itself was socially labelled as yet *another* layer of intersubjective betrayal. As this young man explains:

> You know there is also this quote that says 'depression is a betrayal', they always say this: if you are depressed you are betraying those who died. [. . .]

some people started to make fun of this quote, saying that actually hope is a betrayal. Though I am making fun of this and I always say 'depression is a betrayal, ha' and stuff like that, but deep inside I do believe that depression is a betrayal. I always take some time to remember, remember those who died and remember how they felt about. . . . I mean, how they hoped for change and how they died for this, to make myself more committed. (Interview 27)

And so, what we see here is a deep sense of (powerless) guilt doubling up inside itself: activists not only experienced the violent closure of revolutionary becoming as a personal defect (as a failure to live up to a certain standard of ethical responsibility) but the depression that resulted from this closure and failure was also interpreted as impaired subjectivity: as a personal failure to live up to the ethical demand of the (dead) Other, to do justice by them. This experience of depression as betrayal thus compounded their perception of them having failed.

Indeed, this sense of failure became so pervasive that that it started to inform and transform their way of being in the world. As the lifeworld's horizon of possibility was systematically and violently destroyed through counter-revolutionary colonisation, it was not only the object of revolutionary politics that they interpreted as a failure but their very lives (their existence) as such. This binding of the revolution to their lives of course makes sense not only when we consider the fact that the revolution was an embodied manifestation geared towards life, towards being alive, leading a worthy life, rather than a deadly life of depreciation and abuse. It was about nothing less than their very lives as such:

> It gets down, very down. And you feel that. We have this kind of, yeah, it is a kind of failure. The process is totally turning into failure. You as part of this process are getting this kind of feeling, even my professional life over the last three years felt like a failure, you are grabbing the failure that is in the public sphere into your personal life. [. . .] you feel very frustrated, it is not bringing anything new, we are just losing people, we are losing friends and we are even losing our connections to each other, and it is very frustrating, and that even reflects in your personal life where you are not delivering, you are not making the progress that you would have made if the revolution had not been here. (Interview 31)

NOTES

1. Article 267 of Egypt's penal code criminalises vaginal penetration without consent. However, Article 60 of the penal code overrides the application of the penal code on those who committed a criminalised act out of 'good intention', and

the marriage certificate provides sufficient proof in the Egyptian judicial system that the man did not intend any harm to his wife. Rape is restricted to the penetration of female genitalia, since this is the highest violation of 'honour', and male anal penetration is merely a case of indecent assault, making male rape legally impossible (see Egypt Penal Code 1973; information also based on personal communication with an anonymised Egyptian lawyer (19 January 2017)). Also see (EIPR, 2015; Salama, 2015).

2. For those less familiar with the philosophical debate on representation and intentionality, please see (Jacob, 2003).

3. This for instance has also been incorporated in some of the literature on the experience of teargas in Egypt, which also suggested that activists 'got addicted' to it (Schielke, 2011).

Chapter 10

Deepening Intersubjective Imparity
Turning Violence Inwards

This chapter explains that it was not only the infliction of deadly violence and the lack of revolutionary progress (see chapter 9), due to the colonisation of the political sphere and continued neoliberalisation, that resulted in the undoing of revolutionary potential and the reinstatement of a deadly life, but rather that the spread of traumatic status subordination from the political to the social sphere also played an important role herein. For as traumatic status subordination spread from the political to the social realms, relations previously marked by friendship, love, solidarity and trust were now violently ripped apart. As violent intersubjective imparity was inflicted in the social realm the prefigurative intersubjectivity of Egypt's revolutionary streets and squares was truly turned on its head: having once stood side by side in prefigurative revolutionary becoming, ordinary people now not only celebrated the deaths of other citizens, but also tortured, shot, killed and maimed each other as Egypt became mired in cycles of revenge.

Revenge, it has to be understood, is both a reaction to and the continuation of violent status subordination. In revenge, one tries to regain power over those deemed to have done harm. Revenge is thus a strategic attempt to 'settle the score', or to (re)gain an equal status vis-à-vis the perpetrator. However, revenge may both be directed at the perpetrator, but in the absence of the possibility of addressing the perpetrator directly (which was the case in Egypt), revenge may be redirected to others who stand in or come to replace the perpetrator in the victim's understanding or imaginary. Revenge is, in this sense, hence often a prominent dimension in the victim-becomes-perpetrator dilemma, and frequently degenerates to vicious cycles of violence with no end in sight.

In Egypt, these vicious cycles of revenge commenced with the inward turn of violence at the Presidential clashes in December 2012 and accelerated rapidly in the spring and summer of 2013. The military not only interfered with the Tamarod campaign but also fuelled a strong anti-Brotherhood sentiment through its associated broadcast and print media, leaving some to comment on an emerging anti-Brotherhood hysteria (Diab, 2019). The Brotherhood, feeling increasingly threatened by the 'deep state' and frustrated with its own lack of process itself also added fuel to the fire by digging its heels in the sand and adopting an increasingly antagonistic and violent attitude towards all forms of criticism. This eventually even contributed to the formation of hate speech and lynch mobs wherein Shia minorities were killed (Human Rights Watch, 2013b). Yet, the biggest display of revenge was of course the Rabaa massacre on 14 August 2013, and which followed Morsi's disposal earlier on 3rd of July. Here, Egypt's security forces, behind the back of representatives of the Egyptian government, killed more than 1,000 Brotherhood supporters who had camped out at the Rabaa and Ennahda sit ins (organised in support of the ousted president Mohamed Morsi). This massacre not only established the military as the sole and dominant actor in Egypt's formal political realm, it also further fuelled the vicious cycles of revenge in the social sphere as it fuelled anger and hatred. Some of those who experienced the massacre first hand, or lost loved ones, sought to avenge the dead (targeting both military and security installations but also civilians), while civilians unleashed their violence, anger and frustration onto Brotherhood supporters. Now, the trouble here is not only that the political and social sphere was dominated by a fight between pro-military and pro-Brotherhood supporters, which alienated those who belonged to neither, but also that it accumulated in the brutalisation of everyday life, which further compounded the already existent weight of accumulative death and increased hopelessness (chapter 9).

As Egypt's society became mired in an ever downwards spiral of violence, death and violence became unpredictable and pervasive: one could be confronted with deadly violence at any time anywhere. Interviewees narrated being confronted with the gravest forms of violence at cafe's, street, corners, shops, micro-buses and even inside the family home as social polarisation violently tore family relations apart. In light of such polarisation, they felt ever more deeply estranged from others and the world: the world made no sense anymore: people around them 'had gone mad' and 'stopped thinking' (interview 32). Often, it was the very same the people they used to trust, love and care for that now either celebrated or inflicted violence on them. Having seen the best of people in the revolution of 2011, they were now confronted with the absolute worst. The spread of violent intersubjective imparity into the social sphere not only meant that the injustices suffered in the political sphere remained utterly unrecognised by social others (who even ridiculed or celebrated these injustices) but also resulted in an ever pervasive sense of deep existential insecurity. As the threat of violence was everywhere, there was no respite from it, and activists felt increasingly unsafe and alone in this world. The spread of violent intersubjective imparity into the social sphere also meant that the networks of social support, where one used to experience some recognition of one's equal worth, were now demolished. And unsurprisingly perhaps, this demolisation also manifested itself online, as blocking people with different opinions became a trend. For in the face of relentless multilayered traumatic status subordination that now dominated all the spheres of one's life, it had basically become too hard to tolerate difference – to listen to others, to pierce through the vicious cycles of hate that manifested itself both online and offline.

And so, with Egypt's descent into vicious polarisation, intersubjective relations were violently severed and the potential for creative collective becoming was annihilated. This also affected the functioning of the lifeworld: not only did many experiences a deep sense of disorientation in the face of the relentless (and multilayered) violation of intersubjective parity, but the capacity of meaning- and sense-making was directly affected. The lifeworld's horizon of interpretation, so dependent on communicative relations with others, collapsed: nothing made sense anymore. Activists above all felt disorientated, atomised and above all demoralised. As Ratcliffe explains, in demoralisation it is *the possibility* of meaningful change that dissipates from underneath one's feet (Ratcliffe, 2008). This destruction of meaning- and sense-making also manifested itself physically in interviewees, who not only suffered from inexpicable pains, nightmares, but also deep rooted anxiety attacks. Many resorted to drugs (particularly Tramadol), alcohol, and other such coping mechanisms, but the one mechanism they all resorted to was a retreat into silenced, depoliticised, atomisation. That is, due to the multilevelled pervasive traumatic status subordination they were subjected to, they retreated away from the social and political spheres into their own protective shell. They stopped relating to others and the world, and instead withdrew 'into a protective envelope, a place of mute, aching loneliness, in which the traumatic experience is treated as a solitary burden' (Erikson, 1995: 195).

SOCIAL REVENGE AND THE INWARDS DIRECTION OF VIOLENCE

As Part 2 explained in more detail, the counter-revolutionary marriage of mutual strategic convenience between the Brotherhood leadership and the military quickly turned sour when Morsi was inaugurated as Egypt's president in 2012. While the Brotherhood and the military had benefitted from the strategic co-option of the opportunistic Brotherhood in the military's pursuit of speedy elections and an orderly transition (Stacher, 2020) – as it would ensure a primary political role for the Brotherhood guaranteed to win the elections while the military would gain its newly gained economic benefits – by the time Morsi was inaugurated the happy marriage was more or less over – or at least on much less friendly turns. Morsi turned out to be a president without a parliament and without a constitution (the process of which was controlled by SCAF). Increasingly, frustrated by the military's clipping of the Brotherhood's political wings he thus sought to increase his leverage over the political terrain. This not only accumulated in an increasingly exclusivist constitutional process and a battle with Egypt's judiciary (Reuters, 2012; Khalifa, 2015: 140–141), but also eventually resulted in the presidential declaration of November 2012, wherein Morsi sought to immunise his decisions against any legal challenge, which was rightly interpreted by the anti-systematic revolutionary opposition as an authoritarian move (Teti et al., 2012). At the same time, the Brotherhood itself had increasingly adopted a conspirational framework of interpretation, wherein *all* opposition was cast as part of the deep state, including those of the anti-systematic opposition who had been critical of the military from the beginning. Meanwhile, the military of course fuelled anti-Brotherhood propaganda through its affiliated media outlets and most likely – though proof is difficult to attain – engaged in anti-Brotherhood actions such as the fuel and sugar shortages later in the year of 2012, all of which heightened a strong anti-Brotherhood sentiment.

It was in this way that the stage was set for the radical undoing of revolutionary potentiality through violent social polarisation, wherein social relations would no longer be characterised by intersubjective parity but rather death, injury and suspicion. One of the most important turning points in this trajectory were the presidential palace clashes which occurred in December 2012. Protesters had camped out at the presidential palace in Heliopolis to object against Morsi's constitutional declaration. Rather than trying to de-escalate, the Brotherhood (having adopted a conspirational frame of reference) added fuel to the fire by driving buses full of their supporters to the site of protest, which sparked one of the largest street brawls seen in the history of Egypt. Brotherhood supporters and revolutionaries fought, maimed and even killed each other, while the police and security forces stood by at the sidelines. These presidential clashes constituted the 'first really serious confrontation between groups of the brotherhood and the revolutionaries' (interview 1) and formed a 'benchmark for an increase in civilian violence and also a wider spread of violence all over the country' (interview 19). These events marked a real turning point in the nature of political violence in Egypt because violence was now no longer directed towards the institutions of the state but rather turned inwards as civilians fought each other. What interviewees found shocking was not only that it 'was very reminiscent of high school fights' (interview 19) but also that in these fights neighbours, friends and family members now openly battled each other on Egypt's streets. Rather, what was disorienting about this fight was that relationships previously marked with love, care and trust had now turned violent to the point of death. As this person remarked:

> The events of the Itehedya Palace, December 2012. Actually, that was a turning point for me, I mean, I'm always used to conflict and violence from the police from the army, but what I saw around the palace in December 2012 was traumatic, shocking, so ehm . . . I mean I. . . . It is very hard to see one of your friends, or those who used to be your friends, like . . . I won't say that they are shooting us or anything like that because very few number of them were using weapons, but almost every one of them was throwing stones, being violent with us so imagine that anyone of them could be your friend, your friend your neighbour your brother even and what made me more shocked that I, I always used to be a pacifist, peaceful I did not like silence or conflict or anything like that but that day I was shocked even though my reaction to that. After the Islamists were attacking us, I started attacking back, throwing stones back and I was shocked at my reaction afterwards. I went back home, wondering how I did that. How everything turns me into this, into this violent person, so ehm. . . . That was kind of the turning point for me. (Interview 1)

The presidential clashes thus constituted a turning point wherein traumatic status subordination spread from the political deep into the social sphere. It is significant since it marked the undoing of prefigurative reality of revolutionary unity in the social sphere. Indeed, with the presidential clashes, the prefigurative reality of revolutionary becoming wherein each had been regarded as equal was now truly turned on its head as ordinary citizens battled each other to the point of grave injury and even death. As this young man noted solemnly:

> Hundreds of thousands of people came and weapons were used and on that day again I was hit by khartoush again but insignificant compared to like . . . the idea of like how much hatred and how much; I realized in the moment that the fist fight started that this is a gap that will never be closed. (Interview 19)

The importance of the presidential clashes, hence, lies not only in the gross infliction of the violence itself, which had a huge disorienting impact on interviewees, but rather also with who inflicted it. As neighbours, friends and family members now openly fought each other on the streets, it was not only the betrayal of intersubjective parity through the infliction of violence that was significant but rather also that as traumatic status subordination extended into the social sphere, the lifeworld's taken-for-granted background assumptions were violently undermined. Hence, in the wake of these clashes, many interviewees expressed feeling estranged from the world, unable to make sense of it and deeply suspicious and fearful of others. They narrated feeling numbed, surreal and out of place, as they simply could not make sense of what was transpiring around them.

Now, these clashes of course did not occur out of nowhere but rather were the result of political frustration. They were the direct result of the counter-revolutionary colonisation of the public sphere and the lack of transformative political progress as well as the ever-increasing burden of death interviewees carried on their shoulders. This young man stated that he felt hostile, frustrated and depressed, but 'you feel helpless and you want to do something to make sure that things go back to a certain track of mobilisation but you can't' (interview 32). Hence, political impotence and marginalisation, which was the source of their frustration and anger, also ensured that this very same frustration and anger could no longer be effectively expressed in the political public sphere. Interviewees expressed that they felt increasingly bad tempered, aggressive and short-fused: ready to blow up at any time at anyone. One young man explained that his political frustration had built up to such an extent that he continuously felt on the edge of violent and aggressive outbursts, which were increasingly difficult for him to control. Another young man noted, how the lack of political progress and his own blindness (as he lost both of his eyes to the revolution (the first on the 28th of January and the second on the 19th of November) had directly contributed to his violent eruptions at home, particularly towards his fiancée and his family (interview 13). Or, this young person noted how he had changed from a kind-hearted person to a numbed person who could only feel hatred:

> On a personal level, I would list hatred as the first, as on top. I am a person full of hatred, definitely full of hatred to the Muslim Brotherhood, full of hatred to the army leaders. I am generally a full of hatred person. I would very comfortably, and without thinking, classify myself as a person full of hatred. (Interview 27)

For all these interviewees, the source of such frustration was the lack of political voice, the accumulative weight of death and violence, and the nihilistic meaningless this imprinted upon life and death alike. Increasingly frustration developed into hatred, which lacking a political outlet was no longer only directed towards political institutions but started to broaden to include social others. As this young man narrated:

> During Maspero when I saw what a dead body looked like, how the dead bodies are flattened and they looked like aliens and back then I felt drawn to the idea of revenge, physical revenge, I am being completely honest here again, this is not helpful to my profile. So, there were times when I think about revenge,

obviously comes from hatred and I have like daydreams about hundreds of people, sweeping certain institutions and like running over; them so I remember like during Maspero I was constantly thinking about how like I could easily take part in a poplar execution of the head of Egyptian police, you know. I thought about this. I probably would not do that in reality but I thought about it a lot. And I felt this level of hatred, this is more than hatred I guess, a mix of hatred and a desire for revenge towards like someone the head of the Egyptian police, towards a number of police officers, towards a lot of people. I feel that hatred toward senior brotherhood leaders and sometimes I feel this level of hatred and spite towards people I know. Like a second cousin that I got into debates with about politics. Yeah, I feel like a mixture of anger and hatred and despise. (Interview 19)

Within this context of increasing anger and hatred, revenge formed an important outlet for emotional release. As this young man noted:

Revenge makes you go after your . . . and you forget about the fact that you are not making enough money, the fact that you don't have a job, that the fact that your health care system is . . . is . . . is blah. All of that you're forgetting about that and you're focusing on revenging yourself from some people. (Interview 2)

Other activists also noted that revenge provided some relief for the accumulation of anger and frustration. They explained that sometimes they just felt happy having hit someone on the metro or shouted at someone in the street – that it marked a release of tension, a release of anger. As this young man narrated:

I was in Alexandria and people, you know someone generally asking where you going and I don't wanna talk to him, so he came up to me and he grabbed me and I was really happy that we got into like a fight – I didn't punch him because he was too measly and so on. But I was happy like that people were surrounding us and pushing and so on and I was extremely happy and I shouted and I screamed and like this the kinda stuff. [. . .]. It's not me, I am usually very accommodating, but I'm sick of the bullshit. (Interview 25)

However, the trouble is that while it provided a temporary form of release, it also bound them up in a violent logic of social violence, which they could not only not control but that would in the end leave them even more alienated and isolated. It would give rise to a vicious cycle of violent revenge, wherein the potentiality of prefigurative intersubjective parity and revolutionary creative becoming was destroyed ever further. As this young man remarked:

> If you ask any of my friends [. . .] they would tell you that I get really angry and really frustrated. I want to do anything about it. I feel like it is driving me crazy you know [. . .] human beings [. . .] in my mind, and in my feelings, have to be treated well. Actually, not only human beings but any living thing, so I get angry [. . .]. And this again put us in this vicious circle of violence and revenge. (Interview 17)

Importantly, conceived intersubjectively, revenge is an emotional outlet for accumulated frustration and anger that comprises an assertion of one's strength vis-à-vis another. Or rather, in revenge one tries to violently attain or regain intersubjective power over another after intersubjective parity has been damaged. Hence, conceived intersubjectively, revenge thus entails the attempt to regain intersubjective power through violent means after one has been subordinated and been made to experience a deep sense of powerlessness and often speechlessness. In this sense, revenge is thus both the outcome of a reaction to and the continuation of a distorted mode of communicative action typified by violent status subordination.

Revenge is often directed at the perpetrator(s). Yet, in situations where it is not possible to address perpetrator(s) directly, revenge often gets redirected elsewhere: towards those affiliated to the perpetrator(s) as well as those entirely unrelated to the perpetrators. In Egypt, conspirational victim blaming played a constitutive role in the redirection of political frustration away from political institution inwards into society towards social others. The military started to propagate strong anti-Brotherhood messages through its affiliated media outlets. Herein, the Brotherhood was not only cast as the source of Egypt's political and economic deterioration, but also as constituting an profound existential threat to the identity and security of the nation. At the same time, the military course continued to undermine Morsi's political power behind the scenes, which fuelled the Brotherhood's increasingly suspicious and antagonistic attitude towards all forms of criticism. That is, the Brotherhood increasingly cast revolutionaries as part of the deep state, which constituted an existential threat to the path of legitimacy and democracy. It thereby legitimised violence against protesters of the anti-systematic revolutionary opposition in the name of safeguarding 'legitimacy' and 'democracy'. In doing so, the Brotherhood naturally paid no attention to the revolutionaries criticism of the Brotherhood's anti-democratic, authoritarian measures, such as the constitutional declaration and its opportunistic desertion of the revolutionary field when it partook in the military's transitionary roadmap of an orderly transition. And so, a multilevelled discursive framework of blame occurred wherein other actors and their supporters were cast as constituting an existential threat, the violence was redirected inwards into society. Unable to project frustration onto the political terrain, fights and revenge in the social terrain became not only an emotional outlet but also legitimised: it was a way to get one's right.

> Fights would basically be easy and acceptable option for anybody who wants to kind of let it out, let the frustration and the anger out. And it is the only way to. . . . It doesn't solve a problem but for people who fight it is the only way. Sometimes fights, this is something that is pretty important, also. . . . If we say something like, if you beat somebody, 'ana maghatat haqy', which means I got my right. You know, it is also related to dignity as some kind of . . . you know. . . . You would hear people saying I would never let this pass unless I get my right, and getting your right is basically hitting beating somebody up. (Interview 17)

So, being unable to ascertain one's right in the formal political realm, anger and frustration of having suffered violent intersubjective imparity is redirected elsewhere. In this sense, revenge and the victim-turns-perpetrator dilemma (wherein the victim repeats the violence inflicted on him/her onto another) are actually closely related. Both are a reaction to the experience of intersubjective powerlessness. That is, both are attempts at reasserting one's intersubjective position vis-à-vis another through a display of (verbal and/or physical) force towards the perpetrator and/or social others (who are either affiliated or unaffiliated to the perpetrator). Having been made to feel subordinate, powerless and/or inferior, the victim tries to regain a sense of power, equality or superiority, through the imposition of the other to his or her violent will. It is hence also not surprising that revenge often leads to vicious cycles of revenge, in that the violent attempt to regain intersubjective power over another elicits the same response. Once this logic takes hold in society, it is difficult to stop. It often spreads like a wildfire, leaving a path of social destruction in its wake, while the underlying cause or the real perpetrator often remains out of shot.

In Egypt, this cycle of revenge – aside from violent quarrels and fights in the private and domestic spheres – primarily took the form of violent clashes wherein civilians wreaked havoc on civilians. One such notable example in the spring of 2013 are the Moqattam clashes, which took place in March after revolutionaries marched to the headquarters of the Brotherhood in protest of the Brotherhood's undemocratic domination of the political sphere (El-Dabh, 2013) and the Brotherhood's capture and beating of a female activist a week earlier. The Moqattam clashes were intensely violent, as this young man (part of the anti-systemic revolutionary opposition) narrates:

> we were very very very violent. We were very very . . . I mean yeah the anti-MB camp did some appalling acts, very very seriously. [. . .] But what was shocking to me was that we were involved in some backhand action, when they

captured some from the Muslim Brotherhood, that is not beating, that is torture. This technique is very popular in the poorer areas, it [. . .] means putting a needle like that. They would beat the person really badly with the flat end, not the sharp end. They would beat the person really badly on his skull so his head would be covered in blood and he would lose consciousness. He would suffer a lot of pain, and would be really, really bad but also, he would still be alive but every part of your body is covered in blood you know. And also, they would cut a person repeatedly, not kill him. That is torture, right? I have seen this. I have seen for example a guy from the Muslim Brotherhood. He is around 55 years old, and he was reeeeally afraid. He was frightened when he was caught . . . .eh . . . And the guy himself, he does not. . . . He was standing at the other front, and the other front was armed, and they have their thugs, and the MB have thugs and everything. Everything they have. But the guy himself does not look like he is a thug, and that is why he was caught by the way. If he was a thug or someone like that, he would be able to run. So, he was tortured and beaten up really really badly. He was so afraid to the extent that he was not able to walk actually. He was shaking, and he fell on the ground because he was not able to walk because he was really afraid. And then he kept holding his hands like this on his heart, and then he fainted. I don't know whether he died or whatever, but he was really afraid. And he was full of blood and everything, and people for example . . . there was a woman, who was wearing a niqab, and I was really, really nervous and I was shouting at the protestors to leave the guy. I was shouting 'that is an old guy, leave him, what are you doing blablablablabla'. I was beaten up by the protesters because I was defending him. Okay? And then they put me away, and the woman with this niqab, she was with her husband. And I was really nervous, I was shouting like a crazy person 'see, see what they are doing? Let's go and stop them!'. And then she was like 'go away, I want to see them'. I thought she wanted to see what they are doing, and that she wanted to defend him. She wears the niqab so. . . . I thought she may have some compassion with the Muslim Brotherhood, and then she was like 'So yeah, I want to see him dying'. She was full of anger, and full of hatred. She wanted to see the guy, full of passion for seeing his pain, his torture and see him dying. She was really happy to see this. Yeah, that is it. (Interview 27)

In face of such violence, many interviewees reported a deep sense of disorienting. It was not only the level of violence in these clashes that launched them into a profound sense of alienation (see chapter 9), but rather also that it was inflicted by ordinary people. How could others be so violent? How could they be so violent? In their stories, it is clear that they not only experienced a great level of estrangement due to the overwhelming violence as such (which may be enough to induce a state of disorientation) but rather also that the infliction of such violence by social others violated the interpretative framework of their lifeworld. The violence inflicted by ordinary civilians fundamentally challenged the lifeworld's fundamental taken-for-granted background assumptions about established social norms (namely, the norms that regulate how people will and ought to behave) to such an extent that their sense-making of the world comes crashing down. Hence, in light of such violence, many thus experienced an overwhelming sense of estrangement as they were both unable to influence or stop the violence around them. Unable to change the counter-revolutionary course of direction, a their sense of agency in the world was damaged, at the same time as the deeply uncomfortable realisation that people were simply not who they thought them to be was imprinted upon them. People – sometimes including themselves – could not be trusted. This realisation further undermined their belief in the potentiality of revolutionary becoming, not only was society internally fragmented but many people were increasingly turning into monsters (interview 19) as propaganda battered their brains (interview 2). Hence, one of the most disturbing aspects of social violence is how the infliction of traumatic status subordination in the social sphere resulted in a breakdown of constructive social relations of trust, wherein the fundamental presupposition of intersubjective parity and possibility of meaningful change are undermined, Egypt seemed to be sucked into a violent vertigo that left nothing in its wake but a dark nihilistic hole where nothing made sense anymore.

Many interviewees also particularly experienced a deepening of senselessness in the face of torture, which as social revenge spilled out into the streets of Egypt, also took on a particularly 'social' nature. That is, torture was now no longer inflicted by agents of the state but by citizens themselves:

> It was a bit of shock, because we were used to the policemen doing torture, the army doing torture . . . the politicians doing torture like military police also for intelligence or whatever but for normal people like here in the streets torturing people who they think are thugs or whatever, different from them, dehumanizing people by other people is really shocking. (Interview 22)

What is significant about these practices of torture is not merely that the Brotherhood inflicted a similar traumatic status subordination onto its opponents as SCAF had done before them, but also that this grave violation of intersubjective parity was again inflicted by *ordinary citizens*. Needless to say, such imposition of traumatic status subordination greatly distorted intersubjective relations between the different societal groups and often between individuals who had previously – often including during the revolutionary eighteen days – held more amicable relations. Interviewees were not only angry and enraged about the infliction of such grave violence, it also increasingly left them in a state of disorientation. They felt so devastated 'to see people beating other people and being excited [by violence]' (interview 2). For, this violent extension of traumatic status subordination from the political into the social sphere not only again reinforced the perceived disposability of life (now by social others rather than formal political actors) but also for many also reinforced the perceived pointlessness of revolutionary action. It augmented the point that meaningful change was beyond their reach and that all these martyrs had died for nothing. Politically and socially the revolution was being undone: the revolutionary lifeworld based on intersubjective parity was turned on its head. As social polarisation accelerated, they experienced a growing (brutal) realisation that life is cheap, disposable and worthless. It also impressed upon them the improbability and indeed pointlessness of revolutionary becoming. And worst of all was, again, there was little it seemed they could do about it.

Essential herein was military's careful counter-revolutionary manoeuvring, as it not only set the stage for the Brotherhood's political frustrations (namely the military's limiting of the Brotherhood's actual political power when in office) but also actively sowed anti-Brotherhood sentiment using the media affiliated to the businessmen of the ancient regime. The security forces also directly interfered in the Tamarod campaign (a petition asking for the removal of Morsi through holding early elections) and sought to strategically increase already existent political and economic frustration, thereby pulling Egypt ever deeper into the spiral of social violence, through the sudden withholding of essential goods such as fuel and electricity which resulted in a black-market surge (Hanke, 2013). At the same time, they highlighted that Egypt's economic decline was an indication of Morsi's immense failure and proved that the time for revolutionary action was now firmly over – that it was time to return to security and stability. Meanwhile, the Brotherhood also played its part of course by taking up a sectarian defensive stance wherein the other oppositional voices were violently side cast as traitors of the 'democratic' project – and also managed to raise the blood pressure of many Egyptians through the projection of a culturalist agenda based around their Brotherhood conception of Islamic values and identity. At the same time, the security apparatus withdrew the police from the streets (so as to deepen an underlying existential feeling of unsafety) and the Brotherhood relied on its own supporters for supposed security. This included lynch mobs that attacked Christians, Shias and other groups the Brotherhood deemed part of the 'deep state'. All of this created an atmosphere conducive to vicious cycles of social violence and revenge, an atmosphere wherein the potential of revolutionary unity was ever further undone as intersubjective relations were subjected to the gravest forms of violence as citizens took matters into their own hands:

> At the social level [. . .] we have a lot of fights, and because the police is not like playing a role so people started actually to . . . eh . . . bypass the law and get their own right by their own hands, so . . . yeah. (Interview 6)

Throughout the spring of 2013, social violence between citizens thus intensified, and individuals or groups targeted those they deemed to have oppositional views – or simply those whose faces they did not like, who looked different. As this young woman explains:

> Okay, you can see that in sexual assaults. In random street fights between car – people driving cars. The singling out, like if you take the metro and there is a bearded man you can see people harass him and even if there is a man who looks like a liberal you could also see people harass him. You don't know what exactly what it is that people are after. If you see a veiled woman – when she's in the minority, she's harassed if you see and unveiled woman and she's the minority she's also harassed. So . . . manifested in like you know like . . . singling out the one who's looks different the one who looks different and you direct all your anger and rage at them. Just because you know, you can. (Interview 10)

With the multilevelled infliction of traumatic status subordination, and its extension into the social sphere, we thus see a brutalisation of social life wherein the dynamic of revenge takes hold of the public sphere. For, as noted earlier, the problem with revenge is that it leaves nothing in its wake save the destruction of the communicative realm of the lifeworld. It not only plunges one into an ever-expansive and ever-deeper cycle of revenge but also deepens the wounds of already existent traumatic status subordination as it fails to recognise the injustices suffered while tearing apart social relations, thereby annihilating the potential of collective action and revolutionary becoming ever further and deeper. In this dynamic, a destructive cycle is set in motion based on the betrayal of intersubjective parity wherein nothing less than the violent subordination and annihilation of the Other (the object of one's frustration) is willed. In Levinasian terms, in revenge, the other's particularity is erased as he or she (or they) becomes an abstracted or generalised representation of the Other in whose demise and suffering one rejoices. Pain over pain, strength over strength, violence over violence and so the logic continues until there is nothing left but a radically unsafe world wherein life may be disposed of at any time.

The counter-revolution sought to create a deep sense of existential insecurity wherein it was not merely the state that inflicted traumatic status subordination – through violence, the erosion of political voice or material resources – but rather people themselves. The redirection inwards of violence into society not only ensured revolutionary unity fell apart but also that a general atmosphere of social violence (of traumatic status subordination) was created that would precisely 'legitimise' the necessity of the military's return:

> [Under Mubarak] we felt that ok there is stability in the state, there is stability in the street, there is stability in the community, so we felt that there was a kind

of social security which made you feel like okay it is nice. But soon after the revolution, in the last three years [. . .] we are lacking this kind of psychological feeling of security. I don't feel that okay when . . . Okay when I am becoming more protective because I feel that if something happens for my family in the streets, I feel that, okay, before I felt that people would just be very cooperative and would be more protective than me and they would protect her. And right now, I think people are just feeling that they are not secure and just need to focus on their own issues, they do not have to be involved with other issues and violence is everywhere and people felt that . . . and one of the things that all of the, many, or a huge percentage of the people, they started thinking that government equals police. And when the police disappeared that meant that there is no government. (Interview 31)

Following the trajectory, of counter-revolutionary status subordination and its effects, it becomes apparent that from the very beginning of Egypt's post-revolutionary aftermath the military attempted to create the conditions for its own resurgence to power, not merely through political deals but rather also through gradually shifting the experiential existential structures away from potentiality towards insecurity and the impossibility of change. That is, over the years, it altered the way of being in the world: it changed the existential register away from revolutionary potentiality and equality towards impossibility, insecurity, violence and death. It carefully created a climate wherein existential insecurity was pervasive, as it was this overwhelming feeling of insecurity that would legitimise and underpin the return of a supposedly[2] strong military leader, Abdel Fattah al Sisi. In this existential insecurity increasing economic impoverisation coincided with political disarray and a growing pervasiveness of social violence (again, the conditions of which had all been created by the military) resulted in an atmosphere of 'chaos'. This construction of 'chaos' is of course a classical authoritarian quip, wherein a Manichean dichotomy is created between 'chaotic violence' of the people and the 'stability and security' of the authoritarian leader. It is in this light that we have to understand the increasing spread of rumours by the security-affiliated media, which for instance claimed that the Brotherhood was in fact mobilised by the Palestinian Hamas who were keen to undermine the 'great Egyptian nation' served this same purpose of creating existential uncertainty, fear and disorientation. Similarly, suggestions were made on Egyptian television and radio that without a strong leader, Egypt would follow the same course as the Syrian civil war. As a young female explained, playing on these existential fears, the need for a strong father figure was created – one who would take care of its 'children' who could not do it alone (interview 28). The suggestion was created that the Egyptian the defeatist idea that they could not do it alone: that they needed a strong (authoritarian) leader that would ensure stability and unity. The revolution, and its temporary lived reality of prefigurative collective self-becoming, was thus being radically undone: it was (defeatist) being recast as having been an impractical utopian ideal, one that did not face up to the realities of the day – and that reality of course was that the Egyptian people were not ready for self-becoming but needed a father figure. The ground was being prepared not just for the acceptance but also the glorification of the military, who would rise from the ashes of violence as the saviour of the nation. This leader would necessarily take care of business by being severe and strict, as a good Egyptian father, thereby ensuring stability, security and unity: 'We are very good in making pharaohs, we are very good in making dictators. This is the father's figure thing that we have. And fathers have all the powers' (interview 18).

Now, of course, in this rise of the 'father' only occurred through the redirection of political frustration inwards into cycles towards social revenge but due to popular manifestation of protest which had found its articulation in the Tamarod campaign. Tamarod, though it seemed like a bottom-up grassroots organisation, later turned out to have been carefully directed by Egypt's security apparatus (see chapter 2). It was, however, as a direct result of this Tamarod campaign (in the context of the broader political developments and frustrations sketched out previously) that millions of Egyptians ventured onto the streets on the 30th of June in protest against Morsi's authoritarian rule. Though deeply influenced by the security state, many interviewees did experience this pouring out onto the Egyptian streets as a great moment of elation, as a moment wherein the Egyptian capacity for creative collective self-becoming was manifested again. Many rejoiced and celebrated that in the face of political apathy, collective self-manifestation in the public sphere was nevertheless possible. Others were more sceptical, not only was the political public sphere carefully manipulated by the Brotherhood and the military, with little space for alternative voices, but what was particularly worrying about these protests was that they were negative. As this young man explained, in contrast to the 25 January revolution, the demonstration did not call for positive values such as bread, freedom and social justice but rather was negatively directed *against* something – against Morsi's rule – with no reference to the broader positive values they were striving for. In his words:

> June 30th is certainly the biggest protest that I've ever seen personally and I've been to a lot of big protest. I am not contending that, but they called *against* Morsi, they didn't call *for* anything. And January 25th for me is all about calls for freedom, for all these . . . chants that we had. So, I fear that all our accomplishments are rolled back already public space has been taken away from us, I fear that you know. . . . That's currently my biggest fear. (Interview 11)

And indeed, it was the 30 June demonstration that provided the context wherein the military gave Morsi an ultimatum and subsequently disposed him of his power.

RABAA: MASS MURDER AND THE DESTRUCTION OF POTENTIALITY

Now, faced with the dilemma of having opened up the Pandora's box of political protest and self-becoming (even if articulated in a more negative sense), the military of course had to quickly close this potential and the golden opportunity came in the form of the Rabaa massacre. On the 14th of August 2013, without informing the interim government, Egypt's security forces killed over 1,000 Muslim Brotherhood supporters who had staged a sit-in against Morsi's ouster on the squares of Ennahda and Rabaa. Rabaa massacre was one of the largest displays of direct lethal force by the Egyptian state against its own people and its own subjects, whom it killed en masse in bright daylight. Through this mass erasure of life, the state, de facto ran by the military, sent off a signal, namely that it could commit mass murder without the blink of an eye. It thus sent out a clear message, the state not only possesses superior physical force but also will no longer tolerate any dissent. In the face of dissent, it will commit mass murder. It reinforced the disposability of life in Egypt, its utter worthlessness. Hence, as this *young woman* remarked:

> How can you not be scared after they just killed . . . you know. . . . I mean they say. . . . Initially the court said there were around 400 people and then officially the court said that there were around 1000 people but then they get reports from inside Al Rabaa Adawiyya that say that at least some more people are killed. I don't trust any of them, because I don't trust the state, nor the officials nor the Rabaa people, everybody lies you know and there are so many different accounts. But a lot of people got killed, you know, that is the end of it. And the way that they got killed too, was completely inhumane and how can you not be scared of the state after, after it does that. Of course it is scary yaeny. (Interview 30)

In the face of such overwhelming violence, those who were present (either as participants or as observers) suffered a collapse of the lifeworld. Their subjection to such a grave traumatic status subordination threw them into a severe state of existential disarray and disorientation. They described truly horrific scenes of mass annihilation. One interviewee (interview 20) relayed how he saw his own father being shot twice in the back as he was running away from the violence. His father then collapsed, was arrested and had his wallet stolen by one of the soldiers (who also mocked him and called him names) as he was lying there, bleeding to death on the ground. Another relayed how his Quran teacher, armed with a helmet and a stick, was also shot to death in the middle of the square, while another friend (who was in his early twenties) was shot during the massacre and remains paralysed for life. A female interviewee (interview 6) described how she and her husband lost many friends in the massacre. She also explained that shortly after the massacre, she helped record the names of the dead bodies inside a mosque – for the families who were looking for their loved ones. The smell and sensation of wading through blood-soaked carpets mixed with ice water (as they put ice blocks on the bodies to delay the decaying process) will never leave her and still haunts her to this day. Another young man narrated how he was shot twice in the leg but could not go to a hospital due to the fear of arrest or killings inside these medical facilities. Hence, he had to ask a friend to remove the bullets from his leg (interview 40). Another young man explained how his cousin was shot, taken by the police – and never to be seen again (interview 25). His aunt (his cousin's mother) eventually found out that he survived, and that he is in prison, but they have no idea about the state of his health or medical conditions. He also explained how his family had to give up on the idea of visiting him or seeing him ever again, out of fear of security state repercussions. They gave up on him and move on with their lives, he explained. Yet, another young man who survived the massacre described the following horrific ordeal:

> They were . . . they cornered us in a place, just a square just like this. In this place there were many corners, five corners and if I walk in any place I will be shot – by a sniper. We were in a real battle – noises of explosions and ehm . . . bullets are everywhere . . . and each minute, every minute I see a dead people and people are trying to get it to be healed and solved . . . Ehm, that was for maybe 8 hours or so. . . . They shot us not only by sniper, but they used, if you know – that is a gun by a military carting, a huge gun, that is a big gun. And they shot us from helicopters and there is a video that show the helicopter, the apache, I don't know what it is and it is shooting us. (Interview 15)

Hence, the existential impacts of the Rabaa massacre on survivors were grave. In the face of such a brutal massacre, their lifeworld was destroyed, throwing them into a deep sense of existential disorientation as meaning (or rather the potential for meaning) evaporated into thin air, into nothingness. One young man explained that after Rabaa, he experienced such a state of bewilderment and estrangement that he literally could not speak. He could not communicate for days, not with anyone, not even with his friends who had been there with him. The world, he said, no longer made sense. Another young woman explained how following Rabaa, she and her husband experienced an overwhelming sense of debilitating grief:

> Yeah . . . it keeps coming to me all the time. I mean ehm . . . I don't forget them. I mean ehm . . . yeah, like sometimes, I . . . ehm . . . keep crying . . . when I listen to a song or I see some of the footage or the pictures or remember some people. (Interview 6)

The massacre distorted the everyday functioning of the lifeworld as background of interpretation and social norms wherein we make sense of and derive meaning from the world was ruptured. Instead, in face of the massacre, nothing appeared to make sense anymore. Rather, they suffered deep existential alienation from the world, others and themselves as the massacre threw them into a state of disbelief and shock. It also threw them into serious overwhelming bouts of grief, wherein the world appeared to disappear from underneath them. In grief, our world collapses, as we experience what Stolorow referred to as a 'Being-towards-Loss' (Stolorow, 2011a): the loss or death of (a significant part) the self in relation to another's demise. Again, the impact of this Being-towards-Loss was acerbated by the sheer fact that these deaths were neither an accident nor a natural end of life but rather constituted the mass disposability of life through the malevolent will of the Egyptian security state.

Yet, the trouble is that in a context marked by violent social polarisation, the recognition of this grave injustice by others in the social sphere was deeply compromised. For, rather than receiving support and care in light of these murders, many instead encountered suspicion, hatred and fear, which deeply compounded the existential injuries of the traumatic status subordination they had just endured. Indeed, it appears that with Rabaa, the dynamic of conspirational victim blaming, fuelled by frustration, truly reached its deadly climax with Rabaa in Egypt:

> So, I heard many times, after the 30th of June, especially after Rabaa and Ennahda, people say we need all of them to be burnt, we don't care if they should die or not. So, I mean, some of the people, and I used to hear others saying that they deserve to be burnt, they deserved to be killed. They deserved. And this was shocking for me. (Interview 4)

Indeed, such stories abounded. One young female survivor was distraught and so angry when she found out her friend, a fellow teaching assistant, actively supported Sisi and his attempted annihilation of the Brotherhood. Another young man narrated how his sister's best friend told her that she was happy her father had been shot and arrested during the massacre (interview 15). He also relayed that his other sister's six-year-old daughter came home from school crying one day after her friend had 'told her that she was happy her father (a military officer) killed her father, which left her in tears' (interview 15). And he himself had the following experience as he returned from a visit to Rabaa the day after the massacre (as he wanted to take pictures of the site):

> I returned home with a taxi. So, I was speaking with the taxi driver 'did you see the types of bullets they was so big'. He said to me it is the past massacre or the new one. I told him it's the old one. He told me 'No we want a new one'. So, I don't know how these people lost their humanity. I told them, actually I couldn't say . . . I said a small statement and then I. (Interview 15)

This was not the only intersubjective denial of recognition he endured. Rather, the evening before, shortly after the massacre, he wrote about his experiences on social media, only to find that those around him not only withheld their relations of care to him but also actively sided with the military. As he narrated:

> After these massacres when I returned home – now just writing on Facebook explaining what happened or not explaining or just speaking about my feeling. I was waiting for my friends or my relatives to ask me what happened and to be . . . to side with me or something, but this is not what I've seen no. No, I saw the relatives say that we are holding guns that we are killing the military people that you are standing with terrorists. Actually, when I see one of my friends that was in a place, I have to ask him 'what did you saw' . . . because they are watching the TV, so they are the ones telling me what was there. Actually I am the person who was there and I'm the person who can say what was there, not you. And I am the person who saw my friend has been killed and you have to respect this. So, they did not respect this and they did not respect that I am the one who was there and I saw the whole picture not them. So, they did not respect, they did not even sympathize. Actually, they were sympathizing with the other people, with the military. And they were sharing the dead people, the dead military people and I don't know who killed them but I am sure that I am not the one who killed them. My friends that have been died are not the person who killed them. And I am sorry for them. But don't blame me and don't blame my dead friends of this. (Interview 15)

Survivors of the Rabaa massacre thus suffered a double violation of their intersubjective parity. Not only did the traumatic status subordination that had been inflicted on them often remain unrecognised, the violent reactions to their stories and their ordeals also further undermined the lifeworld's taken-for-granted assumptions about established social norms. In other words, their ability for orientation and meaning-making in the world was also further eroded by the violent verbal and physical reactions they suffered in the social sphere.

Unsurprisingly, therefore, after Rabaa, survivors narrated that they experienced a rapid intensification of feelings of hatred towards the Egyptian state as well as ordinary people. They and their loved ones suffered a mass murder (one of the gravest forms of intersubjective imparity imaginable), and they wanted revenge. This desire for revenge and acceleration of feelings of hatred again originates from the violation of being treated as an equal human being. And so, his young Muslim Brother stated that after Rabaa: 'Actually I hated many people. It's out of my hands if I hate this many people these days. [. . .] after this massacre and all this blood, I think the person becomes . . . nearer to an animal' (interview 15). He saw similar anger and hatred develop in his friends who had also survived the massacre: one friend, who "actually is so lovely girl, but after this massacre she was shouting at the people at the building that are watching us and saying 'you are animals, you are animals, you are killing us'" (interview 15). It is thus not surprising that, in the aftermath of Rabaa, the cycle of social and political revenge intensifies, often targeting Egypt's security apparatus (through attacks on police stations or military facilities) but also social others (especially, but not solely, those they deemed affiliated to the military regime). These violent attacks should not be merely understood as emotional outbursts, but rather also as strategic attempts to regain intersubjective power that had been violated and lost. After all,

> the people who saw burned bodies at Rabaa, [they] want to come back for more blood because [. . .] they will seek justice, I can see my other cousins, who's like a very peaceful religious person, tell me: 'if I go down on those protests I won't go without a gun'. And this is the peaceful one, this is also his way of justice. You can see your seemingly sane friends saying no I will not go down to these protest without Molotov cocktails. And then it's just you know . . . where are we going? What are we doing? I mean, I mean how is it that perfectly normal person would you know one day [. . .] wake up and say I'll make this Molotov bomb. It won't get through my head. And it shouldn't. I don't think it should. [. . .] all the violence express politically because of all the, many ehm . . . like each person who is involved in politics, so you see that after a while they express, you know, their anger and their rage and all those frustrations in being politically violent. [. . .], I'll get hit – I'll hit someone. But I'll just . . . express some of the rage. (Interview 10)

Sometimes such violence was also rhetorically justified by survivors through the deployment of a particularly Manichean religious framework wherein they interpreted their experience as part of a transcendental fight of good versus evil – very much like the fight, the Prophet Mohammed had undertaken throughout his life (interview 37, 20). This interpretation of course re-added significance and meaning to the massacre. Yet, it not only lacked a certain critical self-evaluation about the instrumental role the Brotherhood leadership had played in Egypt's counter-revolutionary unfolding, it also added fuel to Egypt's fire of violent polarisation. One interviewee explained that following the Rabaa massacre and the violent persecution of the Brotherhood, its leadership lost control over many of its younger members who now pursued such a fight of good versus evil by joining more radical groups that targeted the military as well as the ordinary population in a politics of revenge (interview 5).

Hence, Egyptian society got ever more deeply stuck in a vicious and deadly spiral of violence. For, in the aftermath of Rabaa, violence as a 'way of dealing with the situation' became ever more accepted, and death ever more pervasive and normalised (interview 17). Indeed, violence was now actively called for by the Egyptian state itself. As this young female activist explained:

> It is not the kind of violence we have experienced in the revolution of 2011. It is [. . .] basically state sponsored, whether through the media or through direct incitement from the military, from the government, which makes it quite dangerous because you have gone beyond the point of speaking about violence just being condoned by the state or people not being protected by the state. You are going to the point where you face *actual incitement*. [. . .] it has become an officially called for violence against one group, the Muslim Brotherhood. And whether you like them or not, this is not the way you want things to be dealt with. (Interview 28)

The military, she continued, actively called upon its citizens not only to support Sisi's anti-terrorism initiatives but also to fulfil their civic duties: to protect their houses, streets and neighbourhoods from supposed Brotherhood infiltrators. Having found a scapegoat in the partner they used to be strategically wedded to, the military directed citizens' anger and frustration inwards into society and heightened it along sectarian lines (interview 28). Again, a primary role in the instigation of this community-based violent polarisation was played by the media affiliated with the businessmen sympathetic to the military. The media increasingly adopted conspirational framing, wherein the urgency of the existential threat posed by the Brotherhood was heightened, and their Otherness and disposability reinforced. As another female activist explained,

> You cannot blame people honestly, they don't know what they are doing, they are being ignited by the propaganda that says 'they are bad, they are bad, they

are bad, they are bad, they are bad' and 'I am an innocent person, I do not know why they are doing this', so people are being incited. (Interview 22)

And the result of this incitement was that interviewees experienced a direct intensification of community-based violence in their direct social surroundings, including their neighbourhoods, private family homes and in their friendships. For as this female activist stated, in this context:

Political violence? It's becoming way more accepted! Like the most recent catastrophe we have, you know the people who died at Rabaa. Everyone is accepting it; everyone thinks it's legit. Everyone thinks you know, not everyone thinks but most of people you know most of those who don't like the Ikhwan. You know, because now we're polarized. We are terribly polarized. So, it's accepted that, you know, so what 500 people died? 800, so what? It's tolerated. It's actually like you know. When people go affirming Sisi, they're actually cheering for it. They want more blood. So, this is the scary thing about it. If you turn that the other way around. The brotherhood, if you see videos before their fall and when you see their attitudes in Itehedya and cases like that. You see like you know, they were also advocating and cheering for violence. [. . .] you could see each camp cheer for the violence, cheer for the blood as long as he is not the victim. So, this is the scary part. It's not about which political side you're siding you are. It's about accepting violence as like the norm . . . you know. (Interview 10)

As violence entered ever deeper into the social sphere, it became ever more difficult to distinguish political from social violence. Rather, violence just pervaded the everyday:

There is a lot of aggression in general on the streets now, more than before. Ehm, and there is also the constant threat somehow of that something will happen maybe, I don't know, maybe some violence [. . .] Yaeny, political violence is during political events but also daily on the streets. I cannot separate between them. You don't even know who is with you or against you, who is killing who. (Interview 23)

It rather appeared that Egypt had been engulfed in a disorientating vortex of violence wherein the imposition of traumatic status subordination became the order of the day – ready to be imposed and inflicted by anyone, anywhere. Interviewees thus described feeling constantly on edge. In the face of such unpredictability, that continuously impressed their existential unsafety and insecurity on them, they felt constantly threatened, fearful that 'something scary can happen at any time, and this feeling is indescribable' (interview

38). This pervasive existential insecurity was fed by the many instances of community violence, up to the point of grave injury and death, that they directly experienced or witnessed. For instance, as the story of this young man poignantly indicates:

> So, one time I was out with my couple of people, a couple of guys. It was past curfew time so there is only these 1 local cafés, that are open after curfew. Because they are on side-streets. We were sitting on of those side streets and we were having a good time playing cards and then all of the sudden we heard that there were bunch of Ikhwan and that the people had stopped them. They we're like the street protector or whatever they are called. So, we went there and saw two micro-buses filled with people. Looked like they were coming back from one of the demonstrations. And the military police was already there and people were yelling at the people inside. And all of the sudden they were starting screaming bad words in their faces. Calling them names by their mothers, and then the military police started hitting them. They had to take them down from the micro-bus and put them in the military box or whatever you call it in English – the military van so they could take them to jail. There is something called 'feshriba'. Feshriba means you slap somebody at the back of the neck. And each one goes boom boom boom boom. And then one of the guys refused to come down, so the police guard, from what I understood hit him with like an iron thing across the bridge of the nose. So, he couldn't move around and then they tied them with their hands on their back and they threw them. . . . People got very excited, they even said to the police let them be so they can beat them. At least the police didn't do that, I guess they just beat them themselves. But they took them and they were screaming. It was like a 15–20 minutes operation – that was the part we witnessed It was very disappointing to see how violent people are. It's because of the intellectual violence that I was talking to you about, the media pretty much ravaged their brains. Only two weeks prior to that, you could have seen a MB guy on the street and see people walking by. Yes, they wouldn't like him. But they definitively would not have labelled him a terrorist or beat him up. (Interview 2)

After a brief silence, he then added:

> Oh, I forgot to tell you. One of the guys, the Ikhwanis, he was talking to the people standing on the street; he was in the car. So, he was from the window talking to them, so the kid, one of the kids, he is. He took off his shoe and he jumped and he slapped him with his shoe across his face. Multiple times. Every time the guy came to tell us 'we're not gonna lose' or whatever he's saying, he would beat him with his shoe. And it's a kid. Can you imagine? The kid was jumping and they were cheering. It's crazy. That what I'm was talking about. . . . That was a real moment of anger. That was a real moment of sadness. (Interview 2)

Indeed, stories abounded with incidents of civilians fighting civilians along lines of political affiliation up to the point of great injury and death. One young man described walking past a main street in Agouza and seeing a dead body lying in the street, with no one attending to it. Another young woman explained that the Brotherhood marches after the midday prayers in Mohandiseen (the area she lived in) turned into scenes of extreme community violence as people from the neighbouring areas such as Bulaaq descended onto the area where the Brotherhood marched:

> People [. . .] would come out with all kinds if knives and ropes and these large sticks and would stand in front of the Muslim Brotherhood and fight with them. And then all [the] times I saw this I was kind of in between, and then you just want to disappear as you don't have anything to protect yourself with. (Interview 28)

As the infliction of intersubjective imparity had spread from the political to the social realm, deadly violence had become all pervasive: it was ready to erupt and be inflicted at any time. This resulted in a deep uncanny sense of inescapable existential disorientation and unsafety among interviewees: the world, it transpired, was a radically unsafe place. For what was increasingly impressed upon them was the fact that one's equal worth as a human being could be fundamentally betrayed by anyone at any point. For life could be taken by the Egyptian state without the blink of an eye but also others on the street. As this young man for instance narrated:

> I do not feel secure when I am walking on the streets with my girlfriend for example. Comparing to 3 years ago, I think it was better. Seeing people kill each other just for differences in their point of view, their political point of view, which is not connected to the economic and social life of everyday, so their basic daily needs. So, seeing people kill each other not for food, not for housing, just for political disagreement, this for me was like shocking. And also. . . . And ok for religious disagreements it still happens and it also continues to happen in such communities, society. But killing each other just for the sake of political disagreements, for differences in political point of view, ok for me that was shocking. (Interview 31)

Such incidents of extreme community violence, and its active celebration by bystanders, were not only a moment of deep sadness for most interviewees, but many also experienced this as profoundly alienating. The fact that people no longer condemned bloodshed but rather appeared to revel in it (interview

25) was for most interviewees a deeply disconcerting and disturbing realisation. As this young man narrated in disbelief:

> Egyptians were not like this. Egyptians have always totally had a high sense of social solidarity and being supportive to each other, we are not used to seeing blood and, and all of these good things that everyone would think although Egypt is the warmest place of people and and and. Now I found the importance of how the media can change a whole nation into monsters. (Interview 25)

Many thus experienced a profound sense of disbelief: people were not what they expected them to be. As traumatic status subordination expanded to the social sphere and tore apart social relations, it thus crushed their normative expectations about how they had expected people to behave. As people around them cheered on the annihilation of life and the violent betrayal of equality of life, their socio-normative framework of interpretation collapsed – and they experienced a deep sense of estrangement from others and the world around them: 'You feel like people are aliens when you talk to someone [. . .] and its even taking a toll on your family and friend relationships' (interview 19). It was as if 'all the people have stopped thinking' (interview 32). Suddenly, people not only stood at opposite political sides but also inflicted and justified the gravest forms of violence and social aggression. As this female activist explained:

> There are people who maybe your friends they are really kind in front of you and they are really good. But they can practice I guess . . . think that this person does not deserve to be treated like a human being. He is a bad person has to be punished. Normal people who are kind of not psychopathic do the beating and the kind of normal torture. Psychopaths do tend to enjoy torture and do the innovative stuff. But it is mainly about dehumanising the other or seeing that that person is not even a human being. So, like an insect or something, not even an animal, an insect. (Interview 22)

This unreliability of people and the violent spread of dehumanisation also impressed upon them the impossibility or even the futility of change. This contributed to a deep existential hopelessness, wherein the potential for meaningful change was slipping away ever further and further. It was not only that the Egyptian security state did not want or allow for meaningful change, but rather it was the people themselves that refused revolutionary becoming. They thus felt increasingly hopeless: 'you feel like you can't change the people – whatever I tried to do with them I cannot change them. They simply do not want to' (interview 20). Rather, it seemed that instead of embracing life, Egyptians started to celebrate and revel in violence and death: 'Egyptians had become entirely accepting of death: "You feel as if Egyptian people don't want to live. They are appreciating or accepting death as life. Something it seems as if they are looking for this, as if it is something more comfortable than life'" (interview 32).

SOCIAL DEATH AND THE IMPOSSIBILITY OF CHANGE

Indeed, there seemed to be no respite from dehumanisation and the politics of death. Rather, violence was spreading throughout social life, including their family homes. And interviewees were particularly upset as relatives adopted this violent logic of dehumanisation towards their friends and even themselves. They explained that family arguments grew increasingly violent and bitter, not infrequently to the point of the gravest verbal insults and direct physical violence. It tore relationships and even marriages apart as people (including husbands and wives) stood at opposite political lines (interview 19). In a society where the family plays such an important constitutive role, many interviewees experienced this violent familial polarisation as particularly destructive: it pulled away the social network of support from underneath their feet. As their intersubjective parity was violated inside their own homes, they started to experience an ever-expanding, ever more uncanny sense of existential unsafety. What this violent polarisation illustrated was that even the closest relatives did not turn out to be what they appeared to be, even they turned into 'violent monsters' in the context of violent social polarisation. It marked a deep rupture in social relations since it impressed upon them that one was truly alone in this world, unable to rely on anyone. It was through this severing of intersubjective relations that such violence added to their feelings of existential unsafety and threw them ever deeper into a state of existential alienation, isolation and atomisation. Suffering violent intersubjective imparity in the family home also resulted in a huge 'anger ... [that] the family that I am supposed to go to for help does not, is unable to understand' and instead 'calls me garbage and a traitor and everything' (interview 18). Hence, quite a few interviewees left their familial homes in the post-Rabaa period as they did 'not want to see them, [and just] want to leave' (interview 18). Others, who remained with their families explained that they found it difficult to bear the social tension inside their houses and between family members. In order to minimise its existential impact, they adopted a strategy of avoidance: they started to come home late, stay over at friends' places and go straight to their bedrooms as soon as they came home so that they did not have to engage in social interaction with their relatives (interview 4). They increasingly retreated inwards into an atomised protective shell of the self, desperately trying to separate themselves from the violent world around them by cutting intersubjective relations as much as possible.

This process of retreating from social relations intensified and accelerated as violent social polarisation spread. Activists not only retreated from engagement with relatives but also from friends as these relations were also increasingly mired in a dynamic of ever-expanding violence. One young man explained that he cut all his contacts with friends, acquaintances and people he knew in Egypt. He just disappeared, and only regained contact with his father and mother after they chased him for two months. He purposefully moved from place to place so that others would not be able to trace him and contact him. As he put it:

> I had to protect me, for 7 months I did not talk to anyone. I used to stay for days and days at home, not talking to anyone, not doing anything. Just staying on my own. It was a very negative experience. (Interview 7)

In light of all that transpired in Egypt, all this violence and traumatic status subordination, he experienced so much existential pain that the only available option seemed to be to retreat from the world altogether. He was not the only one. Another young man locked himself in his apartment for months, neither answering his phone nor the doorbell as he felt so alienated from the world around him. He simply could not face the world anymore, let alone act in it. Yet another activist found himself frantically pacing in front of the television wearing nothing but his underwear, chain-smoking cigarettes for months on end. He could not find the will to even dress himself. After periods of frantic pacing, he would collapse into a deep state of apathy for weeks and even months on end, where he would not speak to anyone. Another interviewee remarked that he lost nearly all social contacts:

> Generally, my social life is not as it has always been. I don't see my friends anymore. I am always . . . eh . . . and even my friends who would not like to . . . I mean, I don't know. . . . I almost lost all relations with all people. (Interview 27)

While social relations diminished overall, often fractures particularly occurred along the lines of political divisions. For instance, a young man relayed how he broke off contact with a close friend, a Brotherhood member. This was a friend, whom he had carried to safety on the 28th of January, dodging bullets on the way, after his friend was shot in the eye. Only for his friend to then rejoice at the news of his detention and his conviction at a criminal court after Rabaa (interview 5). Such experiences impressed not only the unpredictability of people but also the utter futility of risking one's life – of paying the highest price – for another as many had done in the revolutionary days and its aftermath. Others were mostly upset with themselves, with their inability to cross divisional lines in this context of hardening, violent polarisation. They recognised the normative need to transgress these divisions, to overcome this violent polarisation that strengthened the counter-revolution. Yet, on a personal, intimate level, it often simply proved too difficult. As this one young man narrated, after Rabaa he simply could not get himself to take a picture with an old school friend at a mutual friend's wedding because this school friend was an outspoken Brotherhood member (interview 7). Retrospectively he was upset with himself for not being able to do something as simple as taking a picture, but at the time he felt so much internal disgust and hatred towards the Brotherhood – and thus his friend – that he could not even tolerate his face.

The withdrawal from friendships was not restricted to isolated cases but rather constituted a general trend, as nearly all interviewees relayed stories of friendships being broken and ruptured through politically motivated social polarisation. They relayed having heated arguments, sometimes to the point of physical fights, with close friends and acquaintances. These arguments, they explained, while sometimes providing a temporary emotional outlet for their built-up frustration, were also a great source of frustration and disappointment themselves. As this young woman explains:

> I would be frustrated with some of my friends you know, because we disagree. And like I think that they're being entirely stupid when they're like you know 100% supportive of Sisi. And I am frustrated with some of my other friends you know they're like you know completely brainwashed into you know what political Islam is telling them and like you know. 'Morsi Morsi Raisi' – and like you know, all that stuff. [. . .] I just feel like, I think I ran out of the same people I know, you know, because everyone I mean even the smart ones they would go, like you know, the ones you thought were smart, like the ones you thought were smart, they would go like 'Sisi should have done more killings' or 'no Sisi is a killer!'. [. . .]. I mean it should you know; it frustrates you. (Interview 10)

As she then explains, this resulted in both an avoidance of these topics and a restriction of friendships to those who think the same way:

> You decide not to discuss it further to them because you don't want to say offensive stuff and because you actually like these people. So, I guess I'm seeing the friendships that don't even think this way, like you know. Because you know people would get in into the silly argument. [. . .] And like you know they get all serious about it. And I won't go there, I really won't go

there. Because we shouldn't you know go there and then you know going into a fight over something that really is not won't change a thing you know. (Interview 10)

One of the deep counter-revolutionary effects of multilevelled traumatic status subordination is hence that it contributes directly to social death, the withdrawal from social relations, and thus thereby deepens the improbability of creative becoming. And so, while the revolutionary public realm of the eighteen days incorporated differences in a state of prefigurative intersubjective parity and through that created the potential of profound transformation, any such prospect was being ground down ever further and deeper until there remained nothing but an atomistic, nihilistic abyss. For, unable to address systemic (counter-revolutionary) violence in the political public sphere (through means of equal and open communicative action wherein understanding could be reached) frustration, anger and indignation were redirected inwards onto 'the Other', thereby pulling Egypt ever deeper into a destructive cycle, wherein the potential of revolutionary becoming was torn apart ever further. And so, while interviewees vividly recalled the civil conversations with people from all sections of Egyptian society in the revolutionary square, they now could not stand seeing the closest people around them:

Political decisions and fights have made me really not wanting to see some people, because it always turns tense, it will become a fight. So . . . that definitely has had an impact on my socialisation, some friends I just don't want to see at the moment. This has been the case so much that it really gets on my nerves and we cannot have a normal conversation anymore and we cannot talk about personal stuff anymore it always goes back to politics and we will always fight. (Interview 23)

This retreat from social relations was of course not limited to offline encounters and relationships but also manifested itself on online platforms such as Facebook. In the autumn of 2013 a new fad appeared in the form of 'blocking people':

What happening yaeny, there's like a fashion now, it's called the blocking fashion on Facebook. That everyone every day you can find one of your friends saying that he blocked those who are against him or those who say bad things about his orientations. [. . .]. So far, I was so keen never blocked anybody. But I can say that I was . . . Yaeny I read some things of my friends, and I kept asking myself why am I still friends with them? And they kept getting me angry and I wanted to go fight with them, even online. (Interview 4)

The 'defriending' or 'blocking' of people – or being defriended and blocked – on social media was indeed a common experience among interviewees, with one young man even boasting that

> in the past year, I have removed 70 or 80 people. I now have 1000 friends, but none of them are Islamist, except one or two and I cannot remove them for historical reasons because they are very old friends, and it would be difficult to remove them from Facebook, but you can always hide them so that you cannot see them. (Interview 7)

This blocking thus particularly occurred along the lines of political divisions with people primarily blocking those deemed to be on the other side. As this person remarked: 'now the new phenomenon on Facebook is that all people, they remove even close friends from their town, for example if someone is a Brotherhood or an Islamist, they remove him' (interview 7). This blocking trend itself hardened the social boundaries and divisions between the self and the other, the in- and out group, and not infrequently occurred as a part of build up of frustration or aggression towards the other:

> I mean I am angry and sometimes I will say that I really don't care in a tough language. I don't mind telling that word for some people or unfriend some friends, or block even [. . .] Yaeny, do I comment or do I shut my mouth? Yaeny, wallahy, if I see you, I cannot control myself and I just want to hit you or something like that. (Interview 6)

Blocking people online was of course also both a result and itself contributed to the ever-increasing and ever more destructive logic of violence, namely the inability to listen to others. As this young man put it:

> People, when concerning politics, have developed in such an aggressive manner. So much aggressiveness. All the time you feel that people did not hear each other. They speak but they are not hearing each other. They just want to get out what they can, and they are not hearing you. (Interview 32)

Interviewees explained that they saw this phenomenon everywhere, as people grew increasingly frustrated, short-tempered and angry. In a context wherein violence was directed inwards into society, communicative relations became increasingly distorted through the logic of violence. That is, in face of all that they had endured they simply lacked the patience to relate to others as equal communication partners, instead resorting to the instrumental logic of violence, which distorted communicative and intersubjective relations ever further. And so, any conversation at all, no matter how trivial or superficial, could erupt in a heated verbal argument and fistfights at any time. Again, the potential of violence was inescapable: it was pervasive and unpredictable. And so, activists increasingly resorted to tactics that shielded them from its impact. For quite a few this included adopting the tactic of letting it fall on deaf man's ears, of not listening anymore:

> I just look at them and convince myself that I am not listening. He just talks and we have two ears, not one. Just when I have a chance to talk, I just close the subject very quickly, and maybe I get him to talk about something non-political or otherwise I just tell him I have to go. This works. (Interview 12)

Another young interviewee had taken recourse to headphones as a way of blocking out other people. In his words:

> I found that these kinds of discussions usually turn to the fights or just giving the opinions to each other for no purpose. The other opinions, I decided to put my headphones on and listen to music. Now that is what I am doing in situations like this. (Interview 4)

He was not the only one. Another young man also explained that he deliberately moved house and stopped taking public transport so that he would not have to hear other people's opinions, which would often get him involved in physical fist fights with people in the microbus. Instead, he now walked to work and 'I put headphones in my ear all the time so I am not in touch with any kind of people like this?' (interview 7). This recourse to headphones, wherein conversations were literally shut out, is deeply illustrative of Egypt's society, which was drenched in the counter-revolutionary logic of violence. People no longer listened to each other anymore. Instead, violent social rifts permeated society, as society was re-atomised and the potential of creative revolutionary becoming annihilated. Rather, in face of so much violence, so many instances wherein intersubjective parity was brutally betrayed by political actors and the people around them, interviewees simply retreated into the protective shell of the self, isolated from the outside world, the world that was violently deprived of potential.

Importantly, this societal violence should not be interpreted in cultural essentialist terms but rather was a direct result of the counter-revolutionary curbing of revolutionary potential. And hence the retreat inwards was an indication of the grave accumulative toll that the counter-revolution's relentless, systematic and multilevelled traumatic status subordination had on them. The overwhelming, relentless and multilevelled infliction of violence – both physical and structural – and the seeming utter futility of it all, just left them exhausted and in utter existential disarray:

> It was the yaeny, it is two years of continuous huge emotional variation. Two years of continuous sorrows, two years of continuous fear. Definitely. It affects you a lot. After, . . . It even went so far in Egypt that every day, every hour you find something new. A lot of rumour, a lot of news, a lot of blood . . . yaeny. . . . It is so hard to follow even, you don't have time to yourself. You don't have . . . every time you meet a friend you speak about politics. You meet your friend in the demonstration, you go to work and you speak about politics, yaeny . . . you can feel it in people's eyes everywhere. Yaeny. Definitely. And you feel that you are so exhausted. You are so exhausted. (Interview 32)

Indeed, many complained of just feeling so utterly exhausted. Exhausted with 3 years of existential turmoil, violence and death that seemingly appeared to have been pointless as the potential of revolutionary becoming had been taken away from them by the Egyptian military. Importantly, as Deleuze reminds us,

> Exhausted is a whole lot more than tired. 'It's not just tiredness, I'm not just tired, in spite of the climb.' The tired no longer prepares for any possibility (subjective): he therefore cannot realize the smallest possibility (objective). But possibility remains, because you never realize all of the possible, you even bring it into being as you realize some of it. The tired has only exhausted realization, while the exhausted exhausts all of the possible. The tired can no longer realize, but the exhausted can no longer possibilitate. (Deleuze, 1995: 3)

All the blood, all the fights, all the violence, that they had been subjected to because of the counter-revolution's violent infliction of traumatic status subordination had robbed them of a lifeworld wherein possibility of signification or meaning remained an option. Rather, in the wake of so much violence they were left with a collapsed lifeworld, wherein they, the exhausted, 'renounced all need, all preference, goal or preference' (Deleuze, 1995: 5). Unable to engage in the world, their hurt and existential pain was increasingly transformed into a state of existential indifference, of complete alienation. After all, not only was the political terrain entirely dominated by the violent battle between the military and the Brotherhood, but society and social relations had totally fractured leaving no potential for revolutionary becoming. Some also explained that they were afraid of their own exhaustion, and how it manifested as an exhaustion with life as such. Quite a number admitted that they felt suicidal. As the lifeworld's symbolic order crumbled underneath their feet, they no longer could find their bearing or meaning in the world, while the existential pressure of all those deaths weighed heavily on their shoulders. It was not only the revolution that appeared pointless but in the face of a growing politics of death, so did life itself. If life was disposable, why not dispose of it oneself? In the absence of the potentiality of meaning and meaningful change, they found it increasingly difficult to engage in and with the world and retreated inwards into the protective shells of their individual selves – where the violence continued to haunt them nevertheless.

Many thus also experienced a profound sense of numbing, not just in instances of grave violence but also in the gradual accumulation of violence. The accumulation of violence, the multilevelled infliction of traumatic status subordination, wherein the value of life itself had been systematically destroyed, had ground down the revolutionary lifeworld to its breaking point. Activists were gradually rendered speechless and unable to speak as nothing made sense anymore. They experienced a deep sense of alienation and estrangement from the world (and oneself): an existential uncanniness that is difficult to express in words. Having been subjected to so much physical and structural violence, they experienced a profound narrowing of their available emotional spectrum. For being subjected to such an overwhelming disposability of life, they experienced a shift in the existential structures of possible experience. They were no longer able to relate to the world using the full spectrum of their emotions but rather experienced a deep level of distantiation – of estrangement and numbing. This young man for instance described his numbing in the face of the accumulation of death:

> When the sit in of the Muslim brotherhood was dispersed. . . . It may make you think of 'were they 500 or 900'? Or, 2000 dead, you know you just speak about numbers. Actually, the difference between 500 and 550 is really big but 900 dead that is you know the margin. 500, 700, 900 it is all the same thing. Though of course it is not, it is a really big difference. After some time, you become really cold and it is really dangerous. Yeah, somehow less interested in people's lives . . . ehm . . . and yeah, for example, now, aside from political violence and stuff like that, now if I someone dies I am supposed to . . . when I see someone dying or I lose a friend, I am supposed to be really sad, because I am not really experienced and I did not experience this supposedly, because supposedly I did not experience a lot of people dying. And for example, for my dad, he saw his dad dying and some of his dad's friends were dying, so he is ok with it. For me now, I am very ok with it. I mean if someone who I really knows dies, it is like 'ok he died' or 'ok she died'. And ok move on . . . which is dangerous, because I think that humans need to be sad with it. You need to be affected . . . but I am not. (Interview 27)

He was not the only one to experience such numbing. Rather, it was a common phenomenon among interviewees, with this young woman for instance remarking that 'hearing the stories, you get bored. You just become cold. This person died, this person got raped, those words are becoming very common [. . .] Sometimes I get scared that I become cold with all this stuff' (interview 29). Activists commented on how gradually over time, their available emotional spectrum was being altered. They remarked how in the face of such much violence – no longer merely inflicted by the state but rather by everyone around them – they experienced an increasing estrangement from the world. The world, and others in it, appeared as an increasingly alien place, devoid of meaning and potential. They relayed experiencing greater difficulties in relating to the world and others, with some describing this sensation as a flattening out of their feelings – a zombie-like state wherein the world appeared to pass them by. Hence, the counter-revolutionary aim of destroying the potential of creative revolutionary becoming was increasingly successful. The relentless existential weight of continuous intersubjective imparity accumulated in a retreat from the world as well as an atomistic withdrawal from others. It resulted in a deep nihilistic sense of alienated defeatism wherein the potentiality of self-manifestation in the world was destroyed ever further. No matter what one does, it does not have any effect. They felt increasingly powerless. They felt speechless, as the pain of this powerlessness doubled up inside themselves. In the words of this young woman:

> Sometimes you know I have this situation when you are . . . yaeny . . . you are getting so sad from inside and someone provokes you and you feel like sometimes you cannot talk, you can only cry. You know this feeling . . . yaeny, it is not only because you cannot talk but talking is not going to make a difference so you just scream inside and stop talking. (Interview 6)

Hence, in face of the multilevelled traumatic status subordination that they experienced, they became increasingly demoralised. Importantly, as Matthew Ratcliffe explains, demoralisation entails not just the loss of intentional hope (the hope to achieve a particular end) but rather the loss of radical hope, which is 'a deeper or more profound kind of experience than a loss of all hopes, as one not only loses however many actual hopes but also an orientation that is presupposed by the possibility of hoping for anything' (Ratcliffe, 2014: 120). Radical hope is thus 'not an intentional state with some specifiable content, but, rather, a sense of the kinds of possibility that attitudes of intentional hope depend upon' (Ratcliffe, 2014: 119). It thus runs deeper than the hope for a specific intentional object. Rather, in demoralisation, nothing propels one forward, as the 'ground of hope' itself is lost (Ratcliffe, 2014: 123). Importantly, the demoralised person would be capable of hope if the potential of hope not been so systematically and violently destroyed by the current social and political circumstances. For, as Ratcliffe explains, such demoralisation mostly occurs 'when [other] people offer only threat [and] all those hopes that explicitly or implicitly depend on entering into trusting relations with others are affected' (Ratcliffe, 2014: 124). For, in such contexts (of multilevelled traumatic status subordination), one is likely to develop 'a growing sense of the world as unsafe, of people as bad or dangerous, and of hope as unfounded' (Ratcliffe, 2014: 124). In such situations one loses both active and passive hope: while active hope entails the ability to actively influence and shape one's surroundings (to engage in action), passive hope comprises an ability to rely on other people to work on bringing about the necessary changes (especially in case of one's own incapacitation). It was of course precisely active and passive hope that was destroyed by the counter-revolution: not only did activists appear unable to bring about meaningful change due to the military's structural colonisation of the political and economic spheres, but they also suffered passive hope due to the violent polarisation that swept through Egyptian society. They were not only utterly unable to rely on others to bring about meaningful change, but these others will very likely inflict more violence upon the self.

Hence, a deep sense of demoralisation set in as all their efforts had been in utterly vain: 'Only the faces changed but the system is the same. But now really is the worst time for the political violence' (interview 36). Rather, 'Egypt is controlled by the same 12-25 people, SCAF, nothing has changed since 1956 when Nasser removed the King. Nothing new has happened, nothing has changed' (interview 39). Hence, interviewees felt increasingly betrayed, played like pawns in a game controlled by the military:

> I feel sorry . . . right now I feel that everything we have done is totally for nothing. All the blood we have paid? It is for nothing, nothing has changed. We came back to SCAF ruling, the army's ruling, and people now are worshipping the army. It was all a play. We had to go in and we shared in it also, and we had a part in it. (Interview 3)

Many also looked back at their previous revolutionary selves with a certain sense of retrospective incredulity. Some actively ridiculed their previous revolutionary selves, others remained more understanding while nevertheless expressing their disbelief. How could they have once been so naïve as to have hope? How could they have believed that change would be possible? 'We were so young [laughs]. We were so naïve. I feel quite sorry that I think we have gone through a loop, we have done a big circle and we are back with the military' (interview 28). Or as this young man put it:

> We were very naive, seriously. We were very happy, like we had a lot of expectations though things were really clear. The army was in power and the army was Mubarak's blablablabla, but we were very happy. And then we realised that we were used. And then a whole year of protest during the SCAF period, and then we try to work with the Muslim brotherhood in their first days, and then discovered we were being used. We were used by the Muslim Brotherhood to

vote against Shafiq, and then . . . now June 30th, I am realise we were completely used. We never learn. I thought that actually . . . you know, then that the army yeah you know they are blablablablabla but I had hope that they had learnt and that they don't do this and this and that. And then: the same thing. Even worse. I mean, it is now even worse than before. (Interview 27)

Indeed, it was not only that they were back with military rule but that the political, economic and social conditions had also deteriorated: the political and economic sphere had been colonised by the military, and the social realm lay in tatters. The counter-revolutionary infliction of multilevelled traumatic status subordination had not merely destroyed the object of revolutionary politics as such, but rather its very potentiality. Yet, the difficulty with such a fundamental betrayal of hope is that it completely uproots us, it makes us 'lose our footing in the world' (Ratcliffe, 2014: 71). In the words of this interviewee, the trouble with the loss of hope is that 'being negative and being pessimistic all the time would lead to the idea that you collapse in yourself. [. . .] If you lose hope, if you collapse you know' (interview 9).

And it is precisely here that we see the deeply destructive impacts of multilevelled traumatic status subordination on the subjective realm of the lifeworld: interviewees collapsed. They collapsed inwards into a deep debilitating state of depression where, in the evaporation of significance, they were no longer able to engage with the outside world, with others. Depression, while related to demoralisation, also differs from it: while both depression and demoralisation entail the loss of radical hope, depression also comprises the additional loss of the ability to experience or feel pleasure in the here and now (Ratcliffe, 2014: 131). Hence, while both entail the loss of potential signification and are experienced as a profound estrangement (wherein the world appears static, alien, meaningless and unchangeable) and a 'paralysis of hope' (Brampton in Ratcliffe, 2014: 46), depression also entails the loss of ability to feel joy. Depression is existentially all consuming: as signification retreats, one is drawn inward into a nihilistic abyss. In depression, life is deprived of any meaning, potential and pleasure. Depression therefore, 'involves a change in one's sense of belonging to the world' (Ratcliffe, 2014: 61), which is typified by an erasure of *all* practical significance. The world of the depressed is hence often experienced as colourless, oppressive, suffocating, solitary, inescapable and motionless (Ratcliffe, 2014: 76). Frequently, sufferers described depression as a prison – or a glass jar or bubble – wherein they perceive the world but are not able to relate to it, let alone act in it. Importantly, sufferers not only experience a profound detachment from the world but they also feel as if the *true (nihilistic) reality* of the world is revealed to them in this detached perception. In depression, one sees the world for what it supposedly really is: 'A place of meaninglessness and malevolence, which is experienced as an all-enveloping threat, in the face of which on feels passive, helpless and alone' (Ratcliffe, 2014: 170)

Many interviewees suffered episodes of, precisely, such depression as a result of the continued multi-layered traumatic status subordination they encountered in the political and social spheres. They suffered episodes of serious depression, wherein all signification had retreated, and they felt utterly estranged and isolated from the world around them. These periods of depression ranged from a few weeks to nearly a year, and particularly intensified after 30 June and the Rabaa massacre – namely when violent social polarisation intensified and Sisi rose to power. In light of these events, interviewees described themselves as drowning or even suffocating under the weight of violence, death and repression:

> So weird. I felt I was suffocating. What is this? Should I laugh? Should I cry? This is depression. I did not know until I just led it out through crying. You just. . . . You just feel like you want to scream, and you want to scream at people's faces too. (Interview 6)

In this state of depression and demoralisation, they experienced a profound estrangement from others and the world around them, which now appeared hopeless, unchangeable, meaningless and overwhelmingly violent. They felt themselves flung into a state of alienated disorientation:

> You just walk around the country and I look at it, and I think 'what is this place? How does it look like? Is this a good place? Is this a bad place?' Like when you look at a friend who's done so much good and so much bad, and when you look at their features you wonder 'who are you?'. What are you? Ehm. . . . Should I still love you? Should I try? Should I go? [. . .] What am I going to do? What can I say? It is this feeling of you are just lost, you just walk down the street like you don't connect to anything anymore. And like . . . So, you feel like I am angry at Egypt. I am angry at it. At the country, of course at the system and at the people, but it is everything now, it is the system, it is the people, both sides. Sometimes I even wonder, do I even make sense? [. . .] What should I do, you know? So, the feeling I just described is the normal feeling after what happened with the Muslim Brotherhood, after the fall of Mohammed Morsi. But before it was on and off. Before Mohammed Morsi no, it was still like you had hope, things still happened and even if they did not happen . . . things were still, I mean the violence was not as clear, I guess. But, yeah, no it was not as bad. (Interview 29)

Another activist, a young doctor, described how he experienced his depression above all as a sensation of estrangement mixed with a deep sense of existential loneliness, wherein he felt that 'there is a no hope to make any change. Because

I found that most of the people are accepting it [. . .], and after this I started to feel that I am very alone in this country. Very alone. [. . .]' (interview 32). He then explained that in this depressed state he would withdraw ever further from social life and experienced great difficulty in engaging with the world:

> I sleep a lot. I did not want to meet anyone. I just wanted to be alone. Ehm . . . Lack of interest in the things, and in the news, and ehm. . . . You feel this meaningless feeling. You just want to stay at home [. . .] You feel insecurity inside of you, even if you could not express it. Just you have a feeling of insecurity, a very unpleasant feeling. (Interview 32)

This depression was politically motivated, it was the direct consequence of counter-revolutionary purposeful destruction of hope – the strategic infliction of multilevelled traumatic status subordination, wherein the potential of revolutionary becoming was violently destroyed by the military in its instrumental pursuit of its own political and economic interests. Depression suffered by activists in Egypt is thus above all political: it is rooted in the infliction of a politics of death, violence and the disposability of life and the structural erosion of political voice and creative self-becoming. It is rooted in the counter-revolutionary destruction of the potentiality to live a human, dignified life as an equal peer in relation to others. In light of all this violence, this young man explained, depression became the norm, which changed the existential way of being in the world – one wherein he totally lost himself. In his words:

> I have suffered depression. Depression has come over everyone I have met. [. . .] I was not the same person as I was two years ago. I saw all those dead bodies on the street. And so did my friends. Depression became the norm; it changed the mode of life to zero. My friends said: you look sad, talk to us. But I just did not know how. I lost myself entirely. (Interview 39)

As he then continues:

> Politics entered Egypt's political scene like a train hitting a wall. It leaves a depression one cannot erase. When you want to remove it from your life you realise it is impossible for it to be removed. It is there, and it leaves the impressions of all those things they did inside of you. (Interview 39)

And indeed, this impression of all that they did was so impossible to erase: it changed interviewees' way of being in the world into a being towards loss, wherein they grieved the loss of particular lives as well as the loss of the potential of signification. Rather, as the lifeworld collapsed, they imploded inwards into their atomised selves as signification evaporated into thin air.

But, for many this inwards implosion into the self and retreat from public and social life made matters worse: it increased a deep sense of debilitating existential guilt. As they retreated into their atomistic selves, they were haunted by a deep sense of failure – of revolutionary betrayal. As this young man explained:

> The feeling of guilty makes you sometimes really burned out. Making you afraid, not sharing and make yourself more isolated from your friends, because you don't want to open up deep things or even to look at their eyes. And this and this all these vicious circles takes you eventually to like a state, a chronic state of depression. [. . .] a continuous state of depression. (Interview 4)

Experiencing Existential Pain: Somatic Responses

Such crippling depression and deep existential guilt were also experienced somatically by many interviewees. This is not surprising, since our bodies are of course constitutive in the construction of our existential experience of the world: it 'ordinarily operates as a medium through which the world is experienced' (Fuchs in Ratcliffe, 2014: 96). And so, the change in existential structure of experience is felt in and through the body also. As a medium, (able) persons are ordinarily often not fully aware of its mediating function, until the body's functioning moves from the background of our consciousness into the foreground – mostly upon an experience that makes us particularly aware of our bodily relation to our surroundings (such as disability, illness, pain and pleasure). Bodily feelings are hence profoundly relational (Ratcliffe, 2014: 93), it is not only the medium through which we are experienced and are located in the world, but we also ascribe meaning to the body (and bodily feelings) with reference to an intersubjectively constituted symbolic realm. Or rather, bodily feelings thus include both 'noematic feelings', which entails 'the body as a central or peripheral *object* of experience' and 'noetic feelings', 'where the body is that *through which* something else is experienced' (Ratcliffe, 2014: 94–95 my italics). The body is hence profoundly relational and inherently connected to the shared symbolic realm of the lifeworld. As the lifeworld functioning crumbles, however, our noematic and noetic feelings also change: the body's 'smooth' mediating function falters and we become increasingly aware of the body as an 'object' estranged from the symbolic interpretative flow wherein we previously found ourselves. Hence, sufferers of depression often relay that their bodies become sluggish obtrusive objects – which Ratcliffe refers to as the '"reification" or "corporealization" of the body' (reference). The body thus moves from the background to the foreground of experience as those who suffer depression experience a 'lack of vitality, inability to concentrate, diminished inclination to act and a feeling of being disconnected from things' (Ratcliffe, 2014: 100). As he then explains: 'A world that threatens, overwhelms or suffocates in some inchoate way is at the same time an experience of bodily tension, tightness and pressure' (Ratcliffe, 2014: 97).

The bodily experiences described by interviewees correspond to the somatic state of depression Ratcliffe describes, with most experiencing bodily tension, tightness and pressure. Many interviewees suffered excruciating tension headaches and migraines, as well as extremely painful backs and shoulders. One young man described it as 'a physical manifestation of the anxiety' that he suffered as a result of the intense and relentless stress of Egypt's post-revolutionary aftermath. Moreover, in addition to these aches, as many as twenty-five out of forty interviewees also suffered blood-pressure-related problems – all of which specifically developed during Egypt's post-revolutionary aftermath. One of these interviewees, a female journalist, described how during particular political events her blood pressure would rise to such an extent that she would end up in a 'hysterical' bloody mess. And, all those suffering from post-revolutionary blood pressure problems relayed that they often experienced its effects – which included confusion, chest pains, headaches, tiredness and difficulty breathing – during political events. Their condition particularly deteriorated as the counter-revolution progressed and they were flung ever into a state of hopeless depression.

Many also suffered severe bouts of anxiety, which they experienced as generalised sense of fear and stress:

> Yaeny, one of the things about my anxiety is that it feels like I am being moved by being scared. You know, like I move because I am scared, I do things because I am scared, I do this because I am scared that I miss this or mess up this or you know I am very scared and this is the problem of my anxiety and hence I beat myself up if I don't do things to make things better, you know so . . . I don't know. I think it has to do with the anxiety, the anxiety makes you really scared so you do things to . . . eh . . . eh . . . to stay away from the bad consequences you fear or that you are scared of you know. (Interview 26)

This feeling of generalised fear, of anxiety, in deep inner feeling of restlessness:

> If someone would say what is up with you? I would say nothing and everything you know. Yeah, it happens all the time. I would be restless for no particular reason for no particular reason but for all the reasons. Yeah, it happens a lot. (Interview 27)

Or as a deep sense of nervousness:

> I mean, like . . . sometimes . . . eh . . . I feel nervous . . . even if you are sitting at home and I just feel nervous with no reason. I mean I keep moving from one channel to another. I also have a problem but I am not sure it is related to the political situation. Like, all the time, even if I don't have responsibilities, I have always have the stress of a deadline that I need to catch. This is something that started to be built in. So . . . eh . . . like you cannot feel like you can relax or having a piece of mind. I mean you are thinking of everything all the time, you have a lot of ideas inside your mind. It can be a manifestation of anxiety. (Interview 6)

In face of the relentless traumatic status subordination that they had been subjected to, wherein they were forcefully confronted with the disposability of life, they experienced anxiety in almost a Heideggerian fashion: as an uncanny mode of being in the world characterised by generalised fear. And while it threw them into a state of atomisation, it hardly a process wherein they – as Heidegger would have us believe – could appropriate their authentic ontological being. Rather, in counter-revolutionary Egypt, the possibility of instant demise was hence not something that they could own, it was owned by others. It was not the possibility of death wherein their authentic selves would come into being but rather the potential of murder and suffering wherein they or their loved ones would be violently appropriated by others. For, in the face of pervasive traumatic status subordination, they suffered a paralysing sense of helplessness, the inability to manifest themselves in the world at all. It was this ever-pervasive and generalised existential fear that made them constantly on guard and also resulted in panic attacks:

> I get the panics without understanding their relation to like, you know. Sometimes you get any panics and you don't know how to explain them, because as I tell you I block things. So I know like, you know, lots of things already get you but, you don't know what to do with them you block them. Then after a while you find out that you can't breathe or you can't move and you can't talk and just you know. It's ehm . . . it really gets to you and then like you know. You might after it's gone the panic, you might try to in analyse where it came from. And you really wouldn't know because you blocked the attack. But ehm . . . Yeah I think I can tribute many, many of my panics to the life or that I live here in this country. I mean, the society the . . . just going about your life daily here is bound to bring some threats. [. . .] The . . . many, many things can happen, I mean one is not safe here. (Interview 10)

Yet, participants also noted that this deep feeling of existential unsafety, this sense of panic, could also be triggered by specific places, smells, sounds and sights that brought them right back to the instances of violence and destruction they experienced. For instance, one young man narrated that every day, on his way to work, 'I go through the place I got shot. I see what happened directly in front of my eyes. Also, I always remember the people who died. All of them' (interview 40). Another young man described being haunted by images of his own torture, as well as the clashes wherein 'someone who dies in front of me, someone who dies in my hands, someone who died beside me' (interview 36). Another female activist narrated how she remains haunted by the eyes of her friend, wide eyed, looking at her, pleading for help, as she was sexually tortured by a gang of men in Tahrir Square. And many, including this young woman, described how the sound of fireworks and sirens would remind them of the violence:

> I hate fireworks now, I hate the sound of sirens, they remind me of shotguns, I hate that. And ambulance, fire sirens – any kind of sirens I hate it. When I was in Belgium, in Brussels, the sound of the ambulance was exactly the sound of the CSF car here. And I woke up in the middle of the night hearing it and I was like 'oh my god, it's in my head, it's following me'. And then I talked to my friend in the morning and she's like 'no that's our ambulance'. It is stressful and I am scared. Sometimes there are also particular smell that brings you right back. . . . Vinegar – after Mohammad Mahmoud I can never have vinegar in the house. Vinegar was used to combat the effects of teargas. I can never stand vinegar. (Interview 18)

In light of such existential restlessness, panic attacks and triggers, more than half of the interviewees also suffered sleeping problems and had regular nightmares wherein they were beaten, tortured and found bullets whizzing around their ears. They regularly dreamt about the violent events they had experienced in real life: 'I had dreams about . . . the violence. . . . I don't know. Like you know. The way you see everything that happens always translated in your dreams one way or another. You know' (interview 10). As this person noted, 'when you try and sleep, you hear the bullets all around you' (interview 32). Or, as this young man narrated, after the Rabaa dispersal:

> I always hear the gunshots during my sleep and I would see the number of people who are dead during my sleep or even hallucinations. they happen frequently, like every week. I would wake up stressed but well – this is normal after everything I saw. (Interview 40)

Given the relentless multilevelled traumatic status subordination that they suffered, it is not surprising that the dreams of violence particularly featured the experience of death and dying, with many suffering nightmares wherein they were holding the bodies of bloodied friends and loved ones as they are dying at the hands of the military. Sometimes these were actual martyrs while at other times they comprised family or loved ones who were still alive. One young man narrated that while over the last three years, he had 'generally dream[t] of the dead', these dreams were particularly intense following the martyrs' funeral processions: 'I dream of Mina Daniel, also when I came back from his parade. I dream of Husseini when I come back from his parade, you know stuff like that. Eh' (interview 27). Another person narrated how his friends would wake up screaming at night as they dreamt of the dead during Rabaa (interview 15). Another young man explained he had a recurring dream about smoking shisha with Mina Daniel, one of the revolutionary activists who was killed, who then suddenly asked him how the revolution was going. In their dreams, the dead were hence very much alive – and the encounter with them often instilled a deep sense of existential guilt and anxiety.

In addition to dreaming of those who died, participants also frequently dreamt of their own violent deaths at the hand of Egypt's security state:

> I get nightmares of state security and stuff, and I have been getting them over the past three years. I told our friend A. just two days ago when we went running 'I just had a dream that I got shot by state security', I get dreams like that a lot. It is really weird. [. . .] Yesterday, I had a dream that I was going through a maze type of thing and then I opened one door, there was only one door left and then there was just like a tank and stuff and they shot me at the end . . . in the dream. [laughs] You know they are very simple, it is not like symbolic stuff. It is just like the army, they all shoot me or state security. (Interview 30)

Such dreams of direct personal assassination were often part of a wider array of nightmares wherein interviewees suffered counter-revolutionary death and destruction: 'I have dreams. . . . I was regularly assassinated . . . by the military. . . . I wake up from these dreams. . . . I have had other forms of violence, or dreams of violence. Like being in the middle of a clash, or carrying dead bodies. Yeah . . . things like that' (interview 25). Yet, for some the regular recurring dream did not consist of concrete violent events as such but rather comprised of losing one's teeth – which in psychoanalysis has often been associated with death, loss and personal mourning (Lorand and Feldman, 1955; Capps and Carlin, 2011; Rozen and Soffer-Dudek, 2018).

288   *Chapter 10*

> The main nightmare I have is that I have my teeth in my hand, you know. I find that I am losing all my teeth like sand, and I have them all in my hand and I don't know what to do. [. . .] I have this dream when I am very frustrated. It is a horrible feeling. It is difficult to imagine it. (Interview 7)

Given the prominence of death, anxiety and loss in these dreams, it is also not surprising that the other prominent topics were revenge, betrayal and existential guilt. In terms of revenge, some interviewees dreamt of going on killing sprees or liquidating the Head of the Egyptian police. Others dreamt of 'people and what I want to do to them. I want to kill injustice and I do something brutal in my dreams and I have a lot of anger' (interview 19). While some were haunted by a deep sense of betrayal:

> One time there was a big protest and I could not go for some reason I think I had to work and during the same night I had a dream that eh . . . and then people got killed at the protest. And that day I got a weird dream [. . .] that I was sitting in a park and you know the protesters were inside the building and I told the police where they were, and I felt like I had betrayed them you know. And I get dreams like this all the time. (Interview 30)

Betrayal also clearly appeared as a theme in the dream of another young man, but then at the level of formal politics. He dreamt of shouting at revolutionary politician Khaled Ali who pulled out of the elections at the time. In his dream he was suddenly on a small piece of land with Ali:

> Not a land, a piece of land, which belongs to us, and it has like a wall around it. And someone come and start to take in outside our land. And I talk to Khaled Ali and he was in the office and I say 'come someone is taking our land'. And he said what can I do to him? And I said if you are not, if you cannot protect a small building like this with its land how can we . . . protect a whole country? I think it reflects the kind of disappointment that we took this country, that if we cannot protect ourselves even in small spaces, what about the whole country? (Interview 4)

This sense of revolutionary failure against counter-revolutionary colonisation also featured heavily in this young woman's dream, wherein the car she was driving was stopped by nobody less than SCAF general Tantawi himself. In her words:

> I was in the car, and I was driving. Now a little information, I don't have a car and I don't drive because I am such a loser [laughs]. So, I was driving, and my

dad was sitting next to me and it was after the Port Said incident, the Ultras who died . . . the 74 . . . [. . .] the car next to us someone decided to lean towards us and it was almost as if he was hitting my car and a stop my car and so I was looking [laughs] and now here is the amazing. . . . Who was driving the other car? It was Tantawi [laughs loudly]. The amazing thing is that I got out of the car and I started shouting at him and saying things like just because you think you are an important leader and you are a leader of SCAF and you think that you can do this and that, and we won't let you. And now the weird part of the dream is that my dad stood my grounds, he was very supportive. And I woke up and told my dad to dream, and he said 'are you crazy? If I saw you fighting with Tantawi I would pull you by your hair and we would go run away'. [laughs] [. . .] maybe it is a metaphor that maybe one day my dad will stand my ground that he will change his stance. (Interview 28)

In light of such emotionally charged dreams and violent nightmares, as well as increased levels of general anxiety, it is not surprising that so many activists suffered from insomnia. Not only did they often experience guilt as they were trying to take a rest, to sleep, knowing that while I sleep 'they're beating people and they're shooting people' out there (interview 10), they also had great difficulty falling asleep as they would worry about 'everything and nothing' (interview 27) or be too hyped up with uncertainty about 'what is going on' (interview 37):

You just go to bed and you just can't sleep. And if you slept, if you succeed to sleep, and somebody wakes you up you are not going to sleep again because it is into you and you just cannot get out. And you do not know what is going to happen. And part of it is that living in Egypt for me is not very easy. (Interview 38)

These increased levels of sleep-deprived anxiety enfolded them in a vicious downwards spiral, wherein they suffered ever more sleepless nights. Or if they did sleep, they had difficulty remaining asleep. Many woke up in the middle of their sleep, screaming in a sweat from the nightmares they suffered, while others kept waking up due to a general sense of restlessness – or anxiety. Two interviewees explained that since the revolution they had not been able to sleep more than thirty minutes at a time: 'I sleep and wake up again, sleep and wake up again – like every thirty minutes. It started when all my life changed, when the revolution started' (interview 36). While these two cases are perhaps extreme, most interviewees found that, since the onset of the revolution and counter-revolution, the duration of their nightly rest had been cut to anywhere between three and six hours at the most. As this person remarked:

I have this thing where I may be sleep for three or four hours. Maybe sometimes I am sleeping but . . . eh . . . I am sleeping but . . . eh . . . I am not sleeping, just lay down on the bed and I am awake but I have my eyes closed. I don't know why. (Interview 12)

All of these cases, these somatic pains, these dreams and the inability to sleep are indicative of the extent to which they had personally so deeply affected by the counter-revolution: the counter-revolution had truly impacted their existential and embodied way of being in the world.

COPING WITH THE COUNTER-REVOLUTION: DEPOLITICISATION

It is thus not surprising that in light of this existential shift, activists resorted to a variety of coping mechanisms. Some resorted to taking drugs, or self-prescribed medicine, such as anti-depressants and Tramadol, to ease the stress and exhaustion of counter-revolutionary life in Egypt. Tramadol is an addictive opioid painkiller that has both calming and euphoric effects on the person taking it and has been a popular medicine in counter-revolutionary Egypt to ease the effects of anxiety, stress and depression (Curnow, 2018).[3] In addition to Tramadol and anti-depressants, activists also turned to alcohol. As this young man put it: 'Sometimes I just need to drink alcohol for calming myself down' (interview 32). Or as this woman's anxiety intensified, she found that 'I need a lot of relaxants, yaeny for example in the evening at drink a lot as well because I always need something to calm me down. I am not naturally calm. Ehm . . . yeah' (interview 23).

A handful of interviewees also turned to art – such as writing, music and film – as a coping mechanism, as a way to try reinscribe meaning into their lives. In the context of a lifeworld broken by traumatic status subordination, art is a potentially useful avenue since it provides an outlet for emotions and thoughts. That is, it enables a multifaceted expression of feelings and thoughts in a dialogue with others, thereby reconstructing a (new) symbolic framework wherein meaning may be reinserted into life. Importantly, in counter-revolutionary context wherein real conversations are made increasingly impossible, the audience may be imaginary or imagined – thus enabling the construction of an (imaginary) intersubjective dialogue in an atomised context of isolation and social withdrawal. For instance, one young man started writing diaries to his imagined children:

I'm writing the diaries and this maybe a reflection of the violence and this I have not mentioned before. What happened is that I started to write my diaries to my kids, those who have not been born yet. I am writing to a guy and to a girl, and I keep telling them what is happening, because I feel that there are many chaotic things. And I remember that I wrote a long one to my daughter, my unborn daughter. Telling her that, I don't know what will happen at her time. But I just want to tell her that things are not good but that there is struggle. And I tell her that I feel that she will not be happy with way that women are treated. (Interview 4)

Writing letters to his future imaginary children enabled him to express how he really felt, without having to fear violent repercussions and projecting himself forth (albeit somewhat precariously) into a future. Other interviewees also wrote songs (which they mostly sang to themselves or a small group of friends) and were looking into avenues to create films about human rights and injustice in Egypt – some also resorted to blog writing or keeping journals. As this male revolutionary remarked:

I write to help me. Writing . . . I'd have been much worse off if I wasn't writing, because for me that has been the way to deal with things, but it gets really problematic when I'm too exhausted to – that's the height of it, when I'm too exhausted to even write, yeah, I don't have that energy. So that's when it becomes problematic. (Interview 11)

Many of these writings and artistic expressions were at this stage still political in orientation and expression. Hence, it is not surprising that as soon as Sisi had consolidated his political and economic power, he increasingly closed such avenues through his repressive juridification of the public sphere, which not only included the Protest Law of 2013 but also his New Anti-Terror Law of 2015 and the new Media Law of 2016. The underlying motivation of such repression is clear: it is not only to silence critique itself but rather to destroy the potential of creative collective becoming through mobilisation around such critiques. The point is to destroy the potential of self-manifestation wherein one might come to see a potentiality of being that is different than being lost. Or rather, the goal is to mute activists and throw them into isolating atomisation – keep them imprisoned in the destruction of intersubjective relations. The purpose is to put not just the revolutionary genie, but its very potentiality, back into the counter-revolutionary and authoritarian bottle.

And unfortunately, this project has been largely successful. Not only has the potential of creative collective elf-becoming been systematically destroyed but in the face of its violent and multilevelled destruction, interviewees not only retreated from social relations but also actively depoliticised: they withdrew from anything related to politics and the political. This also meant that activists retreated from the streets, which they no longer regarded as theirs since these had been taken over by the violent urban battles between Brotherhood supporters and Egypt's security forces (Interview 32). And in any case, they remarked, demonstrations had proven pointless, as it had only resulted in more (pointless) deaths:

> We have seen people killed, we have seen blood in the streets, in the last 3 years we have seen thousands of people killed who were part of their larger communities, larger circles, hundreds of thousands of people were affected by this and so far, no change. We just let the sorrow and sadness into the houses of the people killed. (Interview 31)

Not only did participants increasingly regard street politics as futile, they also resigned from formal political parties and other organisations that they had been active in over the last three years. Political parties, they believed, 'are very mediocre so nothing really useful has happened. I mean, all that they do in the meetings is talking, talking, talking as at the same time nothing is being done' (interview 1). Moreover, overwhelmed by years of disappointment and violence, many felt a strong desire 'to be isolated' (interview 4) and 'stopped for example sharing any comments or expressing any ideas' (interview 4). Retreating into their atomistic selves, they also removed themselves from formal organisations that they had been part of:

> Now I don't attend anything anymore for example [. . .] . . . I don't take part in the planning anymore I don't want to hear about it. I don't want to see those people. I don't want to talk to people. [. . .]. I've had an overload, and I'm really tired of discussions and I am sick of some people and I am sick of their views and I . . . yeah . . . I don't want to be near it. (Interview 23)

Not only did they leave the street, political parties and formal organisations, they also withdrew from any form of political participation and engagement, and avoided any exposure to politics, which included the news and conversations with (same-minded) friends. This person reflected the opinion of many participants when he stated 'I need a break from politics [. . .] I don't read the news, don't watch television, I just cut all politics from my life' (interview 37). For, having suffered of multilevelled counter-revolutionary traumatic status subordination, their lifeworld was shattered and they were left in existential disarray. Many felt that they had personally come to embody revolutionary failure not only in their bodies and in their lives but also in light of all the pointless violence just felt so exhausted. In light of all the continuous multi-layered stress they endured, and the counter-revolutionary successful domination of political life, they no longer saw potentiality in politics, only death and exhaustion. The counter-revolution had left them feeling existentially drained, exhausted and demoralised. In the words of this young man:

Dealing with all this takes a lot of time and emotions. You put all your emotions in one basket. You put yourself in the position of the family of those who died. Say you put 100 litres of all your energy and emotions into this basket, then 99 litres are gone just thinking about this stuff. You only have 1 thought or 1% left, it absorbs everything. (Interview 39)

Hence, as the counter-revolution was increasingly successful, interviewees withdrew into an isolated shell of atomised protection. The few relations or friendships they did maintain were mostly with those that were not political at all, or at least no longer discussed politics. For instance, as this young woman explained, the only people she would still hang out with would be a handful of friends who not 'into politics' (interview 30):

I do not talk politics with them at all and they know nothing about what is going on. These are people who would ring me up and go like what is the referendum about tomorrow? And these are my best friends you know. These are people that have nothing to do with the news. And we go out and we drink. We do not discuss politics or religion or anything controversial. This is like my group of friends you know, who know nothing about what is going on in the country. They know nothing, they don't know who the military council is, they don't know. (Interview 30)

Underpinning this retreat into depoliticised atomisation was also a search for existential safety (to not be potentially subject to or party to the infliction of more violent intersubjective imparities). As this woman remarked:

Now I try and avoid discussion. [. . .] Right now it is a feeling that I want everyone to be safe, the good and the bad just need to be safe. There is too much blood. Just be safe. Ehm . . . [. . .] I don't want to discuss all of this now. I talk with people about their work, about how to move on, how to increase productivity, I live in my own Lala-land because that is where I see some change [laughs]. (Interview 29)

Hence, unable to achieve any meaningful change and instead experiencing the systematic erosion of the potentiality of change, they turned inwards, into their depoliticised 'lala-land' where, just perhaps, on a personal level some change (in the form of a new apartment or employment) was still possible. This depoliticised atomisation was thus their last resort, their last chance, of retaining a glimmer of meaning in their lives, when the potentiality of meaningful change had been stolen from them. It was a strohhalm they desperately clang too. For, in an attempt to repair their broken lifeworld, they focused inwards, into their isolated and individualised lives, where they sought to achieve smaller personal successes such as obtaining one's bachelor's degree, finding an apartment or getting some form of paid employment (if possible). Refocusing their attention away from politics and inwards on their own individual private lives they sought regain a sense of control over their lives when all control appeared to have been lost, to regain sense of influence on their surroundings when all influence had been destroyed and thus engage in a (limited form) of self-manifestation when collective self-manifestation had been annihilated. It was at attempt to restore some meaning, when meaning had appeared to have been lost. As this young female activist explained, depoliticising individualisation was an attempt to 'have a life' again:

> I go to work and I do the news and I go home and I watch 'friends' all night or do some silly things like going to the movies or whatever, which is great. I actually started to have a life last year. And yeah, that has been good for me. (Interview 30)

Yet some, like this young man, were also deeply worried about this depoliticised retreat into an atomised existence:

> I am really afraid that people are going to give up. That we are going back to what happened before 25 January, and that people start to be isolated again and that they start to leave the streets and that they start to. . . . Start to feel that it is not their country. That to accept what is going on in the land. Start to feel that they are not represented by the powers. That they are alone. They are already feeling the bullshit of politics. People are not willing to deal with politics any more. After two years of three years of politics nothing has happened. Nothing has happened, and all the time they are feeling that they go to the streets and they have wonderful hopes to change and and and . . . and then something happens and then after that nothing happens. For all the demonstrations nothing has changed on their personal level, like food, transportation and education and reachieving their dreams. Nothing has changed. It is gotten even worse. People now feel really depressed, and after that they start to recognise or accept that really, we did not need any change, we just need to live a normal life and we need to feel that we are safe to go to the street. And this is exactly the message that they wanted to deliver to them, to make them fear again. This is my biggest and worst fear. I fear to be alone again. I have the fear of not even been able to express my feelings and my opinion about what is happening. I fear that I will be like the older politicians that I have seen in Egypt, like in the 70s . . . now they are . . . they do not believe in the revolution, all the time I was an activist I was feeling them dreaming of the Revolution Day that would come and change people. After that I stopped believing in them. No yaeny. (Interview 32)

And indeed, the worries of this young man appeared to have been warranted. The question is whether in this trend of individualised depoliticisation, we do not find history repeating itself. The sad irony seems to be that it is precisely such depoliticisation that many of the interviewees precisely blamed their parents' generation for retreating into their personal lives, for not manifesting themselves politically and for having merely focused on their everyday individual existence. As a young man had stated:

> It is my father's generations, because those people they remained silent for 30 years. So, they wasted the best years of their lives when they were young people, just to eat, marry and to have a normal life. They did not have any aspirations to change the country so they remained silent, and this generation let us down. They will never support us. I don't think that this country has hope, has any, any, any hope, unless young people are in power. After the revolution those people were very resistant to the idea of change. (Interview 7)

Now the question is whether these activists will repeat the patterns of their parents' generation? Will the current processes of depoliticisation persist over time? Or will they enter the political terrain again? Respondents themselves did not know the answers: some insisted that by focusing on education or employment, they hoped to contribute to Egypt's political and economic future in a broader sense. Others sought to leave Egypt altogether in the hope that they might be able to provide a better future for their (unborn) children. Many however felt increasingly unwilling to risk their lives for the 'game' of politics. The short-term prospects for their political mobilisation and regrouping are bleak especially as Sisi's has only intensified the politics of death and the prisonification of society that started to emerge during the time that the interviews take place.

Saying that, small sparks of hope remain. Sometimes in the form of a lone protester carrying a sign saying 'Leave ya Sisi' on Tahrir square, sometimes in the form of simple small protests such as 'Sisi's balls' (Mahmoud, 2017b) and sometimes in the form of larger protests (such as those in light of the Mohammed Ali videos). And so, the long-term prospects for political mobilisation in Egypt, of course, remain an open question. But much here also depends on the extent to which international actors, such as international and European governments, international organisations and institutions finally stand up and raise their voices against Sisi'[s politics of death, prisonification and dehumanisation. And so far, there is not much ground for hope in this respect, as these governments and institutions not only continue to turn a blind eye to Sisi's politics of death but are also rather complicit in the maintenance of his semi-totalitarian regime through increased arms trade, security cooperation around 'counter-terrorism' and migration, as well as engagement in many of Sisi's economic projects. These projects include the Suez Canal, the Siemens factory, Sisi's New Administrative Capital and various projects around ecological and sustainable development (whose primary goal is to greenwash Sisi's regime of death, not least since all the companies involved are part of and serve the military itself). And so, the question we must ask ourselves here is whether these actors continue to believe (and support) the old authoritarian discursive framework of stability (embodied by Sisi's regime) versus chaos (of the people), or whether they are finally willing and able to see Sisi for what he is: a naked emperor who built a violent castle of sand. For, a regime based on the continuous violent violation of intersubjective parity – on the utter disposability of life – can by definition only create instability, chaos and despair. A stable and legitimate political order can only be achieved when all are able to engage in creative collective self-becoming as equal peers. Hence, the question is when the international community will start to value life over death rather than death over life in their engagement with Sisi and his deadly military rule.[4]

NOTES

1. On anxiety in Heideggerian trauma theory, see chapter 2 of this monograph.

2. I use the word 'supposedly' here as in this context I would agree with the distinction Hannah Arendt makes between force and power – while Sisi might have force, his rule and regime has lacked political power since its very inception. This means it is a brittle state, built more on a castle built of sand rather than true stability.

3. While initially the drug was widely available, the government cracked down on the opioid in 2014 making such possession illegal and imposed harsh prison sentences upon such possession. Of course, such repression does not merely consist of symptom reduction but also repeats the same logic of repression that underpinned much of its usage to begin with.

4. Please note that due to a lack of space in this monograph, I have not been able to do justice to the international dimensions of Egypt's counter-revolution. Authoritarian leaders of course never act on their own but also depend on an international network of support. For more on this, please see (Allison, 2019).

Chapter 11

Conclusion

> When I'm stuck in traffic. That's one of my things that at some point if someone as much as talks to me I am going to get crazy. I try to calm down, close the windows, put on some music, but you know, it's not always the best, because I hate to be stuck. For me it's – I'm a bit restless, so if you put me in a metal box, for me a car is a metal box, for more than one hour – you can't do that to me. You are killing my powers of imagination. It essentially kills your dreams, instead of thinking 'I wanna change the world', you think I just wanna get home. Now you're just killing my dreams. (Interview 18)

This young woman compared the existential impacts of the counter-revolution to the suffocating sensation she experiences in Cairene traffic. In the retreat inwards, the closing off from the outside (by closing the windows and putting on music), one's imagination is being killed. Just as one feels stuck in Cairo traffic so did revolutionary activists feel stuck in Egypt's counter-revolutionary aftermath. Unable to move forward, they felt continuously stuck in an ever-eternal present – devoid of imagination, of potentiality, of the possibility of meaningful change. The Egyptian military, through the infliction of multilevelled traumatic status subordination, destroyed nothing less than even the potential to imagine, to dream, to project forward and to create. The potentiality that had burst into Egypt's streets and squares during the 25th January revolution had petrified the army. And so, while riding the revolutionary tidal wave to get rid of Mubarak, as soon as he was ousted, they sought to destroy this through the infliction of grave deadly violence, the procedural colonisation of the political sphere and the further neoliberalisation of the economy that now primarily benefitted the Egyptian military. However, in order to make sense of this kind of complex, multilevelled traumatisation and its exact functioning as a tool of repression, the concept of PTSD appeared to be insufficient not only due to its medicalisation but rather since it abides by a philosophy of the subject. As we saw in chapter 1, the cognitive concept of PTSD not only results in tautological thinking (in that trauma refers to both the causal event and its effects) but was also rooted in a category mistake wherein matters of socio-normative interpretation – of (in)justice – became regarded through the prism of medical observable facts. As we then saw, this was extremely problematic since the ascription of trauma bypassed the boundaries of nosological observation and instead relies on an interpretative moment – wherein causality is established through the ascription of trauma to an event, however, this causality is in fact never accounted – and, as we have seen may never be accounted for through the observation of biomedical facts. This led to a variety of problems, the most important of which is that the cognitivist reduction of trauma resulted not only in a Westocentric projection of particular conception, the problem of a double injury (wherein victims of an injustice are now also told that there is something writing with their mind or brain) but also the inability to account for trauma studies political normative orientation. Even when trauma studies moved to neuroscience as its saviour, aside from its problematic content, all that was established were correlations rather than causation.

This changes when we develop a radical intersubjective theory of trauma, rooted in a meta-theoretical reading of Jurgen Habermas and Nancy Fraser's philosophies, wherein trauma is conceived as the violent betrayal of the counterfactual presupposition of being treated as an equal peer in relation to others. Trauma thus entails a violation of what Nancy Fraser (2003) calls participation parity, as the perpetrator (either a group or an individual) seeks to impose power over the victim (either a group or an individual). In this sense, trauma is hence always already political. For, it comprises the violent imposition of a traumatic status subordination, which is constituted by both grave forms of misrecognition (taken here to mean the failure to recognise our equality as human beings) and maldistribution (the unfair distribution of political and economic resources). Trauma thus entails the betrayal of the counterfactual presupposition of the equal value of each human being in participatory relation to others – and may both be inflicted through violent events (such as torture or killings) as well as structural violence (such as violent marginalisation and excruciating poverty). Indeed, often incidental and structural violence beget each other and constitute a toxic mix through which the lifeworld ruptures and breaks down – leaving one in an incapacitated state of speechless atomisation and disoriented atomisation. Such an intersubjective conception of trauma not only avoids the tautological reasoning of PTSD, in that its cause is the infliction of injustice (intersubjective parity) while its effects are atomising alienation and incapacitation, but also avoids the problems of a double injury and is able to account for its political normative orientation.

Moreover, such a critical theoretical understanding of trauma is able to illuminate why trauma is such a useful tool for political repression. For, underlying trauma is a distinct instrumental rationality which in its violent pursuit of power destroys the presupposition of intersubjective equality. In doing so, it directly distorts the (communicative) foundations of the lifeworld as a background of interpretation and a horizon of possibility. This means that in trauma our meaning-making practices are ruptured, resulting in a deep sense of traumatic alienation and a shift in the underlying structure of experience away from possibility towards an overwhelming sense of the *im*possibility of meaningful change. It thus results in a deep sense of traumatic alienation wherein one loses the capacity to speak back – to manifest oneself in the world and to influence one's surroundings (Jaeggi, 2014). The world and other people in it come to stand over and above us like a malevolent entity that through its violence induces a sense of helplessness in us. It is through this traumatic alienation that the unitary existential structure of experience is shifted away from one of possibility towards impossibility. Drawing on Mathew Ratcliffe's work on depression and illness here (Ratcliffe, 2008, 2014), I argued that trauma thus destroys the horizon of possibility: where demoralisation is so acutely felt that any sense of *the possibility* of meaningful change dissipates from view. And this, I argue is precisely what the counter-revolutionary actors – primarily the Egyptian military, but also its temporary subsidiary the Muslim Brotherhood – achieved when they imposed multilevelled traumatic status subordination on Egyptian activists that spanned across the political and social spheres.

As we then saw in Part 2, traumatic status subordination was inflicted on Egyptian activists through a threefold violent tactic: the infliction of overwhelming physical force, of political procedural monopolisation and of neoliberal economic rationalism – all of which violently marginalised Egyptians from the political terrain and rendered them speechless. While the events of overwhelming physical force left activists in a state of speechless disorientation, political proceduralism ensured that activists were violently marginalised from the formal political terrain. The realm of formal politics was now strategically controlled by the military who – through concealed strategic actions – had co-opted the Brotherhood as its temporary subsidiary and pushed for quick elections all the while safeguarding its own political and economic interests through a series of constitutional amendments. Moreover, neoliberal economic rationalism also deprived activists of the necessary material resources to raise their voice in the public sphere, while the increasing general economic anxiety enabled the military to turn the blame for Egypt's 'chaos' and 'instability' inwards: onto activists themselves, thereby fracturing revolutionary unity. Part 2 hence traced the *mechanisms* of traumatic status subordination – how it was implemented – in Egypt's post-revolutionary trajectory. What we saw here was that the tripartite structure of traumatic status subordination remained remarkably alike under SCAF, Morsi and Sisi – though it should be noted that while Morsi inflicted the same kind of traumatic violations, his political power was seriously curtailed by the military's clipping of the Brotherhood's president's political wings. That is, the military had not only safeguarded its own economic interests but also remained in control of Egypt's post-revolutionary trajectory when it set the conditions of Egypt's constitutional drafting process. It was with Sisi's rise to power in the summer of 2013 that traumatic status subordination accelerated even further and developed into a full-blown politics of death and the prisonification of Egyptian society. Sisi not only rose to power on the ashes of the mass murder of Rabaa but also directly pursued a politics of death and destruction through extrajudicial killings, death sentences and deaths in prisons – the latter also being part of his 'prisonification' of Egyptian society. At the same time that Sisi intensified physical violence, he also accelerated the procedural colonisation of the political sphere, including elections (rife with manipulation, intimidation and violence) and the repressive juridification of the public sphere (including the protest laws, the increased use of the assembly law and media laws, the latter of which made it a crime of national security if one diverted from the governments narrative on issues pertaining to national security). Concurrently, Sisi also accelerated the neoliberalisation of Egypt's economy, ensuring that the military – and particularly those close to him – were the prime beneficiaries.

Now, importantly the counter-revolutionary purpose behind this relentless tripartite infliction of traumatic status subordination is not so much the marginalisation of the object of revolutionary politics, rather the destruction of its very potentiality. That is, the point was not merely to destroy revolutionary politics as such, but rather to eradicate the *potentiality* of revolutionary becoming as such. Hence, it thus sought to alter the underlying structures of being in the world through the violent distortion of activists' lifeworlds' horizons. And so, Part 3 examined how the impact of (deadly) violence – both in terms of the experience of events as well as the accumulative nature of it – in a context of the political colonisation of the political public sphere resulted in a deep existential disorientation. Extensively drawing on the interviews, this chapter thus discussed the effects of traumatic status subordination from a first-person phenomenological perspective, namely how exposure to torture and (near)death (including the experience of being teargassed) clashes and the experience of near-death situations resulted in a deep existential disorientation. It led to a breakdown of the symbolic order of the lifeworld through which we derive meaning in and from the world. Yet, the erosion of the lifeworld's symbolic order occurs not only through the experience of events but also through the gradual accumulation of traumatic violence. Hence, this part explored how the accumulative death of others evoked a profound sense of (Levinasian) ethical responsibility: namely, a refusal to let the particularity of those who died sink in the generalised pit of anonymity. Yet, the ability to ascribe meaning to these deaths through a forward projection of revolutionary becoming was violently curtailed by the counter-revolution, thereby resulting in the accumulative breakdown of the lifeworld's functioning as a background for interpretation. The accumulative weight of death thus pulled interviewees ever deeper into an existential state of nihilistic meaninglessness that hampered their ability to engage in the world.

Then, as the second section of Part 3 indicates, the counter-revolutionary infliction of traumatic status subordination in the political and economic spheres resulted in an accumulation of frustration and anger, which the military and its allies then carefully manipulated inwards – into society – through what I call 'conspirational victim blaming' and social polarisation characterised by cycles of revenge. The result of this was a further deepening of traumatisation through its extension into the social sphere, where relations of trust were violently broken as citizens now battled each other to the point of great injury and even death. Egypt descended downwards into a vicious spiral of revenge. Revenge, as explained in chapter 10, entails the attempt to regain intersubjective power vis-à-vis another through violent means after one suffered status subordination (which gives rise to (relative) feelings of powerlessness). Revenge may be addressed at the perpetrator, as well as redirected elsewhere – onto subjects taken to represent the perpetrator as well as more vulnerable others. In this sense, revenge is thus both the outcome and the continuation of a distorted mode of communicative action typified by status subordination – particularly when it is purposefully redirected away from the (political perpetrator) into the social sphere.

Hence, as a destructive cycle of violent revenge spread through the social sphere, interviewees were subjected to traumatic status subordination there too. This meant not only that the injustices suffered in the political sphere remained unrecognised but also that they were subjected to yet another layer of violent intersubjective imparity, which compounded the injustices suffered in the political realm. It was through this strategic infliction of multilevelled traumatic status subordination that the lifeworld's horizon of potentiality was destroyed. Since violence was pervasive, unpredictable and affected the entirety of their existence, there was not a single space wherein they did not suffer the potential of the violent intersubjective parity. Hence, in light of such overwhelming pervasive violence, interviewees suffered increasing anxiety (also expressed in dreams and nightmares), a deep sense of existential unsafety, deep demoralisation, depression and utter exhaustion. And in the absence of the possibility of effectively addressing this in the social and political sphere, some resorted to drugs and alcohol to numb their existential pain, while a handful of others tried to mend the symbolic framework of their lifeworld through artistic expression. The majority however resorted to depoliticisation and atomisation: a withdrawal from both participation in and exposure to formal and informal politics, as well as a retreat from social relations and an individualistic (atomised) refocusing of their individual lives – towards small achievable goals such as finishing their education, getting an apartment and seeking employment. The uncomfortable truth is not only that herein interviewees repeated the same process of individualised atomisation that they criticised their parents but also that while some regarded this political retreat and individualist refocus as a temporary measure to gain some breath or to re-strategise, the Sisi's violent politics of death and prisonification, ensured that the potential for revolutionary uprising would not arise in Egypt again.

And so, one of the most pertinent questions that remains is how long Sisi can maintain his politics of death. Given Sisi's utter obliteration of alterity in Egypt, the chance of Egyptians engaging in any form of public self-becoming is thin, as in light of Sisi's politics of death and the prisonification of society, the price is simply too high and the pointlessness of it has been forcefully impressed upon them time-and-time again. Though, admittedly, we have seen small sparks of hope here and there: from the lone protester standing on Tahrir demanding Sisi's departure to the children developing a kid's toy (with two balls dangling between one's finger with two pieces of string) calling it 'Sisi's balls' to the somewhat larger protests that erupted in light of Sisi's transfer of the islands of Tiran and Sanafir to Saudi Arabia. However, in a context of relentless, traumatic status subordination, the chances of these efforts resulting in a process of creative self-becoming have been significantly reduced as the very notion of potentiality has been purposefully destroyed.

The trouble is of course that this destruction of potentiality has been aided by the international support Sisi's regime has received from international actors (particularly the Gulf states but also the EU, Western governments and international financial institutions) particularly keen on cooperating with Sisi on matters of counter-terrorism, migration and business deals largely centred around his 'big projects' such as Suez Canal, the new administrative capital and now also sustainable development and eco-technologies (which particularly serves the purpose of greenwashing Sisi's regime). All of these particularly serve the coffers of the military itself. And so, the question here also is whether these actors continue to support and fall for the oldest authoritarian trick in the book, namely the Manichean division between Sisi's supposed stability as opposed to the chaos (of the people themselves). Or will they start to see that it is Sisi and his regime itself that are not only the prime manufacturers but also the main beneficiaries of violence, chaos and death in Egypt. Sisi's force may appears impressive and all-powerful, but really, he is nothing but a naked emperor who built a castle of sand. It will implode one day; the question is, when and what will have been the price paid? For currently, no truer words have been spoken than by this young man, at this moment in time:

> Lives are cheap in Egypt. And people are aware of that. It's a very brutal thought. Life here is superfluous and people here are aware of that. It is a really brutal thought. (Interview 19)

Bibliography

Abdelrahman, M. (2013) "In praise of organization: Egypt between activism and revolution." *Development and Change*, 44(3), pp. 569–685. doi: 10.1111/dech.12028.

Abul-Magd, Z. (2012) "Understanding SCAF – The Cairo review of global affairs." *The Cairo Review*. Available at: https://www.thecairoreview.com/essays/understanding-scaf/ (Accessed: January 22, 2022).

Abul-Magd, Z. (2018) *Militarizing the Nation: The Army, Business, and Revolution in Egypt*. New York: Columbia University Press.

Abuzaid, R. A. (2011) "Chasing after Huntington's third wave of democratization: The Middle East under change." Available at: https://fount.aucegypt.edu/studenttxt/20/ (Accessed: January 11, 2022).

Adly, A. (2017) "Too big to fail: Egypt's large enterprises after the 2011 uprisings." Available at: https://carnegieendowment.org/files/CMEC_65_Adly_Final_Web.pdf (Accessed: January 22, 2022).

Adly, A. (2020) *Cleft Capitalism: The Social Origins of Failed Market Making in Egypt, Cleft Capitalism*. Stanford: Stanford University Press.

Adly, A. I. (2010) "Politically-embedded cronyism: The case of post-liberalization Egypt." *Business and Politics*, 11(4), pp. 1–26. doi: 10.2202/1469-3569.1268.

Adorno, T. (1973) *Negative Dialectics*. New York: Continuum.

AFP (2012) Egypt must stop trials of children in military courts: HRW, Daily News Egypt, 27 March 2012. Available at: https://dailynewsegypt.com/2012/03/27/egypt-must-stop-trials-of-children-in-military-courts-hrw/ (Accessed: 17 August 2022).

Agence France-Press (2015) "Low turnout as Egyptians shun elections designed to shore up Sisi." *The Guardian*. Available at: https://www.theguardian.com/world/2015/oct/18/egypt-parliamentary-elections-shore-up-sisi (Accessed: January 22, 2022).

Aho, K. (2014) *Existentialism: An Introduction*. Cambridge: Polity Press.

Ahram Online (2011) Live Updates: Egypt's 'Friday of One Demand' as it unfolds, Ahram Online, Available at: https://english.ahram.org.eg/NewsContent/1/64/26857/

Egypt/Politics-/Live-Updates-Egypts-Friday-of–One-Demand-as-it-un.aspx/ (Accessed: 15 August 2022).

Ahram Online (2012a), Egypt's Morsi honours retired military brass Tantawi and Anan, Ahram Online, 14 September 2012, Available at: https://english.ahram.org.eg/News/50395.aspx (Accessed: 16 August 2022).

Ahram Online (2012b) "English text of SCAF amended Egypt constitutional declaration." *Jadaliyya*. Available at: https://www.jadaliyya.com/Details/26292 (Accessed: January 21, 2022).

Ahram Online (2014a) "Anan won't run in the upcoming presidential elections." *Ahram Online*. Available at: https://english.ahram.org.eg/NewsContent/1/64/96580/Egypt/Politics-/Anan-wont-run-in-the-upcoming-Presidential-electio.aspx (Accessed: January 22, 2022).

Ahram Online (2014b) "Egypt's Deputy PM Ziad Bahaa El-din resigns." *Ahram Online*. Available at: https://english.ahram.org.eg/NewsContent/1/64/92755/Egypt/Politics-/Egypts-Deputy-PM-Ziad-Bahaa-Eldin-resigns.aspx (Accessed: January 22, 2022).

Ahram Online (2014c) "Shafiq not running in Egypt's upcoming presidential elections." *Ahram Online*. Available at: https://english.ahram.org.eg/NewsContent/1/64/97155/Egypt/Politics-/Shafiq-not-running-in-Egypts-upcoming-presidential.aspx (Accessed: January 22, 2022).

Ahram Online (2020) "Egypt's Sisi ratifies amendments to anti-terrorism law." *Ahram Online*. Available at: https://english.ahram.org.eg/NewsContent/1/64/364938/Egypt/Politics-/Egypts-Sisi-ratifies-amendments-to-antiterrorism-l.aspx (Accessed: January 22, 2022).

Ajdukovic, D. (2007) "Social contexts of trauma and healing." *Medicine, Conflict and Survival*, 20(2), pp. 120–135. doi: 10.1080/1362369042000234717.

al Arabiya (2013) "Egypt army could arbitrate in unrest, analysts say." *Al Arabiya*. Available at: https://english.alarabiya.net/News/middle-east/2013/07/01/Egypt-army-could-arbitrate-in-unrest-analysts-say- (Accessed: January 22, 2022).

al Jazeera (2012) "Many dead in Egyptian football riot." *Al Jazeera News*. Available at: https://www.aljazeera.com/news/2012/2/2/many-dead-in-egyptian-football-riot (Accessed: January 22, 2022).

al Jazeera (2016) "Egypt ratifies new law regulating media outlets." *Al Jazeera*. Available at: https://www.aljazeera.com/news/2016/12/27/egypt-ratifies-new-law-regulating-media-outlets (Accessed: January 22, 2022).

al Jazeera (2019) "UN experts call Morsi's death in Egypt 'arbitrary killing'." *Mohamed Morsi News, Al Jazeera*. Available at: https://www.aljazeera.com/news/2019/11/8/un-experts-call-morsis-death-in-egypt-arbitrary-killing (Accessed: January 22, 2022).

al Masry Al Youm (2020) "Egypt's parliament approves new amendments to terrorism law." *Egypt Independent*. Available at: https://egyptindependent.com/egypts-parliament-approves-new-amendments-to-terrorism-law/ (Accessed: January 22, 2022).

al Nadeem (2013) "Torture in Egypt during a year of Muslim brotherhood rule." Available at: http://alnadeem.org/en/node/439 (Accessed: May 17, 2017).

Al-Ali, Z., Roberts, C., and Toh, A. (2012) "The Egyptian constitutional declaration dated 17 June: A commentary 2012." Available at: https://constitutionnet.org/sites/default/files/commentary_to_june_2012_constitutional_declaration_final.pdf (Accessed: January 22, 2022).

Al-Aswany, A. (2013) "Torture reveals true nature of Egypt's Muslim brotherhood." *Al Monitor*. Available at: https://www.al-monitor.com/pulse/culture/2013/03/muslimbrotherhood-torture-egypt.html (Accessed: December 12, 2017).

Al-Aswany, Alaa (2015) *Democracy is the Answer: Egypt's Years of Revolution*, London: Gingko Library

Alexander, J. C., Eyerman, R., Giesen, B., Smelser, N. J., and Sztompka, P. (2004) "Cultural trauma and collective identity." In *Cultural Trauma and Collective Identity*. Berkeley, CA: University of California Press.

Allinson, J. (2019). Counter-revolution as international phenomenon: The case of Egypt. *Review of International Studies*, 45(2), 320-344. doi:10.1017/S0260210518000529

Alford, C. F. (2016) *Trauma, Culture, and PTSD*. New York: Palgrave.

Alkhshali, H. (2014) "Egypt's el-Sisi vows to finish off the Muslim Brotherhood." *CNN*. Available at: https://edition.cnn.com/2014/05/05/world/africa/egypt-el-sisi-interview/index.html (Accessed: January 22, 2022).

Allen, A. (2016) *The End of Progress: Decolonizing the Normative Foundations of Critical Theory*. New York: Columbia University Press.

American Psychiatric Association (1980) *DSM-III: Diagnostic and Statistical Manual of Mental Disorders – DSM III*. 3rd edn. Washington: American Psychiatric Association.

American Psychiatric Association (2014) *Diagnostic and Statistical Manual of Mental Disorders, Fifth Edition – Coding Update*. Washington: American Psychiatric Association. Available at: http://dsm.psychiatryonline.org/pb/assets/raw/dsm/pdf/DSM-5 Coding Update_Final.pdf (Accessed: January 15, 2022).

Améry, Jean. (1980) *At the Mind's Limits: Contemplations by a Survivor on Auschwitz and Its Realities*. Bloomington: Indiana University Press.

Amin, G. (2011) *Egypt in the Era of Mubarak: 1981–2011*. Cairo: American University of Cairo Press.

Amnesty International (2011) "Egypt: Emergency law biggest threat to rights since '25 January revolution'." Available at: https://www.amnesty.org/en/latest/news/2011/09/egypt-emergency-law-biggest-threat-rights-january-revolution/ (Accessed: January 22, 2022).

Amnesty International (2013) "Egypt: New protest law gives security forces free rein." *Amnesty International*. Available at: https://www.amnesty.org/en/latest/news/2013/11/egypt-new-protest-law-gives-security-forces-free-rein/ (Accessed: January 22, 2022).

Amnesty International (2016a) "Egypt: Hundreds disappeared and tortured amid wave of brutal repression." *Amnesty International*. Available at: https://www.amnesty.org/en/latest/news/2016/07/egypt-hundreds-disappeared-and-tortured-amid-wave-of-brutal-repression/ (Accessed: January 22, 2022).

Amnesty International (2016b) "Egypt: 'Officially, you do not exist' – Disappeared and tortured in the name of counter-terrorism." *Amnesty International*. Available at: https://www.amnesty.org/en/wp-content/uploads/2021/05/MDE1243682016ENGLISH.pdf (Accessed: January 22, 2022).

Amnesty International (2018) "Egypt: Crushing humanity: The abuse of solitary confinement in Egypt's prisons." *Amnesty International*. Available at: https://www.amnesty.org/en/wp-content/uploads/2021/05/MDE1282572018ENGLISH.pdf (Accessed: January 22, 2022).

Amnesty International (2019) "Egypt: Largest wave of mass arrests since President Abdel Fattah al-Sisi came to power." *Amnesty International*. Available at: https://www.amnesty.org/en/latest/news/2019/10/egypt-largest-wave-of-mass-arrests-since-president-abdel-fattah-al-sisi-came-to-power/ (Accessed: January 22, 2022).

Amnesty International (2020) "Egypt: Prisons are now journalists' newsrooms." *Amnesty International Public Statement*. Available at: https://www.amnesty.nl/content/uploads/2020/05/01052020_Journalists-PS-final.pdf?x48668 (Accessed: January 22, 2022).

Amnesty International (2021) "Egypt: 'What do I care if you die?': Negligence and denial of health care in Egyptian prisons." *Amnesty International*. Available at: https://www.amnesty.org/en/documents/mde12/3538/2021/en/ (Accessed: January 22, 2022).

Andrews, M. (2010) "Beyond narrative: The shape of traumatic testimony." In Hyvärinen, M., Hydén, L.-C., and Tamboukou, M. (eds) *Beyond Narrative Coherence*. Amsterdam: John Benjamins.

ANHRI (2016) "There is room for everyone… Egypt's prisons before & after January 25 revolution." *Arabic Network for Human Rights Information*. Available at: http://anhri.net/?p=173532&lang=en (Accessed: January 22, 2022).

Antze, P. (2003) "Illness as irony in Psychoanalysis." *Social Analysis: The International Journal of Anthropology*, 47(2), pp. 102–121. Available at: https://www.jstor.org/stable/23170057?seq=1#metadata_info_tab_contents (Accessed: January 15, 2022).

AOHRUK (2019) "Egypt: Six years of impunity." Available at: https://aohr.org.uk/egypt-six-years-of-impunity/ (Accessed: January 22, 2022).

Armstrong, C., and Thompson, S. (2009) "Parity of participation and the politics of status." *European Journal of Political Theory*, 8(1), pp. 109–122. doi: 10.1177/1474885108096963.

Arendt, Hannah (2017 [1951]) *The Origins of Totalitarianism*, Penguin Books: Milton Keynes

Ashraf, F. (2014) "At least 49 killed, 247 wounded and over 1000 arrested in 25 January anniversary." *Daily News Egypt*. Available at: https://dailynewsegypt.com/2014/01/26/update-at-least-49-killed-247-wounded-and-over-1000-arrested-in-25-january-anniversary/ (Accessed: January 22, 2022).

Atwood, G. E., and Stolorow, R. D. (2014) *Structures of Subjectivity: Explorations in Psychoanalytic Phenomenology and Contextualism*. 2nd edn. London: Routledge/Taylor & Francis Group.

Badrawi, M. (2013) *Political Violence in Egypt 1910–1925: Secret Societies, Plots and Assassinations.* Abingdon: Routledge.

Baghat, H. (2017) "Looking into the latest acquisition of Egyptian media companies by general intelligence." *Mada Masr.* Available at: https://www.madamasr.com/en/2017/12/21/feature/politics/looking-into-the-latest-acquisition-of-egyptian-media-companies-by-general-intelligence/ (Accessed: January 22, 2022).

Bashir, B., and Goldberg, A. (2018) *The Holocaust and the Nakba: A New Grammar of Trauma and History.* New York: Columbia University Press.

BBC News (2018) "Ahmed Shafiq: Egyptian ex-PM withdraws from election." *BBC News.* Available at: https://www.bbc.com/news/world-middle-east-42597803 (Accessed: January 22, 2022).

BBC News (2021) "Alaa Abdel Fattah: Leading Egyptian activist jailed for five years." Available at: https://www.bbc.com/news/world-middle-east-59730354 (Accessed: January 22, 2022).

Beinin, J. (2011) "Workers and Egypt's January 25 revolution." *International Labor and Working-Class History*, 80(1), pp. 189–196. doi: 10.1017/S0147547911000123.

Beissinger, M., Amaney, J., and Mazur, K. (2013) "Who participated in the Arab Spring? A comparison of Egyptian and Tunisian revolutions." Available at: http://www.princeton.edu/~mbeissin/beissinger.tunisiaegyptcoalitions.pdf [Preprint]. Princeton.

Benezir, G. (2009) "Trauma signals in life stories." In Rogers, K. L., and Leydesdorff, S. (eds) *Trauma: Life Stories of Survivors.* New Brunswick: Transaction Publishers, pp. 29–44.

Bergman, R., and Walsh, D. (2019) "Egypt is using apps to track and target its citizens, report says." *New York Times.* Available at: https://www.nytimes.com/2019/10/03/world/middleeast/egypt-cyber-attack-phones.html (Accessed: January 22, 2022).

Bistoen, G. (2016) *Trauma, Ethics and the Political Beyond PTSD: Dislocations of the Real.* Basingstoke: Palgrave MacMillan.

Boon, V. (2009) *On a Europe Without Controversial Learning Curves: Using Habermas Against Habermas*, PhD Dissertation, December 2009, Department of Philosophy, University of Liverpool (UK).

Bracken, P. (2002a) "Listening to Foucault." *Philosophy, Psychiatry, & Pyschology*, (9)2, pp. 187–188. doi: 10.1353/ppp.2003.0022.

Bracken, P. (2002b) *Trauma: Culture, Meaning and Philosophy.* London: Whurr Publishers.

Bracken, P., Fernando, S., Alsaraf, S., Creed, M., Double, D., Gilberthorpe, T., Hassan, R., Jadhav, S., Jeyapaul, P., Kopua, D., and Parsons, M. (2021) "Decolonising the medical curriculum: Psychiatry faces particular challenges." *Anthropology and Medicine*, 28(4), pp. 420–428. doi: 10.1080/13648470.2021.1949892.

Bracken, P., and Thomas, P. (1999) "Cognitive therapy, cartesianism and the moral order." *European Journal of Psychotherapy & Counselling*, 2(3), pp. 325–344. doi: 10.1080/13642539908400816.

Bracken, P., and Thomas, P. (2002) "Time to move beyond the mind-body split." *British Medical Journal*, 325, pp. 1433–1434. doi: 10.1136/bmj.325.7378.1433.

Bracken, P., and Thomas, P. (2005) *Postpsychiatry: Mental Health in a Postmodern World*. Oxford: Oxford University Press.

Bracken, P. J. (1988) "Hidden agenda's: Deconstructing post traumatic stress disorder." In Bracken, P. J., and Petty, C. (eds) *Rethinking the Trauma of War*. London: Free Association Books.

Bracken, P. J., Giller, J. E., and Summerfield, D. (1995) "Psychological responses to war and atrocity: The limitations of current concepts." *Social Science and Medicine*, 40(8), pp. 1073–1082. doi: 10.1016/0277-9536(94)00181-R.

Brown, N., and Dunne, M. (2013) "Egypt's draft constitution rewards the military and judiciary." *Carnegie Endowment for International Peace*. Available at: https://carnegieendowment.org/sada/53806 (Accessed: January 22, 2022).

Brownlee, J. (2007) *Authoritarianism in an Age of Democratization, Authoritarianism in an Age of Democratization*. Cambridge: Cambridge University Press.

Burggraeve, R. (1999) "Violence and the vulnerable face of the other: Violence and the vulnerable face of the other." *Journal of Social Philosophy*, 30(1), pp. 29–45.

Burggraeve, R. (2003) *Wisdom of Love in the Service of Love: Emmanuel Levinas on Justice, Peace and Human Rights*. Milwaukee: Marquette University Press.

Burkeman, O. (2016) "Therapy wars: The revenge of fraud psychology." *The Guardian*. Available at: https://www.theguardian.com/science/2016/jan/07/therapy-wars-revenge-of-freud-cognitive-behavioural-therapy (Accessed: January 15, 2022).

Bush, R. (2011) "Coalitions for dispossession and networks of resistance? Land, politics and agrarian reform in Egypt." *British Journal of Middle Eastern Studies*, 38(3), pp. 391–405. doi: 10.1080/13530194.2011.621700.

Capps, D., and Carlin, N. (2011) "Sublimation and symbolization: The case of dental anxiety and the symbolic meaning of teeth." *Pastoral Psychology*, 60, pp. 773–789. doi: 10.1007/s11089-011-0368-1.

Caruth, C. (1995) *Trauma: Explorations in Memory*. Edited by C. Caruth. Baltimore: Johns Hopkins University Press.

Caruth, C. (1996) *Unclaimed Experience: Trauma, Narrative and History*. Baltimore: John Hopkins University Press.

Caruth, C. (2001) "Parting words: Trauma, silence and survival." *Cultural Values*, 5(1), pp. 7–26. doi: 10.1080/14797580109367218.

CBC (2013) "Egypt clashes leave 27 dead after verdict on soccer riot." *CBC News*. Available at: https://www.cbc.ca/news/world/egypt-clashes-leave-27-dead-after-verdict-on-soccer-riot-1.1314077 (Accessed: January 22, 2022).

CBC News (2018) "Egypt election: Sami Annan, ex-general, arrested after announcing plan to run for presidency." *CBC News*. Available at: https://www.cbsnews.com/news/egypt-election-sami-annan-ex-general-arrested-after-announcing-plan-to-run-presidency/ (Accessed: January 22, 2022).

CIHRS (2018) "Egypt medical neglect of Aboul-Fotouh a prolonged death sentence as political retaliation." *Cairo Institute for Human Rights Studies*. Available at:

https://cihrs.org/medical-neglect-of-aboul-fotouh-a-prolonged-death-sentence-as-political-retaliation/?lang=en (Accessed: January 22, 2022).

Cimpanu, C. (2019) "Egypt government used Gmail third-party apps to phish activists." *ZDNet*. Available at: https://www.zdnet.com/article/egypt-government-used-gmail-third-party-apps-to-phish-activists/ (Accessed: January 22, 2022).

Cooke, M. (1994) *Language and Reason*. Cambridge: MIT Press.

Coşkun, E. R. (2019) "The role of emotions during the Arab Spring in Tunisia and Egypt in light of repertoires." *Globalizations*, 16(7), pp. 1198–1214. doi: 10.1080/14747731.2019.1578017.

Craps, S. (2014) "Beyond eurocentrism: Trauma theory in a global age." In Beulens, G., Durrant, S., and Eaglestone, R. (eds) *The Future of Trauma Theory: Contemporary Literary and Cultural Criticism*. Abingdon: Routledge, pp. 45–62.

Crépon, M. (2013) *The Thought of Death and the Memory of War*. Minneapolis: University of Minnesota Press.

Crossley, N. (1996) *Intersubjectivity: The Fabric of Social Becoming*. London: Sage.

Crossley, N. (2012) "Citizenship, intersubjectivity and the lifeworld." In Stevenson, N. (ed.) *Culture and Citizenship*. London: Sage.

Curnow, W. (2018) "Tramadol abuse addiction sweeping Egypt as part of the world's growing opioid crisis." *ABC News (Australian Broadcasting Corporation)*. Available at: https://www.abc.net.au/news/2018-05-05/opioid-crisis-tramadol-epidemic-sweeping-cairo/9719454?nw=0 (Accessed: January 23, 2022).

Dalal, F. (2018) *CBT: The Cognitive Behavioural Tsunami: Managerialism, Politics and the Corruptions of Science*. London: Routledge.

Daily News Egypt (2011) 12,000 in military courts under SCAF; 2,000 under Mubarak, says lawyer, Daily News Egypt, 7 September 2011, available at: https://dailynewsegypt.com/2011/09/07/12000-in-military-courts-under-scaf-2000-under-mubarak-says-lawyer/ (Accessed: 11 August 2022).

Davidson, C. R. (2000) "Reform and repression in Mubarak's Egypt." *The Fletcher Forum of World Affairs*, 24(2), pp. 75–97.

Davies, T. R. (2014) "The failure of strategic nonviolent action in Bahrain, Egypt, Libya and Syria: 'political ju-jitsu' in reverse." *Global Change, Peace and Security*, 26(3), pp. 299–313. doi: 10.1080/14781158.2014.924916.

Dawoud, K. (2016) "Tiran and Sanafir trials continue to reverberate in Egypt." *Atlantic Council*. Available at: https://www.atlanticcouncil.org/blogs/menasource/tiran-and-sanafir-trials-continue-to-reverberate-in-egypt/ (Accessed: January 22, 2022).

Deleuze, Gilles (1995), The Exhausted, SubStance, 1995, Vol. 24, No. 3, Issue 78 (1995), pp. 3–28.

Descartes, R. (2008) "Meditations on the first philosophy in which the existence of god and the distinction between mind and body are demonstrated: Meditation VI." In Wilkinson, Robert (2008) *Minds and Bodies: An Introduction With Readings*, London: Routledge.

Diab, Osama (2019) Prime-time nationalism: The rational and economic underpinnings of the June 30 nationalist 'hysteria', Ghent University. Available at: https://biblio.ugent.be/publication/8589322 (Accessed: 22 August 2022).

Doss, L. (2013) "Bad spirits: Brotherhood govt targets Egypt's alcohol industry." *Egypt Independent*. Available at: https://egyptindependent.com/bad-spirits-brotherhood-govt-targets-egypt-s-alcohol-industry/ (Accessed: January 22, 2022).

Dunne, M., and Williamson, S. (2014) "Egypt's unprecedented instability by the numbers, Carnegie endowment for international peace." Available at: https://carnegieendowment.org/2014/03/24/egypt-s-unprecedented-instability-by-numbers-pub-55078 (Accessed: January 22, 2022).

Eagle, G., and Kaminer, D. (2013) "Continuous traumatic stress: Expanding the lexicon of traumatic stress." *Peace and Conflict*, 19(2), p. 85. doi: 10.1037/a0032485.

ECRF (2020) "Continuous violation and absent justice Forced Disappearance – A five-year report." Available at: https://www.ec-rf.net/3509/ (Accessed: January 22, 2022).

Edelglass, W. (2006) "Levinas on suffering and compassion." *Sophia*, 45, pp. 43–59.

Edkins, J. (2002) "Forget trauma? Responses to September 11." *International Relations*, 16(2), pp. 243–256. doi: 10.1177/0047117802016002005.

Edkins, J. (2003) *Trauma and the Memory of Politics*. Cambridge: Cambridge University Press.

Edkins, J. (2004) "Ground zero: Reflections on trauma, in/distinction and response." *Journal for Cultural Research*, 8(3), pp. 247–270. doi: 10.1080/1479758042000264939.

Edwards, G. (2007) "Habermas, activism, and acquiescence: Reactions to 'colonization' in UK trade unions." *Social Movement Studies*, 62, pp. 111–130.

Egypt Independent (2014) "Amr Moussa: I will not run for president." *Egypt Independent*. Available at: https://www.egyptindependent.com/amr-moussa-i-will-not-run-president/ (Accessed: January 22, 2022).

EgyptSource (2015) "Egypt's anti-terror law: A translation." *The Atlantic Council*. Available at: https://www.atlanticcouncil.org/blogs/menasource/egypt-s-anti-terror-law-a-translation/ (Accessed: January 22, 2022).

Ehrenreich, B. (2010) *Bright-Sided: How Positive Thinking is Undermining America*. New York: Picador.

EIPR (2015) "A confused step in the right direction: Commentary on the national strategy to combat violence against women." Available at: https://www.eipr.org/en/pressrelease/2015/06/23/2411+&cd=1&hl=nl&ct=clnk&gl=n- (Accessed: November 16, 2015).

EISA (2013) "EISA Egypt: 2011/2012 people's assembly elections results." *Electoral Institute for Sustainable Democracy in Africa*. Available at: https://www.eisa.org/wep/egy2012results1.htm (Accessed: January 21, 2022).

el Amrani, I. (2011) "Egypt: A constitution first Issandr El Amrani for arabist.net." *The Guardian*. Available at: https://www.theguardian.com/commentisfree/2011/jun/12/egypt-a-constitution-first (Accessed: January 21, 2022).

el Ashraf, M. (2021) "A murder not a tragedy; the port-said Massacre." *Audiovisual Projects, American University in Cairo* [Preprint]. Available at: https://fount.aucegypt.edu/audiovisual_student_work/773 (Accessed: January 22, 2022).

el Dawla, A. S. (2009) "Torture: A state policy." In El Mahdi, R., and Marfleet, P. (eds) *Egypt: Moment of Change*. Cairo: Cairo University Press.

El-Dabh, Basil (2012) ElBaradei: constitution will go into the "dustbin of history", Daily News Egypt, Nov 30 2012, https://dailynewsegypt.com/2012/11/30/elbaradei-constitution-will-go-into-the-dustbin-of-history/ (Accessed: 10 July 2022).

el Medni, B. M. E. (2013) "Civil society and democratic transformation in contemporary Egypt: Premises and promises." *International Journal of Humanities and Social Science*, 3(12). Available at: http://www.ijhssnet.com/view.php?u=http://www.ijhssnet.com/journals/Vol_3_No_12_Special_Issue_June_2013/2.pdf (Accessed: August 23 2022)

el Sharnouby, D. (2012) "Morsi's 100-day plan to rebuild Egypt." *Open Democracy*. Available at: https://www.opendemocracy.net/en/morsis-100-day-plan-to-rebuild-egypt/ (Accessed: January 22, 2022).

el Dabh, B. (2013) "Violence flares up in Moqattam." *Daily News Egypt*. Available at: https://dailynewsegypt.com/2013/03/22/193598/ (Accessed: January 22, 2022).

el Fekki, A. (2016) "There is room for everyone' inside Egypt's prisons: ANHRI." *Daily News Egypt*. Available at: https://dailynewsegypt.com/2016/09/05/room-everyone-inside-egypts-prisons-anhri/ (Accessed: January 22, 2022).

El Mahdi, R. (2009) "The democracy movement: Cycles of protest." In El Mahdi, R., and Marfleet, P. (eds) *Egypt: Moment of Change*. Cairo: Cairo University Press.

El-Menawy, A. L. (2012) *Tahrir: The Last 18 Days of Mubarak*. London: Gilgamesh Publishing Ltd.

El-Sadany, M. (2015) "Tracking Egypt's extraparliamentary laws." *Tahrir Institute for Middle East Policy*. Available at: https://timep.org/commentary/analysis/tracking-egypts-extraparliamentary-laws/ (Accessed: January 22, 2022).

Erikson, K. (1995) "Notes on trauma and community." In *Trauma: Explorations in Memory*. Baltimore: Johns Hopkins University Press.

Eyerman, R. (1982) "Consciousness and action: Alain Touraine and the sociological intervention." *Thesis Eleven*, 5–6(1), pp. 279–288. doi: 10.1177/072551368200500120.

Eyerman, R. (2015) "Social movements and memory." In *Routledge International Handbook of Memory Studies*. London: Routledge

Fahim, K. (2016) "Egyptians denounce President Sisi in biggest Rally in 2 years." *The New York Times*. Available at: https://www.nytimes.com/2016/04/16/world/middleeast/cairo-protesters-denounce-egyptian-president-sisi.html?auth=linked-google (Accessed: January 22, 2022).

Felman, S. (1996) *Literature and Psychoanalysis: The Question of Reading; Otherwise, A Johns Hopkins paperback: Literature*.

Felman, S., and Laub, D. (2013) *Testimony: Crises of Witnessing in Literature, Psychoanalysis and History*.

Financial Post (2013) Morsi's financial legacy: Black markets and a shameful economic record, Financial Post, 9 July 2013. Available at: https://financialpost.com/opinion/morsis-financial-legacy-black-markets-and-a-shameful-economic-record. (Accessed 16 August 2022).

Finlayson, J. G. (2013) *Habermas: A Very Short Introduction*. Oxford: Oxford University Press.

Fonagy, P., Rost, F., Carlyle, J. A., McPherson, S., Thomas, R., Pasco Fearon, R. M., Goldberg, D., and Taylor, D. (2015) "Pragmatic randomized controlled trial of long-term psychoanalytic psychotherapy for treatment-resistant depression: The Tavistock Adult Depression Study (TADS)." *World Psychiatry*, 14(3), pp. 312–321. doi: 10.1002/WPS.20267.

Forna, A. (2011) *Memory of Love*. London: Bloomsbury.

Foucault, M. (1995) *Discipline & Punish: The Birth of the Prison*. London: Vintage.

France24 (2013) "'Sisi-mania': Egypt's army chief everywhere from posters to cakes." Available at: https://observers.france24.com/en/20131028-sisi-mania-posters-chocolates-army (Accessed: January 22, 2022).

Fraser, N. (2003a) "Social Justice in the Age of Identity Politics: Redistribution, Recognition, and Participation." In Fraser, N., and Honneth, A. (eds) *Redistribution or Recognition?* London: Verso, pp. 198–237.

Fraser, N. (2003b) "Distorted beyond all recognition: A rejoinder to Axel Honneth." In Fraser, N., and Honneth, A. (eds) *Redistribution or Recognition?* London: Verso, pp. 198–237.

Fraser, N. (2010) *Scales of Justice—Reimagining Political Space in a Globalizing World*. New York: Columbia University Press.

Fraser, N. (2014) *Justice Interruptus*.

Fraser, N., and Honneth, A. (2003) *Redistribution or Recognition? A Political Philosophical Exchange*. London: Verso.

Freedom House (2021) "Egypt: Freedom on the net 2021 country report." *Freedom House*. Available at: https://freedomhouse.org/country/egypt/freedom-net/2021 (Accessed: January 22, 2022).

Frenkel, S., and Atef, M. (2014) "How Egypt's rebel movement helped pave the way for a Sisi presidency." *Buzz Feed News*. Available at: https://www.buzzfeednews.com/article/sheerafrenkel/how-egypts-rebel-movement-helped-pave-the-way-for-a-sisi-pre (Accessed: January 22, 2022).

Fritsch, M. (2019) "Philosophy of the subject/consciousness." In *The Cambridge Habermas Lexicon*. Cambridge: Cambridge University Press.

Gamal, I. (2014) "Ayman Nour boycotts upcoming presidential elections." *Cairo Post*. Available at: https://web.archive.org/web/20140714150950/http://thecairopost.com/news/87508/news/ayman-nour-boycotts-upcoming-presidential-elections (Accessed: January 22, 2022).

Gamal, W. (2019) "Lost capital: The Egyptian Muslim brotherhood's neoliberal transformation." Available at: https://carnegieendowment.org/files/2-1-19_Gamal_Muslim_Brotherhood.pdf (Accessed: January 13, 2022).

Garnham, A. (2019) "Cognitivism." In Robins, S, Symons, J and Calvo, P (eds) *The Routledge Companion to Philosophy of Psychology*. New York: Routledge.

Giry, J., and Gürpınar, D. (2020) "Functions and uses of conspiracy theories in authoritarian regimes." In *Routledge Handbook of Conspiracy Theories*. London: Routledge, pp. 317–350.

Global Post (2011) "Egypt: Uncertainty is bad for business." *The World From PRX*. Available at: https://theworld.org/stories/2011-11-07/egypt-uncertainty-bad-business (Accessed: January 22, 2022).

Goldberg, E., and Beinin, J. (1982) "Egypt's transition under Nasser – MERIP." Available at: https://merip.org/1982/07/egypts-transition-under-nasser/ (Accessed: January 21, 2022).

Guenther, L. (2013) *Solitary Confinement: Social Death and Its Afterlives*. Minneapolis: University of Minnesota Press.

Gur, S. (2016) "The 2015 parliamentary elections in Egypt." *Electoral Studies*, 44, pp. 461–464. doi: 10.1016/J.ELECTSTUD.2016.08.004.

Gutlove, P., and Thompson, G. (2004) "Psychosocial healing and post-conflict social reconstruction in the former Yugoslavia." *Medicine, Conflict, and Survival*, 20(2), pp. 136–150. doi: 10.1080/136236942000234726.

Habermas, J (1992) *The Structural Transformation of the Public Sphere: An Inquiry Into a Category of Bourgeois Society*, Cambridge: Polity

Habermas, J. (1974) *Theory and Practice*. London: Heinemann.

Habermas, J. (1976a) "A positivistically bisected rationalism." In Adorno, T., Dahrendorf, R., Pilot, H., and Albert, H. (eds) *The Positivist Dispute in German Sociology*. London: Heinemann.

Habermas, J. (1976b) *Legitimation Crisis*. London: Heinemann.

Habermas, J. (1979) *Communication and the Evolution of Society*. Boston: Beacon Press.

Habermas, J. (1984) *The Theory of Communicative Action (Vol. 1): Reason and the Rationalization of Society*. Cambridge: Polity Press.

Habermas, J. (1987a) *Knowledge and Human Interests*. Cambridge: Polity Press.

Habermas, J. (1987b) *The Theory of Communicative Action (Vol. 2): The Critique of Functionalist Reason*. Cambridge: Polity Press.

Habermas, J. (1988a) "Morality and ethical life: Does Hegel's critique of Kant apply to discourse ethics?" *Northwestern University Law Review*, 83(1&2), pp. 38–53.

Habermas, J. (1988b) *On the Logic of the Social Sciences*. Cambridge: Polity Press.

Habermas, J. (1990a) *Moral Consciousness and Communicative Action*. Cambridge: Polity Press.

Habermas, J. (1990b) *The Philosophical Discourse of Modernity: Twelve Lectures*. Cambridge: Polity Press.

Habermas, J. (1991) *The Structural Transformation of the Public Sphere*. Cambridge: The MIT Press, an Inquiry into a Category of Bourgeois Society.

Habermas, J. (1992) *Postmetaphysical Thinking*. Cambridge: Polity Press.

Habermas, J. (1993) *Justification and Application*. Cambridge: Polity Press.

Habermas, J. (1995) "Communicative versus subject-centered reason." In Faubion, J. D. (ed.) *Rethinking the Subject: An Anthology of Contemporary European Social Thought*. Boulder: Westview Press.

Habermas, J. (1996) *Between Facts and Norms*. Cambridge: Polity Press.

Habermas, J. (1998) *On the Pragmatics of Communication*. Cambridge: Polity Press.

Habermas, J. (2001a) *On the Pragmatics of Social Interaction: Preliminary Studies in the Theory of Communicative Action*. Cambridge: Polity Press.

Habermas, J. (2001b) *The Postnational Constellation: Political Essays*. Cambridge: Polity Press.

Habermas, J. (2003) *Truth and Justification.* Cambridge: MIT Press.
Habermas, J. (2004) "Religious tolerance—The pacemaker for cultural rights." *Philosophy*, 79(1), pp. 5–17. doi: 10.1017/S0031819104000026.
Habermas, J. (2017) *Postmetaphysical Thinking II: Essays and Replies.* Cambridge: Polity Press.
Hamzawy, A. (2017) "Egypt campus: The students versus the regime." *Carnegie Endowment for International Peace.* Available at: https://carnegieendowment.org/2017/03/06/egypt-campus-students-versus-regime-pub-68207 (Accessed: January 22, 2022).
Hanke, S. (2013) "Egypt: Morsi leaves shameful financial legacy." *Financial Post.* Available at: https://financialpost.com/opinion/morsis-financial-legacy-black-markets-and-a-shameful-economic-record (Accessed: January 22, 2022).
Harding, H. (2016) "Analysis: Egypt's military-economic empire." *Middle East Eye.* Available at: https://www.middleeasteye.net/news/analysis-egypts-military-economic-empire (Accessed: January 22, 2022).
Hatfield, G. (2007) *Neuro-Philosophy Meets Psychology: Reduction, Autonomy, and Physiological Constraints.* Cambridge, Ma: MIT Press.
Hecker, T., Ainamani, H. E., Hermenau, K., Haefele, E., and Elbert, T. (2017) "Exploring the potential distinction between continuous traumatic stress and posttraumatic stress in an east African refugee sample." *Clinical Psychological Science*, 5(6), pp. 964–973. doi: 10.1177/2167702617717023.
Heidegger, M. (2010) *Being and Time.* Albany: State University of New York Press.
Horowitz, M. J. (1983) "Post traumatic stress disorders." *Behavioral Sciences & Law*, pp. 9–23.
Howeidy, A. (2012) "Meet the brotherhood's enforcer: Khairat El-Shater." *Ahram Online.* Available at: https://english.ahram.org.eg/NewsContent/1/64/37993/Egypt/Politics-/Meet-the-Brotherhood%E2%80%99s-enforcer-Khairat-ElShater.aspx (Accessed: January 22, 2022).
Howie, G. (2016) "How to think about death: Living with dying." In Whistler, D., and Browne, V. (eds) *On the Feminist Philosophy of Gillian Howie.* Camden: Bloomsbury, pp. 131–144.
Human Rights Watch (2011) "Egypt: End torture, military trials of civilians." Demonstrators and Journalists Arrested, Abused as Army Clears Tahrir Square. Available at: https://www.hrw.org/news/2011/03/11/egypt-end-torture-military-trials-civilians (Accessed: January 22, 2022).
Human Rights Watch (2013b) Egypt: Lynching of Shia Follows Months of Hate Speech, Available at: https://www.hrw.org/news/2013/06/27/egypt-lynching-shia-follows-months-hate-speech (Accessed 22 August 2022).
Human Rights Watch (2013a) "Why Egypt's new law regulating NGOs is still criminal." *Human Rights Watch.* Available at: https://www.hrw.org/news/2013/06/11/why-egypts-new-law-regulating-ngos-still-criminal (Accessed: January 22, 2022).
Human Rights Watch (2013b) Egypt: Lynching of Shia Follows Months of Hate Speech, Available at: https://www.hrw.org/news/2013/06/27/egypt-lynching-shia-follows-months-hate-speech (Accessed 22 August 2022).

Human Rights Watch (2014) All According to Plan The Rab'a Massacre and Mass Killings of Protesters in Egypt, Available at: https://www.hrw.org/report/2014/08/12/all-according-plan/raba-massacre-and-mass-killings-protesters-egypt (Accessed: 16 August 2022).

Human Rights Watch (2015) "Egypt: Counterterrorism law erodes basic rights." *Human Rights Watch*. Available at: https://www.hrw.org/news/2015/08/19/egypt-counterterrorism-law-erodes-basic-rights (Accessed: January 22, 2022).

Human Rights Watch (2016a) "Death of protesters marks fourth anniversary of Egypt's 25 January revolution." Available at: https://ifex.org/death-of-protesters-marks-fourth-anniversary-of-egypts-25-january-revolution/ (Accessed: January 22, 2022).

Human Rights Watch (2016b) "Egypt: Scores of protesters jailed unjustly." *Human Rights Watch*. Available at: https://www.hrw.org/news/2016/05/25/egypt-scores-protesters-jailed-unjustly (Accessed: January 22, 2022).

Human Rights Watch (2019) "Egypt: Constitutional amendments entrench repression." *Human Rights Watch*. Available at: https://www.hrw.org/news/2019/04/20/egypt-constitutional-amendments-entrench-repression (Accessed: January 22, 2022).

Human Rights Watch (2020) "World report 2020: Egypt." *Human Rights Watch World Report 2020*. Available at: https://www.hrw.org/world-report/2020/country-chapters/egypt (Accessed: January 22, 2022).

Hussin, M. E. (2017) "Toward the emancipation of Egypt: A study on the assembly law 10/1914." *Cairo*. Available at: https://www.cihrs.org/wp-content/uploads/2017/01/Towards_the_em_of_Eg_eng.pdf (Accessed: January 22, 2022).

Hutchison, E. (2013) *Affective Communities in World Politics: Collective Emotions After Trauma*. Cambridge: Cambridge University Press.

Hutchison, E., and Bleiker, R. (2008) "Emotional reconciliation: Reconstituting identity and community after trauma." *European Journal of Social Theory*, 11(3), pp. 385–403. doi: 10.1177/1368431008092569.

ICJ (2012) "Egypt's new constitution: A flawed process; uncertain outcomes." *Geneva*. Available at: https://www.refworld.org/pdfid/530ef8a34.pdf (Accessed: January 21, 2022).

Illouz, E. (2007) *Cold Intimacies: The Making of Emotional Capit*. London: Polity Press.

Ingram, J. D. (2019) "Critical theory and postcolonialism." In *The Routledge Companion to the Frankfurt School*, London: Routledge, pp. 500–513.

Interlandi, J. (2014) "A revolutionary approach to treating PTSD." *New York Times Magazine*, 22 May. Available at: https://www.nytimes.com/2014/05/25/magazine/arevolutionaryapproachtotreatingptsd.htmlhttp://nyti.ms/1m6eTLL (Accessed: January 15, 2022).

Ismail, S. (2006) *Political Life: Cairo's New Quarters*. Edited by S. Ismail. Minneapolis: University of Minnesota Press.

Jacob, P. (2003) "Intentionality." *Stanford Encyclopedia of Philosophy*. Available at: https://plato.stanford.edu/entries/intentionality/#:~:text=In%20philosophy

%2C%20intentionality%20is%20the,or%20that%20they%20have%20contents. (Accessed: January 23, 2022).

Jaeggi, R. (2014) *Alienation*. New York: Columbia University Press.

Janoff-Bulman, R. (1992) *Shattered Assumptions: Towards a New Psychology of Trauma*. New York: Free Press.

Jo, Y. N. (2013) "Psycho-social dimensions of poverty: When poverty becomes shameful." *Critical Social Policy*, 33(3), pp. 514–531. doi: 10.1177/0261018313479008.

Joya, A. (2011) "The Egyptian revolution: Crisis of neoliberalism and the potential for democratic politics." *Review of African Political Economy*, 38(129), pp. 367–386. doi: 10.1080/03056244.2011.602544.

Joya, A. (2017) "Neoliberalism, the state and economic policy outcomes in the post-Arab uprisings: The case of Egypt." *Mediterranean Politics*, 22(3), pp. 339–361. doi: 10.1080/13629395.2016.1219182.

Joya, A. (2020) *The Roots of Revolt: A Political Economy of Egypt From Nasser to Mubarak*. Cambridge: Cambridge University Press.

Jumet, K. D. (2018) *Contesting the Repressive State: Why Ordinary Egyptians Protested During the Arab Spring*. Oxford: Oxford University Press.

Kaminer, D., Eagle, G., and Crawford-Browne, S. (2018) "Continuous traumatic stress as a mental and physical health challenge: Case studies from South Africa." *Journal of Health Psychology*, 23(8), p. 1038. doi: 10.1177/1359105316642831.

Kandil, H. (2013) *Soldiers, Spies, and Statesmen Egypt's Road to Revolt*. London: Verso.

Kant, I. (1724) *Critique of Pure Reason: The Cambridge Edition of the Works of Immanuel Kant*. Cambridge: Cambridge University Press.

Keller, T. and Chappell, T. (1996). "The Rise and Fall of Erichsen's Disease (Railroad Spine)." *Spine (Phila Pa 1976)*, 21(13), pp. 1597–1601. doi: 10.1097/00007632-199607010-000222.

Kenny, P. D. (2010) "The meaning of torture." *Polity*, 42(2), pp. 131–155.

Ketchley, N. (2017) *Egypt in a Time of Revolution: Contentious Politics and the Arab Spring*. Cambridge: Cambridge University Press.

Khalifa, A. (2014) "Maspero: A Massacre revisited." *The Tahrir Institute for Middle East Policy*. Available at: https://timep.org/commentary/analysis/maspero-massacre-revisited/ (Accessed: January 22, 2022).

Khalifa, S. (2015) *Egypt's Lost Spring: Causes and Consequences*. Santa Barbara: Praeger.

Khalil, H. and Dill, B. (2019) "Negotiating statist neoliberalism: The political economy of post-revolution Egypt." *Review of African Political Economy*, 45(158), pp. 574–591. doi: 10.1080/03056244.2018.1547187.

Khan, R., Mahmood, A., and Salim, A. (2020) "Arab spring failure: A case study of Egypt and Syria." *Liberal Arts and Social Sciences International Journal (LASSIJ)*, 4(1). doi: 10.47264/idea.lassij/4.1.5.

Kholaif, D. (2014) "Egypt outlaws anti-Mubarak April 6 movement." *Al Jazeera*. Available at: https://www.aljazeera.com/news/2014/4/28/egypt-outlaws-anti-mubarak-april-6-movement (Accessed: January 22, 2022).

Kienle, E. (1998) "More than a response to Islamism: The political deliberalization of Egypt in the 1990s." *Middle East Journal*, 52(2), pp. 219–235.

Kienle, E. (2000) *The Grand Delusion: Democracy and Economic Reform in Egypt*. New York: I B. Tauris.

Kihlstrom, J. F. (2006) "Does neuroscience constrain social-psychological theory." *Dialogue [Society for Personality & Social Psychology]*, 21(1), 16–17.

Kihlstrom, J. F. (2010) "Social neuroscience: The footprints of Phineas Gage." *Social Cognition*, 28(6), 757–783. doi: 10.1521/soco.2010.28.6.757.

Kihlstrom, J. F., and Park, L. (2016) "Cognitive psychology: Overview." In *The Curated Reference Collection in Neuroscience and Biobehavioral Psychology*. In Reference Module in Neuroscience and Biobehavioral Psychology, Elsevier, 2018. ISBN 9780128093245. Available at: https://escholarship.org/uc/item/06648227 Accessed: August 23 2022.

Kingsley, P. (2013) "Egyptian general calls for millions to protest against 'terrorism' Egypt." *The Guardian*. Available at: https://www.theguardian.com/world/2013/jul/24/egypt-general-sisi-protest-terrorism (Accessed: January 22, 2022).

Kingsley, P. (2014) "Abdel Fatah al-Sisi won 96.1% of vote in Egypt presidential election, say officials." *The Guardian*. Available at: https://www.theguardian.com/world/2014/jun/03/abdel-fatah-al-sisi-presidential-election-vote-egypt (Accessed: January 22, 2022).

Kirkpatrick, D. D., and Stack, L. (2011) "Violent protests in Egypt pit thousands against police." *The New York Times*. Available at: https://www.nytimes.com/2011/11/20/world/middleeast/violence-erupts-in-cairo-as-egypts-military-cedes-political-ground.html (Accessed: January 22, 2022).

Kurzman, C. (2014) "The anointment of Saint Francis Al-Sisi." *IslamiCommentary*. Available at: https://web.archive.org/web/20160502152139/http://islamicommentary.org/2014/03/the-anointment-of-saint-francis-al-sisi/ (Accessed: January 22, 2022).

Laub, D. (1995) "Truth and testimony: The process and the struggle." In Caruth, C. (ed) *Trauma: Explorations in Memory*. Baltimore: Johns Hopkins University Press.

Levinas, E. (2005) *Humanism of the Other*. Baltimore: University of Illinois Press.

Lewis-Fernández, R., and Kirmayer, L. J. (2019) "Cultural concepts of distress and psychiatric disorders: Understanding symptom experience and expression in context." *Transcultural Psychiatry*, 56(4), pp. 786–803. doi: 10.1177/1363461519861795.

Leys, R. (2000) *Trauma: A Genealogy*. Chicago: University of Chicago Press.

Loftus, E. F., and Ketcham, K. (1996) *The Myth of Repressed Memory: False Memories and Allegations of Sexual Abuse*. St Martin: St. Martin's Griffin.

Lorand, S., and Feldman, S. (1955) "The symbolism of teeth in dreams." *The International Journal of Psychoanalysis*, 36, pp. 145–160.

Lotfi, F. (2018) "The presidential candidate supporting his rival." *Meet Moussa Mostafa Moussa - Daily News Egypt*. Available at: https://dailynewsegypt.com/2018/03/25/presidential-candidate-supporting-rival-meet-moussa-mostafa-moussa/ (Accessed: January 22, 2022).

Lynn, S. J., Lilienfeld, S. O., Merckelbach, H., Giesbrecht, T., McNally, R. J., Loftus, E. F., Bruck, M., Garry, M., and Malaktaris, A. (2014) "The trauma model of dissociation: Inconvenient truths and stubborn fictions. Comment on Dalenberg et al. (2012)." *Psychological Bulletin*, 140(3), pp. 896–910. doi: 10.1037/A0035570.

Magdi, A. (2019) "Why executions in Egypt are skyrocketing and why they should end." *Human Rights Watch*. Available at: https://www.hrw.org/news/2019/03/25/why-executions-egypt-are-skyrocketing-and-why-they-should-end (Accessed: January 22, 2022).

Mahmoud, N (2013) Morsi Manages Egypt's Economic Decline, Al Monitor, 7 January 2013, Available at: https://www.al-monitor.com/originals/2013/01/egypt-1970-muslim-brothers.html (Accessed: 16 August 2022).

Mahmoud, M. (2017a) "Egypt's food price crisis: 'How are we supposed to eat?'." *Middle East Eye*. Available at: https://www.middleeasteye.net/features/egypts-food-price-crisis-how-are-we-supposed-eat (Accessed: January 22, 2022).

Mahmoud, M. (2017b) "'Sisi's balls' are no laughing matter for Egypt's police." *Middle East Eye*. Available at: https://www.middleeasteye.net/features/sisis-balls-are-no-laughing-matter-egypts-police (Accessed: January 22, 2022).

Malsin, J. (2021) "Egypt expanded the Suez Canal. It wasn't enough." *Wall Street Journal*. Available at: https://www.wsj.com/articles/egypt-expanded-the-suez-canal-it-wasnt-enough-11616765965 (Accessed: January 22, 2022).

Mamdouh, R. (2018) "Egypt's new media laws: Rearranging legislative building blocks to maximize control." *Mada Masr*. Available at: https://www.madamasr.com/en/2018/07/17/feature/politics/egypts-new-media-laws-rearranging-legislative-building-blocks-to-maximize-control/ (Accessed: January 22, 2022).

Mandour, M. (2019a) "Egypt's political future: Generalissimo Sisi." *Qantara*. Available at: https://en.qantara.de/content/egypt%CA%B9s-political-future-generalissimo-sisi (Accessed: January 22, 2022).

Mandour, M. (2019b) "Egypt's invisible executions." Available at: https://carnegieendowment.org/sada/78998 (Accessed: January 22, 2022).

Mandour, M. (2020a) "Dollars to despots: Sisi's International patrons." *Carnegie Endowment for International Peace*. Available at: https://carnegieendowment.org/sada/83277 (Accessed: January 22, 2022).

Mandour, M. (2020b) "Sisi's war on the poor." *Carnegie Endowment for International Peace*. Available at: https://carnegieendowment.org/sada/82772 (Accessed: January 22, 2022).

Mandour, M. (2021) "The Sinister side of Sisi's urban development." *Carnegie Endowment for International Peace*. Available at: https://carnegieendowment.org/sada/84504 (Accessed: January 22, 2022).

March, J. S. (1990) "The nosology of posttraumatic stress disorder." *Journal of Anxiety Disorders*, 4(1), pp. 61–82. doi: 10.1016/0887-6185(90)90024-4.

Marroushi, N. (2011) "US expert: Leadership of 'Military Inc.' is running Egypt." *Egypt Independent*, 26 October. Available at: https://egyptindependent.com/us-expert-leadership-military-inc-running-egypt/ (Accessed: January 21, 2022).

Marshall, S. (2015) "The Egyptian armed forces and the remaking of an economic empire." *Carnegie Endowment for International Peace*. Available at: https://carnegie-mec.org/2015/04/15/egyptian-armed-forces-and-remaking-of-economic-empire-pub-59726 (Accessed: January 22, 2022).

Marshall, S., and Stacher, J. (2012) "Egypt's generals and transnational capital - MERIP." *MERIP*, 262. Available at: https://merip.org/2012/03/egypts-generals-and-transnational-capital/ (Accessed: January 22, 2022).

Martín-Baró, I. (1994) *Writings for a Liberation Psychology*. Cambridge: Harvard University Press.

Matthies-Boon, V. (2017) "Shattered worlds: Political trauma amongst young activists in post-revolutionary Egypt." *Journal of North African Studies*, 22(4), pp. 620–644. doi: 10.1080/13629387.2017.1295855.

Matthies-Boon, V., and Head, N. (2018) "Trauma as counter-revolutionary colonisation: Narratives from (post)revolutionary Egypt." *Journal of International Political Theory*, 14(3), pp. 258–279. doi: 10.1177/1755088217748970.

Mayes, R., and Horwitz, A. v. (2005) "DSM-III and the revolution in the classification of mental illness." *Journal of the History of the Behavioral Sciences*, 41(3), pp. 249–267. doi: 10.1002/JHBS.20103.

McGrath, Cam (2013) Morsi Slams New Lid on Labor Rights, 1 February 2013, https://truthout.org/articles/morsi-slams-new-lid-on-labour-rights/ (Accessed: 10 July 2022).

Meari, L. (2015) "Reconsidering trauma: Towards a Palestinian community psychology." *Journal of Community Psychology*, 43(1), pp. 76–86. doi: 10.1002/JCOP.21712.

MENA Rights Group (2021) "The practice of 'rotation': How Egypt keeps its dissidents in indefinite detention." Available at: http://menarights.org/en/articles/practice-rotation-how-egypt-keeps-its-dissidents-indefinite-detention (Accessed: January 22, 2022).

Michael, M. (2011) "No booze, no bikinis for Egypt tourists?" *The Seattle Times*. Available at: https://www.seattletimes.com/life/travel/no-booze-no-bikinis-for-egypt-tourists/ (Accessed: January 22, 2022).

Michaelson, R. (2018) "Sadat nephew and Sisi critic drops Egyptian presidential bid Egypt." *The Guardian*. Available at: https://www.theguardian.com/world/2018/jan/15/sadat-nephew-and-sisi-critic-drops-egyptian-presidential-bid (Accessed: January 22, 2022).

Middle East Eye (2016) "Sisi mocked for pleading for 'spare change'." *Middle East Eye*. Available at: https://www.middleeasteye.net/news/sisi-mocked-pleading-spare-change (Accessed: January 22, 2022).

Middle East Eye (2019) "Lone protester arrested in Cairo, Egypt." *YouTube*. Available at: https://www.youtube.com/watch?v=ez6S9oThzI8 (Accessed: January 22, 2022).

Mitchell, T. (2002) *Rule for Experts: Egypt, Techno-Politics, Modernity*. Berkeley: University of California Press.

Moghadam, V. M. (2013) "What is democracy? Promises and perils of the Arab Spring." *Current Sociology*, 61(4), pp. 393–408. doi: 10.1177/0011392113479739.

Mohamed, A. S. (2012) "On the road to democracy: Egyptian bloggers and the internet 2010." *Journal of Arab and Muslim Media Research*, 4(2–3), pp. 253–272. doi: 10.1386/jammr.4.2-3.253_1.

Moore, I. A. (2005) "'Speak, you also': Encircling trauma." *Journal for Cultural Research*, 9(1), pp. 87–99. doi: 10.1080/14797580042000331952.

Mosireen (2011) "Jadaliyya – The Maspero Massacre: What really happened (video)." *Jadaliyya*. Available at: https://www.jadaliyya.com/Details/24609 (Accessed: January 22, 2022).

Mossallem, M. (2017) "Egypt's debt trap: The neoliberal roots of the problem." *CADTM*. https://www.cadtm.org.

Mubarak, H. (2011) "Hosni Mubarak's speech: Full text Hosni Mubarak." *The Guardian*. Available at: https://www.theguardian.com/world/2011/feb/02/president-hosni-mubarak-egypt-speech (Accessed: January 21, 2022).

Naylor, H. (2011) "Mubarak gives 6m Government Employees 15% Pay Increase." *The National*, 8 Feb 2011.

Orange, D. M., Atwood, G. E., and Stolorow, R. D. (2015) *Working Intersubjectively: Contextualism in Psychoanalytic Practice*. New York: Routledge

Pat-Horenczyk, R., and Schiff, M. (2019) "Continuous traumatic stress and the life cycle: Exposure to repeated political violence in Israel." *Current Psychiatry Reports*, 21, p. 71. doi: 10.1007/s11920-019-1060-x.

Pearlman, W. (2013) "Emotions and the microfoundations of the Arab uprisings." *Perspectives on Politics*, 11(2), pp. 387–409. doi: 10.1017/S1537592713001072.

Pearlman, W. (2016) "Narratives of fear in Syria." *Perspectives on Politics*, 14(1), pp. 21–37. doi: 10.1017/S1537592715003205.

Pederson, J. (2008) "Habermas' method: Rational reconstruction." *Philosophy of the Social Sciences*, 34(4), pp. 457–485.

Pendergrast, M. (2017) *The Repressed Memory Epidemic: How It Happened and What We Need to Learn From It*. Cham: Springer International Publishing.

Piazzese, G. (2015) "Scars of Egypt's Port Said massacre refuse to fade." *Middle East Eye*. Available at: https://www.middleeasteye.net/features/scars-egypts-port-said-massacre-refuse-fade (Accessed: January 22, 2022).

Purser, R. (2019) *McMindfulness: How Mindfulness Became the New Capitalist Spirituality: Purser, Ronald: Amazon.de: Books*. London: Repeater.

Radstone, S. (2007) "Trauma theory: Contexts politics ethics." *Paragraph*, 30(1), pp. 9–29.

Raghavan, S., and Mahfouz, H. F. (2019) "In Egypt, when Mohamed Morsi collapsed in court, help was too slow, witnesses say." *Washington Post*, 20 June. Available at: https://www.washingtonpost.com/world/when-egypts-ousted-president-morsi-collapsed-in-court-help-was-not-immediate-witnesses-say/2019/06/20/f4e5716a-9375-11e9-956a-88c291ab5c38_story.html (Accessed: January 22, 2022).

Ratcliffe, M. (2008) *Feelings of Being: Phenomenology, Psychiatry and the Sense of Reality*. Oxford: Oxford University Press.

Ratcliffe, M. (2014) *Experiences of Depression: A Study in Phenomenology*. Oxford: Oxford University Press.

Rehin, G., Eyerman, R., and Jamison, A. (1993) "Social movements: A cognitive approach." *The British Journal of Sociology*, 44(3), pp. 396–536. doi: 10.2307/591836.

Reprieve (2019) "Mass injustice: Statistical findings on the death penalty in Egypt." Available at: https://egyptdeathpenaltyindex.com/wp-content/uploads/2020/11/2019_05_09_PUB-EGY-Egypt-data-report-Mass-Injustice-WEB-version.pdf (Accessed: January 22, 2022).

Reuters (2012) "Egypt's Mursi sacks general prosecutor, appoints another." *Reuters*. Available at: https://www.reuters.com/article/uk-egypt-prosecutor-idUKBRE8AL0NB20121122 (Accessed: January 22, 2022).

Reuters (2016) "Egypt's ElBaradei breaks silence on Rabaa dispersal in rare detailed statement – Egypt Independent." *Reuters*. Available at: https://egyptindependent.com/egypt-s-elbaradei-breaks-silence-rabaa-dispersal-rare-detailed-statement/ (Accessed: January 22, 2022).

Reuters (2018) "Leading member of Egyptian opposition Hisham Genena attacked and badly injured." *Reuters*. Available at: https://www.reuters.com/article/uk-egypt-politics-idUKKBN1FG0CU (Accessed: January 22, 2022).

Reuters (2019) "Egyptian headline inflation rises as food costs jump." *Arab News*. Available at: https://www.arabnews.com/node/1508776/business-economy (Accessed: January 22, 2022).

Reuters (2021) "Egypt's President Sisi ends state of emergency for the first time in years." *Reuters*. Available at: https://www.reuters.com/world/middle-east/egypts-president-sisi-ends-state-emergency-first-time-years-2021-10-25/ (Accessed: January 22, 2022).

Roll, S. (2013) "Egypt's business elite after Mubarak a powerful player between generals and brotherhood." *RP08, Berlin*. Available at: https://www.swp-berlin.org/publications/products/research_papers/2013_RP08_rll.pdf (Accessed: January 22, 2022).

Roll, S. (2015) "Managing change: How Egypt's military leadership shaped the transformation." *Mediterranean Politics* Mediterranean Politics, 21:1, 23-43, DOI: 10.1080/13629395.2015.1081452

Rose, N. (2019) *Our Psychiatric Future: The Politics of Mental Health*. Cambridge: Polity.

Rozen, N., and Soffer-Dudek, N. (2018) "Dreams of teeth falling out: An empirical investigation of physiological and psychological correlates." *Frontiers in Psychology*, 9, p. 1812. doi: 10.3389/FPSYG.2018.01812/BIBTEX.

RSF (2017) "Egyptian intelligence services extend control over media." *Reporters Without Borders*. Available at: https://rsf.org/en/news/egyptian-intelligence-services-extend-control-over-media (Accessed: January 22, 2022).

Ryzova, L. (2020) "The battle of Muhammad Mahmoud street in Cairo: The politics and poetics of urban violence in revolutionary time." *Past & Present*, 247(1), pp. 273–317. doi: 10.1093/PASTJ/GTZ029.

Saad, M., Sayed, M., and Metwaly, A. (2013) "Egyptian artists march against brotherhood-affiliated culture minister - Stage & Street - Arts & Culture." *Ahram Online*. Available at: https://english.ahram.org.eg/NewsContent/5/0/71462/Arts--Culture/0/Egyptian-artists-march-against-Brotherhoodaffiliat.aspx (Accessed: January 22, 2022).

Saker, T. (2017) "Egypt's state of emergency in 2017: Constitutional enforcement and consequences." *Egypt Independent*. Available at: https://egyptindependent.com

/egypt-s-state-emergency-2017-constitutional-enforcement-and-consequences/ (Accessed: January 22, 2022).

Salama, N. (2015) "Egypt's shame: The disturbing legality of marital rape." *Prime Magazine Cairo*, 7 November. Available at: http://www.primemag.me/egypts-shame-the-disturbing-legality-of-marital-rape/+&cd=3&hl=nl&ct=clnk&gl=nl (Accessed: November 17, 2015).

Sanyal, P. (2015) "Egypt: Presidential elections, 2014." *Contemporary Review of the Middle East*, 2(3), pp. 289–307. doi: 10.1177/2347798915604923.

Sarihan, A. (2012) "Is the Arab Spring in the third wave of democratization? The case of Syria and Egypt." *Turkish Journal of Politics*, 3(1), pp. 67–85.

Sarquís, D. J. (2012) "Democratization after the Arab spring: The case of Egypt's political transition." *Politics and Policy*, 40(5), pp. 871–903. doi: 10.1111/j.1747-1346.2012.00381.x.

Sartre, J.-P. (1956) *Being and Nothingness*. Translated by Hazel Barnes. New York: Philosophical Library.

Sayigh, R. (2013) "On the exclusion of the Palestinian Nakba from the 'trauma genre'." *Journal of Palestine Studies*, 43(1), pp. 51–60. doi: 10.1525/JPS.2013.43.1.51.

Schielke, S. (2011) "Longing for the smell of teargas, a book of unfinished stories." Available at: http://samuliegypt.blogspot.com/2011/11/ longing-for-smell-of-teargas.html (Accessed: January 22, 2022).

Schulman, G. I., and Hammer, J. (1988) "Social characteristics, the diagnosis of mental disorders, and the change from DSM II to DSM III." *Sociology of Health & Illness*, 10(4), pp. 543–560. doi: 10.1111/1467-9566.EP10837190.

Selim, Gamal M. (2015) "Egypt under SCAF and the Muslim brotherhood: The triangle of counter-revolution." *Arab Studies Quarterly*, 37(2), pp. 177–199. doi: 10.13169/ARABSTUDQUAR.37.2.0177.

Soliman, S. (2011) *The Autumn of Dictatorship: Fiscal Crisis and Political Change in Egypt Under Mubarak*. Stanford: Stanford University Press.

Solomon, T. (2018) "Ontological security, circulations of affect, and the Arab Spring." *Journal of International Relations and Development*, 21(4), pp. 934–958. doi: 10.1057/s41268-017-0089-x.

Sonay, A. (2018) *Making Revolution in Egypt: The April 6th Movement in a Global Context*. London: I. B. Tauris.

Sorrell, J. H. (2006) "The pleasure of dissent: A critical theory of psychotherapy as an emancipatory practice." *American Journal of Psychotherapy*, 60(2), pp. 131–145. doi: 10.1176/appi.psychotherapy.2006.60.2.131.

Spitzer, R. L. (2007) "Foreword." In Horwitz, A., and Wakefield, J. C. (eds) *The Loss of Sadness: How Psychiatry Transformed Normal Sorrow into Depressive Disorder*. Oxford: Oxford University Press, pp. vii–x.

Springborg, R. (2017) "The rewards of failure: Persisting military rule in Egypt." *British Journal of Middle Eastern Studies*, 44(4), pp. 478–496. doi: 10.1080/13530194.2017.1363956.

Stacher, J. (2020) *Watermelon Democracy*. New York: Syracuse University Press.

Stein, J. Y., Wilmot, D., and Solomon, Z. (2016) "Does one size fit all? Nosological, clinical, and scientific implications of variations in PTSD Criterion A." *Journal of Anxiety Disorders*, 43, pp. 106–117. doi: 10.1016/J.JANXDIS.2016.07.001.

Stevens, G., Eagle, G., Kaminer, D., and Higson-Smith, C. (2013) "Continuous traumatic stress: Conceptual conversations in contexts of global conflict, violence and trauma." *Peace and Conflict*, 19(2), p. 75. doi: 10.1037/a0032484.

Stilt, K. A. (2012) "The end of 'one hand': The Egyptian constitutional declaration and the rift between the 'people' and the Supreme Council of the Armed Forces. 208." Available at: http://scholarlycommons.law.northwestern.edu/facultyworkingpapers/208 (Accessed: January 21, 2022).

Stolorow, R. D. (2007) "Anxiety, authenticity, and trauma: The relevance of Heidegger's existential analytic for psychoanalysis." *Psychoanalytic Psychology*, 24(2), pp. 373–383. doi: 10.1037/0736-9735.24.2.373.

Stolorow, R. D. (2013) "Intersubjective-systems theory: A phenomenological-contextualist psychoanalytic perspective." *Psychoanalytic Dialogues*, 23(4), pp. 383–389. doi: 10.1080/10481885.2013.810486.

Stolorow, R. D. (2018) "Never again! Trauma disrupts the experience of time." *American Journal of Psychoanalysis*, 78(1), pp. 89–91. doi: 10.1057/s11231-017-9126-1.

Stolorow, R. D. (2020a) "Whence Heidegger's phenomenology?" *Human Studies*, 43(2), pp. 311–313. doi: 10.1007/s10746-020-09546-3.

Stolorow, R. D. (2020b) "Worlds of experience: An interview with Robert D. Stolorow." In *Progress in Self Psychology, V. 20*. Available at: https://pep-web.org/search/document/PSP.020.0305A?page=P0305. (Accessed: 23 August 2022)

Stolorow, R. D., and Atwood, G. E. (1996) "The intersubjective perspective." *Psychoanalytic Review*, 83, pp. 181–194.

Stolorow, R. D., and Atwood, G. E. (2014) *Contexts of Being*. Hillsdale, NJ: The Analytic Press.

Stolorow, R. D., and Atwood, G. E. (2018) *The Power of Phenomenology*. London & New York: Routledge.

Stolorow, R. D., Atwood, G. E., and Orange, D. M. (2010) "Heidegger's Nazism and the hypostatization of being." *International Journal of Psychoanalytic Self Psychology*, 5(4), pp. 429–450. doi: 10.1080/15551024.2010.508211.

Stolorow, R. D. (2007) *Trauma and Human Existence: Autobiographical, Psychoanalytic and Philosophical Reflections*. New York: The Analytic Press.

Stolorow, R. D. (2011) *World, Affectivity, Trauma*. New York: Routledge.

Straker, G. (2013) "Continuous traumatic stress: Personal reflections 25 years on." *Peace and Conflict: Journal of Peace Psychology*, 19(2), pp. 209–217.

Strohmayer, E. A. (2007) *Stabilität, Friede und Demokratie im Nahen Osten? 25 Jahre Ägypten unter Hosni Mubarak*. Baden-Baden: Nomos.

Summerfield, D. (1995) "Debriefing after psychological trauma. Inappropriate exporting of western culture may cause additional harm." *BMJ (Clinical Research Ed.)*, 322, pp. 95–98. doi: 10.1136/bmj.311.7003.509a.

Summerfield, D. (2001) "The invention of post-traumatic stress disorder and the social usefulness of a psychiatric category." *BMJ: British Medical Journal*, 322(7278), p. 95. doi: 10.1136/BMJ.322.7278.95.

Susen, S. (2009) "Between emancipation and domination: Habermasian reflections on the empowerment and disempowerment of the human subject." *Pli: The Warwick Journal of Philosophy*, 20, pp. 80–110. doi: 10.1017/S0033291700052569.

Svendsen, L. (2012) "Moods and the meaning of philosophy." *New Literary History*, 43(3), pp. 419–431.

Sztompka, P. (2000a) "Cultural trauma: The other face of social change." *European Journal of Social Theory*, 3(4), pp. 449–466. doi: 10.1177/136843100003004004.

Sztompka, P. (2000b) "The ambivalence of social change triumph or trauma?" *Polish Sociological Review*, 131, pp. 275–290.

Sztompka, P. (2004) "The trauma of social change: A case of postcommunist societies." In Alexander, J. C., Eyerman, R, Giesen, B, Smelser, N. J., Sztompka, P (eds) *Cultural Trauma and Collective Identity*. Berkeley: University of California Press

Tansel, C. B. (2019) "Neoliberalism and the antagonisms of authoritarian resilience in the middle east." *South Atlantic Quarterly*, 118(2), pp. 287–305. doi: 10.1215/00382876-7381146.

Tarek, S. and Maher, H. (2012) "Egypt's Constituent Assembly unveiled amid fears over Islamist dominance – Politics – Egypt." *Ahram Online*. Available at: https://english.ahram.org.eg/NewsContent/1/64/44716/Egypt/Politics-/Egypts-Constituent-Assembly-unveiled-amid-fears-ov.aspx (Accessed: January 22, 2022).

Tasch, B. (2015) "'Build it and they will come': Egypt $8 billion Suez Canal expansion is dubious." *Insider*. Available at: https://www.businessinsider.com/egypts-authoritarian-president-is-celebrating-the-completion-of-an-8-billion-suez-canal-expansion-that-nobody-asked-for-2015-8 (Accessed: January 22, 2022).

Teti, A., and Gervasio, G. (2011) "The politics of Egypt's elections." *Open Democracy*. Available at: https://www.opendemocracy.net/en/north-africa-west-asia/politics-of-egypts-elections/ (Accessed: January 22, 2022).

Teti, A., Matthies-Boon, V., and Gervasio, G. (2012) "The revolution continues: Morsi's miscalculations and the Ikhwan's impasse." *Open Democracy*. Available at: https://www.opendemocracy.net/en/revolution-continues-morsis-miscalculations-and/ (Accessed: January 22, 2022).

Thomas, P., and Bracken, P. (2004) "Critical psychiatry in practice." *Advances in Psychiatric Treatment*, 10(5), pp. 361–370. doi: 10.1192/apt.10.5.361.

Thomas, P., and Bracken, P. (2011) "Dualisms and the myth of mental illness." In Rapley, M., Moncrieff, J., Dillon, J. (eds) *De-Medicalizing Misery*. London: Palgrave Macmillan.

Thomas, P., Bracken, P., and Leudar, I. (2004) "Hearing voices: A phenomenological-hermeneutic approach." *Cognitive Neuropsychiatry*, 9, pp. 13–23. doi: 10.1080/13546800344000138.

Topolski, A. (2015) *Arendt, Levinas and a Politics of Relationality*. London: Rowman & Littlefield.

Totten, M. J. (2012) "Arab spring or Islamist winter?: Three views." *World Affairs*, 174(5), pp. 23–42.

Towfik, A. K. (2011) *Utopia*. Bloomsbury Qatar Foundation.

Trager, E. (2011) "Egypt's military tribunals: Illiberal and destabilizing." *The Washington Institute, Policy Analysis*. Available at: https://www.washingtoninstitute.org/policy-analysis/egypts-military-tribunals-illiberal-and-destabilizing (Accessed: January 22, 2022).

Trager, E. (2016) *Arab Fall: How the Muslim Brotherhood Won and Lost Egypt in 891 Days*. Washington: Georgetown University Press.

Tseris, E. (2015) "VI. Trauma and women's rights ... According to whom? Decolonizing the psychological trauma narrative." *Feminism and Psychology*, 25(1), pp. 34–38. doi: 10.1177/0959353514562820.

van de Sande, M. (2013) "The prefigurative politics of Tahrir square – An alternative perspective on the 2011 revolutions." *Res Publica*, 19(3), pp. 223–239. doi: 10.1007/S11158-013-9215-9.

Vazquez-Arroyo, A. (2018) "Critical theory, colonialism, and the historicity of thought." *Constellations*, 25, pp. 54–70.

Vermetten, E. (2009) "Stress, trauma, en post-traumatisch stress syndroom." *Tijdschrift Voor Psychiatrie*, 51(8), pp. 595–602. Available at: https://europepmc.org/article/med/19658072 (Accessed: January 15, 2022).

Verovšek, P. J. (2021) "The philosopher as engaged citizen: Habermas on the role of the public intellectual in the modern democratic public sphere." *European Journal of Social Theory*, 24(4), pp. 526–544. doi: 10.1177/13684310211003192.

Völkel, J. C. (2020) "The 'chicken and egg' problem of relevance: Political parties and parliaments in North Africa." *Journal of North African Studies*, 25(6), pp 1–16. doi: 10.1080/13629387.2019.1644923.

Weinbaum, M. G. (1985) "Egypt's 'Infitah' and the politics of US economic assistance on JSTOR." *Middle Eastern Studies*, 21(2), pp. 206–222.

Whidden, J. (2017) *Egypt: British Colony, Imperial Capital*. Manchester: Manchester University Press.

Woodside, D., Santa Barbara, J., and Benner, D. G. (2007) "I: Psychological trauma and social healing in Croatia." *Medicine, Conflict and Survival*, 15(4), pp. 355–367. doi: 10.1080/13623699908409477.

Young, A. (1995) *The Harmony of Illusions*. Princeton: Princeton University Press.

Index

Abdel-Aziz, Alaa, 160
Abdel-Ghaffar, Magdy, 193
abstraction, 17, 32, 34, 39, 43
abstract universalism, 21n4
Abul-Magd, Zeina, 153
activists, 2–6, 10, 12–14, 17, 20, 23, 36, 70, 79, 86, 89, 91, 95, 97, 108–10, 116, 118, 126
Al Ahly, 149–50
alcohol, 290
Alexander, Jeffrey, 62
Alford, C. Alfred, 48, 57
Ali, Ben, 113
Ali, Khaled, 288
Ali, Mohamed, 192
alienation: incapacitating, 209; intersubjective, trauma as, 65–91; theory of, 28, 76–80, 108–10; traumatic, 76–80, 108–10, 164
Al Masry, 149–50
Améry, Jean, 140, 221
Amin, Galal, 102, 105
amygdala, 48
Anan, Sami Hafez, 157, 183
Anger, 212, 301
Annan, Sami, 181
anti-Brotherhood rhetoric, 170
anti-depressants, 290
anti-mimeticism, 47, 51, 54, 58–63

anti-systematic revolution, 128–30
Anti-Terror Law, 186–88, 291
Antze, P., 59
anxiety, 7, 68–69, 284, 290
AOHRUK, 198
appropriation, 76–79
Arab Organisation for Industrialisation, 151
Arab Organisation of Human Rights, 198
Arab Socialist Union, 102
Article 60, Egypt's penal code, 243n1
Article 267, Egypt's penal code, 243n1
'Assembly Law' (law 10/1914), 185–86, 188
authenticity, 68
automatic coping mechanisms, 55
Aziz, Mohammed Abdel, 169

Badr, Mahmoud, 169
El Baradei, Mohamed, 159, 175, 235
Bastille Day, 117
'Being-against-Death' (Crépon), 224–33
'Being-towards-Loss' (Stolorow), 237–38, 262
Benezir, G., 4
Bennet, Craig, 48
betrayal, revolutionary, 234–43
Between Facts and Norms (Habermas), 138

Al Bishry, Tareq, 133
blocking of people, 273–74
Bracken, Patrick, 27, 47, 66
brain-wiring, 41

Cairene traffic, 297
Cairo, 18
Camp David Accords (1978), 103
Charcot, J. M., 53
CIHRS, 200
City Eye project, 98n4, 101
clashes, 224–33
cognitive positivism, 41–43, 70
cognitive trauma theory, 54–58
colonisation: of lifeworld, 19, 80–82; theory of, 36, 81–82, 84, 91
communicative rationality: *versus* instrumental rationality, 36; theory of, 34
consciousness, philosophy of, 32–34
conspirational victim blaming, 56, 114–16, 118, 123n2, 126, 142, 147–49, 152, 163, 301; as intersubjective parity, 245–60; during Morsi's rule, 162–63; purpose, 115; as tool, 115
constitutional amendments, SCAF, 133–37
Constitutional Assembly, 133–37
Continuous Traumatic Stress (CTS), 51–53
corporealization of body, 283
counter-revolution: aftermath, 2–3, 13, 93–98; coping with, 290–96; demobilisation, 3; traumatic status subordination, 245; violence, impact of, 1–5, 23
Craps, Stef, 7, 25, 51
creative self-becoming, 12, 36, 78, 217, 282, 302
Crépon, Marc, 224, 234
cross-sectional alliance, 143
CTS. *See* Continuous Traumatic Stress (CTS)
Daniel, Mina, 141, 287
El Dawla, Aida Seif, 107

'The Day of the One Demand,' mass demonstration, 143
death, 221–22, 224–33; being against, 224–33; burden of, 234–43; desire for, 224; Heidegger on, 227; martyrs, 234–43; politics of, 302; revolutionary, 234–43; social, 222, 270–75; violent imposition of, 227. *See also* teargas
deception, 84
defriending, 274
deliberative democracy, theory of, 34
de Mann, Paul, 58
democratisation, 2–3
demoralisation, 10, 29, 36, 70, 90, 108–9, 175, 212, 278, 280–81, 299
depoliticisation, 290–96
depression, 1, 10, 69, 130–31, 212, 232, 237, 241–43, 282–83; somatic state of, 283–90
Derrida, Jacques, 58
Descartes, Rene, 32
El Din, Ziad Bahaa, 175
direct physical force: El Sisi, Abdel Fattah, 190–200; Morsi, Mohamed, 160–65; SCAF, 139–51
disorientation, 228, 230, 232, 233, 300
dissociation, 55
distorted communication, 84–85
DMC, TV network, 188
Doss, Ahmed, 170
Doss, Moheb, 169
double injury, 24
DSMI, 38
DSMII, 38
DSMIII, 39, 44–45, 53
DSMV, 44

EBDA. *See* Egyptian Business Development Association (EBDA)
economic distribution, 11
economic liberalisation, 105–6
Economic Restructuring and Structural Adjustment Programme (ERSAP), 104

ECRF. *See* enforced disappearance of children (ECRF)
ecstasies of temporality, 227
Edkins, Jenny, 61–62
efficiency, 42
Egypt, 98n4; Bastille Day, 117; counter-revolutionary aftermath, 2–3, 13, 93–98; intelligence services, 102; Kifaya (Enough) movement (2004), 111–13; maldistribution, 71–73, 103–5, 298; male rape in, 223; military and civic security forces, relation between, 12–13, 106–7; Nasser's time, 101–2; neoliberal economics, 103–5; political trauma in, 93–98; revolutionary mobilisation (2011), 113–22; security state violence, 105–8; Supreme Council of Armed Forces, 118, 122, 125–54; traumatic alienation, 108–10, 299; traumatic status subordination in, 65–76, 85, 87–91, 93–98, 101–10, 179–208
Egyptian Business Development Association (EBDA), 166
Egyptian Trade Union Federation (ETUF), 106, 167
El-Elaimy, Zyad, 199
electoral politics, SCAF, 130–31, 133
Emara, Adel, 142
emotions, 3
empiricism, 32
enforced disappearance of children (ECRF), 193–95, 208n5
Ennahda massacre, 172–73
equality, 84
Erickson, John Eric, 53
ERSAP. *See* Economic Restructuring and Structural Adjustment Programme (ERSAP)
eventism, 29, 50–51
evidence-based research, 38
evolution, teleological theory of, 18
existential pain, 283–90
Ezz, Ahmed, 153

Facebook, 273–74
Al Fangari, Mohsen, 148
fear, 221, 284
feminisation, 223
fMRI scans, 48
Forna, Aminatta, 7
'For the Love of Egypt' (Gur), 182
Fotouh, Abdel Moneim Abdel, 131, 166, 199
Fraser, Nancy, 5, 9, 19, 24, 28, 71–76, 298; Honneth's model of recognition, criticisms of work, 71–76; on justice, 75–76; on maldistribution, 71–76; on misrecognition, 71–76; philosophy of recognition, 71–76; traumatic status subordination, 71–76, 85, 93–98, 101–10
free-market liberalism, 153
Free Palestine Movement, 96
Freud, Sigmund, 53
frustration, 250, 274

Ganzouri, Kamal, 130, 149, 154n9
Genena, Hisham, 183
German critical theory, 20, 22n18
grief, 235–37
Guenther, Lisa, 200
guilt, 241
Gur, Serap, 182

Habash, Shady, 199
Habermas, Jurgen, 5, 9, 25, 27–28, 159, 298; communicative rationality/deliberative democracy, theory of, 34–35; communicative *versus* instrumental rationality, 36; evolution, teleological theory of, 18; legal discourse ethics, 127; modernity, teleological theory of, 18; Philosophy of the Subject, critique of, 31–36; positivism, critique of, 36; reconstructive method, 17; self, notion of, 32–33; theory of colonisation, 36, 81–82, 84, 91; theory of rational

communication/discourse ethics, 17; traumatic instrumentality, 80–89
Hashima, Ahmed Abu, 189
Hegazy, Mahmoud, 142
Heideggerian trauma theory, 66–70
hippocampus, 47
Holocaust, 60–61
Honneth, Axel, 74–75
hope, destruction of, 282
hopelessness, 246
Horowitz, Mardi, 54
Hosny, Hazem, 182
Howie, Gillian, 226
human-induced trauma, 18, 81, 95
Hutchison, Emma, 62
hysteria, 53

'Ikhwanisation' of society, 163
incapacitating alienation, 209
individual trauma, 11
(in)justice, 11, 87–88, 91, 298
instrumentality, traumatic, 80–89
insult, 24
intentionality, 70
intersubjective imparity, 98n4, 137, 164, 174, 211, 226, 245–96; conspirational victim blaming, 252; counter-revolution, coping with, 290–96; existential pain, 283–90; hope, destruction of, 282; in political terrain, 10; presupposition of, 101, 103; Rabaa massacre, 260–70; revenge, 251–53, 255–57, 259; social death, 270–83; social-normative, 19; social polarisation through, 14; therapeutic practice in, 24; trauma as, 31, 74; violent, 15, 29, 95, 115, 119, 149–50, 162
intersubjective parity: in Egypt's revolutionary public sphere, 212–17; Morsi, Mohamed, 157–59; politics of, 111–23; violence, 85–86; violent betrayal of, 236
intersubjectivity, 31–36; cognitive trauma theory, 54–58; death and, 234–43; equality of all people, 75; lifeworlds collapse and, 55; parity, 62–63, 65, 71–75, 78–79, 81–90, 111–23; self-manifestation of, 84; struggles of, 66–70; trauma and, 64–91, 298
intertheoretic reductionism, 50
interviews, 4–5
intrusions, 55

Jaeggi, Rahel, 19, 28, 76–80, 91, 109, 236
Janet, Pierre, 53
Janoff-Bulman, Ronnie, 54–56
Judges Club protests, 112
juridification, 99n5, 137. *See also* repressive juridification
justice, 7, 9, 75–76; socio-normative, 37; for victims of violence, 25

Kant, Emmanuel, 32
Ketchely, Neil, 116
Kienle, Eberhard, 106
Kifaya (Enough) movement (2004), 96, 111–13
Kihlstrom, J. F., 47

landownership laws, 101
Leone, Sierra, 7
Levinas, E., 238
lifeworld, 55, 65, 71, 85–86, 209–12; being-against-death, 224–33; death and, 219–43; disruption, experience of, 230; symbolic order of, 220; torture and, 220–24
Lifton, Robert Jay, 45
logic of violence, 274

El Mahdi, Rebab, 112
Mahmoud, Abdel Meguid, 158
Mahmoud, Mohamed, 129–30, 135, 142–46, 228
maldistribution, 9, 71–73, 103–5, 209
male rape, 223, 244n1
Mandour, Maged, 198

Manichean dichotomy, 60, 258
Mansour, Adly, 185
marginalisation, 250
Martín-Baró, Ignacio, 88
martyrs, 234–43
Maspero massacre, 141–42
El Masry, Walid, 169
Mead, George Herbert, 32
Media Law (2016), 291
The Memory of Love (Forna), 7
mental health, 41
Metwally, Amr, 195
Metwally, Ibrahim, 195
Middle East, 17–19
military, Egypt, 12–13, 106–7; and civic security forces, 106–7; economisation of, 107; role of, 107
Military Inc, 107
Military Intelligence Directory, 102
Ministry of Military Production, 151
misrecognition, 9, 71–76, 105–8
mobilisation, 62
modernity, 84–85; teleological theory of, 18
Mohi, Ahmed, 207
moods, 69
Moqattam clashes, 163, 253
Morsi, Mohamed, 3, 13, 131, 155–67, 170–71; conspirational victim blaming during, 163, 123n2; direct physical force, 161–65; EBDA, set up of, 166; foreign investors, lower subsidies to, 166; intersubjective parity, 159–60; inward turn of violence, 161–65; neoliberal economic rationalism, 165–67; power, struggle for, 156–61
Moussa, Amr, 181
Moustafa, Ahmed, 182
Mubarak, Gamal, 111, 113–22, 151–52
Mubarak, Hosni, 11–12, 96, 103
Muslim Brotherhood, 3, 12–13, 106, 118, 128–30, 147, 155, 158–68, 247, 252–56, 258–59, 299

Nadeem Centre of the Rehabilitation of Victims of Violence and Torture, 107, 198
Naguib, Mohamed, 101
El Nasser, Abdel Fattah, 11, 95, 101–2
National Services Projects Organisation (NSPO), 151
Nazif, Ahmed, 131
Nazi violence, 68
neo-Kraepelian positivism, 38
neoliberal economic rationalism, 12, 96; El Sisi, Abdel Fattah, 201–7; Morsi, Mohamed, 165–67; SCAF, 151–54
neoliberal economics, 103–5
nervousness, 285
neuroscience, 58
New Administrative Capital for Urban Development (NCUD), 203
New Anti-Terror Law, 186, 291
NGO Law, 156, 160
noematic feelings, 283
nothingness, 68

pain, existential, 283–90
Palestine, 86
Palestinian Hamas, 258
philosophy of recognition, 71–72, 74–75
Philosophy of the Subject, 6–8, 11, 23, 25–27, 87, 93; atomistic individualism characteristic of, 69; Habermas's critique of, 31–36; intersubjectivity and, 57; in trauma studies, 57–58
political activity/activism, 3, 23
political deliberalisation, 106
political impotence, 250
political injustice, 10, 43, 57, 75
political mobilisation, 3
political proceduralism, 97; El Sisi's, 180–84; Morsi's, 156–61; SCAF, 126–33
political public sphere, 14, 72, 76, 84; colonisation, 13, 126–33; intersubjective imparity in, 95–96, 98; repressive juridification,

137–39, 184–90; traumatic status subordination in, 11, 87–91
political trauma, 11, 93–98
politics of violence, 224–33
Port Said massacre, 149–50
positivism, critique of, 36
positivist revolution, 36–44
post-structuralist trauma theory, 58, 60
post-traumatic stress disorder (PTSD), 5, 7, 27, 87, 298; definitions of, 44; emergence of, 36–54; political diagnosis, 57; trauma as, 6, 87
poverty, 204–6
power, 95
prefigurative intersubjective parity, politics of, 111–23; Egypt's revolutionary mobilisation (2011), 113–22; Kifaya (Enough) movement (2004), 111–13
Presidential Bureau of Intelligence, 102
presidential clashes, 249
prisonification, politics of, 16
private/public autonomy, 127
Protest Law of 2013, 156, 185–86, 188, 291
psychoanalysis, 38, 40–41, 59
PTSD. *See* post-traumatic stress disorder (PTSD)

Rabaa massacre, 172–77, 260–70
Radstone, Susannah, 46, 58
rape, 223, 244n1
Rashid, Rashid Mohammed, 166
Ratcliffe, Matthew, 10, 212, 242, 278, 280, 283, 299
rationalism/rationalisation, 32
rationality, 34, 209
recognition, philosophy of, 71–76
reconstruction, 16–17
Regeni, Giulio, 193
reification, 283
reintegration, 55
reinterpretation, 55
reliability, 38

repressive juridification: El Sisi, 184–90; SCAF, 137–39
responsibility, 238
revenge, 15, 150, 251–53, 255–57, 259
revolutionary betrayal, 234–43

Sabahi, Hamdeen, 131, 235
Sadat, Mohamed Anwar, 11, 96, 102–3, 183
Said, Khaled, 113
Salafist Nour party, 130
Saleh, Sobhi, 133
Salem, Hussein, 166
Sawaris, Naguib, 170
SCAF. *See* Supreme Council of Armed Forces (SCAF)
security state violence, 105–8, 116
self, 32, 43
self-deception, 84
self-manifestation, 234–43
self-realisation, 74–76
Selmy document, 143
sense of panic, 286
Shafiq, Ahmed, 131–32, 183
Shahin, Hassan, 169
shame, 206
Sharaf, Essam, 130
Shatan, Chaim, 45
Al Shater, Khairat, 131, 165, 166
'shell shock' syndrome, 53
Siemens factory, 296
El Sisi, Abdel Fattah, 3, 13, 97, 151, 156, 158, 175, 302–3; authoritarian rule, 179; big projects, promotion for, 202; capital gains tax, nullification of, 202; colonisation of political public sphere, 180–84; depoliticisation campaign, 182; direct physical force, 190–200; election, 181–82; General Intelligence Service, 189; neoliberal economic rationalism, 201–7; New Administrative Capital, 203, 290; *versus* predecessors regime, 180; repressive juridification of public

sphere, 184–90; Suez Canal project, 202; tax and deregulatory investment reforms, 202; traumatic status subordination, politics of, 179–208
social death, 222, 270–83
social injustice, 10, 43, 57, 75
socialisation, 32
social relations, 273
social trauma, 11, 62
socio-economic maldistribution, 101–5
socio-normative justice, 37
socio-normativity, 25
Soliman, Samer, 104
somatic state of depression, 283–90
Spitzer, Robert L., 38–39, 45
Springborg, Robert, 107
Stacher, Joshua, 128, 130, 154n1, 181
State of Emergency law, 106, 138
State Security Investigation Service, 102
Stilt, Kristen A., 133
Stolorow, Robert D., 27, 66, 82, 237
Straker, Gillian, 7, 25, 51
stress, 284
structural violence, 29
Suez Canal project, 202, 296
Supreme Council for Judicial Bodies and Authorities, 184
Supreme Council of Armed Forces (SCAF), 118, 122, 125–54; constitutional amendments, 133–37; direct physical force, 139–51; disorientation, 139–51; electoral process, 130, 132, 133; isolation, 139–51; neoliberal economic rationalism, 151–54; political proceduralism, 126–33; repressive juridification, 137–39
Susen, Simon, 83–84
suspicion, 7
Sztompka, Piotr, 62

Tahya Misr (Long live Egypt) fund, 205
Tamarrod, 169–72, 256, 259
Tawasul (intercession) employers committee, 166
teargas, 231–33
terrorism, 106, 110n6, 186–88
'Teslem al Ayadi' song, 177
theory of alienation, 28, 76–80, 108–10
theory of colonisation, 36, 81, 82, 84, 91
thought, 32
thuggery, 138
Topolski, A., 238
torture, 140–41, 164, 219–24
Trager, Eric, 138–39
Tramadol, 290
trauma, 5–16, 24–29, 93; anti-mimetic conception of, 47, 51, 58–63; as broken subjectivity, 23–30, 37, 94, 209; cognitive trauma theory, 54–58; critical theoretical understanding of, 8–9; individual, 11, 93; as intersubjective alienation, 65–91, 298; justice and, 9; as past event, 25; political, 11–14, 17–19; as PTSD, 6, 36–54; social, 11, 222; status subordination, 71–76, 85, 87–90, 93–98, 101–10, 179–208; theoretical understanding of, 299; violence and, 3–4, 9, 13–14, 125–26, 143–44, 219–43
trauma markers, 4
trauma studies, 5–8, 24–26, 93, 298; critical, 65–91; fMRI scans in, 48; Habermas's critique of positivism, 36; neuroscientific, 47; positivist revolution, 36–54; PTSD, emergence of, 36–54
traumatic alienation, 76–80, 108–10, 299
traumatic status subordination in Egypt, 71–76, 85, 93–98, 101–10, 209; El Sisi, Abdel Fattah, 179–208; legacy of, 101–10; Morsi, Mohammed, 155–67; neoliberal economics, 103–5; politics of, 125–67; security state violence, 105–8; traumatic alienation, 108–10, 299
trust, social relations of, 15

unconscious drives, 42
unlimited life community, 83

van der Kolk, Bessel, 8, 26, 49
victim blaming, 56, 114–16, 118, 123n2, 126, 142, 147–49, 152, 163, 212, 252
Vietnam War veterans, 88
violence, 3–4, 9, 13–14, 125–26, 143–44, 219–43; clashes, 224–33; distorted communication in, 85; impacts of, 14; intersubjective parity, 85; inward turn of, 161–65; Israeli, 86; logic of, 274; Moqattam clashes, 163, 253; physical, 210; politics of, 224–33; Port Said massacre, 149–50; potential of, 275; power, 95; presidential clashes and, 249; Rabaa massacre, 172–77; structural experience of, 93; victim blaming, 56, 114–16, 118, 123n2, 126, 142, 147–49, 152, 163, 212, 252
voxels, 48, 64n9

Watermelon Democracy (Stacher), 154n1

About the Author

Prof Dr Vivienne Matthies-Boon is a Socrates Professor in Humanism, Europe and Global Justice and Associate Professor in Political Philosophy at the Radboud University in Nijmegen (the Netherlands). Rooted in critical theory, her work centres around a practical philosophy of (lived) political violence and focuses on the interrelation between structural injustice and experiences of existential vulnerability and fragility. She is particularly interested in the relationship between fragility and political mobilisation, both within and beyond the political contexts of Egypt and the Middle East.

www.ingramcontent.com/pod-product-compliance
Lightning Source LLC
Chambersburg PA
CBHW022008300426
44117CB00005B/90